# THE RETURN OF ULYSSES

–EDITH HALL–

# THE RETURN OF ULYSSES

## A CULTURAL HISTORY OF HOMER'S ODYSSEY

THE JOHNS HOPKINS UNIVERSITY PRESS
BALTIMORE

First published by I.B.Tauris & Co. Ltd in the United Kingdom

First published in the United States in 2008 by the Johns Hopkins University Press

2 4 6 8 9 7 5 3 1

The Johns Hopkins University Press
2715 N. Charles Street
Baltimore, MD 21218-4363
www.press.jhu.edu

Library of Congress Control Number: 2007942538

Typeset in Adobe Caslon Pro by A. & D. Worthington, Newmarket, Suffolk
Printed and bound in Great Britain by TJ International Ltd, Padstow,United Kingdom

# CONTENTS

# ACKNOWLEDGEMENTS

The idea for this book was suggested to me by Alex Wright at I.B.Tauris, who had heard me discussing the topic on Melvyn Bragg's BBC radio programme, *In Our Time*, and developed while I taught BA and MA modules on the cultural impact of the *Odyssey* at the University of Durham in the academic year 2005–6. I would like to thank all the students who enrolled, for their enthusiasm and inexhaustible energy in seeking out new examples of the *Odyssey*'s cultural presence, especially Phil Lofthouse and Joe Platnauer. My doctoral students Charlie MacDougall, Justine McConnell and Rosie Wyles have also helped in all kinds of ways. Others to whom I am grateful include Jennifer Ingleheart, Fiona Macintosh, Margaret Malamud, Luke Pitcher, Richard Poynder, Peggy Reynolds, David Roselli, Polly Weddle, and Richard Williams. Sarah and Georgie Poynder provided trenchant comments on most of the films and all the children's books. Special thanks go to David and Alison Worthington for their copy-editing and proof-reading of the text.

This is the first book to be published under the aegis of the Centre for the Reception of Greece and Rome at Royal Holloway, which was officially opened on 17 December 2007.

# PART I
# GENERIC MUTATIONS

# 1

# EMBARKATION

Muse, sing for me about that versatile man,
who sacked the sacred city of Troy
and then wandered far and wide (*Odyssey* 1.1–2).

In the late Bronze Age, a king from the western islands of Greece was
delayed sailing home after a war in Asia, but did eventually return
to recover his wife, son and throne. His story was told by bards, and
in about 750 BCE one of them – the Greeks said he was blind and named
Homer – put the finishing touches to the epic poem called the *Odyssey*, which opens with the invocation above. This story stays fresh nearly
three millennia later – but why? The recent editor of an anthology of texts
inspired by the plays of Shakespeare admits that Homer, and only Homer,
has proved an equally powerful source of inspiration for later authors.[1]
Another scholar has argued that it can be difficult even to identify 'spin-
offs' from the *Odyssey*, so deeply has it shaped our imagination and cultural
values.[2] My book explores the reasons for the enormity of this poem's
cultural presence.

This is a foolhardy quest. The vastness of the terrain should discourage
all but optimistic travellers. Another deterrent should be the quality of
the previous explorations. In Stanford's *The Ulysses Theme*, the first edition
of which was published more than half a century ago (1954), the reasons
for Odysseus' survival in the literature of later centuries was subjected to
a brilliant analysis. The material that Stanford had collected still arouses
awe in any wannabe successor, even one equipped with online library
catalogues. Stanford's book has already inspired fine epigones, notably the
accessible *An Odyssey round Odysseus* by Beaty Rubens and Oliver Taplin
(1989), and Piero Boitani's heavyweight study *The Shadow of Ulysses* (1994).
Several useful collections of essays have also been published.[3] Yet it seems
to me that a new investigation is timely. Even in his second edition of
1968, and the more popular *The Quest for Ulysses* that he published with

3

J.V. Luce in 1974, Stanford was writing in a world that had not adjusted to feminism, let alone post-colonialism, and in which few movies had engaged with the *Odyssey*.

This book takes a different trajectory from most of its predecessors. It is a study of the influence of the *Odyssey* rather than the figure of Odysseus/Ulysses. It does not discuss textual matters such as the 'authenticity' of the final book of the *Odyssey*, where the hero is finally reunited with his father.[4] Indeed, Laertes supports my argument that one reason for the poem's enduring popularity must be that its personnel is so varied that every ancient or modern listener, of any age, sex or status, seaman or servant, will have found someone with whom to identify. There has been a tendency to see the *Iliad* as a young man's poem, and the *Odyssey* as a poem of old age; the ancient critic Longinus saw its ethical focus as a sign of its author's advancing years: 'great minds in their declination stagger into Fabling', as John Hall of Consett translated it in 1652.[5] But youths relate to Telemachus, and the strength of the entire cast means that it has been possible to rewrite the *Odyssey* from the perspective of old men, of teenage girls, of Elpenor, of Circe's swine, and even of Polyphemus.[6]

Several recent writers have identified themselves with Homer, above all Jorge Luis Borges, who as his own sight began to fail, in his semi-autobiographical *El Hacedor* (1960), spoke of divining the 'murmur of glory and hexameters ... of black vessels searching the sea for a beloved isle'.[7] But my book does not contribute to the controversy about the identity of 'Homer', who was alleged in antiquity variously to have been a lover taken by Penelope, a blind resident of Chios, a descendant of the mystic Orpheus, or a native of Smyrna (Izmir) named Melisigenes.[8] My favourite conjecture is not that the author of the *Odyssey* was a woman (see Chapter 9), but that both Homeric epics were created by Odysseus himself. That nobody else was an eyewitness of both the Trojan War and the voyage of Odysseus was pointed out in all seriousness decades before Herman Melville in *Moby-Dick* (1851) made Ishmael, the sole survivor of another ill-fated voyage, narrate his tale.[9]

The *Odyssey* is attractive simply on account of its great age. The great storyteller J.R.R. Tolkien commented, in connection with H.G. Wells's *The Time Machine* (1895), on the perennial human desire to 'survey' tracts of time. Tolkien's inhabitants of Middle-earth, in the late Third Age, recall the olden days that preceded them.[10] Yet my book is not arranged chronologically, nor does it follow the temporal order of events as presented in the poem. Instead its route travels via responses to the poem grouped according to genres, media, and sociological or psychological topics. But even thematically based discussions have a temporal dimension. Certain aspects of the *Odyssey* have been culturally prominent or recessive at certain times: the Renaissance, seeing it as a charter text of colonial expansion, emphasized the maritime wanderings; the eighteenth century found the teachable Telemachus more appealing than his father; Modernists were obsessed with the trip to the Underworld, and 'made it new' a thousand times.

The cultural manifestations of the *Odyssey* are not here comprehensively covered, and their selection, if not arbitrary, has been personal. There is more discussion of fiction, poetry, theatre and film than of painting and sculpture because I am more at home with texts than images. For a similar reason there is little said about danced versions of the *Odyssey*, for example the Czech ballet company Latérna Magika's epoch-making *Odysseus*, which has been revived repeatedly since 1987. Nor is there much on the many 'crank' theories about the *Odyssey* arguing, for example, that it contains secret instructions for sailing to Iceland across the Atlantic, via Circe in the Hebrides and the Cimmerians in Ulster.[11] Others have suggested that it contains prophecies of later technological developments – for example, that Alcinous' gold and silver guard-dogs (7.91–4) are ancestors of the cyborg.[12] Some, although more scientifically based, fail to see that the epic is not primarily concerned with empirical reality, for example the view that the Sirens were monk seals.[13] Although such readings have an entertainment value, I have not dwelt upon them.

Labels have been attached to our dialogue with the ancient Greeks ever since the Renaissance (the authors whom Bernard Knox, in response to claims that classical culture has been hijacked by Western imperialism, has ironically called ODWEMS, the Oldest Dead White European Males).[14] A late antique rhetorician liked the image of Homer 'sowing the seeds of art'.[15] The old notion of the Classical Tradition or the Classical Heritage takes the idea of a legacy, passed passively down the generations like the family teaspoons.[16] Judith Kazantzis says that Homer's epic of the high seas 'is perennially open to plunder itself and I am a pirate'.[17] The theatre director Peter Sellars sees each classic text as an antique house that can be redecorated in the style of any era, while remaining essentially the same.[18] Taplin proposes the more volatile image of Greek Fire, a substance used as a weapon that burns under water. Greek culture, according to this analogy, is still present in invisible yet incendiary forms.[19] For the Prussian scholar Ulrich von Wilamowitz-Moellendorff, the metaphor of necromancy came from the scene before Odysseus enters the world of the dead: 'We know that ghosts cannot speak until they have drunk blood;

and the spirits which we evoke demand the blood of our hearts.'[20] More ambivalent is Walcott's description, repeated in poems including *Omeros*, of 'All that Greek manure under the green bananas'[21] – the Greek legacy is excrement, but has also fertilized his Caribbean imagination. This beautifully captures the paradoxical nature of ancient Mediterranean discourses to peoples colonized by Western powers.

Various explanations have been proposed for the trans-historical appeal of a few ancient texts.[22] Kristeva suggests that since every text is a 'mosaic of quotations', we must think in terms of *intertextuality*.[23] According to Genette's terminology, the *Odyssey* is a 'hypotext' that has been 'transvaluated' into derivative 'hypertexts' such as the *Aeneid* and Joyce's *Ulysses*, although the hypertexts can subsequently become hypotexts themselves.[24] More satisfying from an explanatory perspective is Vidal-Naquet's argument that ancient literature transcends history because of an unusual *susceptibility* to diverse interpretations.[25] Raymond Williams would have suggested that this was in turn made possible by the ideological complexity of the original epic, according to his notion that any moment in time contains three strands of ideology: old-fashioned ideas on their way out, dominant ideas that the majority of people hold, and *emergent* ideas developed only by avant-garde segments of the population and which may not become mainstream for centuries.[26] On this argument there are things in the archaic *Odyssey* – for example, Penelope's intelligence – that represented *emergent* ideology that might not become dominant for millennia.

'Emergent' ideology corresponds with the Russian formalist Mikhail Bakhtin's notion that literature holds 'prefigurative' meanings that can only be released by reassessments lying far away in what he calls 'great time' in the future.[27] Another way of putting this is Erich Auerbach's concept of 'figura' or 'umbra', which draws on medieval allegorists to develop a metaphor of 'prefiguration' or 'foreshadowing'. According to this argument, an element in an ancient text (e.g. Odysseus' wanderings) can in a mysterious but profound manner prefigure things that happen later (Columbus's voyages of exploration).[28] Vernant further proposes that important artworks *actively condition* the shapes taken by future artworks, whether the conditioning takes the form of emulation, modification or rejection.[29]

Yet none of these models accounts for the two-way nature of the relationship. Every new response to a classic text alters the total picture of its influence. When a great artwork like the *Odyssey* stimulates the production of others, such as Virgil's *Aeneid*, Monteverdi's *Il ritorno d'Ulisse in patria* (1640) and Joyce's *Ulysses* (1922), cultural history changes irrevocably. According to T.S. Eliot, collectively such 'existing monuments form an ideal order among themselves'. But this ideal order will always be 'modified by the introduction of the new (the really new) work of art among them.'[30] Thus Eliot would have seen Walcott's new reaction to the Homeric epic in *Omeros* as affecting the totality of the cultural order and changing forever how we see its precursors: 'for in order to persist after the supervention of novelty, the *whole* existing order must be, if ever so slightly, altered'.[31]

That 'existing order' of cultural history has, moreover, now become international. The *Odyssey* is the intellectual property of the global village. This great quest epic has sometimes shaped the ways in which people in Africa or Mongolia come to understand their own living traditions of epic. This is likely in the case of the *Sundiata* (an African epic narrating the foundation in the thirteenth century CE of the Mali Empire in the western Sudan), which is still evolving in performance by singers called griots.[32] Although the Sudanese give the name Mamoudou Kouyate to the epic's originator, it never became canonized in any single version, and the longstanding French presence makes contact with the *Odyssey* not unlikely. In the global village, in any case, it has become impossible not to be reminded of Proteus in the *Odyssey* when reading about Sumanguru, the shape-shifting sorcerer, or of the scenes in Sparta and Phaeacia when appreciating the hospitality which the exiled Sundiata received at the courts of the kings of Tabon and Ghana.[33]

The two Homeric epics formed the basis of the education of everyone in ancient Mediterranean society from at least the seventh century BCE; that curriculum was in turn adopted by Western humanists. John Ruskin stressed that it does not matter whether or not Homer is actually read, since 'All Greek gentlemen were educated under Homer. All Roman gentlemen, by Greek literature. All Italian, and French, and English gentlemen, by Roman literature, and by its principles.'[34] Hegel had fore-shadowed part of Ruskin's diagnosis in saying that 'Homer is that element in which the Greek world lived, as a human lives in the air',[35] but even from pre-Roman days it was not only the Greek world. We do not know what mother tongue was spoken by the schoolchildren in Olbia in the northern Black Sea in the fifth century BCE, who painstakingly copied out a line in *Odyssey* 9 where Odysseus speaks of the land of the Ciconians, but they felt it had a local geographical reference.[36] For a thousand years countless schoolboys living under the Macedonian or Roman Empires, whose first languages were Syrian, Nubian or Gallic, learned their alphabet through the first letters of Homeric heroes' names, developed their handwriting by

copying out Homeric verses, and the art of précis by summarizing individual books of the *Odyssey*.[37] They also committed swathes of Homeric
hexameters to memory (in Xenophon's *Symposium* 3.5 Niceratus says that
his upper-class father required him to learn *all* of Homer by heart), and
studied them in early manhood when they were learning to be statesmen,
soldiers, lawyers, historians, philosophers, biographers, poets, dramatists,
novelists, painters or sculptors.

All the genres and media these men produced were formed in response
to the great *Ur*-works in the Greek language. Sometimes they adapted
them, and sometimes they quoted them.[38] But the subterranean impact on
the ancient psyche is more important. In the case of the *Odyssey*, no later
author could ever again make a fresh start when shaping a narrative or a
visual representation of a voyage, a metamorphosis, a run-in with savages,
an encounter with anyone dead, a father–son relationship, a recognition
token, or a reunion between husband and wife.

'If the world is to be lived in, it must be founded,' said Mircea Eliade,[39]
and the *Odyssey* was early identified as a 'foundational' text. In one sense,
this status is misleading. The poem represents a late stage in the evolution
of ancient Near Eastern mythical narrative poetry in cultures that had
reached peaks of sophistication millennia earlier, above all the Sumerian
*Epic of Gilgamesh*. Although it also shares material with the biblical story
of Noah and the flood, elements in *Gilgamesh* are related to both the *Iliad*
and the *Odyssey*: like Achilles, Gilgamesh has a beloved comrade-in-arms
whose death he can scarcely abide. But the parallels with the *Odyssey* are
more pervasive. Gilgamesh embarks on a perilous quest which involves
the favour of the Sun God, cutting down trees, building a raft, sexual
advances from a goddess, sacrilegiously killing the sacred bull of heaven,
sailing across the Waters of Death, and an offer of immortality.[40]

The *Odyssey* is also aware of its *Greek* tradition of bardic performances
(see Fig. 1.1), and its language was spoken as early as the sixteenth century
BCE. But if tales of heroic escapades that foreshadow the *Odyssey* were written down in the alphabets used by those Minoan Greeks, no records have
survived. The Homeric poems began to be charter texts at the moment
when, in about 750 BCE, they were inscribed in phonetic script. Their
importance as the possession of Greek-speakers everywhere was identified immediately; knowledge of them became a passport into a psychological community spread over countless coasts and islands. Knowledge of
Homer also spread amongst non-Greeks; Dio Chrysostom said that even
primitive barbarians know Homer's name (*Oration* 53.6), and Homer is
the only Greek author mentioned by name in the Talmud.[41] The influence

of the *Odyssey* can be seen on the *Book of Tobit*, the scriptural tale of the righteous Jew of Nineveh, probably written in Aramaic during the second century BCE.[42]

To allude to the *Odyssey* is to invoke an authority of talismanic psychological power. Certainly composers of epic from Apollonius in Greek Egypt in the third century BCE to Virgil, Tasso, Milton and Walcott have always (if inaccurately) viewed Homer as primary ancestor. So have lyric poets and the playwrights discussed in Chapter 3. But advocates of the superiority of the *Iliad* can only envy the cultural penetration achieved by the *Odyssey*: it is also an ancestral text for cartographers, geographers, navigators, explorers, historians, philosophers, psychologists, anthropologists, occult magicians, novelists, science-fiction writers, biographers, autobiographers, movie directors and composers of opera.

The *Odyssey* has generated other texts with foundational status. Creative people inaugurating a new trend have repeatedly found the *Odyssey* a suitable text on which to rest the burden of their manifestos. The best example is Joyce's *Ulysses*, a founding text of Modernist fiction. Any aspiring novelist since Joyce has had to deal with the *Odyssey* simply because of the magnitude of *Ulysses* in the emergence of contemporary fiction. *Ulysses* has itself been translated into numerous languages, including Malayan and Arabic, and in 1994 become a surprise bestseller in China, which had previously banned it as too obscene.[43] But the list of 'inaugural' responses to the *Odyssey* can be infinitely extended. In the special effects in early cinema, in the early nineteenth-century emergence of children's literature, in the post-colonial revision of the Western canon, the *Odyssey* is invariably to be found in the cultural cauldron when anything interesting is cooking. Its formulaic type-scenes (hospitality, confrontation, seduction by Sirenic females) have even been analysed as an antecedent of *Dallas*, the cult American TV soap opera of the 1970s and 1980s.[44] This situation becomes self-perpetuating. The more that influential thinkers and artists direct their audience's attention to the *Odyssey*, the more likely it becomes that interest in the poem will multiply. People become interested in the *Odyssey* because they are interested in Modernist fiction, Venetian opera or science fiction.

Thinking about the relationship of narrative modes to reality inevitably involves Erich Auerbach's seminal comparison, in *Mimesis* (1945), of the recognition of Odysseus by his scar in *Odyssey* 19 and Genesis 22.1. But it is the relationship with reality in the *Odyssey* itself that avant-garde fiction writers have found inspirational. The poem juxtaposes time levels through dialogues with the dead, prophecies and simultaneous actions in both real, known places and supernatural ones. This complex presentation of time has made the *Odyssey* the basis of the 'fantastic odyssey taking place in the modern literature of Latin America'[45] since the Argentine Jorge Luis Borges' labyrinthine *The Garden of Forking Paths* (1941). This literature involves journeys, deriving ultimately from the *Odyssey*, 'whose destinations do not involve exterior coordinates in time and space', and simultaneity in contrast with linearity. It is often at odds with Western conceptions of cause, effect and sequence.[46] Borges understood the debt that his unorthodox treatments of time owed to the *Odyssey*, and expressed it in *The Immortal* (1947), when the tribune Flaminius Rufus drinks the waters of immortality and realizes that 'in an infinite period of time, all things happen to all men … if we postulate an infinite period of time, with infinite circumstances and changes, the impossible thing is not to compose the *Odyssey*, at least once.' Moreover, 'I have been Homer; shortly, I shall be One, like Ulysses.'[47]

There is realism in the *Odyssey*, but it is combined cohesively with supernatural elements – the morphing Proteus and the 12-footed, six-headed aquatic monster Scylla. This alone explains the poem's attraction to cinema directors, whose medium more than any other can effect visual magic; since George Méliès and his *L'Île de Calypso: Ulysse et le géant Polyphème* (1905), a copy of which can be consulted in the Library of Congress, directors have found the *Odyssey* an ideal text for inspiring special effects. Moreover, the *Odyssey* is often cited as the founding text of 'magical realism', a term which originated in the 1920s but is most often associated with Gabriel García Márquez and the Latin American fiction that began in the 1960s. Theorists require that it contains fantastic elements, never explained 'rationally'; it may often exhibit detailed sensory richness and elements of folklore or myth; it enjoys mirroring events within and between its non-realistic and realist planes, and often leaves the reader uncertain in which to 'believe'.[48]

This catalogue also exactly describes the contents and narrative strategies of the *Odyssey*, composed 2,700 years before Gabriel García Márquez's *One Hundred Years of Solitude*. The epic's synthesis of the empirically plausible and the fantastic accounts for its cultural elasticity. The *Iliad*, despite the epiphanies of gods and one episode involving talking horses, refuses to allow its listener off the painful hook of war.[49] As a deadly serious account of a brutal conflict, it can be transplanted to other situations involving siege or imperialism, but its consistently realist tenor is not open to the multiplicity of meanings that can be found in the non-realist, magical and symbolic figures of the *Odyssey*'s travelogue. As Northrop Frye put it, 'of all fictions, the marvelous journey is the one formula that is never exhausted'.[50]

The *Odyssey* offers an astonishing variety of sensory experience. Both Homeric epics create strong visual worlds: Cicero remarked on the paradox whereby in the case of a poet who was blind 'it is nevertheless his painting not his poetry that we see' (*Tusculan Disputations* 5.39.114).[51] But in the *Odyssey* the interest in the texture, taste, smell and sound of everyday life is connected with its greater diversity of discourses than its more military sister epic.[52] The Troy poem contains little description of landscape or physical environment comparable to several passages in the *Odyssey*, beginning with Hermes' appreciation of Calypso's cave (5.59–73):

> There was a big fire blazing on the hearth, and through the whole island wafted the scent of burning spliced cedar wood and juniper … A luxuriant wood sprang up around her cave – alder and poplar and sweet-smelling cypress. Long-winged birds nested there, horned owls and hawks and cormorants with their long tongues, whose sphere of operation is the ocean. Over the arching cavern there spread a flourishing cultivated vine, with abundant grapes. There was a row of four adjacent springs, with gleaming water, their streams running off in different directions, surrounded by soft meadows that bloomed with violet and parsley.

This is the first *locus amoenus* in the Western tradition, and the visual brilliance of the *Odyssey* has inspired not only novels and poems but visual artworks, such as 'A Fantastic Cave Landscape with Odysseus and Calypso', painted by Jan Brueghel the Elder and Hendrick de Clerck: Odysseus and Calypso sit amidst a precise and lush evocation of the paradisiacal vegetation of Ogygia.[53] Some *Odyssey* paintings have themselves become so famous that, like Joyce's *Ulysses*, they develop a dependent literature of their own. Turner's painting of Polyphemus deriding Ulysses (1829), for example, amazed one poet: Turner had allowed him to gaze upon the Achaian prows gliding by,

> Odysseus in his burnished galleon,
> Nereides that sang him swiftly on
> And baffled Cyclops fading in the sky.[54]

The poem is, in addition, a writer's joy because of its auditory appeal, conveyed in details such as the clanging of the metal bowl in which Eurycleia is washing Odysseus' leg at the moment when she recognizes the scar and drops his foot (19.469). But the poem also stimulates the senses most difficult to replicate in aural or visual art: taste and smell. Much food preparation and eating is described, including the touching scene where Odysseus delights Demodocus by passing him a chunk of roast pork 'with

plenty of fat', sliced from the sumptuous joint (8.475–6). And what stronger evocation of smell can be imagined than Menelaus' description of the
disgusting odour of the seals amongst whom he and his men had to hide
from Proteus, the Egyptian sea-divinity? Proteus' daughter Eidothea was
fortunately on hand to help (4.435–45):

> She, meanwhile, dived down under the broad surface of the sea, and
> brought up four sealskins from the depths, all of them freshly skinned …
> Then she dug out hollows in the seaside sand for us to sleep in … and put a
> sealskin on top of each of us. That would have been a truly dreadful place
> to launch an ambush from, for the fishy stench of the brine-bred seals was
> really disgusting, if the goddess had not herself saved us by devising the
> remedy of putting ambrosia under the nostrils of each one of us, and its
> delicious fragrance did away with the sea-beast's odour.

'The fishy stench of the brine-bred seals' puts the reader of the *Odyssey*
into immediate sensory contact with the seagoing life lived by Homer's
ancient audience. When Hermes flies to Calypso, he swoops down to the
sea, 'skimming the waves like a cormorant that hunts down fish across the
deadly spaces of the barren ocean, dipping its thick feathery wings in the
brine' (5.51–3, see Fig. 1.2).

An ancient epigram memorializes some damage done by immersion in
the sea to a painting of Odysseus, but reflects that the sea can never really
destroy Odysseus, because 'in Homer's verses the image of him is painted
on imperishable pages' (*Palatine Anthology* 16.125).[55] This poet understood
intuitively how the sea explains the *Odyssey*'s cultural immortality. It has
been scrutinized by historians of navigation, and has been described as
the ancestor 'of the port-books and pilot-books of later ages'.[56] The whole
fourth line of the poem is dedicated to the 'many painful things experiences *at sea* that caused him heartbreak' (1.4); by the end of the second
book the first thrilling embarkation takes place, when Telemachus' ship
leaves the Ithacan shore (2.421–8):

> Owl-eyed Athene sent them a following wind, strong and from the West,
> that whistled out across the wine-dark sea … They lifted the pine-wood
> mast, set it upright in its socket, and secured it with forestays; with ropes
> of twisted ox-hide they then hauled up the white sails. The wind filled out
> the mainsail, and the purple wave roared out noisily as the front end of the
> keel sliced through it as the ship pressed on.

The tactile evocation of the tackle, the contrast between the 'wine-dark
sea' (*oinopa ponton*) and the white sails, the sound of the wind and the roar
of the waves have inspired musical pieces, such as Debussy's orchestral
poem *La mer*, Ravel's piano fantasy *Une barque sur l'océan* (both 1905), and

the Homeric tone poem *Oceanides* (1914) by Sibelius.

When ancient artists personified the *Odyssey*, she stood with one foot on a ship, ready to embark, or held a rudder, wearing the conical hat associated with sailors.[57] A relief sculpture from Priene, now housed in the British Museum and known as the Apotheosis of Homer, shows the poet flanked by feminine personifications of the *Iliad* with a sword and the *Odyssey* with a steering oar.[58] Joyce was responding to the *Odyssey*'s focus on the sea in the first chapter of *Ulysses* when Buck Mulligan says to Stephen Dedalus: 'Isn't the sea what Algy calls it: a great sweet mother? The snotgreen sea. The scrotumtightening sea. *Epi oinopa ponton*. Ah, Dedalus, the Greeks.'[59]

The poem presents the sea in different moods, but it dominates Book 5, which includes Odysseus' heroic swimming feat. When the storm smashes his raft and engulfs him in a mighty wave (5.431–44):

> He emerged from the breaker, which disintegrated as it crashed loudly against the coastline, and swam along outside it, looking at the land and trying to identify some shelving beach that could offer a safe haven from the sea. When, as he swam, he encountered a mouth of a flowing river, where he thought he could best reach dry land because it was clear of rocks and sheltered from the wind, he acknowledged the divine presence of the outgoing stream and prayed to it in his heart.

When he reaches land after a three-day ordeal, his physical state is described vividly: 'Both his knees and strong arms buckled beneath him … His whole body was swollen up, and sea-water streamed from his mouth and nostrils. Unable either to breathe or speak, he just lay there, semi-conscious, so total was his exhaustion' (5.453–7).[60] This archetypal narrative moment of shipwreck on a faraway island is one of the greatest gifts that the *Odyssey* has given to the world, often mediated through Defoe's *Robinson Crusoe* (1719); an expert on nineteenth-century boys' fiction has proposed that the island was a crucial site in narratives for maturing boys, since it could serve as 'an appropriately diminutive world in which dangers can be experienced within safe boundaries'.[61] For J.M. Barrie, an avid reader of the nineteenth-century 'island' adventures of Robert Louis Stevenson, shipwreck on an island was even a metaphor for sudden arrival into human existence: 'To be born is to be wrecked on an island.'[62]

Borges once remarked that verse should touch us physically 'as the presence of the sea does'.[63] This sense that *all* poetry has a relationship with the sea helps explain the cultural centrality of the *Odyssey*, which lies behind all sea-voyage poems, however remotely, including Coleridge's

*Rime of the Ancient Mariner* (1798):

> The fair breeze blew, the white foam flew,
> The furrow followed free:
> We were the first that ever burst
> Into that silent sea.

One detail that connects Coleridge's Mariner with Odysseus is that they are both borne sleeping back to their homeland, their ship manned by others.[64] Indeed, when Coleridge wanted to convey the effect of the Homeric hexameter, he exemplified it in two lines that imply that it is like a sea-voyage itself:

> Slowly it bears us along in swelling and limitless billows,
> Nothing before and nothing behind but the sky and the ocean.[65]

Poets have always associated the poem's maritime content with the rolling effect of its broad-sweeping hexameter verse. Robert Fitzgerald said that his translation was improved by being written 'on Homer's sea in houses that were … shaken by the impact of the Mediterranean winter storms on the rocks below'.[66] The sea imagery pervades Homeric reception. Quintilian, a Roman professor of oratory, said that Homer was himself the cultural equivalent of the ocean, 'the source of every stream and river; for he has given us a model and an inspiration for every department of eloquence' (10.1.4). It is in the same tradition that the Restoration poet John Oldham was working when in his ode *The Praise of Homer* he likens the poem to 'the unexhausted Ocean'.[67]

How did the *Odyssey* travel from Quintilian's world to Oldham's? It survived from antiquity in many manuscripts, since the scholars of Byzantium had guarded the Homeric texts carefully ever since the Emperor Constantine had in about 330 CE established his Greek-speaking Roman capital at Byzantium on the Bosporus, renaming it Constantinople. Homer continued to form the basis of education there until it fell to the Ottoman Turks in 1453. Although the earliest manuscript of Homer actually dates from the tenth century CE, there are a dozen from the twelfth. Greek studies started to be exported to Western Europe well before Constantinople was sacked. In the late Middle Ages scholars came west from the Greek-speaking world, bringing their cultural treasures with them. Florence and subsequently Venice were popular destinations, since the aristocratic houses that ruled them followed intellectual pursuits, including the study of Greek.[68] The hero in the story of the arrival of the *Odyssey* as a cultural presence in the West is the fourteenth-century humanist Francesco Petrarch. Like others at the time, he could read an idiosyncratic summary of the *Odyssey* in Book 6 of the medieval Latin prose text *Journal of the Trojan War*, which derives from an original of the first century CE. It is written from the perspective of its narrator, Dictys of Crete, who claims to have fought at Troy and to have known Ulysses.[69] But Petrarch's favourite Latin poet was Virgil, and it was probably this Roman epic that made Petrarch determined to lay his hands on a text of its Greek models. Through a contact working as an envoy in Constantinople, he finally acquired them.

Petrarch and his friend Boccacio both struggled to read the Greek texts, and in the end commissioned their Greek teacher Leontius Pilatus to translate their codex of Homer into Latin, a task he completed in 1369.[70] The die was cast; the *Iliad* and *Odyssey* were finally being read by Western Europeans. It took more than a century before the first printing of the Homeric text in its original form, edited in Florence by the Athenian Demetrius Chalcondylas and printed there by another Greek, the Cretan Antonios Damilas, in two volumes (1488). This precious book unleashed a flood of translations into Latin and modern languages. The Renaissance odyssey of the *Odyssey* had begun.

# 2

# TURNING PHRASES

At the climax of the *Odyssey*, the beggar poised the bow in his hands, and

'as easily as a skilled lyre player and singer stretches a string tight on a new peg, when he has made fast the twisted sheep-gut at both ends, with just as little effort did Odysseus bend the great bow, taking it in his right hand to test the bow-string, which gave out a sound like lovely swallow-song (21.406–11).

Thus, at the moment when Odysseus is about to reclaim his identity, he is compared with a bard whose performances brought the man who he was to life. To string the bow is to string the lyre; to let the arrow fly is here compared with turning thought into poetry.[1]

One explanation of the name *Homeros* is that it means a 'joiner', a man who turned phrases on his lathe, before fixing the poem together.[2] But to 'turn' a poem can also have the Latin sense of *vertere* – to convert it into another language. The *Odyssey*'s many thousand hexameter lines roll forward mesmerically, each arranged around six rhythmical pulses, vocalized in two clusters or asymmetrical half-lines. Hexameters have a measurable physiological impact: medical research has shown that patients' heart and respiratory rates slow down when they read them.[3] Within this rhythmic frame the poem's characters all speak the same dialect of archaic Greek, yet are aware of other languages. Athena, disguised as Mentes, speaks of a foreign port 'where the people speak another tongue' (1.183). The people who produced the *Odyssey* were, from its inception, in contact with other ethnic groups.

Alexander the Great's Macedonian soldiers must have paraphrased the poem to far-flung communities on campaign: Dio Chrysostom claimed that Homer's poetry 'is sung even in India, where they have translated it into their own speech and song' (*Oration* 53.6–7). But evidence for the translation of Homer into other ancient languages is rare, because anybody educated enough to want to read Homer would usually have learnt Greek.

There was one attempt to translate the *Odyssey* into Latin in the third century BCE, by Livius Andronicus, a bilingual poet from the Greek-speaking area of southern Italy. Only a few fragments survive, in a Latin Saturnian metre rather than the hexameter, but they suggest a translation rather than an adaptation.[4]

When the Homeric poems arrived in Petrarch's Italy, it was once again into Latin, then the universal language of scholarship, that they were translated. But after they were printed in 1488, they became central to the Humanists' curriculum, indeed the texts from which students learned ancient Greek. It was therefore inevitable that translations began to appear in languages including Modern Greek, German, Spanish, Castilian and Dutch.[5] The *Odyssey* first saw an English translation with the appearance in 1616 of George Chapman's vigorous version in a ten-syllable metre, a few years after his imposing *Iliad*. There have subsequently been hundreds of translations, into dozens of languages, many of which are catalogued in Young's encyclopaedic *The Printed Homer* (2003). The *Odyssey* could be read in Russian and Danish by the end of the nineteenth century, and soon afterwards in Polish (1904), Hungarian (1905), Provençal (1907), Swedish (1908), Slovenian (1911), Icelandic (1915), Serbo-Croat (1915) and Finnish (1916). A few major non-European languages have had to wait longer – the first Korean *Odyssey* was published in 1991 – but few people in the world today do not know a language in which the epic is available.

Homer has always been central to the theory of translation, whether during the *querelle* between the ancients and the moderns,[6] or in Joseph Spence's essay on Pope's *Odyssey* (1726–27). Individual traditions of Homeric translation, for example in seventeenth-century France, have been discussed well.[7] The debate in England is illustrated by the collection *Homer in English*, edited by George Steiner (1996). Translating Homer became a Victorian national pastime, sparking a controversy between Matthew Arnold and F.W. Newman.[8] Arnold identified four qualities inherent in Homeric poetry: it is rapid, uses plain and direct syntax and language, expresses plain and direct ideas, and is 'eminently noble'. Few translations have even today reproduced these undeniable qualities. Indeed, there have been few remarkable translations of the whole *Odyssey*, although the good ones have been reprinted and studied closely.[9] Into this category fall such hardy perennials as Chapman's version, Alexander Pope's *Odyssey* (1725),[10] Dacier's *Odyssey* in France during the same period, Johann Heinrich Voss's German hexameter version of 1781, and E.V. Rieu's, worldwide, after the Second World War.

The quandaries faced by the Homeric translator differ from those posed by the *Aeneid*, because Homeric epic originated orally. Poetry produced and passed around other bards from memory, without the aid of writing, has distinctive features, such as the typical scene that recurs with minor modifications (guests arriving, sacrifice, divine epiphany). Oral poetry is marked by ring composition, similes, catalogues, doublets and digressions, as well as the feature most obvious in translation – repeated epithets and formulaic phrases recurring in the same metrical positions.[11] Walcott opened his stage version of the *Odyssey* (1992) with a loose hexameter blues rendition of the opening lines, performed by blind Billy Blue. His fifth line is a transliteration of Homer's opening hexameter, with its effect – which combines the poem's interests in sailing and weaving – explained afterwards:

> *andra moi ennepe mousa polutropon hos mala polla …*
> The shuttle of the sea moves back and forth on this line,
>
> All night, like the surf, she shuttles and doesn't fall
> Asleep, then her rosy fingers at dawn unstitch the design.[12]

The challenge facing any *Odyssey* translator can be illustrated with the epithet that appears, programmatically, in that first line – the word *polútropos*, describing Odysseus. *Polútropos* means something like 'much-turning', but the 'many turns' could be connected with Odysseus' many journeys, his many tricks, or his command of every branch of rhetoric.[13] In 1616, Chapman opted for periphrasis and alliteration with the letter 'w':

> The man, O Muse, inform, that many a way
> Wound with his wisdom…

Ogilby (1665) kept complications to a minimum with 'prudent'; the pragmatist Hobbes (1686) simply left it out! Pope picked up on the idea of wisdom in 1725–26, proposing 'The man for wisdom's various arts renown'd'. But Cowper in 1791 branched out with the much more daring opening,

> Muse make the man they theme, for shrewdness famed
> And genius versatile …

'Shrewd and 'versatile' have subsequently become translations of choice amongst the unadventurous. But there have been more noteworthy 'turnings' of *polútropos* meanwhile: Butcher and Lang's proto-boy-scout of an Odysseus is 'so ready at need' (1879); the ingenious Butler's fin-de-siècle hero is 'ingenious' (1900); A.T. Murray's pedestrian Loeb (1919) offered 'the man of many devices', before Caulfield's attempted hexameter *Odyssey* touched a new psychological chord with 'Sing me the restless man, O

Muse ...' in 1923. Rieu's wartime sea captain is 'resourceful'; T.E. Lawrence (1932) and Lattimore (1965) sat on a fence with 'the various-minded man' and 'the man of many ways' respectively, improved by the reliably poetic Fagles as 'the man of twists and turns' (1996), while Shewring (1980) proposed the vague 'man of wide-ranging spirit'. But there is a new intuition in Walcott's version, as sung by Billy Blue, that *polútropos* refers to the multiplicity of tales surrounding Odysseus:

> Gone sing 'bout that man because his stories please us.[14]

That no canonical term has emerged for rendering *polútropos* suggests that no offering has been entirely satisfactory, unlike the oft-repeated Greek formulae within the poem itself. Some are so superb that the bards ceased to improve upon them. 'When rosy-fingered dawn, the early born, appeared ...' occurs 20 times in the *Odyssey*, and the phrase 'rosy-fingered dawn' on an additional five occasions. But even in translation from the beautiful assonance of *rhododaktulos Ēōs*, it is difficult to see how any image could better capture the effect of a dawn morning than pink streaks fanning across the horizon like a woman's fingers (Fig. 2.1).

The oral genesis of the Homeric poems has provoked consistent interest. Cognitive psychologists and even computer programmers have examined how memory functions by systematic analysis of mnemonic processes in Homeric epic; visual images within narrative are symbols that prompt the use of whole clusters of related phrases, speeches and actions.[15] The appeal of the Homeric epics as oral poems is well conveyed in Marvin Bell's poem *Typesetting the Odyssey*, where a typesetter fails to transfer poetic magic into print.[16] Typesetting itself has become obsolete since the advent of electronic word-processing and digital literature. Indeed, because the link-structure in hypertext novels allows for stories without any sequential order, as well as creative input from the 'audient', the notion of the oral epic text has found an unexpected new fan base. There are similarities between the bards' production of their lays and the open-ended nature of digital storytelling, not least the absence of an authoritative printed text with a predetermined conclusion.[17]

The breakthrough in the understanding of Homer's orality came in 1930 and 1932, with publications by the American classicist Milman Parry, inspired by the work of a Slovenian philologist named Matija Murko. Murko collected oral epics in what was then called Yugoslavia. Parry then travelled to Europe to research the South Slavic epic tradition, with the assistance of Albert Lord and a performer of epics – a *guslar* – named Nikola Vujnović. Their collection of recordings, now housed at Harvard University, showed that illiterate singers could improvise massive poems from a repertoire of formulaic language structurally similar to Homer's.[18] This discovery, by knocking Homer off the pedestal he had occupied as a 'consummate literary artist' of the Western tradition, raised the status of traditions of oral epic everywhere, especially in Third World countries. An intense sequence in Walcott's *Omeros* involves its hero, Achille, in a visionary return to his ancestral African home. He listens in his tribe's council hut to the village singer and soothsayer – griot – sing the epic of the African tribes' enslavement and Atlantic crossing; the griot is comparable with Homer and Dante. Just as Walcott uses the content of the Greek *Odyssey* and the form of Dante's rhyming tercets to recreate an African spiritual ancestry, so the Greek Hephaestus, the Christian deity and the African Ogun are all evoked at the Caribbean island's volcano.[19]

Even prior to Parry, Homer's reputation helped to preserve oral performance traditions in developing countries. One tradition, studied by Russian anthropologists in the mid-nineteenth century, was the folk poetry sung by the Kyrgyz people, whose *Manas*, a poem longer than the *Iliad* and *Odyssey* combined, describes the heroism of the Kyrgyz past. Storytellers called Manaschi improvise during emotionally vibrant performances of set pieces at public events such as race meets. The respect which the *Manas* has encountered is related to its perceived affinities with the Homeric epics. On the other hand, there is a price to be paid here, because the term *epic*, which is Western and literary, has affected what type of indigenous oral performances have been recorded; when it comes to African culture, as many oral performances are lost as have been preserved because they are performed with dance, or by women, or do not narrate narrowly defined heroic actions.[20]

Yet the oral genesis of the *Odyssey* certainly helps to explain its significance for black writers. Henry Louis Gates has noticed the importance of Parry's research to the mid-twentieth-century renaissance of black literature, with its oral origins.[21] Ralph Ellison's black American Odysseus in *Invisible Man* (1952) owes his success to his ability as extempore public speaker. Ellison believed in the sophistication of African-American oral traditions and jazz (he initially trained as a musician); in an introduction he wrote to *Invisible Man* in 1981, he spoke of the importance of improvisational forms in its genesis – the rich culture of the folk tales told in barber shops, and the 'wild starburst of metamorphosis' to which a jazz musician could subject a melody.[22]

The jazz French horn player David Amram says, 'Homer was the first great jazz poet or scatter or rapper ... he did the *Iliad* with no notes because he couldn't see. Someone wrote it down later.'[23] The improvisational medium of Rap Music, along with the Hip-Hop culture to which it is allied, has parallels with Greek oral epic. They both depend on a distinct rhythm and dialect featuring conventional formulaic phrases. There are also recognized 'sub-genres' of Rap, involving speech acts like boasting or invective that resemble speech types in Homer. Improvised raps assume a formalized relationship with audience or rival and a particular performance context: the 'Concept Rap' tells a story; the 'Freestyle Rap' is improvised in rivalry with that of another rapper; the 'Battle Rap' relates such a competition, and, like it, includes formulaic elements such as insult, self-glorification and violent metaphors. There are also 'bragging' raps, where the performer boasts about sexual conquests. Rap also has affinities with Homeric epic in terms of its representation of heroes and villains. Rap artists develop an identity that transcends the role of poet: 'they are cultural icons after the fashion of ancient mythic characters';[24] Gangsta Rap and Political Rap music communicate an idealized masculine behaviour.

The *Odyssey* is more interested than the *Iliad* in poetry.[25] From the emotional reaction to Phemius' performance in Book 1, the poem discusses the emotive and aesthetic qualities of enchanting, spell-binding, shapely, honey-sweet song, and offers metaphorical analogies to the art of putting a poem together – weaving and bow-stringing, travelling down pathways, and pleas to the Muse for inspiration. Its terminology informed ancient poetics and aesthetics.[26] All the more self-conscious poets, such as Pindar, Callimachus and Horace, formulated their theories in response to Homer, and the discussions of Poetry in Plato, Aristotle's *Poetics*, Longinus' *On the Sublime* and Horace's *Ars Poetica* all use parameters laid down in the *Odyssey*.[27] These treatises became in turn the foundation texts of aesthetic theory; even now all debates in literary criticism, such as discussion of the impersonal poetic voice which produced the postmodern Death of the Author,[28] build themselves a family tree leading back to Homer.

Artists in prose have been no less mesmerized than poets. Indeed, in the mid-twentieth century the *Odyssey* was felt to be better suited to translation in prose, especially after this was said by T.E. Lawrence, sometimes known as 'Odysseus of Arabia'.[29] Lawrence's own experience of the First World War encouraged him to read Homeric epic as a genre akin to biography.[30] He found that the war in Arabia lived up to epic expectations of battle fostered by his late Victorian classical education.[31] But his guilt at his role in the Arab revolt, as he describes it in *The Seven Pillars of Wisdom* (1922), led to a post-war crisis of identity that found a reflection in Odysseus, the hero who sees the *fallout* of the siege of Troy and the deaths of his comrades. Lawrence certainly stressed to his printer that his experience of the eastern Mediterranean uniquely qualified him to translate the *Odyssey*:

> For years we were doing up a city of roughly the Odysseus period. I have handled the weapons, armour, utensils of those times, explored their houses, planned their cities. I have hunted wild boars and watched lions, sailed the Aegean in sailed ships, bent bows, lived with pastoral peoples, woven textiles, built boats and killed many men.[32]

His 'dazzling mechanical genius', which allowed him latterly to make a living out of speedboat design, fostered a camaraderie with the raft-building Odysseus.[33] His affinity with the master narrator who conceals and distorts the truth at will can be seen in *The Seven Pillars of Wisdom*, which 'vacillates between a historical and personal expression'.[34] Yet the strongest feature of Lawrence's translation is his characterizations. He reacted to the characters in the poem personally (he referred to Menelaus as 'a master-prig' and to Odysseus as 'fish-smelly'),[35] and put finely nuanced phrases into their mouths in the manner of a dramatist.

Aspiring verse translators of the *Odyssey* were also discouraged by E.V. Rieu's Penguin novelistic translation, published just after the Second World War, which became a global bestseller. The founding volume of the Penguin Classics series, costing just one shilling and sixpence, Rieu's *Odyssey* had by 1964 sold over a staggering 2 million copies. Until the publication of *Lady Chatterley's Lover*, Rieu's *Odyssey* was the bestselling UK paperback.[36] The irony is that Penguin was initially concerned about the financial viability of the project, and later its editor-in-chief, William Emrys Williams, downplayed Homer's role by observing that Rieu had 'made a good book better'![37]

The one notable poetic English translation at this time was by Robert Fitzgerald. Educated at Harvard, where he had performed the title role of Sophocles' *Philoctetes* under the direction of Milman Parry, Fitzgerald worked with dictionaries in order to analyse every resonance before translating the words, as he insisted, into another poem altogether. His flexible blank verse was unafraid of weighty epithets ('Hermes the Wayfinder') and unexpected word order (Odysseus 'racked his own heart groaning').[38] No higher tribute to his work could be made than Seamus Heaney's poem 'In memoriam: Robert Fitzgerald', which uses the flight of the arrow from Odysseus' bowstring, as it 'sang a swallow's note', to evoke the lasting impact of Fitzgerald's translation:

> The great test over, while the gut's still humming,
> This time it travels out of all knowing

Perfectly aimed towards the vacant centre.[39]

The ancient Greeks had also already seen the potential offered by the *Odyssey* to poets in smaller-scale genres,[40] and it has since resurfaced in every conceivable genre – epigram, satire, elegy, ballad, lyric, poetic monologue, haiku, sonnets, prose poems – some examples of which will be encountered later in this volume. It is a favourite with enthusiasts of the limerick, who are now publishing their versions of the *Odyssey* online, as in the contributions by one Chris Doyle in the *Omnificent English Dictionary in Limerick Form*:

> Here's Aeaea, the Island of Dawn,
> Where Odysseus brandished his brawn
> In a battle with Circe.
> Removing her curse, he
> Turned swine back to men and was gone.[41]

Yet the genre in which the presence of the *Odyssey* has been most fully investigated is the European tradition of epic, from Apollonius to Walcott, via Virgil, Tasso, Dante, Milton and Kazantzakis.

The voyages conducted by Apollonius' Jason and his four-book *Argonautica*, written in the third century BCE, revisit some of the places where Odysseus travelled, including the island of Circe. The first six books of Virgil's Roman epic the *Aeneid*, especially the wanderings that Aeneas narrates at the court of the Carthaginian queen Dido in Book III, are a brilliantly conceived response to the *Odyssey*; the premise is that the Trojan survivor (Aeneas) and the Greek survivor (Odysseus) are *simultaneously* sailing around the Mediterranean in frustrated quests for their respective destinations. The unseen presence of Odysseus is felt particularly in the rewriting of the Cyclops episode. Virgil gave this story to a new narrator, an eyewitness to the bloody confrontation, the Ithacan Achaemenides. He had been left behind in the Cyclops' den when Ulysses had hurried to escape (3.613–54). In Ovid's miniature version of the *Odyssey*, incorporated in Book 14 of his epic *Metamorphoses*, he capped the eyewitness account of the Cyclopes by telling the story of Circe from the perspective of Macareus, a member of Odysseus' crew, who had been changed into a pig: 'I began to bristle with hair, unable to speak now, giving out hoarse grunts instead of words ... I felt my mouth stiffening into a long snout, my neck swelling with brawn' (14.277–84).

But even epic traditions where influence is less easy to prove show obvious parallels with the *Odyssey*, such as the *Chanson de Roland* and other *chansons de geste*, in particular the dangerous sea-voyage undergone by the hero of the thirteenth-century *Huon de Bordeaux*. Specialists in

French epic have pointed out the importance of the *Odyssey* in the creation of a more 'romantic' hero than was supplied by the *Iliad*.[42] The presence of the Homeric poems has certainly led to the production of other kinds of epic in European history, especially since the mid-eighteenth century when the 'discovery' of old 'druidical' ballads began to be linked to rising national identities. Welsh harp players were likened to Homeric bards (see Fig. 2.2), and in Scotland James Macpherson published *The Poems of Ossian* (1760–93), supposedly by a third-century Gaelic songster.[43] Although mostly Macpherson's own invention, these poems inflamed some of the best minds across eighteenth-century Europe,[44] thus spurring on poets to record their own people's ancient songs and to look afresh at Homer in their attempts to create a national literature.

One result can be seen in *The Old Soldier Gorev* by Pavel Katenin (1835), an architect of Russian literature. His *Achilles and Homer* (1826) is in a Russian hexameter, but his long *Odyssey* poem uses a demotic pentameter more acceptable to the Russian ear. Moreover, the poem transfers the story of the *Odyssey* to a real, Russian contemporary community. The peasant Makar Gorev leaves his wife and son, and sets out for the Napoleonic wars. He is taken prisoner and is the last to return home, after ten years of wandering. On home-coming Gorev is taken for a beggar, and becomes a guest in his own house. Stylistically, Katenin adapts to his Russian form many Homeric features, including similes, formulae, epithets and direct speech. But he also replaces gods with Russian peasants, and Homer's wily Odysseus with the credulous Gorev. His self-seeking 'Penelope' can identify a suitable new husband, and his competent 'Telemachus' takes over his father's estate and impedes his return. This is a truly Russian *Odyssey*, both in form and content.[45]

The *Odyssey* has also inspired translations that have *themselves* in turn inspired new poetic creativity. Keats penned a famous sonnet after first looking into Chapman's translation of Homer (see Chapter 6). Yet the palm here must surely go to Ezra Pound's first *Canto* (1930), the introductory poem in his *A Draft of XXX Cantos*, which translates the first 65 lines of Book 11 of the *Odyssey* (the description of the journey from Circe to the land of the dead), and compresses the subsequent 90. But Pound's project is more than a Modernist plunge into the abyss of myth: he is creating his own version of the poet's traditional homage to the *Odyssey* as the very text that he rightly believed constitutes the source of the Western poetic subject.[46]

Pound's father's first name was Homer, and from an early stage his guiding myth was that of Odysseus; his attraction to Mussolini's politics was based on his idea that the Italian leader was rebuilding a lost Ithaca in his homeland.[47] Canto I translates the passage in which Odysseus travels to the Underworld to speak with Tiresias. Like Odysseus, Pound seeks knowledge in the minds of men long dead. He cannot speak to them directly, as Odysseus does, but their ghosts linger in old books. In Paris he had picked up a Renaissance Latin translation of the *Odyssey* by Andreas Divus, published in 1538, and it is this version that he himself translated in Canto I. However, in translating it, he used poetic conventions derived from Old English verse. Pound knew that the shape of Odysseus' quest has survived through millennia, but he also knew that the means for its survival have been all the many metamorphoses it has undergone into the particular words of new places and new times. If we want to see ancient visions, we must seek them wherever they have reappeared in successive cultures, and in Canto I Pound reveals the complex filter of language and altering culture which is his only way to view the past.

Hugh Kenner's book *The Pound Era* documents the encounter with the epic undergone simultaneously by the other Modernists Eliot and Joyce. Long before *Ulysses* (also 1922), Frank in *The Dubliners*, in his yachting cap, reveals Joyce wrestling with the Odyssean hero.[48] But Joyce's attraction to the *Odyssey* raises the question of children's versions, because it was through one such book, Charles Lamb's *The Adventures of Ulysses* (1808), that Joyce first experienced the epic.[49] Indeed, a reason why the *Odyssey* has achieved such cultural penetration is because it has been regarded as suitable material for children's books, and latterly children's theatre, cartoons and videos. Many people have had their imaginations fired by the *Odyssey* in childhood, and the tradition of children's versions leads back to the one that inspired Joyce, which was reprinted many times.[50]

Lamb's *The Adventures of Ulysses* was the idea of William Godwin and his new wife Mary Jane, who had together established a publishing house; these impoverished Godwins, whose combined household contained five children, had experience in storytelling for the young. After Lamb's retelling of stories from Shakespeare for children in 1807, it was the turn of the *Odyssey*. In his preface Lamb admitted his debt to Chapman's translation and Fénelon's *The Adventures of Telemachus* (see pp 50–1). This is to frame the *Odyssey* as a moral tale for the education of boys. Lamb compressed the story of Telemachus, cut much dialogue and changed the order in which the episodes are told by reverting to chronological linearity. Lamb's Ulysses appreciates beautiful goddesses, but does not sleep with them, nor even with Penelope, because this retelling stops just short of Ithacan bedtime. This is a gentler person than the Homeric Odysseus. But the book, if morally sanitized, is beautifully written and calculated to appeal to children. At this time Charles was drawing strength from his unorthodox religious convictions in order to keep control both of his own drinking and his sister Mary's sanity; after stabbing their mother (who had neglected her as a child) to death in 1796, Mary had only been allowed out of the asylum because her brother had promised to oversee her. Mary's input into Charles's writing during these years was immense; much of the first children's version of the *Odyssey* may have been written by a childless manic depressive who had murdered her own mother.

There are now many ingenious versions of the *Odyssey* for children. *Odysseus in the Serpent Maze* imagines Odysseus' boyhood adventures, involving Penelope and Helen as children, pirates, a satyr and the inventor Daedalus. *Waiting for Odysseus* tells Odysseus' story through the eyes of Penelope, Circe, Athena and 'his old nanny Eurycleia'; *The Pig Scrolls, by Gryllus the Pig* is told from the perspective of one of the crewmen turned into a pig.[51] Other children's versions include Marcia Williams's touching comic-strip cartoon (1996), and Rosemary Sutcliff's *The Wanderings of Odysseus* (1995), which preserves the melancholy tone and brutality of the original, although she does censor the relationships with Calypso and Circe. Also related to the Lamb tradition are the numerous stage versions of the *Odyssey* for children that have been performed recently. These include Tom Smith's hilarious *The Odyssey* (Polyphemus is a myopic schoolgirl),[52] and John Murrell's exciting Canadian version of the travelogue, performed in June 2005 at the Ottawa International Children's Festival.

Children's versions of the *Odyssey* have included TV serializations, comic-strips such as *Classics Illustrated* no. 81 (1951),[53] and animated cartoons, most recently the reductive 47-minute *Odyssey: Written by Homer* released by Burbank Films in 2004. These emerge from the traditional relationship, dating from the early twentieth century, between the *Odyssey* and cinema, in which 'translation' has taken on new meanings alongside new technologies by which epic may be transferred to (audio)visual media. Paradoxically, the movie of the *Odyssey* that has reached the widest audience exists only in snippets. It is a film being made within the frame plot of a movie integral to French New Wave Cinema – Jean-Luc Godard's *Le Mépris* (*Contempt*, 1963). The director of the art-house version of the *Odyssey* under construction is Fritz Lang, acted by himself. There is one scene where the rushes are scrutinized, and they include dazzling white statues of the gods against azure skies, who seem to be coming to life. Penelope stands against a bright yellow wall, adorned with heavy make-up suggesting Mycenaean frescoes; there are shots of sea-nymphs and Odysseus swimming towards a rocky outcrop.

The film was adapted from Albert Moravia's novel *Il Disprezzo* (1954, usually translated as *A Ghost at Noon*), but stressed the triangular tension between Odysseus, Penelope and the vindictive sea-god Poseidon, and their real-life counterparts, the French screenwriter Paul Javal (acted by Michel Piccoli), his wife Camille (Brigitte Bardot) and the cynical American film producer Jeremy Prokosch (Jack Palance). In the 1950s Moravia, after repudiating the use of third-person narrative, was experimenting with the first person, and his Odysseus-figure narrates the novel. The film, however, consistently adopts the wife's perspective.

The marriage of Paul and Camille breaks up, just as the Lang movie collapses because of tensions between artistic and commercial motivations. But *Le Mépris* explores the process of translation itself – not only between languages and historical periods, but between media. As Godard has himself insisted, written discourse 'automatically' changes when it is turned into film.[54] During the rushes sequence, the discussion turns to European poetry in different languages – Dante and Hölderlin. Indeed, Godard's alterations to the Moravia novel *heighten* the focus on translation. In the novel, the producer believes that while the Anglo-Saxon countries have the Bible, the Mediterranean has the *Odyssey*.[55] But in the film, the *Odyssey* film is to be made by a German director (because Schliemann discovered Troy), shot in Italy and produced by a North American. Godard's *Odyssey* is far more international; his Odysseus has travelled further than Homer's.[56] Godard himself wrote that *Le Mépris* could actually have been entitled *In Search of Homer*;[57] the *Odyssey* itself is irrecoverable, fragmented into an ever increasing number of different retellings.

Yet *Le Mépris* itself retells some of the themes in the *Odyssey*, at least as Godard interpreted it. Paul assaults a neoclassical statue of a woman during his quarrel with Camille; in their apartment, just as in the world of Odysseus, 'one must be careful not to anger the gods'.[58] Moreover, Camille reads a book arguing that it solves nothing to murder a sexual rival, which brings to mind not only her husband's jealousy of Prokosch, but the carnage in *Odyssey* 22. Later, Paul and Camille themselves rewrite, despite their estrangement and Camille's sudden death, the marriage of Odysseus and Penelope.

Just one year after Alberto Moravia published *Il Disprezzo*, his compatriot Mario Camerini, a renowned director of thrillers, achieved what the filmmakers in Moravia's novel fail to create: a coherent film of the *Odys-*

*sey*. This achievement has rarely been equalled (except by another Italian, Franco Rossi, who in 1968 directed an admired eight-part Italian TV serialization entitled *Odissea*, now almost impossible for anyone outside the charmed circle of Italian media historians to access). *Ulisse* has an almost all-Italian cast except for Kirk Douglas (pre-Spartacus) as the hero, and Anthony Quinn as a horrid Antinous. Silvia Mangano plays both a dignified Penelope and a sinister Circe. The movie, with its unexpected ethical complexity, has stood the test of time. The psychological struggle of Ulisse was avant-garde in its time and stills works. Douglas intelligently portrays a man torn between his family and adventure – a conflict brilliantly evoked during the Sirens episode. They are never shown, but are given the seductive voices of Ulisse's wife and son as the camera offers a long dolly-in on his face. An authority on epic cinema has written that Camerini's version works because it combines a level of persuasive authenticity (the impression is passably Mycenaean) with a sense of the supernatural power surrounding Odysseus; the colourful special effects by Eugen Schüfftan, moreover, helped the film (which preserves the chronology and sequential flashbacks of the original) to develop its story 'in an intelligent, notably urgent style'.[59]

There has been one film realization of the *Odyssey* subsequently, Konchalovsky's version (1997), discussed in Chapters 8 and 14. But the *Odyssey* has a more complicated relationship with cinema than this implies. It has held a special place in aspiring screenwriters' lore since Christopher Vogler's bestselling handbook *The Writer's Journey* (1992). The formula for a successful screenplay that Vogler advises is structured around quotations and archetypal figures that he traces to the *Odyssey* – the wise elder figure (Mentor or Obi Wan Kenobi in George Lucas's 1977 *Star Wars*), the Herald figure (Hermes or the telegraph clerk in Fred Zinnemann's *High Noon* (1952)), the Shape-shifter (Proteus and countless morphing superheroes and their adversaries), and so on. Another analysis of Hollywood plot structure emphasizes the importance of the 'classical storytelling technique' that involves two parallel protagonists who pursue, simultaneously, different courses of action although they end up working together towards a shared goal. This formula is exemplified in Richard Donner's *Lethal Weapon* (1987), but it could have been lifted straight from the *Odyssey*, with its separated father and son's parallel travels and eventual reunion.[60]

The perceived affinities between film and epic-heroic narrative have, however, produced regular allegations that there were parallels being consciously drawn by screenwriters of movies that may superficially bear little relation to the *Odyssey*. Examples I have encountered include the figure of the nerdish Seymour in both the original 1960 film *Little Shop of Horrors* and its 1986 remake,[61] *Watership Down* (1978), *Captain Corelli's Mandolin* (2001, an adaptation of Louis de Bernières' novel, directed by John Madden), *Waterworld* (1995), Tim Burton's *Big Fish* (2003), and the maritime adventures in *The SpongeBob SquarePants Movie* (2004), which include one-eyed foes and an angry sea god. The important point is no longer whether any particular screenwriters have drawn on the *Odyssey*, or indeed ever read it, but that they would almost all self-consciously cite the *Odyssey* as a key text in the history of adventure narrative. This epic's status, at least in Hollywood, has once again – and in a new sense – become a matter of legend.

# 3

# SHAPE-SHIFTING

In Shakespeare's *Henry VI Part 3*, Richard boasts, 'I can add colours to the cameleon,/Change shapes with Proteus, for advantages' (Act 3, Scene 2), and of all the words that the *Odyssey* has given us, the term 'protean' is one of the most familiar.[1] It stems from Menelaus' account of his meeting with the sea-divinity Proteus, who slept on a beach on an island named Pharos, north of the mouth of the Nile. Proteus is the archetypal shape-shifter; his labile nature is related to his identification with the mutable element of the sea. It is also reflected in the colony of seals of whom he is the herdsman, and with whom he is so intimate that he sleeps amidst them on the sand. Experts in shamanic lore know that the seal, as a mammal similar to humans in voice, size and ability to cry real tears, holds a special place in the metamorphosis tales of many cultures; in Celtic myth, enchanted seals turn into irresistibly handsome male visitors who sexually comfort the widows of men lost at sea.[2]

Proteus' own repertoire of physical presentations, his daughter Eidothea tells Menelaus, includes water and fire as well as every beast on the earth; when Menelaus and his men did finally apprehend this slippery old being, he responded by turning into a lion, a snake, a panther, a giant boar, running water and a huge leafy tree (4.417–18, 455–9). There were other shape-shifters in this league to be found in early Greek epic poetry, such as Periclymenus (the son of another sea-divinity, Nereus), and the females Nemesis and Mestra.[3] But the *Odyssey* provides the only extended account of serial metamorphosis in archaic Greek literature, which explains why Proteus achieved his archetypal status.

Most shape-changing beings in Greek myth do not have full membership of the immortal pantheon, but are intermediate figures, inimical to both gods and heroes.[4] Proteus' gift for changing shape is in his own power; he uses it at will and to his own advantage. But ultimately he is worsted and must give Menelaus something as a result of the contest; his gift is special knowledge. There are parallels with the biblical story of Jacob wrestling all night with a mysterious being – whether a man (according to Genesis 32:24) or 'the angel' (according to Hosea 12:4) – and winning thereby knowledge of the parts of animals that can be eaten by Jews. Menelaus acquires instead god-like omniscience, for Proteus shares with him the secrets of past, present and future. The knowledge brings him both grief and joy. He hears the fates that befell the other Achaeans after Troy – the drowning of his comrade Ajax, and the murder of his brother Agamemnon. He learns that Odysseus has survived, but is stranded on Calypso's island. Menelaus is taught the ritual sacrifices to Zeus and the other gods that he must himself perform in order to win safe passage back home from Egypt. But finally, Proteus gives him the knowledge denied almost all men – the circumstances of his own death and the nature of the afterlife that he will enjoy: he will not die at home in Argos, but be taken by the gods to the Elysian plain at the end of the earth. This blissful place knows only fair weather and soft winds, and offers men an easier life than anywhere else in the world.

The reason Proteus supplies for Menelaus' immortality is that he was married to Helen, daughter of the immortal Zeus. But the story as it is told implies that the supernatural knowledge and the immortality are somehow prizes for beating Proteus in the contest of strength – for remaining unchanged in the face of the very principle of change itself – just as Jacob was rewarded with special insights into God's will because he subdued the mysterious all-night wrestler. Menelaus, like Jacob, has faced and known 'the reservoir of change from which all futures flow'.[5]

The theme of metamorphosis, however ancient, chimes with much more recent challenges to the unitary, Western notion of a changeless, secure identity. Emerson wrote of Man in his *Essay on History*:

> The philosophical perception of identity through endless mutations of form, makes him know the Proteus. What else am I who laughed or wept yesterday, who slept last night like a corpse, and this morning stood and ran? And what see I on any side but the transmigrations of Proteus?[6]

As Marina Warner puts it, the principle of physical change as manifestation of organic vitality and the pulse in the body or art not only 'lies at the heart' of classical myth, but also, not coincidentally, 'runs counter to notions of unique, individual integrity of identity in the Judaeo-Christian tradition'.[7] Moreover, it has become easier for people to take delight in the idea of transformation – witness the interest in shape-shifting powers in recent children's cinema – now that raising ontological questions no longer flies in the face of Christian suspicion of the supernatural, and terror of the pagan concept of metamorphosis.[8] Yet the zoomorphic (animal-form) transformations of the *Odyssey* pose questions about the nature of the subject, of consciousness and its relationship to the body and time. In what sense is Proteus still Proteus if he has become an animal, let alone an element? The men whom Circe transforms, we are told, still retain the same minds – yet surely a 'self' cannot withstand such material alteration?[9] The same question is asked, in poetic form, by the member of Odysseus' crew who wakens in Thom Gunn's 'Moly' to a

> Nightmare of beasthood, snorting, how to wake.
> I woke. What beasthood skin she made me take?[10]

On Circe's island, Odysseus' lieutenant Eurylochus takes an advance party of 22 men to her palace, where she wines and dines them. But Eurylochus himself stays outside, hidden, to observe what happens and report back to Odysseus. The wine is drugged, and makes the crewmen forget their homes; when Circe uses her magic wand on her dazed victims, they instantly acquire the body, bristles and voices of pigs (10.239–43), while retaining their human consciousness (see Fig. 3.1). They can only be restored when Circe applies a different drug, in the form of an ointment, to their porcine forms, whereupon they lose their bristles and become the same humans again – only even better looking than before (10.388–99).

Circe – the *maga famosissima*, 'most famous sorceress', as St Augustine called her (*City of God* 18.17) – is probably the most famous figure in the *Odyssey* besides its hero, Penelope and Polyphemus. Part of the power of the Circe story is that changing a man into a pig has a resonance particular to the attributes of the animal, especially in a peasant society like ancient Greece where humans lived in physical proximity to their farm animals. Pigs are symbolic of dirt and animal appetites, but they are also often perceived as having a rather sinister 'dead-alive look', and their mouth takes on the same position whether they yawn or squeal. Either way, they can look to humans as if they are laughing.[11] Transformation into animal form is a motif attested in the mythologies of every world culture, and in the code of pre-literate societies it has much to say about primeval patterns of belief.[12] Anthropologists would include hunting and sacrifice rituals entailing homeopathic or sympathetic magic, initiation rites involving ritual enactments of animal identities, totemism, shamanism and reincarnation. But in the Western tradition, it is Circe's transformation of Odysseus' crew into pigs that is the ancestor of all our countless tales of forcible human–animal metamorphosis from ancient Greece via Ovid and Apuleius to Kafka and recent fiction.[13]

Skulsky has classified the meanings of the fantasy of transformation in major literature. In the *Odyssey*, he argues, metamorphosis is a way of talking about enchantment. Odysseus' men are pigs because they forget their own pasts and are enchanted by Circe, losing the human power of intelligent autonomous agency. It is crucial to this story that Odysseus himself can use his brain and resist the enchantment (see Fig. 3.2); this is with the help of Hermes' gift of the plant *moly* which acts as an antidote to Circe's power, alongside tactical advice to respond to her magic with violence.[14] This story contrasts with Ovid's Latin epic *Metamorphoses*, where human–animal transformations are just one type amongst several (human–plant, human–constellation, god–animal). Moreover, they express a more wide-ranging ontological and metaphysical anxiety about the instability of the self and the beloved, the self and the universe, matter and mind, empirical reality and the world beyond, and therefore about the boundaries that demarcate all these categories from each other. The transformation of Lucius into an ass in Apuleius' Latin novel *The Golden Ass* has, according to Skulsky, a different literary purpose: it becomes a satirical tool used to attack superstitious belief in the form of an entertaining fiction that yet, in a curious manner, ends up affirming religion. But nearly two millennia later, when Kafka turns Gregor Samsa into a beetle, he is offering a metaphor for 'alienation without grace' – an almost Absurdist expression of the futility and bleakness of the human condition.

In a wonderful satirical dialogue entitled *On the Rationality of Animals*, Plutarch staged a debate between Odysseus and Gryllus, or 'Grunter', one of Circe's pigs who refuses to turn back into a man. The relative virtue practised by humans and beasts is examined in pseudo-philosophical style, with the beasts getting the better of the argument. Because Plutarch elsewhere protested against excessive cruelty to animals, and offered arguments in support of vegetarianism, this ancient response to the Circe episode in the *Odyssey* became in the early seventeenth century a foundation text in the history of animal rights.[15] But Warner has pointed out that the dialogue, which is really a joke against people, 'is an inspired early satire in the great fabric of the literature of folly', and that Gryllus became the emblem of a certain kind of refusal, from Machiavelli to Pieter Breughel, 'of a laughter that mocks self-righteousness'. Such refuseniks were called *grylli* because they used wit to point out human shortcomings.[16]

Perhaps the most famous pig-humans of them all, where the metaphor has a transparently political rather than generically satirical purpose, are those featured in George Orwell's picture of totalitarian tyranny in *Animal Farm* (1945). But the technique he used, strictly speaking, was not animal metamorphosis but zoomorphism (also used in a rather different way by Anna Sewell in *Black Beauty* (1877), written from the perspective of a real horse). Napoleon, Snowball and Squealer may be thinly disguised humans, but they have always been pigs, and always will be. True metamorphosis does occur, however, in the case of Marie Darrieussecq's *Pig Tales* (*Truismes* (1995), subtitled in English *A Novel of Lust and Transformation*). The female narrator is a sex-industry worker who turns into a sow. She has a relationship, as the subject of metamorphosis, with Ovid's sexploited heroines, but a more specific one with the Lucius of Apuleius' *Metamorphoses*, a foundation text in the history of the Western novel (on which topic Darrieussecq used to lecture at the University of Lille). The relationships between Homer's Circe, Apuleius' ass-hero and Darrieussecq's pig-heroine have excited less attention than her more oblique references to individuals in Kafka and Orwell, but they are revealed in several features.[17] This female writer (an avowed feminist) makes her point about male treatment of women's bodies through transformation into a pig, thus inscribing her own subjectivity on both the *Odyssey* and Apuleius' novel, two of the paramount foundation texts of subjectivity in fiction.

Proteus is emblematic of the whole *Odyssey* because of the central position it gives to transformation and disguise – indeed acting of parts: it is significant that for post-Renaissance theorists of theatre, Proteus became an enduring metaphor for the actor's pliability.[18] Odysseus himself has always been an accomplished actor: Helen remembers how, long ago at Troy, Odysseus had entered the city on a reconnaissance mission; he had disguised himself as a household slave by inflicting blows on his own body and wearing rags (4.244–8). He was to revive this role a decade later on the Ithacan stage. He lived in a world in which it was half-expected that visitors might turn out to be gods play-acting, a possibility of which the other suitors try to warn Antinous (17.483–7). And the prize for best actor in the *Odyssey* must indeed go to Athena, from the moment that she appears on the very threshold of the Ithacan court disguised as a 'leader of the Taphian people' (1.103–5). When she assumes her second disguise, as the sensible senior Ithacan Mentor, 'she seemed identical to him both in looks and in voice' (1.268). She is not only a great actress *en travesti* (even Odysseus is not required to perform transvestite parts), but her roles include the youthful Telemachus (whom she impersonates at 2.383), can be sustained at length (she keeps up her Mentor disguise throughout the voyage to Pylos and the first part of Telemachus' encounter with Nestor), can deceive even best friends (in the case of Nausicaa, 6.22), and include several avian forms (1.320; a vulture at 3.371–2). At the poem's close she again wears the form and voice of Mentor, in order to create peace between the families of the suitors and of Odysseus (24.548). Indeed, the concluding formula of the entire poem is 'having likened herself in form and body [to Mentor]'.[19]

Even the stage actor's power to affect his audience psychologically seems pre-empted by the way that such appearances are connected with the *Odyssey*'s interest in emotional change. The first visit of the disguised Athena to Telemachus leaves him 'full of spirit and courage', a change that astonishes him because he can *feel* it in his heart (1.320–3). The ageing actor's ability, in a mask, to impersonate a beautiful young person also seems strangely foreshadowed by the de-ageing makeover that Athena offers Odysseus whenever he needs to maximize the impact of his looks and virility. On Phaeacia, Athena 'made him look taller and stronger, and made his locks hang in curls from his head, like Hyacinth petals'. As a craftsman inlays gold on silverware, she 'poured pleasing grace on his head and shoulders' (6.229–35). With such divine assistance in his toilet, it is scarcely surprising that Nausicaa conveniently helps him because he seems to offer promising husband material.

The *Odyssey*'s fascination with transformations and disguises is undeniably greater than that of the *Iliad*, which contains no serial shape-shifter like Proteus and no humans turned into animals at all. Indeed, the only surviving rival of either Proteus or Circe in archaic literature is the god Dionysus, one of whose own so-called *Homeric Hymns* (7.38–53) relates the myth of his escape from pirates who had abducted him in his true shape – that of a handsome youth. Dionysus first made the ship sprout vines and ivy, and then himself changed into a lion and a bear before turning his adversaries into dolphins. It is no coincidence that this shape-shifting god, once theatre was invented at Athens in the sixth century BCE, became its tutelary deity and the patron of the acting profession. Nor is it any coincidence that theatre was invented in Athens at the same time that it was first enjoying regular, formal recitals of the Homeric epics at public festivals. In this historical context, the *Odyssey* looks heavily pregnant with the art of theatre, a condition brought to fulfilment by the innumerable dramatic works that it has subsequently inspired.

The *Odyssey* was adapted into all three genres of drama – tragedy, satyr play and comedy – invented in Athens; under the Roman Empire, itinerant troupes of actors included in their repertoires the enactment of scenes of bloodshed 'drawn from Homer', perhaps including the Ithacan showdown.[20] Odysseus' catalogue of dead women in Hades (11.225–332), who include Tyro, Oedipus' wife and mother Epicaste (later known as Jocasta), Leda, Phaedra, Ariadne and Eriphyle, not only magnifies Odysseus' status as the only man who has been in contact with all departed humanity, but reveals another facet of the *Odyssey*'s relationship with theatre: these women are included because their genealogies and marriages were distinguished and their fates memorable – the features that subsequently made them so attractive to tragic poets, even if only the ancient Greek plays about Phaedra and Jocasta happen to have survived.[21]

Yet in antiquity the *Odyssey* itself does not seem to have been felt suitable for tragedy. Odysseus of course does make important appearances in tragedy, since he was identified by the fifth-century tragedians as the type of ruthlessly effective public man, driven by motives of expedience, whose actions necessarily cause tragedy in the lives of others (Ajax, Philoctetes, Iphigenia, Hecuba, Polyxena). The way he was configured in Athenian tragedy had much to do with the fact that he was not an Athenian hero. Moreover, he was a supporter of the Peloponnesians at Troy, and it was the Peloponnesian Spartans against whom the classical Athenians waged their longest war in the fifth century. Odysseus plays a significant role in three surviving tragedies, Euripides' *Hecuba* and Sophocles' *Ajax* and *Philoctetes*. All use his reputation for brilliant rhetoric (indeed, he becomes the symbol of the master-sophist/demagogue) and his ability to think up cunning strategies in order to achieve his goals. His *political* instinct and genius are played up far more than in the *Odyssey*, where he is not shown operating in contexts such as the assembly or the management of open war. An exponent of callous *Realpolitik* and *force majeure*, the tragic Odysseus always argues that the more powerful party must win and that resisting this inevitable outcome is a futile, sentimental waste of time.

In every single case he proves *effective*. Odysseus *always* gets what he wants, while creating the tragedies for other people to suffer. This is Odysseus inspected from the point of view of the fifth-century democratic citizen – what role does a man with his particular 'skillset' play in a democratic *polis* where the good of the group is placed higher on the agenda than the good of the individual aristocrat? In *Hecuba* (as later in *Iphigenia in Aulis*, where he does not physically appear, but operates as a terrifying unseen presence), two new features appear: ruthlessness in the face of the suffering of the completely innocent, and a disregard for personal loyalties previously acquired. In *Ajax* he is both humane and cynical, the winner who can afford to be charitable; in *Philoctetes* his role is complicated. He behaves appallingly in any human, moral sense, and yet there is a level on which he is right: getting the war over and done with has become a priority for the entire Greek community, and it would be irrational to allow Philoctetes' personal pride and grudge against the Greeks to jeopardize the greater good. In this play Sophocles uses Odysseus to examine both

(1) the Utilitarian argument that society needs to aim at achieving the greatest happiness for the greatest number (which inevitably means the unhappiness of dissenting minorities), and (2) the ethical conundrum of whether moral ends can justify immoral means.

But why did Odysseus not offer the prototype of a convincing tragic protagonist himself? One reason is that he is neither kin-killer nor committer of incest, and is destined to die peacefully in old age. Moreover, his pragmatism, self-discipline, unerring intelligence, and above all his invariable achievement of successful outcomes in all forms of conflict, have always militated against the development of plot lines that offer theatre spectators tragedies entailing either fall or error. His biggest mistake in the *Odyssey* is his unnecessary, boastful revelation of his name to the blinded Polyphemus, a tactical error that results in the deaths of many of his comrades. Yet the nature of the Cyclops as supernatural giant, and the childlike tenor of much of the way that the story is told (see Chapter 7) made it difficult to present Polyphemus' tale in a tragic mode, although there were satyr plays on the theme (including Euripides' *Cyclops*) and several comedies.[22]

Of Aeschylus' lost *Odyssey* plays, his *Penelope* and *Ostologoi* ('Bone-Collectors') may have been satyr dramas, and his *Psychagōgoi* ('Ghost-raisers'), which had something to do with the *nekuia*, is deeply controversial.[23] On the other hand, Sophocles' lost *Odysseus Acanthoplex* ('Odysseus Spine-Struck'), adapted by the Roman Pacuvius in his *Niptra*, dealt with adventures after the end of the *Odyssey*, and offered the tragic poet the opportunity for his characters to retell famous episodes from the epic, including the descent to the Underworld.[24] But this exception may nevertheless help to prove the rule, since the tragedy was, in Aristotelian terms, less one of action or even character than one of *pathos*: both plays were remembered for the scene in which Odysseus lamented the pain caused by a wound (Cicero, *Tusculan Disputations* 2.48–9).

When it comes to comedy, the picture looks different: indeed, the *Odyssey*'s scenes between husband and wife, or young adult and slave, lie at the foundations of the whole genre of domestic comedy as practised by Menander, Terence and Molière, of televised sitcom, and of romantic comedy from *As You Like It* to Hollywood.[25] But actual episodes from the epic were dramatized comically in Theopompus' *Odysseus*, in which the returning Odysseus describes the fine texture of a tunic that he has been brought to wear;[26] the same poet also composed a *Penelope* and a *Sirens*. Philyllius' titles include *The Washerwomen* or *Nausicaa*. One of the saddest losses in the history of *Odyssey* reception must be *The Odysseuses* by Cratinus, Aristophanes' brilliant rival. This comedy, indeed, inaugurated an important new trend in the ancient comic theatre by relying entirely on the humour to be derived from burlesque rather than jokes at the expense of contemporary individuals. The burlesque stage version of the epic had a chorus of Odysseus' Ithacan comrades, and seems from its outset to have featured Odysseus' ship as a dominant part of the stage design; the main focus was on the Cyclops, portrayed as an expert cook.[27]

Since the Renaissance, there have been numerous stage versions of the *Odyssey* aiming at laughter;[28] the only one that has made me laugh out loud on reading it, however, is *Odysseus from Vraa* by the Danish poet Jess Ørnsbo, a dark satire on the seedier corners of post-war Danish society. When Odysseus turns up disguised in sunglasses to the dingy boarding-house run by his wife in Vraa (a faded seaside resort with a reputation equivalent to the English Morecombe), she tells him that her husband, although not very bright, 'was good with dogs'.[29] Their son Telle is a delin-quent teenager obsessed with cars. He kills everyone in the boarding-house with rat poison to make room for his errant father.

But until the twentieth century, although there were tragedies created by rewriting individual episodes, such as Goethe's *Nausikaa*, written in Sicily in 1787,[30] there were no successful versions of the *Odyssey* as a whole that we would regard as tragic. Perhaps the Renaissance literary theorist Giraldi Cinthio was correct when he named the *Odyssey* the classic exam-ple of 'happy tragedy' – *tragedia di fin lieto*.[31] Perhaps Aldous Huxley was right when he declared, in 'Tragedy and the Whole Truth', that Homer in the *Odyssey* 'refused to treat the theme tragically', because he insisted on telling the Whole Truth: men in the *Odyssey* who have been terribly bereaved still attend to the cooking of their supper.[32] As Milton perspica-ciously asked, Odysseus is sad – but does that make him unhappy?[33] These profound insights into the essentially untragic conception of the *Odyssey* are contradicted by neither Giovanni Falugi's self-styled *tragicommedia in terzine* entitled *Ulixe paziente* (circa 1535), an adaptation of Books 16–23 of the *Odyssey*,[34] nor Giambattista della Porta's counter-Reformation *Penelope* (also styled a tragicomedy) of 1591. This was one of the few poetic works attempted by this titan of Renaissance science and natural philosophy, and in a spirit of Christian didacticism presented the heroine as a veritable marvel of chastity and constancy.[35] In the same year as the publication of della Porta's Italian *Penelope*, William Gager's Latin *Ulysses Redux* was performed at Christ Church, Oxford. Styled a *Tragoedia Nova*, it ends in cheerful triumph, with little ethical, metaphysical or psychological depth, to the accompaniment of much ordering of food for the reunion festivities.

The atmosphere is clouded only to a minimal degree by the prospect of the suitors' vengeful families.[36]

Even that master of pathos, the eighteenth-century tragedian Nicholas Rowe, found it difficult to produce a tragedy out of the *Odyssey*; indeed, as we shall see in Chapter 9, he ultimately fails. Rowe resorts to adding depressing metaphysical ruminations for Ulysses to utter at the end in order to cloud the joy of the final moments:

> Like thee the Pangs of parting Love I've known,
> My Heart like thine has bled.– But oh! my Son,
> Sigh not, nor of the common Lot complain,
> Thou that art born a Man art born to Pain,
> For Proof, behold my tedious Twenty Years
> All spent in Toil, and exercis'd in Cares ...[37]

It is not surprising that the eighteenth-century stage transferred its interest from Odysseus and Penelope to the more exciting scenes of youth encountering supernatural beauty offered by Fénelon's Telemachus novel (see below).[38]

In the nineteenth century, the *Odyssey* provided material for a few light-hearted musical burlesques (discussed in Chapter 5), and for elaborately costumed and staged *tableaux* linked by dialogue and songs in George Warr's *The Tale of Troy*, staged in London in 1883 and 1886, in both ancient Greek and in English-language performances.[39] In the aftermath of Schliemann's excavations at Troy, this production offered lavish spectacle informed by archaeological research – seven tableaux were selected for their glamorous or violent content (they included illustrations of 'Calypso parting from Ulysses' and 'The retribution of Ulysses') – but it certainly was not tragedy. Nor was Stephen Phillips's verse drama *Ulysses*, which opened on 1 February 1902 at His Majesty's Theatre (then the most prestigious venue for Shakespearean productions), directed by Herbert Beerbohm Tree (who starred as Ulysses). It ran for a lucrative 132 performances,[40] and was revived at the Garden Theatre in New York the following year, where Tyrone Power Senior played Ulysses. Tree's production was as lavish and spectacular as usual, making much of 'the summit of Olympus, an amphitheatre of marble hills in a glimmering light of dawn', a scene of the suitors 'dancing in abandonment with the handmaidens' in front of the palace 'richly decorated in the Mycenaean style' in Act I, and an extended *nekuia* complete with flitting ghosts and much wailing in Act II.[41]

*Ulysses* was an elegant attempt to render the *Odyssey* suitable for an audience that liked Shakespearean blank verse, staged splendidly. Phillips was pleased that the set and costume design reflected 'recent discoveries of the Mycenaean age', rather than the 'conventional classical costumes and familiar building styles of later Greece'.[42] The souvenir programme (now a collector's item) that was issued to celebrate the 60th performance, a few months later, contained lavish colour plates of the leading players in costume, reproduced from oil paintings by Charles Buchel.[43] But the ethical interest of the play lies in its very blandness and inability to face up to the level of violence and brutality of the homecoming, indicated by its wholesale excision of all the problematic elements. Phillips makes the vengeance against the suitors almost exclusively a divine affair, and excises the punishment of the disloyal women altogether. His Ulysses has no moral complexity.

How very different was the version that Stanisław Wyspianski published in Poland only five years later (1907). *The Return of Odysseus* (*Powrót Odysa*), first staged in 1917 (it is still revived in Poland), focused on the tension between son and father. 'Oedipal' struggles with both Odysseus and Laertes were here developed more subtly than in the Freudian readings of Greek myth associated with Eugene O'Neill two or three decades later. Wyspianski's hero is recognized not by the scars that he has suffered, but by those he inflicts on others; he is also the first of many twentieth-century stage Odysseuses, from Gerhart Hauptmann's emotionally realistic *Der Bogen des Odysseus* (1914) to Walcott's stage version of the *Odyssey*, to exhibit the depression and derangement that ensue from a career of killing and vagrancy.[44]

One serious English-language version of the *Odyssey* was given a British performance as a radio drama during the Second World War. Edward Sackville-West's *The Rescue* was subtitled *A Melodrama for Broadcasting based on Homer's Odyssey*: Sackville-West used the term 'melodrama' in its old sense, as designating a serious drama with music, provided in the form of an orchestral score by Benjamin Britten. It was broadcast in November 1943, when Greece was under occupation, and the author drew attention to the painful parallels between the situation there and the Ithacan palace, occupied by the suitors. But this grave reassessment of the epic also allowed some criticism, placed in the mouth of Telemachus, of the irresponsibility of the upper-class Odysseus: his father's absence has caused incalculable suffering to the 'people of Ithaca', who have lost 'homes and goods and lands and even their children and relations – through starving and ill-treatment'. In Sackville-West's hands, the *Odyssey* not only addressed the class tension that was to prove explosive at the general election two years later, but became a call to its British listeners *across* the class spectrum to take arms and assume responsibility for liberating all the lands threatened by Nazi 'suitors'.[45]

Even before this, a tradition of politically charged Odysseys had been established in the aftermath of the Spanish Civil War.[46] It seems from the history of staging the *Odyssey* that this epic, unlike the *Iliad*, can only become sufficiently dark to make it susceptible to tragic realization as a result of radical re-topicalization or extensive surgery on the psyche, politics and motivations of its hero. Either the happiness of the reunion with child, wife and ageing father must be undermined, or the sense of tragedy imported from an extrinsic socio-political context. Yet there will inevitably always be theatrical performances – comic, tragic-comic, musical, danced, poetic – based on the *Odyssey*. In the wake of Walcott's stage version, there has recently been a wave of stage productions, in every continent, unprecedented in the history of the epic. The Kohinoor Theatre, a venerable mobile troupe based in Pathsala, has toured with its Assamese adaptations of both the *Iliad* and the *Odyssey* as well as Shakespeare and versions of well-known films. Meanwhile, in London, Jatinder Verma directed his Tara Arts Theatre Company in *2001: A Ramayan Odyssey*, which staged an intercultural collision between the Indian and Greek epic heroes – but only after developing his ideas about the *Odyssey* in *An Asian Song-Line* (1993), an encounter in north-west Australia between Aboriginal, British and Asian performers. In Winnipeg, Rick Chafe's psychologically intense and physically experimental *Odyssey* play was performed outdoors in the ruins of a Benedictine monastery in 2000. Indefinite Article's retelling of the *Odyssey* with the help of sand poured onto an overhead projector intrigued the audience at the Lyric Studio in London in January 2004. A few months later, Leszek Bzdyl's Polish *ODY-SEAS* was billed as 'a wandering event/performance' created jointly with the visual artist Robert Rumas. The audience was taken on foot and by boat through the historical Gdansk shipyard, during which it experienced the myth of Odysseus through visual and performing arts. This production also toured to Baltic ports in Lithuania, Russia and Latvia.

The following year, Tom Wright's Melbourne Festival of the *Odyssey* resonated with the Australian experience of war at Gallipoli. An anti-war point was also made by a Croatian production called *Odyssey 2001*, conceived by Damir Saban, the artistic director of the GUSTK theatre workshop, in the open air theatre at the Cairo opera house during the 2006 Cairo International Festival of Experimental Theatre.[47] By projecting onto a screen vast video images of contemporary figures, including George W. Bush in the role of the god who had ordained 'the New World Order', the play's satirical message was unmistakable, using iron oil barrels variously as tanks and war planes, archaic sailing ships, or scattered to represent islands.

The very image of oil barrels from Croatia scattered across an open air space in Egypt, where once Menelaus wrestled with the shape-shifter Proteus, reminds us that the *Odyssey* is a shape-shifting object in itself. The poem has so many strands, some prematurely truncated, others winding through the text to re-emerge later, that it can safely be said, through a mysterious alchemical fusion, to reflect its content in its form. This Protean text also absorbs so many different types of verbal performance – lament, dream-telling, prayer, insult, compliment, invitation, order, praise, prophecy, description, anecdote, advice – that it is a kaleidoscopic representation of a pre-literate society in intense verbal interaction. Yet it also mutates ceaselessly into a different type of story – the *Odyssey* is a *generic* shape-shifter, changing from a heroic epic into a quest narrative, a revenge tragedy, a domestic comedy, a romance, *Bildungsroman* and biography. Like Proteus, whenever you try to pin it down, it turns into something else; like Circe, countless dramatists and writers have tried to reduce it and fix its meaning as something both more definable and less fluid and wonderful than it is.

# 4

# TELLING TALES

A t the Phaeacian court, Odysseus is treated to a feast, dancing and a bardic performance, before being invited to tell his story. He speaks of Calypso and of the voyage from Troy – the Cyclops, Aeolus, Circe and the trek to the edges of Ocean. We listen, enraptured, as Odysseus narrates his invocations of the dead; he describes his encounters with the deceased Elpenor, Tiresias, his mother Anticleia and a procession of famous heroines. At this spooky point Odysseus suddenly halts, announcing that the time for sleep has come. He has, of course, not yet got to the part that everyone has been waiting for – his dialogues in the Underworld with the other Trojan War heroes, specially Agamemnon and Achilles.

At this tense moment, where the external tale is arrested as violently as Odysseus has interrupted his own act of narration just before its climax, the epic formulates what is virtually a defence of fiction. We are desperate for Odysseus to continue, like Alcinous, who would be happy 'to stay up in this hall until the divine dawn' to hear his guest (11.375–6). But Alcinous has just drawn a distinction between Odysseus and liars, or perhaps between Odysseus *and other liars* (11.363–9):

> Odysseus, as we look upon you we cannot imagine that you are a fraud and conman of the kind that the dark earth breeds so many – liars who come from heaven knows where. On the contrary, in the words that you speak there is grace and good sense. You have told your tale with the skill of a bard.[1]

Alcinous does not seem to mind whether Odysseus' tale is true or not, so skilfully and with such wisdom has he delivered his bard-like performance. The same idea underlies Eumaeus' account to Penelope of the stranger, who he says is a Cretan gifted at telling the story of his adventures (17.513–21). Eumaeus is lying. He knows Odysseus' true identity, and that the tales of the 'Cretan' are thus untrue. But by this point in the *Odyssey* it is clear that truth is not a good criterion by which to judge the success of a story.

The tales told in the swineherd's shed have become a byword for all tall
stories subsequently, the yarns spun by any booze-befuddled old mariner,
sitting 'on the deck of a bungalow'; in some ways a pathetic figure, such
a man knows an important secret – 'the joy of never arriving,/making it
up, the next tale and the next', as a recent poem entitled 'In the hut of
Eumaeus' has put it.[2] In the *Odyssey*, in other words, untrue narratives that
offer pleasure are celebrated for their own sake.[3] This is why this non-novel
has so often been called, not only by novelists themselves but by theorists
and historians of fiction, the very birthplace of literary fiction, 'the best
novel that ever was written', as the hero of a Victorian novel described it
before reading it in translation to schoolgirls holidaying in the Alps.[4]

In 1932, T.E. Lawrence (no mean storyteller himself) wrote in the introduction to his translation that the *Odyssey*, 'by its ease and interest remains
the oldest book worth reading for its story and the first novel of Europe'.
Aldous Huxley explained this by pointing to the poem's humane vision
of life as a whole: the *Odyssey*'s influence over later 'Odyssean' fiction such
as Fielding's *Tom Jones* (1749) lies in its unremittingly untragic perspective. Huxley emphasizes the ending of *Odyssey* 12, where after watching
Scylla devour six of their comrades, Odysseus and his men prepare their
supper 'expertly' on the beach. Homer, says Huxley, 'prefers to tell the
Whole Truth. He knew that even the most cruelly bereaved must eat
… He knew that experts continue to act expertly and to find satisfaction in their accomplishment, even when friends have just been eaten …
Homer refused to treat the theme tragically.'[5] Joyce made a similar point
in 1917, when discussing his attraction to Odysseus (although he drew on
the ancient tradition that Odysseus had tried to avoid going to war, which
is not itself included in the *Odyssey*):

> The most beautiful, all-embracing theme is that of the *Odyssey*. It is
> greater, more human, than that of *Hamlet, Don Quixote*, Dante, *Faust* …
> I find the subject of Ulysses the most human in world literature … After
> Troy there is no further talk of Achilles, Menelaus, Agamemnon. Only
> one man is not done with; his heroic career has hardly begun: Ulysses.[6]

The *Odyssey*'s status as the archetype of all fiction – the mother of all stories
as well as the mother of tall stories – has been anatomized in an essay by
Calvino, 'The Odysseys within the *Odyssey*', which stresses the plurality of
tales echoing the master theme of wandering and return. Eumaeus, Eurycleia, Telemachus, Nestor and Menelaus all have their own Odysseys.[7]

This formal elevation of both Homer and Odysseus to magisterial status
in the history of fiction has led to Odysseus' regular personal appearances
in postmodern, self-conscious novels that explore the nature of story-

telling: one outstanding example is Christine Brook-Rose's tendentious *Textermination* (1992). At a conference held at the San Francisco Hilton, not of scholars but of literary figures defending their places in the canon, Odysseus rubs shoulders with another sea captain, Ahab from Melville's *Moby-Dick*, with Huckleberry Finn, and characters from Rushdie's *The Satanic Verses* who (hilariously) pose problems to security. John Barth's *The Tidewater Tales* (1987) is a narrative in the first-person plural involving a voyage down the Chesapeake and encounters with such titans of world fiction as Don Quixote, Odysseus and Scheherazade.

One 'novelistic' feature of the poem is that its form mirrors its content. The travelling across geographical space is represented aesthetically by the meandering narrative, with all its false trails, mini-biographies, digressions and embedded anecdotes. Homer could still teach a thing or two to students of creative writing. David Lodge cites the temporal structure of the *Odyssey*, which loops backwards and forwards in time, as the textbook example of 'timeshift' in fiction.[8] The poem's self-consciousness has even generated several novels, with onion-like layers of complication, about making *movies* of the *Odyssey*. The most famous, because it was subsequently itself filmed, is probably Albert Moravia's *Il Disprezzo* (discussed on pp 27–8). But there are others. Simon Raven's *Come Like Shadows* (1972) explores translating an epic poem to images and dialogue when an academic with the Odyssean surname Arrowby becomes involved in making such a movie on Corfu. A film of the *Odyssey* is being planned throughout much of Iris Murdoch's *The Sea, The Sea* (1978). The *Odyssey* is used in all these novels to signify the difficulties involved in transferring content between different narrative media.[9]

The *Odyssey* was already important to novelists in the ancient world.[10] A neglected factor in the eighteenth-century rise of European fiction was the cultural presence of the ancient novels. The earliest surviving example (first century CE) is Chariton's Greek love story *Chaereas and Callirhoe*. Travel, pirates and suitors separate the titular newly-weds; to ensure the readers are aware of its literary ancestry, the text quotes Homer repeatedly.[11] Translated into Italian in 1752, French in 1763 and English in 1764, this novel's impact on the development of romantic fiction was considerable. The more sophisticated *Leucippe and Clitophon* by Achilles Tatius, on the other hand, had made into a modern language (Italian) as early as 1546, and into English by 1597; it includes references to Penelope, Odysseus, the Sirens and to Homer himself.[12] At a similar date there became available in modern languages Heliodorus' long *Ethiopian Story*, which actually equates the star-crossed lovers Theagenes and Charicleia with

Odysseus and Penelope (e.g. 2.19–21, 3.4–5, 4.5, 5.17, 22, 6.7, 14, 10.16).

A different debt to the Homeric epic is discernible in the earliest surviving burlesque novel, Petronius' obscene and parodic Latin *Satyrica* (first century CE, the archetype of Federico Fellini's movie *Satyricon* (1969)). The hero-narrator Encolpius, an educated rogue, has offended the sex-god Priapus just as Odysseus had offended Poseidon, and travels through the sleazy southern Italian demi-monde on a quest for renewed erectile function (see p 192). He laments that 'just as Ulysses was terrified of Neptune's kingly power, so now upon me, too, the restless hatred of Priapus falls, hounding me on, over land and sea, on and relentlessly on' (139). With his companion Giton, Encolpius experiences not only a storm at sea but escapades in the bedrooms of Pannychis ('All-nighter'), Oenothea ('Wine-goddess'), Tryphaena ('Luxury') and a female named Circe. The one allegedly chaste woman is seduced without difficulty. The adventurers meet an aspiring epic bard and professors of rhetoric named Agamemnon and Menelaus. They are entertained at a banquet held not by a Phaeacian king, but by Trimalchio, a vulgar *parvenu* with terrible taste, whose walls are decorated with paintings of the Homeric epics (30).

The *Odyssey*'s travel theme also underlies the ancient novels dealing with marvels on the edges of the known world, precursors of the hundreds of 'imaginary voyage' stories published in the eighteenth century alone,[13] and of modern 'fantasy' fiction. Most of the ancient examples are now known only through summaries and fragments,[14] but in Lucian's *True Narratives* there survived to the Renaissance perhaps the best of them all, from which time it exerted a profound influence on the European imagination. It was published in a Latin translation as early as 1476, into Italian by 1525 and English by 1634. What made it so fascinating was the narrator's journey through space to the moon, which led to its identification as one of the founding texts of science fiction (see Chapter 6).

Equally important is this novel's epistemological dimension. It explicitly discusses the nature of truth and fiction, which makes it the most obvious ancestor of the self-reflexive novels of the later twentieth century. The title – *True Narratives* – flags veracity as its major interest; the Lucian-narrator says that the teacher of all mendacious discourse is Homer's Odysseus, especially in his stories told to the Phaeacians. Lucian insists that he himself only took to lying because he had 'nothing true to relate, since I have had no adventures of significance' (1.4). But he is an *honest* liar. He warns his audience that he is writing about things 'which I have neither seen, nor had to do with, nor learned from others, which in fact do not exist at all' (1.4). Lucian has understood that joyous revelling in the unreal and untrue is a special feature of the *Odyssey*.[15]

An even stronger impact was made on the Renaissance mind by Apuleius' Latin novel *Metamorphoses*, also known as *The Golden Ass*. English-speaking readers enjoyed William Adlington's vivid translation (1566), and Italians the novel's influence on Boccaccio's *Decameron*. In Apuleius' tale, the narrator Lucius, after his transformation into an ass, is forced to take an inland journey involving a series of arresting encounters. This book is thus the ancestor of the picaresque novel and ultimately of the 'road movie' from *Easy Rider* (1969) to *Thelma and Louise* (1991), as aficionados of these genres are aware.[16] The taverns and farmhouses through which Lucius treks underlie Cervantes' configurations of his hero's misadventures in *Don Quixote* (1605–14), and subsequently Alain le Sage's *Gil Blas* (1730), Fielding's *Tom Jones* (1749) and Smollett's *Humphrey Clinker* (1771). But the linear ancestor of these cultural titans is Homeric, since Apuleius stresses how much his novel owes to Odysseus' wanderings by opening an important travel section with an explicit identification (9.13).[17] He rewrites the Elpenor episode (4.12), and there are allusions to Calypso (1.12), Circe (2.5) and Polyphemus (8.12–13).

The *Odyssey*'s impact on prose storytelling in antiquity was one factor in its contribution to some of the early Christian narratives concerning the apostles' journeys and tribulations.[18] This relationship seems to have been clearest in the apocryphal New Testament *Acts of Andrew*, an exciting narrative about one of the more shadowy disciples, which was translated into numerous languages and read in early Christian Africa, Egypt, Palestine, Syria, Armenia, Asia Minor, Greece, Italy, Gaul and Spain.[19] The *Acts of Andrew* featured seafaring, shipwrecks, pirates and cannibals, as well as a *nekuia*-like encounter with dead souls. Andrew's loyal wife Maximilla waits at home, resisting the advances of a predatory suitor. The hero is a fisherman who possesses extraordinary powers of endurance (he takes four days to die after being crucified). As a Christianized Odysseus, he proves the difficulty faced by the inhabitants of the ancient Mediterranean, raised on Homer, in conceiving any heroic travel story on lines that departed much from the *Odyssey*.[20]

Children's versions, feminist revisions and science-fiction novels dependent on the *Odyssey* are discussed in other chapters, but there have also been relatively straightforward retellings of the epic. John Erskine's *Penelope's Man: The Homing Instinct* (1929) is a wry and light-hearted prose adaptation that retains the ancient Greek setting. Rather more emotionally turbulent is *Return to Ithaca: The Odyssey Retold as a Modern Novel* by Eyvind Johnson (1952). In *The Voyage Home* (English translation 1958), the former naval captain Ernst Schnabel rewrote the wanderings until the moment when Odysseus returns to Ithaca.[21] C.S. Lewis's *After Ten Years* (*c*.1959) is a fragment of a novel, eventually published in 1966. After completing the Narnia books (which appeared between 1950 and 1956), Lewis returned to the classical authors he had studied as an undergraduate, and struggled to complete this study of the relationship between Helen and Menelaus as portrayed in *Odyssey* Book 4. At this time he underwent emotional upheaval, encompassing both happiness and despair, portrayed in the film *Shadowlands* (1993, dir. Richard Attenborough). His wife Joy, who had been in remission from cancer since 1958, died in 1960, repeating the pattern of agonizing loss he had suffered as a small child when his mother died. During this period he worked out his views on marital love, through the mirror of the strange, sad, redeemed marriage of Helen and Menelaus.

Alastair Fowler, Lewis's student, believes that he intended a philosophical tale about the ethical meaning of life. He was, says Fowler, fascinated by Menelaus as the cuckold who yet possesses his heart's desire and whose life therefore has meaning despite the way he is perceived by others: Menelaus 'had all that mattered: love'.[22] The first section of the novel narrates Menelaus' reunion with Helen during the siege of Troy, and his shock at her changed appearance – plumper, wrinkled, greying;[23] the second fragment is set in Egypt. Lewis wanted to use the ancient tradition (first evident in the lyric poet Stesichorus)[24] that Helen had never actually gone to Troy, since the gods had sent a manufactured image of her there, to comment on the gap between the image of the person with whom we are in love and the actual, physical individual onto whom that fantasy is projected.

The most historically influential of all novels that develop one figure or episode in the *Odyssey* is Fénelon's *Les Aventures de Télémaque* (1699, see p 64), like John Bunyan's *The Pilgrim's Progress* (1678–84) a travelogue which is also a *Bildungsroman* ('rite-of-passage' or 'education' novel). In the nineteenth century, especially in North America, the traditional travelogue evolved into a dark genre featuring obsessive mariners who travel to the edges of the globe, suffer shipwrecks and sometimes encounter savages. The most illustrious example is Melville's *Moby-Dick* (1851), the story of the captain of a whaling ship and its shipwreck, but it was preceded by Edgar Allan Poe's two stories *Manuscript Found in a Bottle* (1833) and *A Descent into the Maelstrom* (1841), as well as the longer *Narrative of A. Gordon Pym* (1838).[25]

It was in the later nineteenth century that the *Odyssey* began to lend itself to avant-garde statements about the form and language of fiction. Experimental novels could make their forward-looking message clearer by looking to familiar content, while gaining the weight of canonical authority in support of their controversial argument, One of the most moving is Andreas Karkavitsas's bitter satire *O Zitianos* (*The Beggar*, 1896), the first novel published in demotic Greek – the language spoken everyday by Greeks who had not experienced an elite education. The story of a beggar's escapades, it asks how the *Odyssey* would look if it happened in poverty-stricken provincial Greece at the end of the Turkocracy. By choosing to downgrade one of the canonical flagship-texts of the conservative and prosperous classes, Karkavitsas's commitment to using the ordinary people's language acquired greater force and irony (see pp 135–6).

In Modernist France, the potential of the *Odyssey* as a vehicle for experimental fiction was seen in 1919 by Jean Giraudoux in his *Elpénor* (English translation 1958), an intellectually demanding but witty existentialist telling, from the perspective of the least intelligent of Odysseus' crewmen, of the Cyclops, Circe and Phaeacian episodes; the Cyclops is bored to sleep by his Greek visitors' incessant practice of philosophical dialectic. In his *Les Adventures de Télémaque* (1922), on the other hand, Louis Aragon produced a radical venture into Dadaist surrealism that parodies both the *Odyssey* and Fénelon, especially the seventeenth-century conventional use of epic models, extended descriptions and moral didacticism.

It was at exactly this time that Joyce's monumental *Ulysses* was first published as a complete, unexpurgated text in Paris (February 1922). As the pioneering and paradigmatic 'Modernist' novel, *Ulysses* changed the history of prose fiction forever. Joyce claimed that he had taken the general outline from the *Odyssey*, and the 18 chapters are known by the headings under which they were published in *The Little Review* between 1918 and 1920 (before its editors were prosecuted for publishing obscene material), even though the novel itself omitted them.[26] *Ulysses* tells the story of what is done on 16 June 1904 by the two Dubliners Stephen Dedalus (Telemachus and in part an autobiographical substitute for Joyce, inherited from *Portrait of the Artist as a Young Man* (1916)) and Leopold Bloom (Ulysses and a Jewish advertising canvasser). They go about their separate business, encountering a gallery of memorable Dubliners as they teach, eat, walk, argue and masturbate. Thanks to the book's interior monologues, the reader overhears their thought processes. *Ulysses* is such a major work that it has produced a veritable flood of scholarship, amongst which are several studies of its relationship with the *Odyssey*.[27] Joyce, although introduced to the epic by Charles Lamb's version for children, scoured Homer's text with the literal 'crib' by Butcher and Lang (1879), which explains his obsession as much with the details of Homeric diction as with the overarching story.

There are several reasons why *Ulysses* is so important in itself as well as in fixing the ancient epic forever in the constellation of key texts in the history of fiction. If Modernism is defined as the movement that removed the necessity of realism as a goal in the novel, substituting the world and sensual cognition as they are phenomenologically and linguistically perceived, then it is fascinating to see how Joyce uses Homeric figures and scenes as topic headings under which to organize cognitive experience. For Leopold Bloom in Chapter 5, lotus-eating can take several forms, from the oriental harem, complete with eunuchs and opiates, to the tranquillizing rituals of the Roman Catholic church, the seductions of betting on race-horses and adulterous postal flirtations that relieve quotidian pain. In some chapters, the Odyssean resonance is tied to experiments with language, as 'Eolus' includes not only metaphors to do with wind, but inflated rhetoric (see Fig. 4.1). The Modernist love of puns, riddles and intertextual games also illuminates the way that Joyce handles his ancient Greek co-text, as he asks readers to supply meanings in the story of Leopold, Molly and Stephen from knowledge of Odysseus, Penelope and Telemachus.

Joyce was not the first author to relocate the plot of the *Odyssey* to a contemporary context; there are examples as early as the eighteenth century (see pp 134–5). But it was *Ulysses* that prompted the flood of updated *Odyssey* plots in the fiction and cinema of the twentieth and twenty-first centuries. Curiously, the anti-realist Joyce was drawn to describe the detailed map of Dublin and its architecture from the tower where the novel opens to the layout of Leopold's household, by the vogue for Homeric archaeology in the first decade of the twentieth century. Joyce was fascinated by Wilhelm Dörpfeld's excavations on Ithaca, which had begun in 1890, and Victor Bérard's *Les Phéniciens et L'Odyssée* (1902), which had traced a plausible itinerary for Odysseus' voyage along the Phoenician merchants' trading routes. By 1906 Joyce, inspired partly by this concrete, archaeological Homer, had decided to write a fictional version of the *Odyssey* mapped onto an equally real, concrete Dublin.[28]

The relocation allowed a platform for subtle expression of Joyce's own socio-political views, especially the need for sexual, ethnic and religious liberalism, as we shall see later in Chapters 7 and 14: in his case, it is hard to agree with Eagleton's claim that Modernism's return to myth was a profoundly conservative move.[29] Yet as Joyce himself wrote, *Ulysses* is 'the epic of two races (Israel-Ireland)',[30] and it helped to make writing an *Odyssey* novel an obvious choice for those using prose fiction in order to create national and ethnic *traditions*. Karkavitsas's *The Beggar* offered a demotic Greek *Odyssey* at a time when 'Modern' Greek literature was inventing itself. But it was during the twentieth century, and especially during and shortly after the Second World War, that there appeared a cluster of novels in which an indigenous Odysseus figure experiences a period of history crucial for his people. Hugh MacLennan was writing for Canada in his *Barometer Rising* (1941), a saga of the emergence of national self-consciousness, set during the First World War. Neil MacRae returns from France to Halifax (the capital of Nova Scotia), where Penelope Wain (who bore a baby in his absence) is now living. The character types in the *Odyssey* – the returning wanderer, the waiting woman and the fatherless child – surface in most of MacLennan's other novels, especially *The Watch that Ends the Night* (1958).[31] Canadian authors have remained attached to the *Odyssey* when exploring questions of identity, especially as emigrants from Ireland (see Chapter 12).

Rom Landau's earnest *Odysseus: A Novel* (1948) explores the choice a man faces between his Russian, German and English selves on the brink of the Second World War. Ultimately he unfurls his flag for Britain, 'the only country he was certain of … he knew in his very bones that she would be ready to sacrifice everything in defence of her ideals'.[32] Landau was a spiritual writer, drawn to Eastern mysticism and Islam as well as Christianity, and the hero of his novel, in a tribute to John Bunyan, is named John Pilgrim. He makes his choice about national identity only after encounters with priests and mystics. Pilgrim is himself a writer who, before the war, had written a novel entitled *Odysseus among the Apes*, the story of a man who grew up in Germany but had become disenchanted with the barbarism he witnessed in the early 1930s. After travelling the world (his novel-within-the-novel was even made into a Hollywood movie under the title *Ulysses among the Apes*), he settled in England just before the Anschluss. Pilgrim (not unlike Landau) was of complicated identity: his Russian mother, after her English husband had died, had settled in Germany to raise her son. Landau's novel is strong meat; published in 1948, it indicts everything that had gone wrong in Germany and he felt was going wrong in the Soviet Union. At the end, you can almost hear the British national anthem being played.

The *Odyssey* novel that raises ethnic struggle to epic proportions while drawing on Joyce as much as Homer is Ralph Ellison's epoch-making *Invisible Man* (1952), which tells the story of an Odysseus from the Deep

South; his alienation is born of a history of slavery and racial oppression; his journey to New York is also his quest for an identity as a black man. After attempting to work for an honest living, and becoming disillusioned with the Communist Party, he eventually decides to become invisible and efface himself, like the hero of Dostoevsky's *Notes from the Underground* (1864). The novel is dazzling, 'a veritable *Ulysses* of the black experience',[33] and, as Ellison himself always insisted in middle and old age (see Fig. 4.2), the black experience was integral to America: 'You cannot have an American experience without having a black experience.'[34] It is not just the black *Ulysses* but the North American one.

Ellison signals the Homeric link in the figure of Homer Barbee, the blind minister who proffers to the students at the state college for negroes (modelled on Tuskegee College, Alabama, where Ellison studied) an idealized, pious vision of their past. Barbee's moral epic substitutes 'sweet harmonies' for the reality of the psychological chaos of Afro-American life.[35] *Invisible Man* takes the basic trope from the return sequence of *Odyssey* – that a man unwanted by his society must enter it in disguise, or entirely effaced – and transforms it into an indictment of the absence of dignified ways of being a black man, post-slavery, in the USA. Besides a few stereotypes of what was still then called 'The Negro', several of which are explored in the novel, there was no model on offer of a prosperous, fulfilled black male to which the narrator could turn. In the opening paragraph, he explains:

> I am invisible, understand, simply because people refuse to see me ...
> When they approach me they see only my surroundings, themselves, of
> figments of their imagination – indeed, everything and anything except
> me.

By the end of the first page the reader is in the middle of a physical fight, started when a blond man, unprovoked, called the narrator 'an insult-ing name'. But the narrator, despite being roused to fury, decides against slitting the racist's throat when, as he explains, 'it occurred to me that the man had not *seen* me, actually; that he, as far as he knew, was in the midst of a walking nightmare'. The blond man had seen a non-existent but terrifying phenomenon – what he *expected* from an African-American male when, alone and vulnerable, he encountered him on a dark night. The impossibility of achieving any kind of true selfhood, recognizable by other people, is the central cause of the Odyssean disguise assumed by the narrator of the novel.

During its course he himself tries out the few roles available to him: diligent and grateful college boy, permitted (if he never puts a foot wrong) to move a certain distance up the white totem pole; industrial worker (but without the union rights available to the white proletariat); gang-land criminal; revolutionary; sexual partner of frustrated white women. The stereotypes that white culture imposed on him are also dramatized – mugger, boxer, sufferer from mental illness, primitive sex god. The narrator is never named, which adds mysterious power to the accounts of his experiences. His Odyssean features are many: his odyssey of self-discovery took 20 years; his grandfather, a slave freed in his 80s, was a cunning individual like the Odyssean Autolycus who advocated destroy-ing the enemy – the white man – through absolute servility: 'Live with your head in the Lion's mouth. I want you to overcome 'em with yeses, agree 'em to death and destruction, let 'em swoller you till they vomit or bust open.' He is self-possessed; after Mr Norton, a college benefactor, confides in him, he comments: 'That was something I never did; it was dangerous.'[36]

With Chapter 1 begins the 'Telemacheia', the account of his own early manhood. Its explosive opening depicts blindfolded black youths boxing at a macho party of the leading citizens of a small Southern town. Before being blindfolded the boys are made to stare at a naked white woman; then they are herded into the ring. After the battle royal, the narrator, his mouth full of blood, is asked to give his high school valedictorian's address. As he stands under the lights, his accidental reference to equality nearly ruins him; but in Chapter 2 he takes up his scholarship to college, where he is introduced, amongst other things, to Greek plays.[37]

Ellison's novel is one of the most important reasons for the attachment to the *Odyssey* of African-Americans, and people of African descent in Latin America, the Caribbean and Europe.[38] As we shall see, this attach-ment has played a significant role in discussions around the possibility of a literature that has put colonialism behind it. Some African writers living in exile have also come to see the *Odyssey* as embodying a deeply felt ambiva-lence towards their mother continent in general and their own nations of origin in particular. Conspicuous amongst these is Nurrudin Farah's dark novel *Links* (2004). Jeeblah, the principal character, is returning from New York to his native Mogadiscio (Somalia) in north-east Africa for the first time in 20 years. The country is beset by warlords and clan-based militias, but Jeeblah is intent upon finding his mother's grave, in a story that contains echoes of both the *Odyssey* and Dante's *Inferno*.

There are few species of the genus prose fiction that have not produced at least one example that uses the *Odyssey* directly. There are many short stories based on individual scenes in the epic.[39] The lucrative market for 'fantasy fiction' (a diluted version of science fiction with less science, more exotica and more erotica) is particularly drawn to the world of Odysseus' wanderings, for example in Gene Wolfe's *On Blue's Waters* (1999). In Edward S. Louis's *Odysseus on the Rhine* (2005), the hero leaves Ithaca to visit survivors of the Trojan War who now live in the north with golden-haired Teutonic women. The best moments in this novel are actually provided by Orestes, who is now almost completely insane. Even more extreme syncretism of different mythical complexes is demonstrated in *The Fabulous Riverboat* (volume 2 of a series called *Riverworld*) by Philip Jose Farmer (1971). This involves Mark Twain's alter ego building a riverboat to traverse the waterway on his distant planet, a task for which he needs the help of the Viking Erik Bloodaxe, Bad King John of England, Cyrano de Bergerac, the infamous Nazi Hermann Göring and, of course, Odysseus. Even sub-genres according to distinctions wholly baffling to the non-initiate, such as Cyberpunk, like to signal their Odyssean credentials. Jon Courtenay Grimwood's well regarded *Pashazade* introduces mythic depth to his freakish world by Homerically calling his sea 'wine-dark'.[40]

The *Odyssey*'s influence on the novel has worked in several different ways: as a direct model, as the submerged model whose influence is mediated and sometimes concealed by the secondary work, and as a text with which the secondary work is in constant, conspicuous dialogue. It has also focused generations of writers on the nature of the act of narration, which has been examined in relation to Ralph Ellison's exploration in *Invisible Man* of the double consciousness of reliving a story as both narrator and protagonist.[41] It is often said that the nineteenth-century novels of Eliot and Hardy used the form and content of Greek tragedy, but in the twentieth century the *Odyssey* was surely the most important ancient text in relation to the art of fiction. In his *Theory of the Novel* (1920) Lukács diagnosed the crisis he saw in the genre as resulting from the realistic mode that it had assumed in the previous century, and called for it to be replaced with a renewal of epic – a form with a much larger, more societal vision, encyclopaedic inclusiveness, and especially range through time and space. It is this plea that illuminates why the *Odyssey*s of Joyce and subsequent novelists were needed so badly.

The notion of a more collective perspective, an updated prose epic, elicited many experiments in the following decades, and radically affected the type of fiction that was to be written. Novels appeared with multiple perspectives and worlds contained within them, and narrative that can veer off into other storylines at numerous junctures, as Jorge Luis Borges (a lifelong admirer of the *Odyssey*) demonstrated so famously in

*The Garden of Forking Paths* (*El jardin de senderos que se bifurcan*, 1941). This new compositional strategy, in which a book narrates several different storylines happening in different locations, beginning with any one of them, prefigured features of the hypertext of the electronic age,[42] as well as interactive computer games and movies. The narrative mode of pre-literate epic, above all the *Odyssey*, has come back under the spotlight as we enter what some cultural commentators are already calling a *post*-literate world, a new oral age. The notion of a bard in an oral society, who could enter the world of heroes at any point in their activities and extemporize a new song, taking his audience down any branch of the tree that comprised the organic *epos*, has found a descendant that resembles it in the least expected of places – a computer screen.[43]

# 5

# SINGING SONGS

One explanation of Homer's name is that it derives from a Babylo-
nian noun meaning 'a person who sings',[1] and in the story of the
Sirens, the narrative celebrates the power of the singing voice to
enchant the listener. Forewarned by Circe that the voices of the Sirens are
irresistible, Odysseus has sealed his men's ears with wax and had himself
bound hard to the mast. But as he sails close to their meadow, the Sirens
let forth their 'high, clear song' (12.186–8):

> No man has ever passed by us in his dark ship before listening to the honey-
> sweet sound of our singing voices; he sails away a more knowledgeable
> man after first feeling great joy.

The aural effect of the song of the Sirens 'is of unusually rich melody even
for Homer, a melody which inheres in the original Greek and is lost in the
translation'.[2] Odysseus has heard the most beautiful singing that can be
heard anywhere, the price for which privilege is usually death, and lives
to tell the tale.

Other vocalists in the poem are Calypso in Book 5, who 'sings with
a lovely voice, moving to and fro at her loom', Circe, the bard Phemius
in Books 1 and 22, Demodocus in Book 8, and Menelaus' palace bard
at the beginning of Book 4. Three millennia later, the *Odyssey* has been
adapted to several genres of popular song. In the lyrics of heavy-metal
music, which celebrates high-pitched, theatrical vocal lines, the Sirens
regularly appear; the band Sirenia's album *An Elixir for Existence* included
a haunting instrumental 'Seven Sirens and a Silver Tear', a prelude to
their major *Odyssey*-inspired work, *Sirenian Shores* (2004).[3] The queen of
contemporary American folk, Suzanne Vega, recorded 'Calypso', a lament
in the voice of the ancient goddess, on her 1987 album *Solitude Standing*, which made her an international star. Geoffrey Oryema's synthesis of
Ugandan and soul music discovered in Homer the emotional range for his
album *The African Odysseus* (1993). In *O Brother, Where Art Thou?* (2000),
the Coen brothers mined a rich seam of American folk and popular song,

from the chain gang's opening 'negro spiritual'-derived *Po' Laz'us*, intoned in time with their smashing pickaxes. The recurring bluegrass song 'Man of Constant Sorrow', which the film suggests was invented impromptu by Ulysses Everett McGill, was actually first recorded by the Virginian Stanley Brothers in 1950, and brought to the world on Bob Dylan's debut album (1962). The Coen brothers drew an inspirational connection between this old folk song, from the oral culture of the American Deep South, and Odysseus' formulaic epithet *polutlas*, 'much-enduring'.

Yet the only composer who, to my knowledge, has set his own translations of Homer to his own music is the Cornishman Inglis Gundry, who had studied Classics at Oxford. He was set on fire by T.E. Lawrence's translation, and like many opera composers before and since, it was by Penelope that he was primarily inspired. What, he wrote in his autobiography, could provide better material for an aria than her rebuke to the bard Phemius at 1.337–44 (see Fig. 5.1), when he has reduced her to tears with his song of Troy?

> Leave this bitter tale that always
> Tears at my heart reminding me
> Of that unforgettable sorrow
> That crushes me above all women,
> For I remember – ah! with how much longing
> The dear head of my husband whose sad story
> Rings in the voice of every poet and singer
> Throughout the world. [4]

The vividness with which characters in the *Odyssey* express their emotions is an obvious reason for its attractiveness to composers of opera. But even more significant has been the authoritative status of the subject matter, which has led several major composers (Monteverdi and Fauré especially) to use it as the basis for a libretto when they wanted to make avant-garde musical statements.

The story must begin – and often return – to the first great musical version of the *Odyssey* to be created after the Renaissance, Monteverdi's beautiful *Il ritorno d'Ulisse in patria* (1640), the work of his old age and artistic maturity. It is a retelling of the second half of the *Odyssey*, set on Ithaca at the time of Ulisse's return. It is a fairly faithful adaptation, although there are alterations reflecting contemporary aesthetic expectations. It opens, for example, with a superhuman scene in which the allegorical figure of Human Frailty is taunted by Time, Fortune and Cupid, who claim to control man's fate. The scene turns the collusive audience into guests of the gods, inspecting Ulisse's return from a privileged perspective. Other important developments are in the figure of Melantho (whose role is elaborated as Eurymachus' co-conspirator), and the beggar Iro, who is given a colourful sung confrontation with Eumaeus and a pathetic suicide scene.

*Il ritorno* was the first work that Monteverdi ventured for the public opera of Venice, at the age of 73, following a long gap since his previous operatic venture. Indeed, he was probably only persuaded by the blandishments of his friend Giacomo Badoaro, the author of the libretto. Badoaro subsequently wrote that he had submitted drafts of several scenes to Monteverdi in order to allow him to alter them in ways that would release his musical inspiration.[5] The opera was revolutionary in its passion, realism and vitality,[6] and the recognition scenes were written with a superb sense of theatre. In consequence, *Il ritorno* was a huge success: performed ten times to crowded audiences in Venice, and taken by a travelling company to Bologna where the performers were celebrated in a series of sonnets,[7] it was even revived the subsequent year in Venice, at the time an exceptional mark of honour.

The brilliant Monteverdi scholar Ellen Rosand has suggested that in the figure of Ulisse, disguised as an ageing beggar, Monteverdi recognized himself – an elderly man, tempted out of a longstanding retirement from the art form in which he had excelled, to teach the young claimants to the throne of opera a lesson. Perhaps what persuaded Monteverdi back into opera was the presence in Badoaro's libretto of a nonpareil disguised as an elderly nonentity. Certainly, the words sung by Monteverdi's Ulisse as he picks up the bow can be heard as a warning to younger composers: 'My Queen, within this body/there's a soul so undaunted/it summons me to the contest.'[8] This opera clearly stunned his rivals, and was early admired because of its melodic representation of relationships and intensely fluctuating emotions. In III.8, for example, the nurse Ericlea tries to decide whether to reveal to Penelope the beggar's identity. Monteverdi gives even this lowly woman a moment of emotional vacillation, expressed in sections of varying size, each with an intensifying *ritornello*, culminating in a loaded question – what *will* you do, Ericlea?[9]

In *Il ritorno* Monteverdi was addressing an aesthetic challenge. In his earlier operas *Orfeo* (1607) and *Arianna* (1608, which is almost completely lost) he was still justifying recitative as a way of representing speech: formal arias were kept to dramatic situations where singing was inherently plausible. This illuminates the choice of Orpheus, a professional singer, as a protagonist: indeed, legends concerning musicians were still being recommended as the material most suited to opera in the 1630s. Some types of character – gods, allegorical figures and lower-class comic figures – were conventionally expected to sing. But *Il ritorno* allows dignified characters such as Odysseus and Penelope, at least in emotional states, to sing arias *regardless* of their dramatic situation. Monteverdi actually chose *not* to put Phemius in the opera at all, a decision which may have been connected with the aesthetic statement he wanted to make. Carter has argued this case through the figure of Penelope, who sings only recitative throughout much of the opera, but bursts finally into an ecstatic moment of emotional release in her love song at the climax ('Shine bright, O heavens'). Monteverdi thus draws attention to the problematic status of aria within operatic endeavour. He 'shows us how individuals can – must – sing rather than speak', and thus makes a pioneering statement about the nature of sung drama as a whole.[10]

The success of *Il ritorno* inevitably led to plans for an opera dramatizing the earlier part of the *Odyssey*, and Badoaro began to compose such a libretto. But Monteverdi died in 1643. The music was supplied instead by their colleague Francesco Sacrati, and *L'Ulisse errante* was performed at the Teatro SS Giovanni e Paolo in Venice in 1644. The stage design was by the incomparable Giacomo Torelli.[11] Unfortunately Torelli never produced the set of engravings that he had promised would illustrate to the world the labours he had undergone in order to display the heroes of Ulisse's day.[12] There is some compensation in the survival of several illustrations of Torelli's baroque stage designs for other operas on mythical themes, which give an indication of how he would have handled the visual requirements of Ulisse's most exotic adventures. Fine examples are the lovely seascapes for his *Ermiona* (Padua 1636) and *Bellerofonte* (Venice 1642), along with the cave scene, also for *Bellerofonte*.[13]

The opera on the wanderings was constructed on unusual lines, with five *attioni*, each of which formed a self-contained episode and required a different exotic setting – the islands of the Cyclops, Circe, Calypso and the Phaeacians, via a trip to the Underworld. Yet the manner of telling the story is altered by the active role of both Amore and Mercurio, in whose hands Ulisse, presented with a succession of desirable females, is less psychologically autonomous than in the original epic. The first episode retells the same Cyclops story as *Odyssey* Book 9, but adds the figure of Galatea, mourning the death of her beloved Acis, which Badoaro had discovered in Ovid's *Metamorphoses* Book 13. The Circe episode provided the material for the second *attione*, but added the extravagant spectacle in which Circe's palace fell in ruins, and her statues returned to life as the spell is removed. In the third *attione*, Ulisse arrived in the Elysian fields.

Instead of meeting old Trojan warriors, he encountered the imported Teutonic warrior Frode, who caused Ulisse to hallucinate, seeing Penelope in the jaws of a monster, and his country overrun. This inaugurated the trend towards mixing Odysseus and figures from the *Odyssey* with characters from other mythological systems, which was to become extremely popular in the twentieth century, from movies such as *Hercules, Samson and Ulysses* (1963, directed by Pietro Francisci) to avant-garde fiction (see pp 47, 56).

The most erotic *attione* was the fourth, which developed the story of Calypso told in *Odyssey* Book 5 by staging a struggle between Amore and Mercurio. The four lovely Seasons appeared to tempt Ulisse into accepting Calypso's offer of immortality, but he refuses, and the episode concluded with a ballet performed by the Months. The final *attione* took Ulisse to Phaeacia, to an encounter with Nausicaa, a tournament and the arrival of Sonno (Sleep). The opera ended with Alcino, king of the Feaci, ordering the sleeping Ulisse to be taken back home to Ithaca, and Love exhorting the other gods to make peace.[14]

During the eighteenth century, however, interest in the operatic potential of the *Odyssey* took surprising turns. The only distinguished serious musical staging of a story about Odysseus was *Penelope*, a *Dramma per musica* in two acts by Domenico Cimarosa to a libretto by Giuseppe Maria Diodati. First produced in Naples, at the Teatro del Fondo, in the carnival atmosphere of Boxing Day 1794, it was revived over the next 20 years in Livorno, Florence, Paris and St Petersburg.[15] It went down well in London in 1817, where the *The Morning Chronicle* declared it the best of all Cimarosa's operas.[16] The aim seems to have been to increase the number of romantic scenes and provide showcase arias for soprano castratos, including the superstar Girolamo Braura, who played Telemaco. The role of Telemaco needed to be upgraded. The result was the addition of rather absurd complications surrounding Ulisse's return to Ithaca.

Before Ulisse (tenor) returns, Evenore (bass), the king of the island of Lesbos, arrives in Ithaca in order to woo Penelope. His daughter Arsinoe (soprano) is also in love, reciprocally, with Telemaco. A plot against Ulisse organized by Evenore and Perimede (another soprano castrato) leads to his imprisonment. Telemaco rescues him and is given the perfect opportunity for a terrifically demanding aria in which he is torn between his love for Arsinoe and his filial obligation to kill his father's enemy Evenore (her father). The opera is a vehicle for some powerful expressive sentimentalism, and was no doubt an aural treat. But in contrast with Monteverdi's version it diminished the humane quality of the epic contributed by its lower-class individuals and did little to advance the serious standing of the *Odyssey*.

Cimarosa's focus on Telemachus was symptomatic of the broader eighteenth-century pattern which saw Odysseus' son virtually upstage his father. At this time, the most important text through which the epic was mediated throughout Western Europe was François de Salignac de la Mothe-Fénelon's version of the myth, *Les Aventures de Télémaque* (1699).[17] A didactic novel, it was designed to demonstrate to Fénelon's pupil, the Duke of Burgundy (heir apparent to the French throne), the correct – non-autocratic – way to govern. Fénelon expanded on the Homeric Telemacheia in order to portray Télémaque passing through a series of ordeals, trials and adventures while he searches for his father. He is accompanied by his moral guide and tutor, Minerva in disguise. Télémaque is shipwrecked in Book 7 of the novel on Calypso's island, and resists her advances because he is himself in love with a shepherdess, Eucharis. When Calypso tries to hold them by setting fire to their ship, his tutor pushes Télémaque into the sea and they escape in a passing ship (see Fig. 5.2).

Many eighteenth-century operas followed Fénelon's version of the Telemachus story. These began in 1714 with a spectacular production at the Théâtre du Palais-Royal in Paris of *Télémaque ou Calypso*, a five-act lyric libretto by Simon Joseph Pellegrin, set to music by André Cardinal Destouches. This influential opera was itself revived several times, and imitated in new Italian and French-language versions.[18] In Capece's *Telemaco* for Alessandro Scarlatti, the shepherdess's name is Erifile and she is revealed in the end to be Antiope, the daughter of Idomeneus of Crete, whom Telemachus is destined to marry. Other librettos, based on different episodes in Telemachus' travels, include Sografi's *Telemaco in Sicilia* (Padua; music by Calegari, 1792), and various accounts of Telemachus' alliance with Circe. Coltellini's *Telemaco, ossia L'isola di Circe*, set to music by Gluck, was performed in Vienna in 1765 and revived at Sadler's Wells in 2003.

Odysseus did not find his champion in the Germanic musical tradition, on the other hand, until the late nineteenth century and the euphoria that followed the unification of Germany after the Franco-Prussian War. Max Bruch wrote to his sister in 1871 that he had been reading the *Odyssey*, and the 'scales had fallen from his eyes': he now saw a secular, patriotic antidote to the 'Christian lamentation and the poetic tears of Bach's cantatas'.[19] His oratorio *Odysseus* (1873) is a lucid and accessible alternative to the Wagnerian conception of national mythology, even if the sentiments in the 'large resounding final chorus, glorification of mari-

tal love and fidelity, and of the homeland' have dated.[20] After the famous
G-Minor Violin Concerto, *Odysseus* was certainly Bruch's most successful
work. The heroic bass-baritone role of Odysseus is taxing, indeed 'requires
a voice with the qualities of a Wotan' and acting skills, especially in the
expression of rage at the suitors.[21] It was popular until the First World
War, but Modernist aesthetics and the demise of the oratorio as viable art
form meant that only recently has it enjoyed a revival. The work premiered
in 1873 and by the end of 1875 had, remarkably, received over 42 performances. Brahms chose to conduct the work himself in 1875 at the last
concert of his career as Director of the Viennese Society of the Friends
of Music. In 1893, when Bruch was awarded an honorary doctorate from
Cambridge University, the celebratory concert opened with an excerpt
from *Odysseus*. For Bruch's generation, Homer offered an alternative to
the mystical unreality of Wagnerian music drama. Its late nineteenth-
century Hellenism was fundamentally an extension of the idealization
by eighteenth-century Enlightenment thinkers of classical antiquity for
its philosophical thinking, rationality, control of emotion and perceived
orderly aesthetic values.

Yet Bruch's magnificent oratorio ran into controversy fast and badly. In
the context of the Weimar Republic, it was reminiscent of the imperialist
enthusiasms of the 1870s, and seemed too straightforward and sentimental. In Germany, after the catastrophic fallout from the First World War,
Bruch, moreover, became a convenient symbol of an older generation's
error-filled ways. This was partly because, following the success of *Odysseus*, he had written a much less brilliant *Achilles* and even a *Leonidas*.[22]
These efforts mirrored a romance with ancient Greece and the defeat of its
enemies, Trojan or Persian, that had flourished after Germany's defeats of
Austria and France.[23] In the early 1870s, in the eyes of its subjects, imperial Germany seemed poised to take the place in modern history occupied
by the Greece of antiquity. Antiquity was perhaps the only subject matter
that could rival the nationalism evident in the Nordic and Germanic
themes of Wagner's music dramas.[24]

Bruch's *Odysseus* remains, nevertheless, a beautiful musical work and
a more important achievement than August Bungert's vast project *Die
homerische Welt*, also known as *Die Odyssee*, which recast the epic on a
Wagnerian scale. He refused to call the four constitutive pieces 'operas',
preferring the term 'Musik-Tragödie' ('music-tragedy'), to be called collectively a 'tetralogy' on the model of the productions of Greek tragedy at the
ancient Athenian festivals of Dionysus.[25] They were to be entitled *Kirke*,
*Nausicaa*, *Odysseus' Heimkehr* (*Return*) and *Odysseus' Tod* (*Death*) respec-

tively. Bungert, inspired by Voss's translation (see p 18), wrote the libretto himself. He conceived this monumental idea (since he was patronized by Bruch's sister, very likely from noticing the attention paid to Bruch's oratorio) before he met the young Friedrich Nietzsche in 1883, but it was not until 1896 that *Odysseus' Heimkehr* received its premiere in Dresden in a lavish production culminating in a crowded stage;[26] this was the only part to be revived subsequently. Bungert's conception of the poem was nationalistic, and conceived as a rival to Wagner's Ring Cycle – indeed, Bungert dreamed of building a festival theatre to house repeated productions of these *Homeric World* operas at Godesberg.

What the operatic reception of the *Odyssey* desperately needed by the early twentieth century was a dose of aesthetic Modernism, which it thankfully received in 1913 with Fauré's *Pénélope*. The *Odyssey* appeals to elder statesmen in the musical community: Monteverdi turned to the *Odyssey* when he was over 70 years old, and Fauré when he was over 60. He later said that he had previously turned down a stream of poems offered to him 'that all seemed equally idiotic'.[27] The list of operatic projects he had rejected included a *Manon Lescaut* and an *Ondine*: it was only with the Greek stories of Prometheus and Penelope that he actually produced operas. He had no hesitation in agreeing to make an opera of the *Odyssey* and always felt that the material had virtually been made for him.[28]

*Pénélope* premiered in a three-night run in Monte Carlo in March 1913, before beginning a triumphant season at the new Théâtre des Champs-Elysées in Paris in May, with brilliant sets and costumes. From its first performance onwards it elicited extreme reactions; it has been described as both a 'failure' and a 'masterpiece' (Fauré himself believed it was his best work, and dedicated it to his devoted friend Camille Saint-Saëns). Although it is performed from time to time, it has yet to become a favourite in the repertoire,[29] perhaps because the music is sometimes experimental. Fauré worked on it from 1907, in his favourite haunts by the Swiss lakes, and began with the idea that Penelope herself was 'in G minor, that she spoke in a beautiful middle-register voice and raised it only rarely'.[30] He already had his Penelope in mind – the incomparable Swiss-German soprano Lucienne Bréval (one of the highest-paid opera stars in history), a dark-haired, dignified singer and accomplished actress. Fauré juxtaposes Penelope's sad G minor theme with the confident, bracing intervals that sound for Odysseus – major seconds and rising fifths. The serving women at their spinning wheels sing over continuous runs of semi-quavers; in the F minor 'shroud theme' (Act I, Scene 7) a chromatic flute figure, within a sustained chord, suggests the thread running through the fabric that

Penelope is unpicking; the opera concludes with calm grandeur, as Odysseus' rising fifths ascend through the orchestral bass.[31]

Fauré was trying to find a new type of operatic voice. His *Prométhée* (1900) had been a lyrical tragic drama, in which sections of spoken text alternated with vocal and orchestral panels. It is often performed under concert conditions. By the time of *Pénélope* Fauré had composed more than 70 songs, and in attempting to liberate himself from the orchestral dominance he associated with Wagnerian opera, he invented his own new style. Continuously flowing, all-sung but restrained, its dramatic power emerges from what has been called its 'wholly inward type of musicality',[32] through mobile vocal lines, descending octaves and sustained flights of lyricism. It synthesizes all previous operatic styles, recalling especially the operas of Monteverdi.[33]

The opera marks a particular cusp in opera history. It stands at the end of the old line of 'tragédies lyriques' that stretches back, via Berlioz and Gluck, to Rameau and Lully. But it also marks a crucial stage in the development of melodic Modernism. The year 1913 was indeed an epochal one in the arts in Paris: just a week after *Pénélope* opened, Nijinsky leapt into the history books with his shocking choreography for Stravinsky's even more shocking music for the *Rite of Spring*. And the musical style and harmonies of *Pénélope* are of their time. The Modernism of the piece staggered Saint-Saëns, who wrote in 1913 of his 'superhuman' efforts to come to terms with it:

> I simply can't get used to it never settling down in any key, to consecutive fifths and sevenths and to chords demanding a resolution that never comes ... At a stroke Fauré has placed himself in a position of authority at the head of the young ... But what an example for students to see their master constantly breaking the rules they're being taught![34]

Fauré's librettist, René Fauchois, also wrote a three-act tragedy on the Homeric theme of the death of Patroclus (1917) and the libretto for a two-act opera *Nausicaa* (composed by Reynaldo Hahn, 1919). But he is today more famous as the writer of *Boudou Saved From Drowning* (*Boudu sauvé des eaux*), a play which was in 1932 made into a classic movie directed by Jean Renoir. It has subsequently been remade as both *Down and Out in Beverley Hills* starring Nick Nolte (1986), and *Boudou* starring Gérard Depardieu (2005). In Fauchois' story the tramp Boudu is saved from the Seine and taken home by a Parisian bookseller. Boudou beds not only the bookseller's wife, but his maid and his mistress as well. He finally throws away his new-found fortune and becomes once again a solitary vagrant. Fauchois' comedy is indebted to the *Odyssey*, indeed is an *Odyssey* which takes the comic premise that the filthy vagrant who arrives from the water to claim the bed of the householder's wife is exactly that – a filthy vagrant. Fauchois had replaced the serious emotional lens through which he had viewed the *Odyssey* for Fauré with a darkly humorous one suitable for the comic stage.

The saddest 'missing link' in the history of the vocal reception of the *Odyssey* must be the unpublished *Ulysses Africanus* by Kurt Weill and Maxwell Anderson, on which they worked in 1939. The songs for this production have attracted the interest of musicologists,[35] and the Homeric scholar Robert Rabel, a Kentucky Classics professor, is preparing an edition of the surviving score, only two copies of which are known to exist. The plot concerns a freed slave named Ulysses, who leaves his wife Penny for a life of adventure during the American Civil War. A Circe-like figure ushers him into a scene reminiscent of the Underworld in Book 11 of the *Odyssey*. As a result of his adventures, Ulysses becomes a theatrical entrepreneur, and in Act II he stages his own version of Homer's *Odyssey*. The focus on slavery and the performance-within-a-performance would have made this musical exceptionally interesting. When, after the war, the *Odyssey* did become transformed into this distinctively North American type of musical theatre, the result was very different. *The Golden Apple* (1954) is a chirpy Broadway resetting of both the *Iliad* and the *Odyssey* set in the American north-west in the early twentieth century. John Latouche wrote the words and Jerome Moross the music; they juxtaposed the Greek material with folksy American settings and added waltzes, ragtime, blues and vaudeville. True to the tradition of opera composers using the *Odyssey* to avant-garde ends, *The Golden Apple* upset traditional audiences by offering them no dialogue at all, and thus seeming very 'operatic'. This highbrow feature has been blamed for the lack of success of the piece following its opening season.

The *Odyssey*'s cultural elasticity could not be better illustrated than by the contrast between *The Golden Apple* and the next major sung version of the epic, Luigi Dallapiccola's *Ulisse* (1968). Like Monteverdi and Fauré before him, Dallapiccola produced his *Odyssey* at an advanced age, in his 60s, and saw it as a consummation of his life's work and aesthetic project. He was also using a myth which to him seemed to offer a transcendent promise of answers to the aesthetic and philosophical questions that obsessed him, precisely because he felt that it stood both at the dawn of Western culture and at the dawn of Western opera, with Monteverdi's version. *Ulisse* is Dallapiccola's most ambitious composition, and after its première it was criticized for its lack of theatrical qualities and slow pace. It certainly has no 'tunes' or even melodic lines to help the listener untrained in the ways of the musical avant-garde, although later performances are said to have revealed that a more stylized and oratorio-like production can make a more accessible impact.

As a philosophical meditation on modern man's search for a meaning to existence, *Ulisse* is never likely to be seen by the uninitiated as a musical treat. But it is a literary tour-de-force. The composer's own libretto incorporates references not only to Homer but to Dante, Shakespeare, Thomas Mann, Cavafy and the Spanish poet Machado. The first act is a compacted version of the wanderings, including Calypso (soprano) gazing out to sea, lamenting that Ulisse (baritone) has left her. But Ulisse's existential crisis – the true subject of the opera – is signalled in her warning that he is entirely isolated: 'Alone, once more, are your heart and the sea', which is actually a line from Machado. The intellectual project is moved forward by Circe, who tells Ulisse that the monsters and vagrancy are within his mind, not in the external world. Here it becomes apparent that the conflict Dallapiccola is trying to resolve is one inside the intellect and psyche. His Ulisse has a quest that points within himself – an attitude encapsulated in the words with which the opera opens and which are repeated throughout: 'To search, to wonder, and to search again and again'. There are reminiscent of the Tennysonian Ulysses' catechism, 'To strive, to seek, to find, and not to yield' (see pp 211–12).

In the climactic feast scene, the suitors make Melanto dance, giving her the bow of Ulisse as inspiration. But she is interrupted by the arrival of Telemaco, whom the suitors believed to be dead. They have not recovered from their surprise when Ulisse enters and reveals his identity. He orders the guards to hang Melanto, strings the great bow and strikes down the suitors one by one before Penelope appears. After a symphonic intermezzo, the original part of Dallapiccola's opera ensues. Ulisse is once more at sea, gazing at the stars while he undergoes an existential crisis. Failing to comprehend what has happened to him, he prays for illumination. The opera draws to a close as he is rewarded with a vision of God.

Dallapiccola's understanding of the Odysseus myth owes much to the tradition of philosophical, less dramatic, interpretations of the *Odyssey*, especially those of Dante, Pascoli, Tennyson and of course Joyce. Dallapiccola's earlier theatre pieces centred on the struggle of man against a superior force, but Ulisse's struggle is above all a struggle against *himself*, as the philosopher-theologian who sets himself the task of understanding the cosmic mystery. He can only do this truly alone, but the divine vision allows him to transcend fear and doubt. Dallapiccola wanted to come to terms with the existence of God and to find comfort in a faith that he had earlier lost.

Although sung versions of the *Odyssey* are particularly popular in Greece, these days musical compositions and productions inspired by the *Odyssey* can be seen in theatres and heard on the airwaves across the world. At one extreme of eccentricity stands the alternative rock tonality of Andreas Ammer's *Odysseus 7* (1997), a 'radio space opera', which takes Odysseus into outer space to the accompaniment of the theremin (a futuristic electronic instrument with a vibrato effect).[36] At another stands Edward Rushton's *Barks*, an opera for ten singers chained to the stage like dogs and impersonating the sounds they imagine Odysseus' dog Argos made when he recognized his master.[37] Somewhere between these extremes lies *Odysseus Unwound*, an opera in which the story of Odysseus is merged with knitting and spinning in an unprecedented type of performance, composed by Julian Grant and Hattie Naylor.[38]

The centuries-long stream of inventive musical responses to the *Odyssey* seems inexhaustible. But although opera composers have used the epic in order to make avant-garde musical statements, and in the case of Dallapiccola a philosophical one, the musical theatre is not the place where politics and the *Odyssey* have usually met. The situation might have been different if Kurt Weill's ex-slave Ulysses Africanus had ever found a public voice in performance. But in 2003 an unusual step was taken by Rinde Eckert when he composed *Highway Ulysses*, a 'contemporary musical response to Homer's Odyssey' that received its premiere from the American Repertory Company in March 2003. *Highway Ulysses* was in its own way musically experimental, since Eckert adopted the open intervals of the perfect fourth and fifth, inspired by the ancient pentatonic scale. But it is in the political stance of this opera that its greatest interest is to be found. As in many movies (as we shall see in Chapter 10) Eckert's story of the returning warrior is transferred to lower-class life in contemporary North America; his Ulysses is a Vietnam veteran whose quest to find his son involves him in encounters with a truck-stop waitress, gaoled sirens and a woman in a tattoo parlour. But these lowlife contacts actually enable Ulysses to confront his violent past and locate his long-lost child.

In an interview, Eckert has called himself a literary 'predator', who has stolen from the *Odyssey* the questions it asks 'about the relationship between a returning war hero and the operations of a state'. This is, of course, hardly surprising in the USA in 2003, when war was once again being declared on Iraq. But Eckert's reading of the *Odyssey* makes the hero an irresponsible leader, refusing to acknowledge the crimes he has committed either abroad or at home:[39]

> Odysseus is responsible for the loss of over five hundred men ... You have
> to admit what you've done ... In American history, you can't sweep under
> the rug the treatment of Native Americans. Let's be clear about our own
> past. I think that's the sine qua non of civilized society.

For Eckert, Odysseus is a problematic hero because, like the North American establishment, he won't own up, even to himself, to the damage he has done. Moreover, Odysseus' trickery 'makes him a quintessentially modern figure ... During the Vietnam era, there was outright lying. Odysseus is not a figure of antiquity, he has great contemporary relevance because of his strange relationship to truth.' And that note is an appropriate one for the argument of this book to move from Section I, which has focused on the media in which the *Odyssey* has been adapted, to Section II, which explores the way it has been used in relation to the real-world concerns of politics and society.

# PART II
# WORLD AND SOCIETY

# 6

# FACING FRONTIERS

When Odysseus describes the Cyclops' island, he speaks with the discerning eye of the colonist (9.131–6):

The land is not at all bad, and could produce every kind of seasonal crop. For there are luxurious irrigated meadowlands along the coast, by the white-topped sea, which would support vines throughout the year. The soil would be easy to plough, and tall ripe crops could always be harvested, for underneath the topsoil the earth is very rich. There is also a good natural harbour there.

Odysseus the mythical explorer is related to the real-life Greeks who in the archaic age sailed into unknown waters across the Mediterranean and Black Sea. Tiresias also tells Odysseus that he must later go on another journey (11.121–5), until he comes 'to men who have no notion of the sea, and do not add salt to their food. These men have no knowledge of ships with crimson cheeks, nor of the poising of oars which serve as wings for ships.' Here Odysseus is configured as the master mariner who can yet travel deep inland, thus becoming not only 'the symbol of all sea-based civilizations',[1] but of every subsequent explorer of sea, land or indeed outer space. Keats had a profound intuition when he composed his sonnet *On First Looking Into Chapman's Homer* (1817).[2] The poet-narrator equates his own literary journey with Odysseus' explorations, by echoing the first lines of the *Odyssey* in saying that he himself has 'many goodly states and kingdoms seen' on his travels 'round many western islands'. But when his poetic voyage took him to Chapman's translations of Homer (9–14),

Then felt I like some watcher of the skies
  When a new planet swims into his ken;
Or like stout Cortez when with eagle eyes
  He star'd at the Pacific—and all his men
Look'd at each other with a wild surmise—
  Silent, upon a peak in Darien.

Keats's thrill of discovery must resemble what an astronomer feels when he

75

first identifies a new planet through the lens of his telescope, or a Spanish explorer in the New World when he first gazed from a peak in Panama on a vast ocean he never knew existed.[3] The poet had recently read William Robertson's *History of America* (1777), which had fired his imagination as much as Homer.[4]

Keats's similes were adopted by the space-race community in the 1960s. The lines about the watcher of the skies, much cited in NASA publicity documents, have been quoted in newspapers ever since the first walk on the moon by Neil Armstrong of the Apollo 11 mission, at 10:56 pm EDT on 20 July 1969. The prime minister of Australia famously wrote in the visitors' book at the Australian mission-control centre assisting the Americans, 'Mankind now can "gaze at each other with wild surmise" as to what future travel in space may bring.' Keats had put his finger on two key frontiers – the Americas in the Renaissance and interplanetary space – that have indeed been significant in the history of the *Odyssey*'s influence.

The epic evokes the danger and excitement of traversing unknown seas to distant lands (see Fig. 6). But although, as we shall see in the next chapter, it has been read as validating the ancient Greeks' conquest of indigenous peoples in remote territories, it did so in a sophisticated form. Odysseus' adventures are not known itineraries; he is no straightforward equivalent of the early Mediterranean explorers whose real names we know, such as Scylax of Caryanda (see below) or Hanno the Navigator.[5] The resistance that Greek tradesmen encountered abroad informs the poem, but is mediated by the vocabulary of myth, so that the ethnically other is transformed into the supernatural and inhuman.[6] The colonization myths of other world cultures similarly conceptualize the enemy as bestial or supernatural. In the *Rāmāyana* the Sri Lankans resisting Aryan conquest are portrayed as monkeys, demons and bears, while the Chinese 'civilizer' hero Yü visits the winged people and the black-teethed people.[7] A study by Romm (1992) has shown how the notions of the world's boundaries that arrived in the Renaissance, although informed by Seneca, Tacitus, Lucian and ancient literary versions of mariners' handbooks, ultimately derive from the *Odyssey* and other epic poetry. This explains why, when the Persian king Darius I sent Scylax of Caryanda (the first Greek to visit India) to the Far East for 30 months (Herodotus IV.44), he returned with a logbook that catalogued peoples with strange deformities. Scylax's Greek audience was raised on the *Odyssey* and its influence was impossible to evade.

Three recent books study the frontier mentality articulated in the *Odyssey*. Malkin (1998) ties the emergence of the poem to archaeologically identifiable waves of colonization, arguing that it reflects 'proto-colonial' heroes who needed money and authority before they could launch an expedition. They indeed wandered the seas to trade, but did not build or settle communities abroad. Hartog (2001), meanwhile, focuses on the epic's impact on later mental maps. The poem underlay ancient and therefore Renaissance notions of geographical space, topography and cartography. The Greek travellers and thinkers whose models of the world were ineradicably informed by the journeys of Odysseus include Pythagoras, Solon, Anacharsis, Pausanias, Plutarch, Alexander, Polybius, Dionysius of Halicarnassus, Strabo, Aelius Aristides and Apollonius of Tyana. On a more literary level, Dougherty (2001) has suggested that Odysseus' itinerary, symbolized by his raft, is a 'metapoetic' device for moving the poem's listener around in the imagination.

For the Romans, the *Odyssey*'s travelogue symbolized the expansion, centuries before, of civilization to Italy and the islands off its western coast. They were aware that already in the early Greek epic that contained the divine genealogies, Hesiod's *Theogony*, Odysseus appears as the father of Italian colonists via the sons Circe was sometimes said to have borne to him (1011–16): Agrius, Latinus and Telegonus, who 'ruled over the famous Tyrseni [i.e. Etruscans], far away in a recess of sacred islands'. It was important to Roman identity that this Telegonus was said to have founded Praeneste (in Latium, east of Rome) and Tusculum (also Latium, south-east of Rome).[8]

Frescoes depicting scenes from the *Odyssey* adorn a rich tomb of the fourth century BCE at Etruscan Tarquinia (the Tomba dell' Orco); one depicts the blinding of the Cyclops, and others the Underworld. Several Etruscan funeral urns with *Odyssey* scenes have also been discovered. Some scenes may relate directly to the individual being buried: the *Odyssey* would have resonances, for example, in the burial of a faithful wife. But Farrell suggests that since the most common scene types represent Odysseus' journey, which was early understood as taking him to Italy and Sicily, these Etruscans accepted Odysseus as the hero who brought their people westward and wished to assert a continuity of cultural identity with him.[9]

The Romans of the Augustan and Imperial periods used illustrations of the *Odyssey* in internal décor. One series of panels found in a Roman house on the Esquiline, and now in the Vatican museum, was painted in about 30 BCE. The series is similar to those in the Tomba dell' Orco, which

suggests, says Farrell, that this programme was 'of a type that was familiar throughout Italy from at least the fourth century onwards'.[10] Indeed,
Vitruvius, an Augustan architect, names scenes from the wanderings of
Odysseus (*Ulixis errationes*) as traditional subjects for wall-paintings in
fine homes (7.5.1–2). In 1957 a seaside cave was discovered at Sperlonga,
which had served as a shrine of the nymphs and as a summer dining area.
It contains massive sculptural recreations of Scylla attacking Odysseus'
ship and the blinding of Polyphemus – scenes thought to have taken place
in the Italian area. Elite Romans, following the Etruscans, surrounded
themselves with visual Odysseys that linked the heroic past to their Italian present, suggesting that 'Odysseus was an Italian culture hero and
even the ancestor of some peoples'.[11] The blinding of the Cyclops reminded
dinner guests of Odysseus' role as mythical colonizer. The victory over the
Cyclops was emblematic of the Roman domination of the Ligurian and
Tyrrhenian seas.

Geographers took Odysseus ever westward as the Roman Empire
expanded, and he became the mythical founder of cities in Spain and
Portugal. The name of the capital of Lisbon is a modification of its ancient
name *Olissipo* or *Ulyssipo* (i.e. Ulysses' polis) under the influence of the
story of a city founded by Odysseus in Iberia. But the name acquired
new resonances as Portugal built up the first great Western global empire
during the sixteenth century in Africa and India. By 1400, the Ulysses in
Dante's *Inferno* describes his ships passing through the Pillars of Hercules
at the Straits of Gibraltar, where he exhorted his crew like a prefigurative
Columbus, urging them across the Atlantic: 'O brothers who through a
hundred thousand dangers have reached the West … choose not to deny
experience, following the sun, of the world that has no people.'[12] Although
Dante had in mind the ill-fated expedition to circumnavigate Africa that
Ugolino Vivaldi had led through the Pillars of Hercules in 1291, never
to return, this new narrative was grafted on to the story of Odysseus, as
well as other ancient texts. Both Dante and Columbus knew the mysterious passage from Seneca's *Medea*, which seems to offer a prophecy of the
Renaissance maritime adventure, speaking of the epoch in centuries to
come 'when Ocean loosens the bonds of the world and the earth lies open
in its vastness, when Tethys will disclose new worlds and Thule not be the
farthest of lands'.[13]

For the Portuguese, the Ulysses who was fulfilling Seneca's prophecy symbolized their imperial aspirations. They focused their expansion
in the Atlantic Ocean, discovering the islands of Madeira in 1418 and
the Azores in 1432. Bartolomeu Dias and Vasco da Gama explored the

sea route around Africa to India, whereas other Portuguese sailors like
Ferdinand Magellan worked for the Spanish Empire in the Pacific. *Os
Lusíadas* (*The Lusiads*) by Luís Vaz de Camões is the Portuguese national
epic, published in 1572, that celebrates Vasco da Gama's voyage round the
Cape of Good Hope to India. The poet announces that he will sing of

> Arms and the Heroes, who from Lisbon's shore,
> Thro' seas where sail was never spread before,
> Beyond where Ceylon lifts her spicy breast.[14]

The *Aeneid* is the major inspiration, but there are pointers to the *Odyssey*,
including Sirens, idyllic islands and the instruction to Fame that da Gama
has outdone Ulysses: 'with wonder name the Greek no more,/What lands
he saw, what toils at sea he bore'.[15] This identification of the Portuguese
colonial navigators with the heroes of ancient Greek and Roman epic
suggested to the mystical nationalist Fernando Pessoa that in his *Mensagem*, a poetic rewriting of his country's history (1934), he make Ulysses,
the man who arrives by sea (*que aqui aportou*), the image on which the
Portuguese identity as a nation of seafarers was founded.[16]

The association of the Indian frontier with those faced by Odysseus and
Aeneas lurks in the title of an account of the mercantile Greek community
whose presence in Bengal and northern India can be traced back to the
early 1600s – *Ulysses in the Raj*.[17] But when it comes to what the Europeans
called their 'discovery' of America, Columbus's own journal (1492) reveals
that he saw himself as a descendant not only of Marco Polo and John
Mandeville but of the quest-heroes of mythology. The journal is not an
objective account but the story of a latterday Odysseus, Jason or Sinbad.
The author, Columbus, is the hero of his own fable and what we read is a
subjective account that reveals how he imagined his heroic role as well as
what he might actually have seen (see Chapter 7).

When the Connecticut patriot Joel Barlow attempted a national epic
poem celebrating the 'discovery' of America, he eventually decided on
the Homeric title *The Columbiad* (1807).[18] More recently, a novel by Max
Yeh, *The Beginning of the East* (1992), leads its hero to Seville to investigate
Columbus, but his figure and those of Marco Polo and Odysseus become
intertwined: Columbus is tied to the mast, credited with the words, 'nemo
… no-man is my name', and dreams of a land where an oar would be
misidentified as a winnowing fan (see Chapter 15). Columbus's men find
a skull with one eye socket, eat lotus plants and butcher cattle despite a
prohibition.[19] Another novel, Daniel Panger's *Black Ulysses* (1982), makes
explicit the analogy between the *Odyssey* and the narrative of the European
'discovery' of America, although with a twist. This Ulysses is a black slave

from Morocco, who left Spain with Alvar Nuñez in 1537. From Trinidad they arrive in Florida, and travel along the Gulf of Mexico to Texas and finally California. They face terrible ordeals and keep losing men, their quest for the western lands lent a mythic aura by the references to a vicious one-eyed governor, the Sirens, aggressive fish-spearing natives, Hermes and angry seas.

In the twentieth century the frontier that dominated the world's cinematic imagination was still the Western one, which now provided the setting of films belonging to the genre known as the 'Western'. In the broadest sense almost all Westerns are 'mythic' and 'heroic'; they are also 'Odyssean' in that they involve archetypal masculine figures in combat and ordeal on distant frontiers. But with John Ford's *The Searchers* (1956), made in Utah's Monument Valley, the relationship with Homer becomes more specific. This was after Ford filmed *Stagecoach* (1939) with John Wayne, thus making this actor's career a symbol of the American frontier spirit.

From the day of its release, rumours circulated about *The Searchers'* relationship with the *Odyssey*. The influential magazine *Look* called it 'a Homeric Odyssey … a Western in the grand manner'.[20] These rumours were compounded by a scene in the movie about the screenwriting business that Ford made the following year, *The Wings of Eagles* (1957). A copy of the *Odyssey* lies on the table between the film director John Dodge (based on Ford himself) and his screenwriter Frank Wead, a crippled naval officer (played by John Wayne). This Odyssean allusion was inserted on the instruction of Ford. But although Ford himself described *The Searchers* as 'a psychological epic',[21] no scholar has ever proven that he consciously incorporated ideas from the *Odyssey*. They may have been the result of an unconscious casting of the protagonist Ethan from the mould of the itinerant, lonely hero. But the *Odyssey* was on the film industry's mind in 1956, after the release of Camerini's *Ulisse* with Kirk Douglas, and there are some striking parallels: the opening scenes of both films offer a dark, silhouetted figure viewed against a frame. Moreover, Ford was an obsessive devotee of Irish culture, who in 1951 had made an emotional pilgrimage to his parents' birthplaces in western Ireland, and would certainly have encountered Joyce's *Ulysses*. Indeed, he considered filming a short story by Joyce.[22] *The Wings of Eagles* allusion implies that he enjoyed the rumours spread by the article in *Look*, even if they were unfounded. It is anyway more significant that the parallel with the *Odyssey* has haunted the critical responses to *The Searchers*, and thus constitutes an important filter through which the meaning of the movie is created by its viewers.

Some of the parallels, even if they are not echoes, are clear. The opening credit sequence of *The Searchers* is accompanied by a recording of a group called Sons of the Pioneers singing verses that ask:

> What makes a man to wander?
> What makes a man to roam?
> What makes a man to leave bed and board
> And turn his back on home?

Ethan is established as a wanderer, and 'the reason why he wanders is established as the central question'.[23] At one point the Reverend Captain Clayton says to Ethan, 'You fit a lot of descriptions' – he is *polútropos*, a man of many identities. Ethan in *The Searchers* is also Odysseus-like in his quest to reclaim his kin and wreak revenge for assault on the nearest thing he had to a household, in his epic journey, and in his relationship with Martin, the Telemachus figure. It has recently been argued that in his rage he is more a latterday Achilles than an Odysseus,[24] but as the man of complex morality, who undergoes both inward and outward journeys, his resemblances to Odysseus are stronger.

Ethan is the consummation of the paradoxes that Ford had imputed to the Western hero since *Stagecoach*. He is both hero and anti-hero, outlaw and soldier, bloodthirsty and chivalric. He has no Penelope to mark the end of his quest because Martha, the woman he loved, was his brother's wife and she has now been killed.[25] Ford said that the film was actually 'the tragedy of a loner ... [who] could never really be part of the family'.[26] At the end Ethan turns to go back into the desert from which he arrived. Of course, it was not uncommon in the genre for the hero, after fulfilling his function, to leave the community rather than integrate himself.[27] But in combination with the other Odyssean features of the film, it could be understood as a reference to Tiresias' prophecy that Odysseus will go on the road one more time.

The film was adapted from a 1954 novel by Alan Le May, originally serialized in a newspaper as *The Avenging Texans*. This contains no obvious reference to the *Odyssey*, and Ford's film is more philosophically profound. Like the *Odyssey*, *The Searchers* is focused on epistemological issues, making viewers ask how they understand what is going on from the signs they are given.[28] The film's treatment of the perilous margin between 'Western' civilization and the unknown society beyond the frontier is mysterious: Ethan is both close to the native Americans and violently opposed to them. Indeed, *The Searchers* is regarded as the turning point in the history of the Western because white violence and brutality, as displayed by Ford's pioneers, Texas Rangers, and homesteaders, suddenly increase in comparison with both the violence of Native Americans and the violence of white men in earlier Westerns.[29]

From the western to the northern frontier: travellers to the Canadian Arctic have been reminded of the *Odyssey*. As Al Purdy sailed to the Kikastan Islands, he expected to see signs reading 'Castles for sale/Apply at Circe's Island'.[30] The Canadian novelist Robert Kroetsch, who as a young man spent months amongst the Inuit, has compared the act of writing to facing a frontier:

> To write is, in some metaphoric sense, to go North ... One goes North at the very point on the page where the word is in the process of extending itself onto the blankness of the page.[31]

Kroetsch's own *Odyssey*-inspired novel about frontiers, *The Studhorse Man* (1969), stands out for its literary bravura as a picaresque adventure set in rural Alberta. Hazard Lepage's quest to breed the perfect horse is signalled as an absurdist parody of Odysseus' wanderings.[32] The novel opens in 1945 when Lepage decides to leave his fiancée of 14 years to search for a mare worthy of coupling with his blue stallion Poseidon. His shape-shifting, delays, narrow escapes and epic sexual encounters are recorded by Demeter Proudfoot, the novel's clinically insane narrator, who is writing in a bathtub. Kroetsch is convinced that 'no story can be told only once', but that in every retelling the original story 'can no longer be'; he finds 'in the narrative necessity of myth not meaning at all, but a potential for meaning'; we are 'entrapped' in the ancient mythic stories and face the choice of surrendering to them, or telling our way out – always on that frontier of discovery.[33]

Tracing the role of the *Odyssey* in representing frontiers must now move from the far west and north to space, the final frontier. There are links between the frontier monsters encountered by ancient Greek quest heroes and the aliens inhabiting other planets in science fiction;[34] with Stanley Kubrick's film *2001: A Space Odyssey* (1968), the Homeric epic became forever welded in the world's imagination with space travel. The satellites currently sent into orbit by the company Sea Launch, from an oceanic cosmodrome on the Pacific equator, ascend from a floating launch platform named Odysseus. NASA's Mars Orbiter, which arrived at the Red Planet in October 2001, is itself called Odyssey. But the history of the relationship of the *Odyssey* with travel beyond Planet Earth goes much further back into history.

The term 'science fiction' (SF) was coined in 1929 by Hugo Gernsback; scholars of the form routinely trace it back to the *Odyssey*, usually via Lucian's *True Narratives*,[35] in which the narrator describes his trip to the moon. One element missing from these ancient texts in comparison with

SF is the science: the journey through space in Lucian contains no interest in the mechanical means by which it might be effected. Yet the novel does play with astronomy, anthropology, geography and natural history, all of which had developed in the near-millennium since Homer, especially in terms of empirical observation and taxonomy.[36] The doyen of the history of SF, Sam Moskowitz, has trenchantly put it, 'in an era when the "entire world" was thought to be confined to the Mediterranean basin ... a pack donkey or a sailing ship was every bit as good a device as a spaceship for locating strange and bizarre civilizations and boldly seeking out fantastic adventures on the rim of the world'.[37] Moreover, in taking the journey off Planet Earth, Lucian's plot-type was breaking new ground, in the wake of another novel lost to posterity, Antonius Diogenes' *Of the Wonderful Things Beyond Thule*, which also contained a moon journey.[38]

Controlled scientific speculation, as well as the 'sense of wonder' earlier SF theorists thought was definitive of the genre,[39] are offered by Lucian's ice-sailing, and the well and a mirror in the extra-terrestrial world that allow terrestrial activities to be heard and seen. But the most influential definition of SF recently has been Darko Suvin's model of 'cognitive estrangement' – a process by which we imagine a world alternative to our own, but to which we relate through significant knowledge systems.[40] Perhaps the true claim of *True Narratives* to SF status lies not in its celebrated depiction of interplanetary travel but in its scrutiny of the moon-world and sun-world as parallel and analogical universes.[41]

It is also true, of course, that there is no trip to the moon in the *Odyssey*. Yet Lucian's *True Narratives* could never have been conceived without the entire history of 'wonder' travelogues, and Lucian makes numerous allusions to the *Odyssey* as his prototype,[42] even before the discussion of the alternative world to be found on Circe's island (2.35–6). Moreover, as Suvin has insisted, Jules Verne's Captain Nemo's electrical submarine in *Twenty Thousand Leagues Under the Sea* (1869) anticipates by decades the invention of SF set in space, but without leaving Planet Earth. This crucial figure in the evolution of SF, moreover, is informed by Homer's Odysseus. Not only does his name, the Latin for 'Nobody', invite the comparison, but he is an Odysseus because he displays 'both superior technology and liberating aims'.[43]

The importance of the *Odyssey* in relation to SF has long stimulated writers to base new stories on it. Arthur C. Clarke's story *The Sentinel* (1948), from which the idea for *2001: A Space Odyssey* was derived, did not include Homeric references, but other SF writers had explicitly used the *Odyssey* before the movie. Early examples are the stories by Stanley

Weinbaum written in the 1930s, which creatively adapted the *Odyssey* in order to explore what were in Weinbaum's time frightening futuristic scenarios: *The Lotus Eaters* (1935) imagines the world from the perspective of intelligent plant life, and *Proteus Island* (1936) reads the shape-shifting sea god as a study in genetic engineering.[44]

There are also pronounced Homeric features in *David Starr: Space Ranger* (1952) by Isaac Asimov, a titan in the history of SF who read Homer and Greek mythology voraciously during his New York boyhood. The earthling David Starr has defeated a Martian attempt to poison the human food supply (the head of the Defence of the Homeland is called Hector). A resourceful and untruthful hero, in Chapter 9, 'Into the fissure', Starr embarks on a dangerous fact-finding descent into the dusky abyss of the Martian interior,[45] and meets a feminine energy force. Like Calypso, she is immortal, and wistful about the emotional richness of experience that mortals enjoy. In an encounter with a male being, who Tiresias-like delivers prophecies, the newly renamed Space Ranger is given a personal force-field in the form of a strip of an energy mask. It saves his life in the lethal Martian sandstorm, in a reference to the scarf which Leucothea, the sea-goddess who had once been a mortal woman, bestows upon Odysseus to save him from the storm sent by Poseidon. In the five subsequent Starr novels, Odyssean traces include the revenge theme and barbarous space pirates of *Lucky Starr and the Pirates of the Asteroids* (1953), the colonial civilization beneath the boundless seas in *Lucky Starr and the Oceans of Venus* (1954) and the deadly giant robot of *Lucky Starr and the Big Sun of Mercury* (1956).

Three years before the Kubrick movie, the British SF hero Dr Who had an intense relationship with Odysseus when he time-travelled to the Trojan War in *The Myth Makers*, a four-part story broadcast in Autumn 1965 but sadly wiped from the archives (the audiotape survived). In an Odyssean allusion, Dr Who himself, played by the white-haired William Hartnell, was assumed by the ancient Greeks and Trojans to be Zeus, in a beggar's disguise. When, less than a year later, NBC broadcast the first episode of *Star Trek* (8 September 1966), Captain Kirk said for the first time, 'These are the voyages of the starship *Enterprise*, her five-year mission to explore strange new worlds, to seek out new life and new civilizations', as well as 'to boldly go where no man has gone before'. Any TV viewer acquainted with the *Odyssey* will instantly have noted the similarity with its opening, 'Tell me, O muse, of that ingenious hero who travelled far and wide after he had sacked the famous town of Troy. Many cities did he visit, and many were the nations with whose manners and customs he was acquainted.' As the authors of an insightful study of *Star Trek* concluded, the TV series may offer 'a new set of wineskins, but the mythic fermentation within is as old as Apollo'.[46] Although the crew of the *Enterprise* never actually encountered Odysseus in the TV series, Kirk and Spock certainly got involved in the *Odyssey* in spin-off versions by the late 1970s (see below). Actually coinciding with, and therefore not deriving from the Kubrick movie, there was also Lafferty's *Space Chantey* (1968), a humorous novel postulating the need for storytelling in the oppressively logical space age of the future, which intersperses its futuristic narrative with sections of poetry. Captain Roadstrum, a survivor of a terrible ten-year space war, leads his crew to the pleasure planet Lotophage, with its bar, The Sleepy Sailor. He deals with the Polyphemians, xenophobic shepherds. But for this futuristic Odysseus there is no home to go to, and he concludes the novel like Dante's Ulysses, adjuring his men to arise: 'To come to the end of the journey is to die. We go again!'[47]

There had, therefore, been SF Odysseys before *2001: A Space Odyssey*. But it is only in its wake that specialists in SF have promoted the *Odyssey* to cult status. The name of the hero, David Bowman, is an obvious compliment to Homer's champion archer, and the monocular computer HAL has Cyclopean features (see p 92). But it is difficult to press specific points of resemblance, despite the attempts that have been made by fervid allegorists.[48] Resemblances are certainly not to be found in the short story which originally inspired Kubrick, *The Sentinel* by Arthur C. Clarke (1951). When Kubrick approached him, Clarke began a new novel expanding his idea, entitled *2001: A Space* Odyssey, and collaborated with Kubrick on the screenplay. It was at this point that the Odyssean resonances crept in. The point of connection is, in fact, more profound than narrowly intertextual readings imply. Kubrick and Clarke were underlining the importance of Odysseus as the first great quest hero with a claim to global, universal status in the history of the Western (and arguably the human) psyche: he has a vital generative role in humanity's journey into the space age. We *are* Odysseus as we travel collectively from ape to human and eventually, after leaving the planet, to starman-angel.

Kubrick's film can lay claim to a foundational status as one of the most significant statements about its own medium. The International Association for the Fantastic in the Arts chose as the theme of its 2001 conference what else but 'Once and future Odysseys'. *2001* is felt to have achieved an epochal breakthrough in the epistemological potential of SF, as the first film to use space as a metaphor for the evolution of intelligence. In Odysseus' mendacity, reflected in the deception programmed into the computer

HAL at the beginning of the mission, the tragic dilemmas of the power to distort the truth that accompanies human intellectual prowess is ironically explored. Like Odysseus, HAL understands the terrible tension between the need to control circumstances by deception and the need to search out new knowledge; sadly, the controlling, effectively murderous, impulse wins.[49] Such has been the critical response to the film's philosophical depth that it also prepared the way 'for the birth of a rigorous and informed body of science-fiction film criticism'.[50]

SF novels using Homeric epic have multiplied since Kubrick's film.[51] The more enjoyable include the *Dies Irae* trilogy by Brian Stableford (1971), which draws on the *Iliad* in the terrible Beast War of Part I, and on the *Odyssey* in Part II, *In the Kingdom of the Beasts*. Besides the overriding theme of Circean zoomorphism incarnated in the foully obese beast-woman, the hero Mark Chaos repeats many of Odysseus' adventures in hyperspace: his 17-year captivity on Calypso's World, a flesh-eating hairy giant, and a lovely Nausicaa figure named Yvaine. This author cleverly sees that the narrative complexity of the *Odyssey*, and the games it plays with linear time, are similar to the licence allowed to an SF writer by postulating a cosmic time gap.

After *2001*, the epic finally became fused with *Star Trek* in *What Fools These Mortals Be*, issue number 53 (July 1978) of the comic-strip version published by Gold Key between 1967 and 1979. Accidentally beamed down to a beautiful planet, Spock soon tells Kirk and McCoy that they are in the middle of the *Odyssey*, 'one of your ancient Earth legends about a general returning from battle. He had similar problems with his crew, when they came to a place called "The Land of the Lotus Eaters". He, too, met up with cannibals, and battled a one-eyed giant called Cyclops, I believe! It happened after an encounter known as the Trojan War!' An Olympian tells them from the sky that the gods have decamped to another planet, and abandons the doughty crew to suffer winds blown by Aeolus, the Sirens' song (only Captain Kirk does not need earwax), Scylla and Charybdis. Eventually the planet's inhabitants are liberated by the visitors, who knock Zeus off his aerial throne with a deflected tractor beam. The crew achieve, as they are told, what even Odysseus could not, and are beamed back smugly to the *Enterprise*.

Fans of the several *Star Trek* series argue that they became successively more Homeric. Most comparisons have been drawn between Odysseus and Katherine Janeway, star of *Star Trek: Voyager* (1995–2001). Janeway has been catapulted many light years away, into the unknown Delta Quadrant, and her voyage home to her husband will take her 75 years; moreover, in episode 162, *Favorite Son* (March 1997), there is an explicit retelling of the story of how Odysseus outwitted the Sirens. The *Odyssey* was, however, more central to the cult TV animated cartoon series *Ulysses 31*, which premiered in 1981 but which has been enjoying a revival since its release on DVD. In this charming, innovative adventure series, the *Odyssey* was transported to the thirty-first century by a French–Japanese collaborative production team. Ulysses, the viewer is told at the beginning, killed the giant Cyclops when he rescued 'the children' and his son Telemachus. But the gods of Olympus are angry and are enacting a terrible revenge. Ulysses has been sentenced to travel through the universe of Olympus on a quest to find the Kingdom of Hades. Only then will he be able to return to earth and to his beloved Penelope.

The futuristic visual environment abounds in Ionic columns, the space-station of Troy in the episode *Vengeance of the Gods* is in the shape of a Greek hoplite helmet, and the space ships are built to replicate Poseidon's trident. One episode is actually set on Ithaca, but the story-writer, Jean Choplin, uses the *Odyssey* wittily in every episode. In *Song of Danger,* Ulysses disables the robot Nono's circuits in order to hear the Sirens. Charybdis, the deadly whirlpool, in *The Black Sphere* becomes a lethal gravitational field, strewn with wrecked spaceships. The main alteration is in the rewriting of the character of Odysseus. This hero of the future is morally sanitized (there are no sexual partners) and a wonderful father. Cronus in *Cronus, Father of Time* says he is actually naive. The audience of *Ulysses 31* watches a boy-scout leader with flowing locks and a Grecian tunic. But this was the version of the *Odyssey* through which millions of fans in the 1980s were introduced to Greek myth, and some still greet each other with Ulysses' catchphrase, 'Computer, give me all possible options at once!'

# 7

# COLONIAL CONFLICT

When the blinded Cyclops hurls his rock at Odysseus' escaping ship, he effectively creates the entire action of the epic by entreating his father Poseidon to frustrate all the Ithacan's attempts to return home and to ensure that he finds trouble when he does arrive (11.528–35). Odysseus, explorer and frontiersman, must learn that there is a price for arrogant trespassing on others' land. The brilliant satirist Lucian, an Asiatic subject of the Roman Empire himself, had already realized in the second century CE that, to the Cyclops, Odysseus and his men must have seemed to be nothing more than common robbers.[1] It is hardly surprising that the same poem that to explorers, pioneers, conquistadors and astronauts has always symbolized the human impulse to boldly go where no man has gone before has meant something rather different to the beings inhabiting the new worlds and new civilizations into which such travellers and colonial settlers have stumbled. Every society that has tried to run an empire has had – sooner or later – to pay for the wrongs it has committed.

In the Renaissance it begins to be possible to see how non-Western cultures reacted to the *Odyssey*, to which they were introduced by Western travellers. In one of the earliest examples, the *Odyssey* was fused with an indigenous heroic tradition. The medieval Japanese narrative *Yuriwaka Daijin (The Great Lord Yuriwaka)* celebrates the feats of the young nobleman Yuriwaka, who is selected by the gods (in a council scene unique in Japanese literature) to command the Japanese forces in a the thirteenth-century war against the Mongols. He leads a vast fleet to victory, with the help of Shinto and Buddhist deities, after a three-year stalemate. But on his way home he is abandoned in a death-like sleep on an island by his lieutenant, Beppu, and only returns to Japan years later. His appearance has so altered that nobody recognizes him, not even his most devoted servants. Beppu has taken over his province and wants to sleep with his lovely wife, but may not marry her until she fulfils a vow to transcribe a sacred Buddhist text a thousand times. Yuriwaka works as a servant until he can establish his identity by stringing a stiff iron bow, and punish his uppity rival by trussing him to a pine tree and mutilating him.[2]

The startling parallels with the *Odyssey* have led Japanese scholars to ask how the Mediterranean story might have arrived in Japan in time to inform the sixteenth-century *Yuriwaka Daijin*. Some have suggested that Marco Polo might have told the story in Peking, from where it travelled with the Mongols to Japan. But it is generally accepted that the conduit was the mission that accompanied Francis Xavier, a learned Basque who visited Japan in 1549–51. He was accompanied by the Portuguese Jesuit Juan Fernández, who was fluent in Japanese. Everyone in Portugal was familiar with the story of Ulysses, the traditional founder of Lisbon, and their pronunciation of the beginning of his name would have been heard in Japan as *Yuri*.[3]

Yet for many peoples coming into contact with Western powers, it must have been difficult to identify with the pioneer hero Odysseus. Instead, at least during the twentieth century, Odysseus' arch-enemy Polyphemus the Cyclops became the focus of a particular kind of attention. The Cyclops episode in the *Odyssey* is one of its most famous, and one of its most frequently represented. David Bader, the irrepressible composer of English-language haiku, condensed the *Odyssey* into these 17 syllables:

> Aegean forecast –
> storms, chance of one-eyed giants,
> delays expected.[4]

In antiquity the tale was the most popular of all the *Odyssey* themes in the visual arts, and the earliest vase portraying it, from Eleusis, is as old as the seventh century BCE.[5] It captured the Renaissance imagination immediately; Erasmus's opinionated, bibulous servant Felix of Ghent was nicknamed 'Polyphemus', and even incorporated under this name into *Cyclops*, one of his master's *Colloquies*.[6] It has had an important role to play in introducing children to mythology, through children's versions, of which since Charles Lamb's version there have been several hundred (see pp 26–7); many have featured a Cyclops as their cover illustration.[7] This has been on the assumption that the Cyclops, as an anthropophagous (human-flesh-eating) monster, deserved everything that he suffered. Until recently children's versions have followed Lamb's characterization of the incident, which he upgraded to take centre place in his first chapter. Lamb's Cyclops is described more pejoratively than Homer's; he is an 'uncouth monster', with a 'brutal body', and 'a brutish mind'; Lamb also dictated the story's meaning for his juvenile readers by adding that it provided 'manifest proof how far manly wisdom excels brutish force'.[8] Lamb was taking his cue from the ancient intuition that Odysseus' travels somehow symbolized colonial expansion.

Although the occasional ancient controversialist spoke up for the Cyclops,[9] the poem was almost always understood from the perspective of Odysseus the wayfarer, the *homo viator*, and the victory over the Cyclops came to symbolize the Roman domination of the western Mediterranean. By 1400, the Ulysses in Dante's *Inferno* tells how he exhorted his crew like Columbus, urging them across the Atlantic to new lands. At the same time, rumours spread of deformed giants that peopled the new worlds, and it was with a potential reality in mind that the accounts of monstrous races on the edges of the world – including one-eyed giants – in Pliny's *Natural History* and other ancient compendia were canonized in the medieval period.[10]

The Cyclops is the original man-eater, but reports of cannibalism the world over have been exaggerated. The problem facing anthropologists is that allegations of its practice are a standard trope in the xenophobic polemic of nearly every culture and era.[11] The missionaries in Africa feared that they might end up in an indigenous casserole, but some of the natives believed that the white invader was interested in eating the local people he encountered. Columbus's first letter discusses the Caribbean people of Caniba, terrible cannibals (said in other sources to have only one eye), the image of whom was to underlie the creation of Caliban – the barbarous native just ripe for subjugation – in Shakespeare's *The Tempest*. Columbus also noted how native peoples couldn't handle alcohol, an element in the presentation of the Cyclops in the *Odyssey*, and in the literature of colonial encounters between Europeans and their subjects everywhere (see Fig. 7).[12] The Cyclops then flourished during the great age of teratology (monster studies), which coincided with the first great wave of European colonial expansion, as numerous fabulously illustrated books attest.[13]

By the end of the seventeenth century, when John Locke wrote the second of his *Two Treatises of Government* (1689), the expanding mercantilism of the West needed examplary situations in which disrespect of political authority was legitimate: Locke chose Ulysses' defiance of the barbaric Cyclops' right to govern his own island.[14] Charles Darwin had absorbed the Odyssean myth of the barbarous cannibal; in his *Beagle* diaries he expresses his trust in Captain Cook's description of the Cyclopes-like New Zealand natives who throw stones at approaching ships, shouting 'come on shore and we will kill you and eat you all'.[15] The myth of Odysseus' subjugation of the Cyclops was deemed an exemplary tale for everyone living under Britannia's rule. In the *Royal Readers*, six standard schoolbooks, the episodes in myth and history selected for their instructive value included the Vikings, Napoleon, the Roman Empire, the conquest of Ireland and Odysseus blinding the Cyclops.[16]

The Cyclops thus long represented the savages who inhabited shores ripe for invasion. Yet Immanuel Kant began a new trend to redefine the one-eyedness of the Cyclops as narrow-mindedness. Kant captured this distinction in his contrast between the *sensus privates* (views that are only formed through privatized experience), which he called 'Cyclopean thinking', and the *sensus communis*, common or public sense. For Kant, it was possible to be an erudite Cyclops who knew a good deal about natural history, philology and mathematics. But without the enlarged thought that comes from engagement with diverse viewpoints, the learned person fails to think *philosophically*.[17] Closely related to the narrow cognition of the Kantian Cyclops is the widespread association of the one-eyed giant with the Orwellian Big Brother and his sinister, electronic Eye of surveillance: the most familiar example is Stanley Kubrick's intelligent computer HAL in his movie *2001: A Space Odyssey* (1968). But there had long before been real-life, sinister self-appointed agents of surveillance: when the Ku Klux Klan structured itself into the Invisible Empire of the South at a convention in Nashville, Tennessee, in 1867, the lieutenants of the presiding grand wizard were given the titles 'grand dragons', 'titans' and 'exalted cyclopses'. The 'Cyclops' chapter of Joyce's *Ulysses* (1922) is perhaps the first text *critically* to identify Cyclopean monocularity with ethnic narrow-mindedness: there, drinking in his 'cave' within Barney Kiernan's pub, is the huge, belligerent Cyclops; imagined with a granite spear and 'mighty cudgel rudely fashioned out of paleolithic stone', the obsessive Fenian anti-semite Citizen baits the Jewish hero mercilessly.[18]

In Ellison's *Invisible Man* (1952), the first Cyclopes the hero meets are when, Odysseus-like, he refuses to give his name to the medical staff subjecting him to electroconvulsive therapy: one doctor inspects him with 'a bright third eye that glowed from the centre of his forehead', and another has 'a circular mirror attached to his forehead'.[19] In the final chapters, however, it is revealed that the autocratic white leader of the tyrannical brotherhood, a thin disguise for the Communist Party of the USA in the early 1950s, has only one functioning eye. This Cyclops' fanatical tunnel vision has masqueraded as a concern for the African-American population.[20] In Walcott's stage version of the *Odyssey*, the Cyclops is a totalitarian tyrant who will brook neither dissent nor laughter in his grey police state.[21] And post-colonial theory has associated the myth with the Algerian activist Frantz Fanon's work on the privileging of vision by colonial powers. When Odysseus challenges the Cyclops, like Fanon, he offers a *critique* of the inadequate colonial 'look of surveillance', the 'single mode of colonial (super)vision maintained in the evil eye of objectification'. The Cyclops loses the tyrant's power, because he, like the French in Algeria, discovers that monocular, racist vision actually sees 'nobody' at all.[22]

Even Salman Rushdie has made use of this Cyclopean tradition in reference to George W. Bush's government and its attitude towards the Islamic world. In the aftermath of 9/11, with its masterminds still at large, Rushdie memorably compared the USA to a

> blind giant, flailing uselessly about: like, in fact, the blinded Cyclops Polyphemus of Homeric myth, who was only one-eyed to begin with, who had that eye put out by Ulysses and his fugitive companions, and who was reduced to roaring in impotent rage and hurling boulders in the general direction of Ulysses' taunting voice.

Rushdie contemplates how the episode might reflect Osama bin Laden's own fantasy construction of the global order:

> Polyphemus, after all, is a sort of evil superpower, a stupid creature of great, brute force who respects no laws or gods and devours human flesh, whereas Ulysses is crafty, devious, slippery, uncatchable and dangerous.[23]

The USA, as run by the former governor of Texas, was thus framed by Rushdie as running the risk of presenting itself to the rest of the world as the stupid, all-devouring, ugly, blundering giant outwitted by a smaller, cleverer hero. The flexibility of this type of comparison, it must be borne in mind, has meant that the North American press has been able to counter this possibility by pointing out that Bin Laden's notorious lieutenant Mullah Mohammed Omar is one-eyed and currently resides in a cave – 'the Cyclops of al-Quaeda'.

But the story doesn't end here, for the Cyclops has become not only a totemic but a *contested* figure. There is yet another twist in the tale of the re-envisioning of the Cyclops. In 1993, when Davies, Nandy and Sardar published their polemical *Barbaric Others: A Manifesto on Western Racism*, they took it for granted that the roles of good guy and bad guy in the story of Odysseus needed to be inverted. In their reading, Polyphemus returns to the status of the colonized subject, but now it is as a *victim*, the earliest and most influential example of 'the analytic categories that swayed the minds of Columbus and his successors'. The Cyclops is here the colonized and brutally subjected savage of archaic myth.[24] The stupid monster who became Big Brother has now turned into a victim of racist oppression.

By 1889, the American historian Henry Adams implied sympathy for the Cyclops as colonized subject when he was describing the American reaction to a British naval attack on the unprepared USS *Chesapeake* in 1813: 'The brand seethed and hissed like the glowing olive-stake of Ulysses in the Cyclops' eye, until the whole American people, like Cyclops, roared with pain and stood frantic on the shore, hurling abuse at their enemy, who taunted them from his safe ships.'[25] But the most important factor in the rehabilitation of the Cyclops was the twentieth-century, post-Freudian reappraisal of Odysseus,[26] which inevitably led to the re-evaluation of his victims. In philosophy, the major assault on Odyssean heroism came towards the end of the Second World War, when Theodor Adorno and Max Horkheimer collaborated on *Dialektik der Aufklärung*, first published in New York in the dark days of 1944. In an increasingly irrational world they sought to activate every resource made available through philosophical reasoning, but simultaneously identified the deadly role played by reason in the creation of humankind's problems, at least in the form of means–end calculations and the specious objectivity of ideologically motivated science. When they traced the genealogy of the dark underbelly of Western reason, it was the voyage of Odysseus which they selected for their allegorical case-study, thus tracing the destructive potential of reason to the *Odyssey*, one of the earliest charter texts of Western culture. They argue that this Odyssean rationality, already bound to identity, inevitably represses singularity and difference. Reason offers humans extraordinary, unhoped-for success in dominating nature through scientific and intellectual advancements, but inevitably leads to the domination of some men by others, and of most women by most men.

For the Frankfurt School, then, Polyphemus the Cyclops, in his ideal pastoral existence, is the creation of an imagination already racked with sorrow at its alienation from the environment. Polyphemus, they recognize, becomes the model 'for the evolving line of stupid devils of the Christian era right up to Shylock and Mephistopheles'; they argue that the stupidity of the giant comes to represent 'something better as soon as it is subverted by the one who ought to know better'.[27] They are the first to recognize that Odysseus *abuses* his intellectual powers on the Cyclops' island – that he is trespassing with all the arrogance of a colonial master, and creates a situation which can only result in bloodshed. The Dialectic of Enlightenment means that Odysseus cannot assert his superiority without dialectically beginning to behave as badly as his supposed inferior. This is always the conundrum of empire – that its justification (the ascent from primitive barbarism) is inevitably cancelled by the physical or

cultural violence required to impose it. Even more importantly, the critical theorists see that the minute Odysseus behaves this badly, the *stupidity*
of the Cyclops begins to look more like benign naivety.[28]

Closely allied with the Frankfurt School's reading is the last reason
for the recent vigour of the Cyclops as cultural presence: the proposition
that his eye is no more nor less than a marker of radical *difference*. For
this group of interpreters, the Cyclops represents the way that ancient
Greek colonizers *imagined* the different types of human that they encountered on their marauding voyages. Their own different appearance, diet
and mode of production, and the fear they feel become projected on to
the figure of the primitive ogre and crystallized in him. What is now
needed, it is being argued, is not identification with the Greek adventurer
as he invades the home of the Cyclops, devours his food, intoxicates and
blinds him – a triumphalist celebration of the Greek's right to subdue
and dominate – but a reading that tries to imagine what it *felt like to be
the Cyclops*, that turns him into the *subject* of the narrative rather than its
*object*. This line of argument owes much to the readings of Polyphemus'
close relation Caliban in Shakespeare's *The Tempest*, the colonial agenda
of which was pointed out with the greatest eloquence by Aimé Césaire in
his 1969 French version of the play *Une Tempête*.[29] In David Dabydeen's
*Coolie Odyssey*, which explores the difficult relationship between a black
man and a white woman, configured as Caliban and Miranda, there is
also the mysterious presence in the modern woman's world of a man with
'a prehistoric eye' who delivers to her 'strange usurping tales of anthro-
pophagi/And recitation of colonial texts'.[30]

The position has been taken furthest by Sylvia Wynter, Professor
Emerita at Stanford University, who proposes that black readers should
practise what she calls 'a Cyclopean poetics of reading'. She argues that the
Cyclops defines radical difference within the repertoire of images encoded
in Western culture, on the level of 'marvellous reality'.[31] For Wynter, the
Cyclops episode in the *Odyssey*, on the level of the imagination – of magical realism – is profoundly important in the history of racism. Wynter
is offering a counter-mythology to other lineages proposed by black and
post-colonial writers. These include Orlando Patterson in *The Children of
Sisyphus* (1964), in which being condemned to roll stones uphill symbolizes the experience of extreme poverty in Jamaica; Wole Soyinka, who in
the context of praising Nelson Mandela has pitted the African 'Herculean'
burden-carrying archetype against the Odyssean Dr Livingstone archetype;[32] and the numerous writers who have followed Ellison in defining
black experiences through Odyssean quest-narratives. Wynter denies that

it is possible to square the contradiction between Odysseus' relationship with white colonization and the black poets' desire to identify their own quest for freedom with Odysseus' pursuit of his goals. For Wynter, if you side with Odysseus in *Odyssey* Book 9, you *inevitably* end up conspiring in the binary oppositions that have figured people of African descent as Other. Wynter therefore makes explicit what has been implicit in some black writing previously, that the time has come to embark on 'the as yet still unexplored nature of *what must be* the quest of the Cyclops', a new poetics which has as the goal of 'its Cyclopean quest ... the assumption and revalorization of the being and perspective of *alterity*'.[33]

Historians of popular culture have suggested that the mutant *X-Men*, invented by Marvel Comics in 1963, written by Stan Lee and illustrated by Jack Kirby, were a covert or unconscious fantasy exploration of the civil rights crisis, since their physical alterity leads them to face state-sponsored bigotry, prejudice and lynchings.[34] Their leader, Scott Summers, is known as 'Cyclops' on account of the visor that protects his powerful eyes. Cyclops' parents are enslaved; the mutants' patron, Professor X, has been likened both to Martin Luther King and Malcolm X.[35] In *Sea Grapes* (1976), Walcott suggested that the Cyclops was actually involved in *creating* the epic *Odyssey*. The feature of the Cyclops which is here given primacy is the blindness he shares with Homer, the author of the epic: 'the blind giant's boulder heaved the trough/from whose groundswell the great hexameters come/to the conclusion of exhausted surf.'[36] It is with the image of the Cyclops' boulder that Walcott reminds us that *nothing* – not even the glories of ancient Greek poetry – can ever compensate adequately for the pain of cultural loss and dispossession. In Walcott's *Omeros*, too, Odysseus is fleetingly linked with the clever European persecutor of the black children of the Caribbean, themselves associated with the Cyclops' flock, in stories 'we recited as children lifted with the rock/of Polyphemus'.[37]

Instances of the Cyclops becoming a point of identification by oppressed ethnic groups, or anti-colonial polemicists, can now be multiplied; he has recently been used to make the case for the Hawaiian movement for independence.[38] But the roots of the new Cyclops extend back to a passage in Aimé Césaire's prose poem *Return to My Native Land* (1939). This Martiniquan intellectual trained as a teacher of Latin and Greek at the prestigious École Normale Supérieure.[39] The poem relates his quest for identity in Paris and back home, and Gregson Davis has shown how subtly Césaire exploits the association of his black author-narrator with Odysseus.[40] In one episode, having become an Odyssean victor-figure in Paris, he encounters on a tram another enormously tall black man, malodorous and with 'gigantic legs', whose eye socket has been hollowed by poverty. The narrator betrays his race by smiling at him in cowardly complicity with two white women.[41] Wynter names this stunning section *Encounter with the Cyclops on a Paris Tram*, and her identification rings especially true if we read the final speech Césaire gives to Caliban in his anti-colonial adaptation of *The Tempest*. It could equally well have issued straight from Polyphemus' mouth, if instead of 'Prospero' we insert the vocative 'Odysseus':

> [Odysseus] you are the master of illusion.
> Lying is your trademark.
> And you have lied so much to me
> (lied about the world, lied about me)
> that you have ended by imposing on me
> an image of myself.
> Underdeveloped, you brand me, inferior,
> that's the way you have forced me to see myself.
> I detest that image! What's more it's a lie.[42]

Stupid monster, Big Brother or victim of racism – the experience of our Cyclops over the last hundred years have been varied indeed. If after travelling with the Cyclops through time we now go back to Homer's text, we will also learn to be wary of translators, convinced that they understand the moral outlines of the story and have often imposed meanings of their own: one influential version introduces the term 'race' where Homer simply says 'the Cyclopes'.[43] The phrase that introduces Polyphemus is usually translated something like '*a giant* who used to pasture his flocks far afield, alone' (9.187–8), but the Greek actually says 'a huge *man*' (*anēr pelōrios*).[44] The Greek marauders enter uninvited, light a fire and eat food. The Cyclops does not notice their presence until he has returned home and sealed his cave in order to keep his flocks inside. When he realizes what is going on he does eat Odysseus' men, but (anthropophagy apart) is this form of self-defence really so shocking? Odysseus, after all, later kills the suitors who exactly mirror his own actions in the land of the Cyclopes, since the suitors are also intruders who sit uninvited at another man's hearth and consume his livelihood. Moreover, the Texas Penal Code article 9.42, 'Deadly Force to Protect Property', argues that it is justifiable to kill a trespasser on your property when 'the actor reasonably believes that deadly force is immediately necessary to prevent the other's imminent commission of arson, burglary, robbery, aggravated robbery, theft during the night-time or criminal mischief during the night-time'. classical scholars have now had to accept that, at least in a Texan court, the Homeric Cyclops would today have a watertight defence![45]

Polyphemus and his struggle with Odysseus have had such wholly conflicting reverberations in recent times that they can be read as a symbolic paradigm of the struggle over the classical canon. Their showdown metaphorically represents both the conflicting views about the contents of the canon suitable for a post-colonial age, and the ways in which those contents should be read. How can enjoying the 'Western Classics' be compatible with opposition to Western imperialism and cultural or racial oppression? One way of responding to this question comes from a neglected study by the classicist Norman Austin, published more than 20 years ago. Austin pondered on the difference in tone between the Cyclops episode and the rest of the epic, noticing correctly how childlike the two leading characters are (which partly explains their enduring fascination for children).[46] Odysseus wants lots of presents like a child in the Christmas holidays; Polyphemus is a playground bully asserting the rights of the king of the castle over the dirty rascal; they bicker and squabble and brag. Unlike most of Odysseus' adventures, this one offers no grown-up erotic interest, nor even palace coup: two men-boys slug it out, to the point of death and mutilation, over a few dairy products. Austin proposes, in a reading that owes much to Melanie Klein, that what the Cyclops' cavernous dairy represents is the womb and the breast, and that what we are facing here is the most regressive and infantile sibling rivalry. Not only does Austin's psychoanalytical discussion apprehend the *tone* of the story better than anything I have read, but in the post-colonial global village the notion of squabbles between brothers under the skin can perhaps help the survival of *all* cultures, indigenous, Western, pre-Christian pagan, and non-Western alike. The myth represented in the *Odyssey* belongs to everyone and no one. Narrow-mindedness, childishness and sibling rivalry know no ethnic boundaries.

The defiant anger of Polyphemus as he hurled great rocks at the escaping ship featured in Joseph Turner's awe-inspiring Romantic oil painting *Ulysses Deriding Polyphemus: Homer's Odyssey* (1829), in the National Gallery; here Polyphemus looms over Odysseus' galleon like a configuration of dark, angry clouds, an elemental force of nature. John Ruskin commented that 'Polyphemus asserts his perfect power'.[47] Jean-Léon Gérôme subsequently took a rather less mystical approach to the same episode, but his painting is interesting because the viewer is invited to see the casting of the boulder very nearly from Polyphemus' viewpoint.[48] This seems to be the perspective taken in a very ancient Armenian story about a giant, and looking at other myth systems provides a second possible

answer to the problem presented to the global village by the values traditionally attached to the Western canon.

The Armenian hero Turk Angeleay, who has forebears as early as
Mesopotamian myth, bears striking similarities to Polyphemus, including great size and some special quality to his eyesight. Yet for the Arme-
nians, Turk was always a celebrated figure precisely because he fought off
wicked pirates, brigands and looters who sailed too close to his country's
coastline, by tossing huge boulders at them. An eminent scholar of Armenian myth has recently written of Turk:

> When we stand with him on the Pontic shore as he hurls boulders at a
> pirate ship, it may come as a shock that some Odysseus is aboard: this
> is the Anatolian mirror-image of Greek heroism, from an Anatolian
> source.[49]

The *Odyssey* represents just a single cultural expression of a far more
ancient set of stories shared by cultures wherever *homo sapiens* has ever
travelled. In the version of the Central Asian oral epic *Alpamysh*, sung by
the nomadic Karakalpaks, the 'exile and return of the husband' theme is
so similar to the *Odyssey* as to have convinced Russian scholars that there
was a common Eastern tale that preceded Homer by many centuries.[50]
The type of the Cyclops figure is manifested in a wide range of myths
recorded the world over.[51] One etymological explanation of Polyphemus'
name is that it means 'speaking many languages' or 'spoken of in many
languages': large mythical shepherds have always transcended cultures
quite as much as clever mythical travellers. The monocularity of the pastoral giant, living cheek-by-jowl with his flocks and herds, was probably a
response not to anything remotely to do with ethnic difference but with a
universally occurring genetic abnormality that all primitive humans will
have observed occasionally amongst the premature foetuses aborted by
their sheep and cows.[52]

Yet the third and most important response to the challenge of disentan-
gling the Western classics from the terrible legacy of empire, must come
from the new strategies being developed in the work of contemporary
'transcultural' writers. In Paul Coelho's recent novel *The Zahir* (English
translation from Portuguese, 2005), a renowned author-narrator goes in
search of his missing wife, on a quest explicitly paralleling that of Odysseus, which takes him to Central Asia. The story uses a global language
by combining Islamic mysticism with Greek myth and a contemporary
setting. The Cyclops story certainly appeals to Wilson Harris, born in
Guyana (then called British Guiana) in 1921. His parents combined Amer-
indian, African and European blood, and he objects to being ethnically

categorized. He also refuses to be forced into a choice between rejecting or embracing any literary traditions simply because of the contingent
values that they have historically embodied. In his visionary novel *The
Mask of the Beggar* (2003) Harris fuses the *Odyssey* with the pre-Colum-
bian Aztec figure of Quetzalcoatl to ask whether humans can spiritually
transcend their tragic history of mutual barbarism through stressing the
threads that connect their imaginative lives. For Harris, the labile figure
of the Cyclops sometimes represents the innocence of the peoples massa-
cred by the conquistadors, but at others the blindness of societies still
today imprisoned by obsolete hostilities.[53]

The Maori poet Robert Sullivan draws his ancestry both from the very
Nga Puhi people of New Zealand's North Island of whom Darwin was so
terrified, and also from Galway in western Ireland. Sullivan has recently
used the myth of Orpheus to explore the legacy of Western imperialism
in the south Pacific in his libretto *Captain Cook in the Underworld* (2002),
where the opening chorus absolves Cook for the temerity of his claim to
have 'discovered' a land that could not be discovered because it was inhabited already:

> Forgive the Ulysses
> of his day, for the mores of his age,
> for overlooking the inhabitants with his claim.[54]

But Sullivan has also imbued with intense Odyssean resonances a collection of poems about Maori seafaring, *Star Waka* (1999, a 'waka' is a canoe).
These offer the reader a jumble of voices that explore the contradictions
within the indigenous New Zealanders' relationship with the Western
canon. One voice is able to acknowledge the bravery of the poor European settlers who sailed to New Zealand 'over the edge of the world/
into Hades/the infernal Greek and Latin-ness of many headed creatures'.
Another angrily derides Odysseus for depriving him of his rightful place
in the poem and subjecting the Maoris to the curious stare of anthropologists. Yet to be heard within this complicated polyphony is another, more
reflective voice offering a message about culture and its now inevitable
globalization that seems both resigned and somehow more hopeful:

> Do not mind the settler. I observe
> The rules of this mythology (see how he did not
> place a star or ocean or a waka
> in his pageantry). I am Odysseus,
> summoned to these pages by extraordinary
> claims of the narrator. I run through all narratives.[55]

# 8

# RITES OF MAN

In the panoply of Greek mythical heroes, most of Odysseus' qualities are shared by another individual: Hector is as brave, Daedalus is as inventive, Heracles as good an archer, Jason as experienced a voyager and Achilles nearly as good an orator. But a few of Odysseus' characteristics are more idiosyncratic and integral to his particular model of the hero – one that has traditionally been seen as a 'new' type of heroism with an intellectual element that represents an advance on the physically indomitable but simpler warriors of the *Iliad*.[1]

A study of the connections between heroes from Greece to Spiderman has argued that Odysseus' distinctiveness does indeed lie in the inspired application of his intellect, the cunning intelligence (*mētis*) celebrated in his epithet *polumētis*, but that it is of a special kind associated with interiors, undercover operations and darkness. Odysseus' closest parallel amongst imaginary modern superheroes is Bruce Wayne/Batman, with whom he shares both his mortal parentage (unlike the divine or extra-terrestrial parents that Heracles, Achilles and Superman can claim), and his craftiness, practised in the dark. Odysseus operates covertly in Polyphemus' cave, in the wooden horse or, in *Iliad* 11, on nocturnal raids, whereas Achilles and Heracles, like Superman, perform feats of physical prowess under open skies in daylight.[2]

There are two other characteristics that define Odysseus. One is the self-control that he learns en route: indeed, by the time of Plato, an uneasy parallel had developed between Socrates and Odysseus, based on their shared capacity for stringent self-control. In Xenophon's *Memorabilia* only self-restraint is said to have saved Odysseus from the gluttony that would have turned him into one of Circe's pigs (2.6.10–12; 1.3.7). In Plato's *Republic* (4.440e–441c) Socrates uses Odysseus to illustrate his proposition that reason and passion must comprise separate parts of the psyche. He points to the episode in the *Odyssey* where its hero, angry to discover that some of his slave women have slept with the suitors, controls his emotions in order to apply the patience that will enable him later to attain the outcome he wants (20.17).[3]

The other Odyssean characteristic is implied by his epithet *polútropos*, one meaning of which is that he is 'able to turn his hand to many things', or 'versatile' (see pp 19–20). This is allied to another of his epithets, *polumētis*, 'capable of many kinds of cunning'. Odysseus has a plethora of skills; he is an all-rounder, an archetypal 'Renaissance man', who would in the twenty-first century be as at home in a DIY store as at a university seminar or on a football pitch. He is a gifted carpenter, who builds a seagoing vessel in four days, from tree-felling to sail-making (5.228–62); he also once fitted a whole bedroom for himself and Penelope (23.184–204). An expert navigator, he can steer his route by the stars (5.269–75). He is a confident peasant farmer, even as a child given by his father his own orchard and vineyard, and who could beat Eurymachus in a ploughing race any time (24.340–2, 18.366–75). But these manual skills sit alongside his aristocratic training in athletics:[4] he is champion wrestler (4.341–5), discus-thrower (8.186–98), spear-thrower (8.215–33) and boxer (18.88–107) as well as the earliest 'epic' swimmer in Western literature (see p 13). There is scarcely a manly pursuit for which he does not offer himself as an idealized forerunner.

The arenas in which manhood is tested are today as likely to be Wall Street or the corporate board room as the battlefield. En route to Ithaca, Odysseus does indeed acquire several gifts, or capital assets, which he carefully hides in the cave of the nymphs before taking on the suitors. But by losing his ships and allowing his livestock to be consumed for years without replenishment, he perhaps does not make the ideal model for modern businessmen. This has not prevented two North American professors of management from analysing what Odysseus can tell the business community in *The Classic Touch: Lessons in Leadership from Homer to Hemingway*.[5] He is, we are told, the archetypal example of MBO, or Management By Objectives, as a certain school of strategic management techniques is labelled. He avoided distractions to the achievement of his goals. In the tale of Scylla and Charybdis he 'faced a classic management decision', the choice between two 'no-win' situations, in which his only rational course of action was to cut his losses. Odysseus' strength was that he 'knew how to augment his rapidly dwindling resources by forging informal linkages ... across organizational lines', especially in the cases of Aeolus and Circe, who both controlled intellectual property and equipment that he needed. As their modern parallel to Odysseus, the professors propose C. Michael Armstrong, whose stellar performance as chief executive officer at the American telecoms corporation AT&T between 1997 and 2002 was the result of his ruthless objective-led management style. 'Whether the goal is returning home after ten years, achieving a sales objective, increasing earnings per share, or bringing about a productivity improvement, it is the "Odyssean" focus that gets results.'[6]

Star businessmen are usually ruthless with employees, and so perhaps Odysseus is an illuminating model for moguls because where he performs *worst* is in the personnel department. The curious proem to the *Odyssey* gives disproportionate attention to a single incident – the loss of his men when they ate the cattle of the Sun: Odysseus, we hear, suffered at sea in his attempts to bring his comrades home, and failed only because of their own folly. Yet Odysseus had been warned by Tiresias to avoid that island; however exhausted they were, it was irresponsible of him to give in to his crewmen's demands. The stress laid on his men's sacrilege is therefore designed to pre-empt any charges of negligence towards them (see 24.426–8).

But Odysseus lands his men in danger elsewhere. It is his idea to sack the city of the Cicones (where six of them die), and he who boasts to the Cyclops. No fewer than 11 of his ships are destroyed by the Laestrygonians, and the hungover Elpenor breaks his neck falling from Circe's roof; Scylla eats another six men. Although the *Odyssey* takes its hero's part virtually throughout, dissident voices occasionally ensure that the audience is left slightly uneasy about Odysseus' managerial competence. On Circe's island, Odysseus had sent out a reconnaissance cadre of 22 men under the leadership of his kinsman Eurylochus, who returns to report that all the others in the advance party have been turned into swine. Eurylochus, reasonably enough, discourages the remaining crewmen from taking such a risk themselves. His rebuke to Odysseus sounds mutinous (10.431–7):

> Poor us! Where are we off to now? Why do you want to risk going to Circe's household, where she will turn us all into pigs or wolves or lions, and where we will be forcibly compelled to guard her great palace? That's like the Cyclops – when our comrades were in his yard in the company of rash Odysseus. It was his irresponsibility that destroyed them, as well.

Odysseus' poor performance as leader makes it all the more paradoxical – or cynics might say appropriate – that his archetype has influenced our daily perceptions of our heroes and leaders, both fictional and actual.

Popular culture, disseminated through recreational activities, creates meanings that communicate 'aspects of social and political myth'.[7] One of its key procedures is displacing archetypal myths to new settings. This reaffirms old certainties and values in contexts that otherwise seem

alarmingly uncertain. Thus *Star Trek* was successful because it took one
of the oldest myths – the voyage of discovery with the invariable survival
of the leading traveller – and displaced it into worlds and futures that in
reality offer only unknown dangers. Odysseus' indestructibility is transformed through its contribution to the myths of both the Western hero
and the intergalactic traveller.[8]

What sociologists have called the 'American monomyth', embedded
in the consciousness of every US citizen, is the story of the 'committed
and incorruptible hero who single-handedly saves the community from
evil'.[9] This hero-type derives from what the myth-scholar Joseph Campbell seminally defined as the 'universal hero archetype' or 'the classical
monomyth' in *The Hero with the Thousand Faces*:

> A hero ventures forth from the world of common day into a region of
> supernatural wonder: fabulous forces are there encountered and a decisive
> victory is won: the hero comes back from this mysterious adventure with
> the power to bestow boons on his fellow man.[10]

Odysseus, like Aeneas, is one of the thousand such heroes, moulded
upon primeval rites of initiation, in which the youth departs from his
community, undergoes trials and returns to be re-integrated as an adult.
This conception of the hero, based on ancient religious practices, has
also become identified with the universal model of the human psyche as
defined by the psychologist Carl Jung (see Chapter 12).

Yet some analysts see the hero less as a universal, psychological
constant than a phenomenon that adapts culturally, as history changes,
while nevertheless staying *relatively* stable for generations because the
hero's symbolic function is central to the society that constantly reinforces
it. Robin Hood, who steals from the rich to give to the poor, has remained
a constant favourite in societies with unfair distribution of wealth, but
might mean less to a society where poverty had been eradicated for centuries. The historically contextualizing approach to heroes is exemplified
by Slotkin's study of the functions performed by frontier myths during
the industrial revolution.[11] Another study proposes that there is just one
difference between the figure defined in Campbell's 'classical monomyth'
and the American monomyth: the modern plot is informed by the idea of
redemption rather than initiation.

The pagan model of heroism, according to this view, was indelibly modified by the Judaeo-Christian redemption plot, producing a socially consci-
entious and self-sacrificial hero who renounces his past wrongdoings and
undergoes some Damascene conversion, or who leads a moral campaign
on the side of right.[12] This altruistic, socially responsible figure can be

seen as early as the frontiersmen Daniel Boone (explorer and Kentucky settler), Davy Crockett and Wyatt Earp.[13] Their legends were created by a society which was Christian but whose imagination was shaped by the pagan classics.[14] Moreover, there is a constant dialogue between the communal perceptions of such folk heroes and those of *historical* leaders, from George Washington to Martin Luther King and Bill Clinton. But one constant is that, like Odysseus, the modern culture hero must have a goal, set out on a long journey to reach it, and at some point descend into darkness, from which he emerges better equipped to restore order in his community.[15] In American politics, the Odysseus-heroes are sometimes from humble backgrounds (Jimmy Carter the peanut farmer), and sometimes from quasi-royal dynasties (the Kennedys); Odysseus, the farmer, king and beggar rolled into one, can supply mythic resonance for any of them.

A study of the North American frontier hero in fiction and cinema has identified four traits that resurface in his portrayal: 'genteel qualities' such as self-control, 'clever traits' such strategic thinking, 'prowess' shown by prevailing over numerous foes, and 'epic significance', which denotes the glorification of individual exploits.[16] But at the heart of the sense of national identity in the USA has always been the notion of *conflict*.

> As a frontier nation, the idea of struggle was inbred into the American monomyth; the hero's struggle was one of vertical mobility, raising himself from humble beginnings until he had forced society to recognize him as a successful individual.[17]

The notion of the struggle that precedes victory is certainly what explains Odysseus' attraction to the creators of national traditions. Previous chapters have already noticed how the Renaissance Portuguese and imperial Japanese identified the ordeals undergone by their own nations with Odysseus' fight to regain control of his household, and there have been other examples. In nineteenth-century Russia, Gogol believed that the *Odyssey* offered the ideal model for the creation of a new Russian identity, which fused Western, progressive elements and the spiritual power that he identified with his Ukrainian – indeed Cossack – ancestors. Gogol wanted to become the 'Thucydides of Little Russia', but the epic grandeur of his novel *Taras Bulba* (1839), narrating the defence of the Cossack realm by Bulba and his sons, suggests, rather, the title 'Homer of Little Russia'. Throughout the nine years he was writing *Taras Bulba* he was close to the Romantic poet Vasily Zhukovsky, who was preparing his epoch-making translation of the *Odyssey* into a Russian dactylic hexameter. Zhukovsky, as a friend of Goethe (a passionate admirer of Homer), had talked to

Gogol about the Homeric poems for years.

Zhukovsky's translation made a huge impact on Russian culture when it was published in 1849. The role allocated to the *Odyssey* by Zhukovsky and Gogol was to provide the basis on which a national aesthetic could be built. 'The publication of *The Odyssey* will mark the beginning of a new era. *The Odyssey* is without doubt the most perfect work of all the centuries,' wrote Gogol.[18] The translation, 'a kind of miracle', is 'not a translation, but rather a re-creation, a restoration, a resurrection of Homer'.[19] Forget the poem's pagan polytheism, says Gogol – Zhukovsky has shown how Russian Orthodox Christians can understand God through watching Odysseus' nobility in the face of his afflictions. The *Odyssey* triumphantly affirms true-hearted adherence to ancient customs that every Russian can emulate.[20]

Gogol even naively believed that the *Odyssey* could save Russia from class antagonism and revolutionary discontent:

> *The Odyssey* strikes with the majesty of the patriarchal, ancient mode of life, with the simplicity of uncomplicated social lives … In *The Odyssey*, our nineteenth century will hear a strong reproach.[21]

A sense that Odysseus could help create national consciousness later became evident in Poland. In the introduction to his translation of the epic (1924), which he began during the First World War, Józef Wittlin proposed that Homer could help writers fuse the best of the old 'humanist' European epic tradition with the values of 'Young Poland', the Modernist literature that sought to forge a Polish cultural identity. At the same time as American, Irish and English Modernists were responding so strongly to the *Odyssey*, Wittlin's translation committed the 'Young Poland' writers to recovering an ancient, European and Mediterranean tradition of epic literature.

Odysseus can partly be adopted as a national or ethnic leader because he is not a completely lone hero, even after losing his men. He does *not* triumph over the suitors single-handedly. He is assisted by two loyal slaves and by Telemachus, who had himself very nearly strung the bow, which would have put him in the awkward position of having won his own mother's hand in marriage. It was a warning from Odysseus that had forced this Oedipal upstart to 'stop short in his eagerness' (21.128–30). Indeed, the relationship that is arguably most important in this poem does not involve Penelope: it is this intense father–son bond. It is also implausible, because in reality the return of any soldier after a period of years is a psychologically explosive event. The problem is often expressed in the disastrous failure to relate to his children – above all first-born sons

– born shortly before or during his absence. Real-world studies of these relationships have revealed precisely the tensions that the *Odyssey* touches upon, especially the child's extreme attachment to the mother.[22] The anxieties that afflict the father are often connected with his ability to impose discipline, his physical alienation from the intimacy of family life (often exacerbated by his sexual experiments abroad) and fears about his wife's fidelity. But the overriding concern relates to whether or not his children will like him, and whether the father can himself 'feel' anything at all in response.[23]

Far more plausible is the sense of competition between Odysseus and Telemachus for the status of the poem's most important hero. Telemachus has his own wanderings, and is suspended on the verge of a sexual initiation after the gorgeous Helen provides him with a robe that he can bestow on a future bride (see pp 189–90). Indeed, he fits the pattern of 'initiation hero' better than his father, as ancient admirers of Homer were aware. Some stories they told contained obvious initiatory motifs, such as the tradition reported in Plutarch's treatise *On the Rationality of Animals* that Telemachus fell into the sea (ordeal and symbolic death in an alien environment) and was saved by a dolphin (miraculous rebirth and contact with a wild creature); as requital, his father had dolphins engraved on his ring and emblazoned on his shield (equipping him for combat and marking him as such). Telemachus' suitability for the role of initiation hero also explains why he could become the *Bildungsroman* star, especially after Fénelon's *Télémaque*, as well as inspiring many children's books,[24] and poems in the persona of a young man reflecting on his relationship with his father.[25] For in the course of his father's poem Telemachus does significantly alter, from tearful adolescent to confident public speaker and warrior (see Fig. 8). Moreover, he has an essential accoutrement of the *Bildungsroman* hero: a wise mentor – indeed, the original Mentor, Athena in disguise.

The ancient commentators saw that the three generations of the Ithacan royal family (Telemachus, Odysseus, Laertes) in the *Odyssey* had a message for a man in every stage of his life: 'Homer is first, middle, and last for every boy, for every man in his vigorous prime, and for every man in old age,' wrote Dio Chrysostom (*Oration* 18.8). Heraclitus, an interpreter of Homer also working in the early Roman Empire, warmed to this theme:

> Our earliest infancy was entrusted to the care of Homer, as if he had been a nurse, and while still in our swaddling clothes we were fed on his verses, as if they had been our mother's milk. As we grew to youth we spent it

with him, together we shared our vigorous manhood, and even in old age we continued to find our joy in him … There is but one terminus for men and Homer, and that is the terminus of life itself' (*Homeric Problems* 1.5–7).

Underlying these statements is Homer's place in ancient education, a matter which fathers arranged for their sons. Plutarch's fascinating treatise *On How a Young Man Should Study Poetry* sets forth the principles of a literary education suitable for his sons. He invokes Odysseus himself as the ideal paternalistic guide and censor (15d). When texts show immoral actions, we should not refuse to let our young men study them, should not 'stuff their ears with wax, but we should set them against an upright standard of reason and there bind them fast'. Odysseus understood that he could listen to the Sirens' dangerous song, but needed to have an inbuilt mechanism that prevented him from following their injunctions. In the mast of Odysseus, Plutarch finds a symbol of the moral guidance that the teacher can offer his pupils.

Telemachus played an important role in ancient paedagogy, which explains the relative abundance of papyri of the Telemacheia books written out in schoolboys' handwriting.[26] The audience of the *Odyssey* knows that Telemachus has really grown up at the archery contest, when he addresses these peremptory words to his mother, excluding her from the event that will determine her future, and she obeys him (21.350–3):

> Return now to your quarters and attend to your own sphere of influence – distaff and loom – and tell your women to attend to their work. The bow shall be the responsibility of men, and my responsibility most of all. In this house I am the one in charge.

Telemachus takes over the reins of power for just long enough to allow his disguised father to string the bow and begin the slaughter of the suitors. The true business of the epic – men wreaking revenge on rival males – requires that he dismiss Penelope: indeed, the poem hints at potential for conflict between them. Telemachus says that he can't be sure who his father is, whatever his mother tells him (1.215–16) – a standard complaint of men in the days before genetic testing. But his greater concern is that Penelope may be persuaded to remarry by the men in her natal family (her father and brothers), removing some of his patrimony from Ithaca when she moves on (15.14–19).

Masculinity, and the male initiation rites that signify its maturation, are in every culture defined by being Not Feminine. Much of the *Odyssey*'s energy is produced from tension between females and the masculine hero. It defines the ancient Greek social system anthropologically by sending Odysseus into encounters with feminine power of several kinds.[27] It explores the male mindset that underpinned patriarchy by presenting varieties of the feminine – nubile (Nausicaa), sexually predatory and matriarchal (Calypso, Circe), politically powerful (Arete), domineering (the Laestrygonian king's huge daughter and mountainous wife), monstrous and all-devouring (Scylla, Charybdis), seductive and lethal (the Sirens), loyal, domesticated and maternal (Penelope).

One woman who could have been more significant is the hero's mother Anticleia. Initiatory heroes usually have important relationships with their mothers: in the *Epic of Gilgamesh* the hero is helped by his goddess mother Ninsun; in the *Iliad* Achilles has a powerful ally in his divine mother Thetis, and in the *Aeneid* Aeneas' mother Venus watches over him and his son Ascanius constantly.[28] But Odysseus' self-sufficiency is stressed because his mother was human, is now dead, and seems always to have been ineffectual. Nothing better distinguishes Odysseus from similar heroes.

Different eras have emphasized different aspects of Odyssseus. For the Renaissance poet Samuel Daniel, he epitomized the man of action seeking fame upon the high seas, and scorning sensual pleasures: when the Siren invites him to 'joy the day in mirth the while' with her, he sternly replies that 'manliness would scorn to wear/The time in idle sport'; the honourable man goes around the world in case called on to fight, so often has he seen 'a wicked peace/To be well chang'd for war'.[29] Pope's translations created a restrained, Augustan ideal of male heroism by reducing the tears and emotions displayed by Homer's men.[30] The *Odyssey* became central to the Victorian male's attempt to understand his ethics, religion, treatment of women, sexuality, manners and public self-presentation. The public schools' ideal of competitive athletics, and the celebration of versatility and cunning intelligence required by the imperial service, found ideological grounding in the Odyssean hero.[31] As early as 1830 Henry Nelson Coleridge argued that Odysseus was a more impressive figure than Achilles (not at all the received view at that time), since he:

> shines by his own light, moves by his own strength, and demolishes all obstacles by his own arm and his own wit ... Ulysses has a passion, a vehement desire ... Ulysses is homesick ... This brings him at once in contact with the common feelings of every man in the world.[32]

The scene in which Odysseus lands back in Ithaca well explains his special attractiveness in the nineteenth century: the same he-man who can fight to the death to protect his property and assert sexual control over his women slaves is also an urbane gentleman. As Athena says, 'that is why

I cannot desert you in your misfortunes: you are so civilized, so intelligent, so self-possessed' (13.331–2). William Gladstone was impressed with Odysseus' gentlemanly handling of the insult from the Phaeacian prince who said that he resembled a merchant rather than an athlete. Gladstone commented that it demonstrated 'more than any composition … up to what point emotion, sarcasm and indignation can be carried without any loss of self-command'.[33]

This elite admiration for Odysseus translated into the more populist heroes of nineteenth- and early twentieth-century fiction as they were configured in the *Boy's Own Paper*;[34] these young heroes were athletic, resourceful, competitive, adventurous, successful with ladies, but fundamentally decent chaps. Reading the *Odyssey* at school or university will have offered a conceptual parallel. The novels for boys by W.H.G. Kingston (who was also editor of *The Colonist* and a self-help book on how to emigrate) revolved repeatedly around the same Cyclops-like plot in which a brave young man endured shipwreck and the threatened savagery of indigenous tribesmen.[35] Andrew Lang, a translator of Homer and writer of poems on the topic of Helen of Troy, was also leader writer for the *Daily News*. His reviews of fiction shaped the form taken by popular novels, and his criteria were informed by the heroes of ancient epic. He liked men to be athletic, noble, uncomplicated and unimpeded by domestic life; he encouraged novelists who wrote for boys, like Stanley Weyman, whose heroes were always going 'on the road'.[36]

That Victorian schoolboys experienced a reflection of classical heroics in the heroes of imperial fiction is demonstrated by Rider Haggard's protagonists, not only in *She* (see Chapter 14), but also Sir Henry Curtis in *King Solomon's Mines* (1885) – a golden-haired, bearded hero, the best fighting man in the book, who also happens to have 'taken a high degree in the Classics'.[37] Not dissimilar is the Odyssean hero of *Benita* (1906) – broad-shouldered and 'sealed with the indescribable stamp of the English gentleman', whose feats include a dangerous voyage down the coast of Africa and an epic swim. Finally, the Homeric parallels are explicit in *The Four Feathers* by A.E.W. Mason (1902); the Odyssean hero, Harry Feversham, leaves behind his loyal fiancée to face perils on a lonely journey through the Sudan to help his friends. These include Colonel Jack Durrance, who is less clever but a brave soldier: 'Hector of Troy was his ancestor; he was neither hysterical in his language nor vindictive in his acts … stern when occasion needed and of an unflinching severity'.[38]

In antiquity, the masculinity of most heroes was at some time challenged or compromised. Even Achilles, in some versions of his story, was brought up dressed as a girl, and Heracles was enslaved to a domineering Asiatic queen called Omphale. Moreover, many ancient Greek heroes have sexual interests in men as well as women, but Odysseus is not among them. Thus although many twentieth- and twenty-first-century Odysseuses have been psychotic, or unheroic, they are usually emphatically masculine and heterosexual. As we have seen in the earlier chapter on colonial conflict, and will shortly be seeing in the chapter on women's work, such a configuration of the male hero is these days inherently problematic. Heroism is now 'so irrevocably a gendered and "raced" a concept' as to be practically unusable in any of its old forms.[39] The intimate association of the idea of the hero with celebrations of physical valour and macho posturing, often in a colonial context, has been condemned by many recent cultural critics for devaluing such 'feminine' and 'community' values as cooperation and nurturing.

It was in reaction to the relatively uncomplicated Victorian models of manhood that the great early twentieth-century writers – Joyce, Pound, Eliot – found Odysseus so suitable an archetype of their new anti-heroic Modernist literary subject. But he was still a profoundly masculine one. Ralph Waldo Ellison's Invisible Man was a new type of Odysseus as a hero of the civil rights endeavour, but one whose road to self-knowledge, and political understanding, passes through relationships with undeveloped female characters – both helpers and exploiters – whose subjectivities are ignored.[40] It is illuminating at this juncture to see how, in another fascinating post-war North American example, the Odyssey was used in an exploration of the particular constructions of masculinity and heroism involved in the marketing of professional sport.

The moment in the Odyssey when Odysseus hurls a discus unbelievably far in order to silence the insults of a Phaeacian (8.158–93) is, in modern screen history, best replicated in Barry Levinson's baseball classic The Natural (1984), starring Robert Redford. With all odds against him, old, injured and reviled, Roy Hobbs smashes the ball that soars far enough to begin a series of four home runs and take his (fictional) team, the New York Knights, to a glorious victory. The movie also takes Hobbs back to his long estranged fiancée, and the son he had unwittingly sired 16 years before. The prominent Odyssean references consolidate the mythic power of what is regarded as the best baseball movie of all time (it was also a financial and critical success).

When the young Hobbs is first held fast in conversation by Harriet Bird, a sexually enthralling Calypso-like lunatic with an avian name and feathery headgear, she asks him whether he has ever read the epics of

Homer. For most of the film the self-controlled, tortured and mysterious Odyssean persona of the fast-forwarded Hobbs, now in his late 30s, keeps the viewer guessing as to what he had been doing throughout his absence. In addition to Harriet there is another murderous seductress, 'Memo' Paris, who threatens Hobbs's memory of who he really is by appealing, Circe-like, to his animal desires. But the white-robed, backlit figure of Iris, the patient farmer-fiancée named after one of the Homeric messengers of the gods, can inspire him into heroic deeds of sporting prowess. Their son, on her own admission, has arrived at an age where he needs a father figure. The corrupt gambler Gus Sands, Hobbs's arch-enemy, covers one of his own eyes, Cyclops-like, in order the better to scrutinize his adversary. The baseball bat which gives Hobbs his heroic status as hitter has a totemic power, since it was carved by him from a tree that was struck by lightning in his youth; like Odysseus he is both farmer and carpenter.

The screenplay for the film version of *The Natural* was written by Robert Towne, adapting Bernard Malamud's novel, to which the *Odyssey* is both more and less important. Malamud portrays pitchers and hitters in a far more violent and epic way than the film expresses: he frames the opening competition between Hobbs and The Whammer as combat between Homeric warriors. The two vocations of farming and fighting (in the form of baseball) come over more clearly as alternative heroic arenas in the film than the novel. Harriet Bird does ask him whether he has read Homer,[41] and the Sirenic associations of the black-feathered hat in which she shoots Roy make better sense in the written version. The crazed girl is both 'less and more than human', and her assault on Hobbs is cast in Homeric terms: she had left him 'cut down in the very flower of his youth, lying in a red pool of his own blood'.[42]

The novel also works with a series of fantasy images in Roy's consciousness, above all the swim in green waters, like Odysseus' rite-of-passage swim between Calypso's island and Phaeacia. In the novel Gus is more truly Cyclopean: he has one working and one glass eye.[43] Roy's physical breakdown is caused by over-eating massively at a festive buffet, when Memo, who knows that his appetite for food is his great weakness, plies him with plate after plate. As the Circe figure, she almost literally turns him into an animal until his stomach, which has never properly healed, explodes and he is rushed to hospital. Roy does sell out, agrees to connive in losing the crucial game, and ends the novel alone, disgraced, weeping 'many bitter tears'.[44] The degree of alteration to the conclusion in the movie is breathtaking, and actually makes it far more like the *Odyssey*: Iris's role is enormously upgraded, and she has a grown son by Odysseus:

they end up a happily reunited all-American nuclear family back home on their Midwestern farm.

The difference between the novel and the film versions of *The Natural* crystallizes the tension in current reactions to Odysseus as a hero. In the novel it is precisely the masculine values of sexual appetite, competitive sport and macho business culture that bring the story of Hobbs – who fails to make a lasting relationship with a woman – to a tragic conclusion; in the movie, it is Hobbs's identity as a decent Midwestern male, rooted in his soil and his frontier values, that saves him and his all-American family. This Odysseus, therefore, both is and is not a good husband and father. Such an ambivalence certainly underlies one of the most bizarre appearances of the *Odyssey* in recent culture, as a model for disaffected men seeking to rediscover their inner hero.

Robert Bly, an American poet, in 1990 intervened in post-feminist debates by writing a self-help bestseller for men. Bly had been giving talks on mythology, and found that the Brothers Grimm tale *Iron John* hit a nerve with men. His resulting book about this age-old story helped establish the men's movement, and his group encounters inspired its drum-beating, tree-hugging stereotype. In early seminars, Bly asked men to re-enact the scene from the *Odyssey* in which Odysseus raises his sword as he approaches 'the symbol of matriarchal energy', Circe (see p 189). Peace-loving clients were unable to lift the sword, so fixed were they on the idea of not hurting anyone. These were men who had come of age during the Vietnam War, and they wanted nothing to do with a manhood which, 'to feel its aliveness', required an enemy. Instead of the single-mindedness of the 1950s male, they had a receptivity to different viewpoints.[45]

The world may be a better place for these 'soft males' – they are lovely human beings, Bly admits – but he believes that they are also distinguished by their emasculation and passivity. Bly tried to teach these men that flashing a sword didn't necessarily mean you were a warmonger, but that you could show 'a joyful decisiveness'. *Iron John* is about taking men back, through myth, to the source of their masculinity, and finding a middle path between the greater awareness of the 'sensitive new age guy', and the power of the warrior. Bly believes that New Age thinking about harmony holds a dangerous attraction to naive men. Mythology, he claims, beckons them to enter fully into life, with all its blood and tears and joy; women, apparently, should welcome any male efforts to revive such an Odyssean, forceful, spirit of masculinity.[46] How they have actually reacted to Odysseus will be seen in the following chapter.

# 9

# WOMEN'S WORK

Arguably the most important symbol in the *Odyssey* is neither Odysseus' bow nor Phemius' lyre but Penelope's huge loom. The weaving Penelope has reappeared in countless paintings, sculptures and tapestries over the centuries. Walcott's sad Maud in *Omeros* creates a quilt embroidered with the birds that symbolize the voyage to and from Africa. Another dying woman, the protagonist in Marina Carr's play *Woman and Scarecrow* (2006), evokes Penelopean resonances by knitting incessantly as she laments her husband's errant ways. In the *Odyssey*, Penelope's making and unmaking of the same shroud for her father-in-law is also the primary image of the oral poet's endless re-creation of his song.

It is possible that ancient Greek women sang epic stories: the catalogue of famous women in the Underworld (11.336–41), enjoyed by the Phaeacian queen, may contain vestiges of the types of women's traditional song that have been recorded in Indian villages.[1] But it is certain that fabric production was central to women's lives. Domestic task-forces spent long days turning wool into fabrics for soft furnishings and clothes.[2] At the houses' thresholds they received from their menfolk the fleece culled from the flocks in the outdoor world, removed the grease and scoured it clean. They dried it, dyed, combed and teased it into roves, spun yarn from them with distaff and spindle, and then loaded the warp yarn, weighted, onto looms.[3] It was only at this point that weaving could begin.

Because both male and female labour is required to produce textiles, weaving became a symbol of male and female collaboration, and the *Odyssey* stresses that marriage is a cooperative enterprise. But because the male and female parts of the process were separated, weaving also symbolized the demarcation of the masculine from the feminine, the exterior and the interior spaces. Weaving is also, more abstractly, a symbol of technology, of taming the natural world until it becomes serviceable to humans. Although the analogy between weaving and making poetry can linguistically be traced back far earlier than the *Odyssey* into the Indo-European tradition,[4] the analogy with the intellectual skills associated with the Odyssean hero lends the association in this epic particular intensity.[5]

When Aristotle summarized the *Odyssey* in his *Poetics*, he neglected to mention any female at all:

> A man is away from home for many years; he is watched closely by Poseidon; further, things at home are such that his property is being wasted by suitors and his son is being plotted against. He arrives, storm-tossed; he causes certain recognitions. Attacking, he survives, and destroys his enemies. This is proper [to the poem's plot]; the rest is episodes (1455b.17–23).

But Penelope, at least, lurks mysteriously even beneath Aristotle's diction: whom are these wasteful 'suitors' wooing? Even with Aristotle's peerless intellect and the best patriarchal will in the world, it proved impossible to delete all traces of the enigmatic Penelope from the story.

This may explain why it has often been denigrated as 'feminine' and 'elegant'.[6] In the late nineteenth century, personifications of the *Odyssey* tended to be decidedly ladylike.[7] Richard Bentley argued that while Homer had composed the songs constituting the *Iliad* to perform at festivals in front of men, those in the *Odyssey* were designed for women.[8] William Golding agreed, saying 'anyone who prefers the *Odyssey* to the *Iliad* has a woman's heart'.[9] Very recently it has been argued that 'Homer' was in fact female, on the unscientific grounds that both epics seem 'sympathetic' to women and sometimes to question violence.[10] But a better case was made over a century ago by Samuel Butler, who, in *The Authoress of the Odyssey* (1897), suggested that while the manly ethos of the *Iliad* was unquestionable, the poet of the *Odyssey* was female.

The most reputable scholars are still divided on the question of whether Butler believed his own arguments,[11] or was writing a parody of the earnest, archaeologically informed Homeric hypothesis that had been such a feature of nineteenth-century scholarship, in Britain especially after William Gladstone's *Homer and the Homeric Age* (1858). I am inclined to believe Butler's biographer when she argues that in *The Authoress of the Odyssey* he was irreverently debunking both Victorian scholarship and the patriarchal values it embodied. No one

> could go as unerringly to the heart of Victorian prejudices as he. The very title of his book … was calculated to offend the entire establishment nurtured on Gladstone's notion that a classical education, a grounding in the political and military tactics of Homer's *Iliad* and the navigational prowess of the *Odyssey*, was the best preparation for young men whose task was to rule the empire.[12]

The idiom of Butler's work also catches the tone of the historicist studies of Homer then in vogue; to document his treatise, he travelled with his camera not only to Greece and Schliemann's excavations at Troy, but to Sicily. There he recorded images of the impoverished home of his 'authoress' – small sailing boats, dusty courtyards and farm animals, especially pigs.

Butler claimed that the *Odyssey* was a domestic tale about a journey within Sicily, composed by a Sicilian woman. Butler's project was supported by his fluent prose translations of the *Iliad* (1898) and the *Odyssey* (1900), which challenged the archaizing style of verse translation then in vogue and, as he said, aimed at an audience of young girls uneducated in Classics. Bouncy Edwardian suffragists certainly had their own way of reading the *Odyssey*, if the *Nausicaa* written by Mary Hoste (a tutor at Lady Margaret Hall, Oxford) for performance in girls' schools is anything to go by: she recommends Nausicaa as a role model because she 'is strangely modern' and 'active, self-reliant, and courageous … well able to take care of herself': after all, she can harness mules as well as supervise the laundry.[13]

Butler was giving mischievous expression to the current state of scholarly controversy. There was a long tradition arguing that the domestic *Odyssey* was not authored by the same poet as the warlike *Iliad*. This had culminated in F.A. Wolf's proposal that many bards had contributed to their composition.[14] But the Victorian defenders of the unity and greatness of Homer, including Gladstone and Matthew Arnold, preferred to praise his 'grand style' and patriarchal focus. Butler, in caustic response, cast doubt on their values and grandiloquence by claiming that the canonical author of one of these works of genius was in fact a woman.

His theory inspired Robert Graves's novel *Homer's Daughter* (1955), narrated by a high-spirited Sicilian princess named Nausicaa, who grafts onto legends the names of her own friends, foes and slaves. This in turn was adapted into *Nausicaa*, one of the few *Odyssey* operas written by a woman, Vaughan-Williams's student Peggy Glanville-Hicks. Her 'grand opera' premiered in Athens in 1961,[15] and outraged the male-dominated Greek establishment, although Glanville-Hicks insisted (disingenuously) that she despised feminism. She understood the insouciance of Butler's project better than the French scholar who as late as 1977 borrowed his arguments in order to prove the same hypothesis.[16] But Butler's irreverence is worth taking seriously. Writing at the moment when women classical scholars were beginning to emerge, he was poking fun at the pompous Victorian philological establishment while drawing attention to epic's status as a male preserve.

By 1856 Elizabeth Barrett Browning had fulfilled her childhood dream of becoming the 'feminine of Homer' by making a female the narrating subject of her verse epic *Aurora Leigh*,[17] just as H.D. (Hilda Doolittle) was to feminize epic conventions by rewriting the *Iliad* from Helen's perspective in *Helen in Egypt* (1961).[18] During Aurora's voyage to Genoa, she refers to Odysseus' visit to the Underworld as she watches the mountains 'straining past' one another like 'grand dull Odyssean ghosts,/Athirst to drink the cool blue wine of seas/And stare on voyagers'.[19] But to *translate* Homer seems to have been seen as beyond some mutually agreed pale (even today most women poets adapting the *Odyssey* have chosen lyric or lyric-narrative form).[20] With the exception of Anne Dacier, whose French translations were often reprinted, no woman has ever made a name by translating either Homeric epic.[21] Anne Dacier's public image was that of devoted wife to her husband André, and mother to his children. When her *Odyssey* came out in 1708, this image of wifely devotion no doubt allowed the reader to fuse the epic's translator with its heroine, Penelope. This fusion will have been supported by the translator's eloquent refutation of the charge that the *Odyssey* is inferior to the *Iliad*; on the contrary, Dacier argues, although a less frenetic poem, it offers models of wisdom and constancy, along with recognitions and vicissitudes.[22]

Yet Dacier did not defend the *Odyssey* on the specific ground of Penelope's virtue, and the problem of understanding Penelope's consciousness has long frustrated scholars. The enigma begins when she summons the beggar, outraged at the suitors' treatment of him. This, she says, could never happen if Odysseus came back. At this point Telemachus sneezes *and Penelope laughs* (17.543–50). Before she has met the beggar, she tells the suitors to bring bridal gifts; the narrator comments, 'Odysseus saw with glee how she lured them to make presents to her, stealing their souls with persuasive words though her heart meanwhile was set elsewhere' (18.281–3). This raises the possibility that Penelope believes that Odysseus is about to return, or even that she has seen through his disguise.[23]

When the two finally converse, she weeps as he tells her that Odysseus is alive and will be home before the year's end. We hear that Odysseus represses his pity for his weeping wife (19.209–12), but are given no information about Penelope's suspicions or lack of them. When she confides her ominous dreams and her impulse to set up an archery contest, he tells her to organize it for tomorrow. Penelope is presented as believing his assurances that Odysseus will arrive before the bow can be strung; she then retires to her bed where she dreams that Odysseus lies physi-

cally beside her (20.88–90). She is woken by the nurse who tells her that
Odysseus has returned. Even after being told about his scar she is not
convinced: in a rare description of her feelings about the man who claims
to be her husband, the narrator says that 'she sat for a long time in silence,
with bewilderment upon her heart, because as her eyes searched his face
she thought him one moment like Odysseus and then again could not see
him so because of his miserable rags' (23.90–5).

This picture is perplexing. Does the archery contest occur to her because
she believes that the crisis must finally be resolved one way or another?
Does her *subconscious* mind recognize Odysseus while her consciousness
does not? Is she an irrational creature so emotionally confused that it
is pointless to look for consistency of motive? Whichever way the story
is read, it is sexist: we are asked to collude with this woman's husband
and son in scrutinizing her misery (see Fig. 9.1). In pre-feminist times
some women identified with Homer's Penelope on an uncomplicated
level; Pope's translation reached a wide female readership, and lay behind
Angelica Kauffman's repeated portraits of Penelope in lonely distress.[24]
Many women wept at Nicholas Rowe's tragedy *Ulysses*, first performed in
1706. Rowe invented the type of bourgeois drama known as 'She-Trag-
edy', in which a virtuous woman in distress, usually a mother, was torn
between conflicting loyalties. Accordingly, his stage version of the *Odyssey* was really Penelope's play (see Fig. 9.2). It tests not only her virtue but
the very possibility of a virtuous woman, an issue raised by the elderly
Aethon when he says that there is no such thing as a wife who cannot be
persuaded out of fidelity.[25]

Yet Penelope's virtue is unassailable until the dastardly Erymachus
contrives a situation in which he forces her to agree to marry him, by
arresting Telemachus and decreeing that the youth will be executed unless
she complies. A psychologically sado-masochistic confrontation ensues;
once she is tearful and obedient, she is likened to another famous Homeric
mother:

> So Silver *Thetis*, on the *Phrygian* Shore,
> Wept for her Son, foreknowing of his Fate.[26]

The suicidal Penelope is suddenly saved by the appearance, from the skies,
of the goddess Pallas. It transpires that Odysseus has been testing her all
along, disguised as the aged Aethon. In this sentimental playhouse celebration of Penelope's chastity, the eighteenth-century mixed-sex audience
found a version of the *Odyssey* that corresponded with their social agenda.[27]
More recently, the epic has become embroiled in controversies concerning
women's and men's abilities and proclivities. At base the classic love story,

in which a well-matched couple faces adversity before being reunited, it is simultaneously much more.

Odysseus values Penelope's intelligence, and the poem celebrates the desirability of 'like-mindedness' within a marriage (see 6.181–4). It was to Penelope that Odysseus delegated the responsibility for his household by making her his regent (18.259–70).[28] The satisfactory outcome of the poem depends as much upon Penelope's qualities as on those of Odysseus.[29] This makes her almost unique in Greek mythology, where clever women have a tendency to misbehave, and feminine docility is valued more than shrewdness.[30] Nor does the portrait of Eurycleia, Odysseus' nurse, underestimate the power that even a slave woman could exert: both Telemachus and Odysseus trust her, and with reason.[31]

Yet the poem has presented problems to the female reader, at least since the late nineteenth century. 'What a long slog through centuries of misogyny,' concluded Judith Yarnall in her study of Circe.[32] Penelope's intelligence may be celebrated in her epithet *periphrōn*, 'mindful', which occurs 50 times; but her intelligence is confined to a single, domestic sphere, whereas Odysseus' 'intelligence' epithets, *polumēchanos*, *polumētis* and *polutropos*, emphasize the variety of venues in which he displays his many skills.[33] Although Penelope's subjectivity is explored occasionally through her dream-life, no modern reader can find her emotionally plausible. She is not angry at being abandoned or deprived of more children, sexually frustrated, suspicious of her husband's fidelity, satisfied at being in charge of the household, or resentful of having to relinquish space when Odysseus returns. She does not even complain when, on their first night together, he says that he will leave her again (23.266–87). The reader must make guesses to 'fill in' the gaps in Penelope's psychological profile, thus giving her a strange extra-textual status of her own. Is she suppressing these negative emotions, or has she a secret life? It is in having to respond actively to Penelope's characterization that over the last century many authors have found inspiration.

It has a precedent in Ovid's *Heroides*, poems taking the form of a letter from a heroine, the first of which imagines what Penelope might have written to Odysseus/Ulysses. This Penelope sounds angry and real. She complains about lying alone in bed, about rage, about her suspicion that he has a lover, about losing her looks. *Heroides* 1 has long attracted female poets, such as the Restoration Anne Killigrew, who imitated it.[34] Yet even Ovid never suggests that such a long separation might undermine the couple's ability to communicate. This was perhaps first proposed in a poem penned in 1875 by an American named Jemimah Makepiece Sturt.

Fig. 1.1. Bard on a fresco in the Mycenaean palace
at Pylos in Greece, courtesy of the Archive of
Performances of Greek and Roman Drama.

Fig. 1.2. Hermes skims the sea. Copper engraving
taken from Andrew Tooke's *The Pantheon* (1729
edition), facing p 51.

Fig. 2.1. 'Rosy-fingered dawn'. Copper engraving taken from Andrew Tooke's *The Pantheon* (1729 edition), facing p 133.

*S. Shelley pinxt.*                    *C. Taylor sculpt.*

Fig. 2.2. Homer at the Eisteddfod. Charles Taylor, late
eighteenth-century engraving of a painting inspired by
Thomas Gray's Celtic-revival poem *The Bard* (1757).

Fig. 3.1. Circe and the pig-men in Derek Walcott's stage
version of the *Odyssey* (1992), courtesy of the APGRD.

Fig. 3.2. Circe outwitted by Odysseus: black-figure vase from
Thebes, fifth century BCE, courtesy of the APGRD.

Fig. 4.1. Aeolus, god of the winds. Copper engraving reproduced from Andrew Tooke's *The Pantheon* (1729 edition), facing p 164.

Fig. 4.2. Ralph Waldo Ellison in the 1970s, courtesy of the APGRD.

Fig. 5.1. Phemius, the Ithacan bard, in a painting by Charles
Buchel reproduced from the souvenir programme for Phillips's
*Ulysses* (1902), courtesy of the APGRD.

Fig. 5.2. Mentor pushes Telamachus into the sea.
Engraving by Thomas Stothard, reproduced from John
Hawkesworth's translation of Fénelon's *The Adventures of
Telemachus* (1784), between pp 172 and 173, courtesy of
the APGRD.

Fig. 6. Ulysses at sea with his crew. Illustration, by Charles Buchel, on
the cover of the original programme for Stephen Phillips's verse
drama *Ulysses* (1902).

Fig. 7. Odysseus offers wine to Polyphemus in the
illustration by John Flaxman, *c.*1805.

Fig. 8. Telemachus gets ready for action, in a painting by
Charles Buchel reproduced from the souvenir programme for
Phillips's *Ulysses* (1902), courtesy of the APGRD.

Fig. 9.1. Penelope in distress, in a painting by Charles Buchel reproduced from the souvenir programme for Phillips's *Ulysses* (1902), courtesy of the APGRD.

Fig. 9.2. Penelope in Nicholas Rowe's *Ulysses*. Engraving by Thornthwaite of Mrs Hunter (published 1778). Reproduced by courtesy of the APGRD.

Fig. 10.1. Eumaeus the swineherd, in a painting by Charles Buchel reproduced from the souvenir programme for Phillips's *Ulysses* (1902), courtesy of the APGRD.

Fig. 10.2. Odysseus in the beggar's disguise, painting by Charles Buchel reproduced from the souvenir programme for Phillips's *Ulysses* (1902), courtesy of the APGRD.

Fig. 11. Athena, goddess of wisdom, in a painting by
Charles Buchel reproduced from the souvenir programme
for Phillips's *Ulysses* (1902), courtesy of the APGRD.

Fig. 12. The Alexandrian poet Cavafy, *c*.1895.

Fig. 13. 'The Slaughter of the Suitors', frontispiece with title page to Anne Dacier's translation of the *Odyssey* (1716 edition).

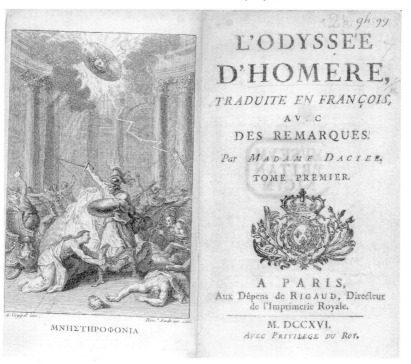

Fig. 14.1. The Odyssey personified as the loyal Penelope in Lecomte du Nouy's *Homer* (1882), reproduced from the *Illustrated London News*, 3 June 1882, courtesy of the APGRD.

Fig. 14.2. Calypso of the beautifully braided hair, in a painting by Charles Buchel reproduced from the souvenir programme for Phillips's *Ulysses* (1902), courtesy of the APGRD.

Fig. 15. Elpenor appears to Odysseus. Detail from Athenian red-figure vase about 475–425 BCE. Boston Museum of Fine Arts 34.79.

Steiner's Penguin collection *Homer in English* includes it, but, by patron-
izingly describing it as an 'amateurish lyric', fails to see its path-breaking
importance.

> Thy limbs have lain in witches' arms,
> I know the cunning of thy charms.
> Why have you come to claim my heart,
> When we so long have dwellt a'part?
> When I can hear within your blood
> The changing dalliance of the flood?
> Stay with me, if you must, a'while.
> The stars shine cold in your soft smile,
> The desert winds sing in your breath,
> I know I'll be alone at death.[35]

This Penelope grudgingly lets Odysseus stay, but has emotions that are
independent of him: she is of interest *in her own right*.

With Dorothy Parker's caustic 'Penelope' (1928), the independent wife
raises another question. What is the nature of courage, and which of them
is really brave?

> In the pathway of the sun,
> In the footsteps of the breeze,
> Where the world and sky are one,
> He shall ride the silver seas,
> He shall cut the glittering wave.
> I shall sit at home, and rock;
> Rise, to heed a neighbor's knock;
> Brew my tea, and snip my thread;
> Bleach the linen for my bed.
> They will call him brave.[36]

The other significant pioneer in the rewriting of the *Odyssey* was
H.D. (Hilda Doolittle), whose relationship with it culminated with the
Penelope-narrator in 'Winter Love' (1958).[37] Less well-known is Katherine
Anne Porter's *A Defense of Circe* (1954), a story about a 'sunny-tempered,
merry-hearted young enchantress', who is misunderstood by history. This
Circe is an autobiographical cipher for Porter's own struggles with men
who abandoned her, and with alcoholism and childlessness: she points out
that, unlike Odysseus, Circe can be *trusted* to keep her word. Nor did she
turn any man into a pig: her drugs simply cause men to reveal their true
natures.[38]

In the tidal wave of feminist versions of the *Odyssey* engulfing the literary scene over the last few decades, the important ideas are private space,

weaving and quest. As early as 1972, Martha Collins's poem 'Homecoming' expresses Penelope's fear of losing her Woolfian room of her own – Ithaca in Odysseus' absence.[39] Clayton has shown how French literary theorists' taste for weaving metaphors fostered the poststructuralist rediscovery of Penelope, which contributed to her recuperation by feminists. In the early 1970s Roland Barthes proposed the term *hyophology*, or 'theory of the web/textile', as a way of thinking about written discourse.[40] Luce Irigaray and Hélène Cixous were meanwhile turning to mythical females, especially Medusa, to illustrate their theories about feminine writing. Mythical weavers inevitably excited attention. One was Arachne, punished for creating a beautiful artwork by being sentenced to create webs whose only function was food-processing. Arachne is silenced. 'Cut off from the work of art, she spins like a woman.'[41] But Penelope could be appropriated as the founding mother of *écriture féminine*, since she did create an artwork, but its conclusion was endlessly deferred.

Feminist frustration can find expression through the image of Penelope's unweaving. In Katha Pollitt's savage poem 'Penelope Writes' (1981), she dreams nightly that she tears down her household after attacking her loom with such violence that her fingers bleed.[42] But the landmark text was Carolyn Heilbrun's 'What was Penelope unweaving?' She first delivered it to a conference in 1985, claiming that 'the old stories confirm that women wove, not to conceal, but to reveal, to engage, to counter male violence. For this they are punished, but not before "the voice of the shuttle" had been heard, if only to be silenced again. Women's weaving was women's answer to their enforced silence about their own condition, their own mutilation.'[43] Heilbrun argues that women have no story other than marriage and motherhood by which to shape their lives. The problem for Penelope was that hers was an unwritten story: 'how a woman may manage her own destiny when she has no plot, no narrative, no tale to guide her'.[44]

Seamus Heaney begins his poem 'The Stone Grinder' with the envious sentiments of his workman-narrator:

> Penelope worked with some guarantee of a plot.
> Whatever she unweaved at night
> might advance it all by a day.[45]

Penelope was in a plot; Penelope springs to the mind of a working-class labourer looking for a poetic figure with whom to compare himself. But Heilbrun suggests that Penelope 'had' no story because the *only* story women are allowed to tell is the romance, the 'marriage plot, the erotic plot, the courtship plot, but never, as for men, the quest plot'. The absence of female quest heroes prevents women from escaping the single narrative line in which they have been configured. For women even now, Heilbrun suggests, few narratives help prepare them for entry into public life rather than the marriage market, kitchen or nursery.

Heilbrun's focus on women's exclusion from quest narrative has had striking results. One is the reconceptualization of domestic toil as quest, in, for example, Marilyn Hacker's poem 'Mythology' (1986), which asks what does a girl do,

> but walk across the world, her kids in tow,
> stopping at stations on the way, with
> friends to tie her to the mast when she gets too
> close to the edge.[46]

Another consequence is that Dorothy, the heroine of L. Frank Baum's novel *The Wonderful Wizard of Oz* (1900), has been identified as the first significant female 'quest' hero. The startling idea that a girl from Kansas could search for something other than romance illuminates why the *Odyssey* has been so important to gender politics: it assigned, for more than two millennia, the role of quest hero exclusively to men. Seeing the importance of Dorothy, moreover, led to a new interest in Baum's support of women's suffrage, and the suspicion that in his gutsy heroine he was channelling the energy he derived from his suffragist wife and his mother-in-law Matilda Joslyn Gage, a prominent feminist.

There is one female quest hero related to the *Odyssey* who had appeared as early as 1984, in Hayao Miyazaki's ecological manga *Nausicaa of the Valley of the Wind*. Miyazaki's Nausicaa celebrates Homer's Phaeacian princess because she acts to save her latterday utopian environment from pollution and invasion. A direct female heir to Odysseus himself is the comic-strip adventuress Tank Girl, summoned by her television-obsessed son Tele to rescue her husband from suitors, despite the 'siren call' of Gothic Rock.[47] But Heilbrun's fascination with Penelope underlay other developments, especially the feminist rewriting of philosophy. Adriana Cavarero's classic *In Spite of Plato* begins with Socrates' recommendation in *Phaedo* 84a–b that the philosophical man, who must untie the soul from what binds it to the pleasures and pains of the body, strive to be *unlike* Penelope: she constantly untied her weaving, only to reconstitute it. Cavarero identifies in this passage a new, Penelopean way for women to be philosophers: they can weave together what men have undone – the relationship between mind and body, between thought, birth and death.[48]

Heilbrun's essay also suggested to female writers that they write an alternative history – just as Penelope used weaving rather than epic song, so women could draw on their letters and diaries to challenge the idea that history must consist of a narrative of public affairs: in Lyn Hejinian's prose poem *My Life*, the autobiographical subject compares herself to 'Penelope reworking the twill', an expanding patchwork into which she can always insert new material.[49] Heilbrun also saw Penelope, who wove the same pattern anew, as emblematic of the feminist project of rewriting the literary canon. Penelope is author of a text, but also the object of new texts which women write as they put male interests under the feminist spotlight. The task facing women authors, argued Heilbrun, is to form new fictions for themselves, but women must 'transform old tales, and recognize how women have transformed old tales in the past'.[50]

Few Greek or Shakespearean heroines have not been the subject, over the last two decades, of feminist re-envisioning: Clytemnestra has been justified, Jocasta transformed into a freethinker, and Shakespeare's Kate from tamed shrew to rape victim. In her hilarious poem 'Circe', Carol Ann Duffy's pig-keeper swerves vertiginously from talking about pig-men she has slept with to recipes for cooking pork.[51] But Penelope has been allowed to weave her own subjectivity. Just two years after Heilbrun's incendiary lecture, the first of several novels rewriting the *Odyssey* was published in Austria – Inge Merkel's *Odysseus and Penelope: An Ordinary Marriage*.[52] This rewrote the *Odyssey* from the perspective of the women left behind – above all Penelope, but Eurycleia is also upgraded.

Merkel draws on Greek tragedy by adding the songs of choruses including the elders of Sparta, mothers celebrating childbirth, soon-to-be-widows of Ithaca, Fates singing as Troy falls, abandoned mothers, nymphs in their Ithacan cave and maids listening at the bedroom door. Penelope appreciates Odysseus for his diligence in bed, and the depressive Anticleia presents no challenge as a mother-in-law: the important relationship is with Eurycleia. Merkel uses the old nurse, who has produced several children but never known a husband, to articulate insights into gender relations. When Odysseus is nervous about Penelope's impending labour, Eurycleia sarcastically points out that it is rather late for him to worry.[53] Odysseus becomes jealous of the suckling baby, whose noisy presence puts a stop to his sex life. He says of the urge to go to Troy that 'a man can be truly at home only if he has returned from some other place'. His excitement mounts: 'we'll have a men's outing', he thinks, 'a loud, boastful, brilliant, mindless merriment only for men, untroubled by a guilty conscience, by the memory of a weeping woman'.[54]

Penelope eventually finds her sexual starvation agonizing. She develops an eating disorder, varicose veins and a drink problem. She stops washing and resorts to black magic. She nearly has a lesbian affair; she climbs into bed with Amphinomus before getting cold feet; she flirts with Antinous. The narrator tells us that although Penelope's three affairs were all unconsummated, both she and Odysseus 'had committed adultery. He in the way of men and she in the way of women.' [55] Merkel asks what constitutes a heroic ordeal. Penelope says to her self-obsessed husband, 'We women, my Odysseus, are seldom drifting on the swaying waters of the bleak sea, but we are familiar with other bleaknesses, bleaknesses of the despairing heart through which we drift with suffering and torment.' [56]

Although denying that she is a feminist, Merkel owes much to the feminist tradition of reading Greek myths instantiated in Christa Wolf's *Cassandra* (1975). Merkel claimed that she just wanted to write about marriage.[57] Yet her men are less admirable than her women, and the differences seem grounded in nature. When Odysseus resists the hallucinatory pleasures of the lotus, his quest drive is grounded in libido: 'by the urging of his manhood, by his sex'.[58] Merkel finds Homer's picture of his supposedly intelligent queen of Ithaca insulting. Her Penelope knows everything about Odysseus' affair with Calypso (an 'island tart'), and she is not hoodwinked by her husband's vagabond disguise. From a woman's perspective, this makes for a more emotionally satisfying read than the *Odyssey*, where Penelope is scrutinized for the effect men's actions are having on *her*, rather than vice versa.

Merkel's innovative book has received little attention in comparison with the two 'Penelope' novels published in 2005, Adèle Geras's *Ithaka*, told by an orphaned granddaughter of Eurycleia, and *The Penelopiad* by Margaret Atwood, which she subsequently, in 2007, adapted into a stage play that was performed by the Royal Shakespeare Company in collaboration with Canada's National Arts Centre. Like Merkel, Atwood alternates prose narrative with choruses. Her innovation is to give the task of narration to dead women: Penelope and the 12 maids who are executed in Book 22. *The Penelopiad* wittily portrays Penelope using slang: when she first saw Odysseus 'he had the manners of a small-town big shot, and had already expressed several complicated ideas the others considered peculiar'. Rumours come that during his absence he is lingering in 'a high-class Sicilian knocking shop – the courtesans there were known for their musical talents and their fancy feathered outfits'. Penelope recognizes him straightaway, but strategically decides to play along with his theatricals: 'if a man takes pride in his disguising skills, it would be a foolish wife who would claim to recognize him'.[59]

Unlike Merkel, Atwood makes her Penelope as obnoxious as her

Odysseus. She is arrogant, vain, insecure, unsympathetic and sexually possessive. She is tyrannical with her slaves; it is she who orders the 12 'disloyal' maids to hang around the suitors 'using whatever enticing arts they could invent'.[60] Penelope has here displaced Odysseus as an epic hero, as Atwood's title implies (at least one scholar, impressed by Penelope's prominence, long ago described the poem as the *Penelopeia*).[61] Atwood's Penelope is granted agency, intelligence and gifts as a raconteur, but is difficult to like. This is post-feminism at its most cynical; not only have women reclaimed the old stories, but they have reclaimed the right to be vile.

There have also been innumerable Penelopes reassessed by women poets and dramatists. Linda Pastan's seven-poem lyric cycle 'On Rereading the *Odyssey* in Middle Age' weaves into an imitation of the poem the responses of a mature reader.[62] Carolyn White's 'The Voyage of Penelope' (1993) presents Penelope's heroic journey through her dream-life and her textiles; she wants Odysseus to stay away so that he can never shock her with 'the pig eyes of greed/The perfume of a lesser woman in his hair'.[63] 'Penelope serves Odysseus breakfast' (2000) by Karen Bjorneby has the wife of a prosperous businessman announce that *she* is going on a cruise. The focus of Louise Glück's lyric cycle *Meadowlands* (1996) is also a failing modern marriage; she uses sequences from the *Odyssey* for exploring the subjectivities of the son (Telemachus) and the 'other woman' (Circe) as well as the husband and wife.[64] The most extreme feminist updating was Rachel Matthews's radio play *The City at Night* (broadcast on BBC Radio 4 on 4 November 2004). Her Ulee, a former man who has undergone a sex-change operation, is now searching for her fiancé on the Newcastle quayside. *Current Nobody* by Melissa James Gibson, performed at the 2006 Sundance Institute Theatre Laboratory, involves another kind of sex role inversion by having Penelope going away as a war photo-journalist, leaving Odysseus at home with a teenage daughter, Tel, who grapples with the cost of her mother's epic ambition.

Indeed, creative writers turned to the *Odyssey* more quickly after the 1970s feminist revolution than did the Classics establishment. Although rescuing Penelope is now standard amongst Homer scholars,[65] it was not ever thus. It was Helene Foley who as long ago as 1978 first showed how the *Odyssey* uses 'inverted sex role' similes to underline the tensions in the marriage and under patriarchy, for example, when Penelope finally accepts her husband and clings to him as shipwrecked men grasp dry land (23.233–8).[66] But it was not until 1987 that Sheila Murnaghan's outstanding *Disguise and Recognition in the Odyssey* broke new ground within Classics by arguing that Penelope is construed as a heroic type who achieves her goals by cunning intelligence, only to be knocked down as such by an ideological imperative inimical to male–female equality.[67] Marilyn Katz's *Penelope's Renown* (1991) is perhaps the first feminist study to make a virtue out of the ambiguity of Penelope's presentation, showing how the poem's audience is kept guessing about the type of wife that she will turn out to be – an adulterous Helen, a murderous Clytemnestra or an exemplar of fidelity and virtue. Penelope, as the constantly evolving and least determinate figure in the poem, is thus the paramount symbol of its poetics. Three years later, Nancy Felson-Rubin acknowledged Penelope's power as a signifier of open-endedness, but focused on the engagement of the listener/reader with the unfolding of the story to ask whether subjective ways of identifying with the emotional vicissitudes in this text are in themselves irredeemably gendered.

An excellent range of less polemical approaches to all the female figures in the *Odyssey*, not only Penelope, was edited by Beth Cohen in 1995, the same year that Lillian Doherty in *Siren Songs* found it impossible to square her sexual politics with her love of the poem. She argues that it seduces female readers into adopting a masculine perspective and construing its female figures, including the heroically intelligent Penelope, purely on Odysseus' terms, thus betraying their own interests as women. Besides anything else, Homeric women do an enormous amount of work, as women have always done in time of war.[68] They especially do the domestic labour that became a symbol of oppression during the women's liberation movement. As Diana Blakely's Circe tartly puts it, Odysseus' men 'missed/clean clothes and forks. At home/they'd had their beds changed, the sheets tightened,/uncreased.'[69] Penelope may weave, but it is the slave women who scrub houses, wash clothes, bathe men's bodies, cook, pack provisions and manage store cupboards. They even dispose of corpses. Perhaps the women whose treatment in Homer it is most difficult for any modern reader – female or male – to understand are the 12 slave women who are executed on the grounds of their 'disloyalty' (22.446–54):

> All the women came down in a flock, wailing dreadfully, in floods of tears. The first thing they did then was carry out the corpses of the slain, and lean them up against one another in the porch leading to the enclosed courtyard. Odysseus himself kept them at it with his commands, so that they were forced to continue the hauling under duress. Then they cleansed the chairs and handsome tables with water and porous sponges.

As Odysseus' slaves, these women's vaginas, like the rest of their bodies, belonged exclusively to him. They were committing a crime against his property by letting others use them without his permission. But the point that comes over most forcibly to me, as a woman who is untalented at vacuum cleaning, is the form taken by their punishment. Even when they are about to be strung up in the courtyard, they are forced to do the cleaning.

In the late twentieth century, the world waited for the return of Nelson Mandela to oust the white politicians who in 1948 had imposed apartheid, and to claim his proper role as leader of his country. For decades, vast numbers of disfranchised South African women struggled to eke out a livelihood by cleaning rich people's houses. Thousands were also waiting for the return of husbands from political exile, imprisonment or absences imposed by the system of migrant labour. The parallel between the plight of the women of South Africa and the suffering of Penelope and her slave women was not lost on the writer Njabulo Ndebele, himself a longstanding political exile. Now the vice chancellor of Cape Town University, he has developed the parallel in his novel *The Cry of Winnie Mandela*, which addresses the still unhealed psychological wounds inflicted on individual women and their marriages by the brutalities of the apartheid system. For nearly three decades Winnie Madikizela-Mandela, the wife of their incarcerated leader, was the global symbol of all waiting wives. But the primary focus of Ndebele's novel is less this powerful Penelope figure than four of her more ordinary equivalents.

In the real world their stories inevitably fail to live up to the idealized fidelity and happy reunion dictated by the *Odyssey*. One actively pursues her husband only to discover that he is a bigamist. Another has a child while her husband is away studying and ends up divorced. Mamello's husband was imprisoned on Robben Island, but he abandons her to marry another woman on his release. The fourth wife's husband dies after a long career of adultery. As each of them tells her personal story, she engages in a dialogue with Winnie Mandela, as the most visible 'Penelope' in the land.

The novel, although not at all blind to Madikizela-Mandela's vanity, her megalomania, her dissembling and violent leadership style, rescues her from the hatred and calumny to which she has been internationally exposed by offering instead a more objective picture of a passionate woman under unbearable pressure. The coercive ideal embodied in the Penelope archetype is revealed to be a patriarchal fiction serving only men's needs and causing quite unnecessary psychological suffering, especially to a figure as exposed to the public gaze as the wife of the most famous hero on the world political stage. The agony of deprivation and vulnerability underlying the true experience of waiting women – an agony glossed over by the *Odyssey* – is exposed throughout this heartbreaking novel. But it receives its most explicit expression in the real letter that it quotes, written from prison by Nelson Mandela himself, to his beautiful young wife:

> Your love and support, the raw warmth of your body, the charming children you have given the family … the hope of enjoying that love again, is what life and happiness mean to me. I have somebody I love who is worthy to be loved and trusted, one whose own love and patient support have given me so much strength and hope … Yet there have been moments when … I have wondered whether any kind of commitment can ever be sufficient excuse for abandoning a young and inexperienced woman in a pitiless desert, literally throwing her into the hands of highwaymen.[70]

When real life produces such authentically moving sentiments as these, even Ndebele's expert and humane mythologizing method very nearly becomes superfluous.

# 10

# CLASS CONSCIOUSNESS

This dog's owner has died far away ... Now his situation is hard, because his master has died away from his homeland, and the women do not look after him. Slaves never work properly when their master is not there to govern them, for far-thundering Zeus removes half a man's capacity when the day of slavery takes him down (*Odyssey* 17.312–23).

S uch is the comment that Eumaeus the swineherd makes to the beggar he does not yet know is Odysseus, when the faithful dog Argos recognizes his disguised master and dies. The position the speech takes on slavery is complex, not least because the person who delivers it is himself a loyal slave, to whom the old hound offers an implicit parallel. But Eumaeus also believes that slaves are insubordinate, needing constant supervision. Acknowledgement of the deleterious effects of slavery on the human being is rare in the *Odyssey*. Its dominant picture portrays idealized, harmonious inter-class relationships. Eumaeus himself, an exemplar of virtue (see Fig. 10.1), conveniently turns out to be an aristocrat who was kidnapped as a child (15.351–484). In 1829 an Ithacan scholar claimed to be a direct descendant of Eumaeus, but he emphasized Eumaeus' origins as son of the king of another island rather than his status as slave and swineherd.[1]

One reason why the *Odyssey* has proved susceptible to adaptation is that its characters are not confined to an elite, aristocrat group: besides the significant slave characters (Eurycleia, Eurynome and Melantho as well as Eumaeus), the poem includes an ordinary rower (Elpenor) and the beggar Irus: in *Il ritorno d'Ulisse in patria*, Monteverdi upgraded the character of Irus significantly, giving him social aspirations and a serious suicide scene.[2] The *Odyssey* includes stories about merchants and pirates, and much backbreaking peasant labour. The setting on rugged Ithaca contrasts with the luxury of Phaeacia and Menelaus' opulent Sparta. Little wonder the Renaissance critic Julius Caesar Scaliger, who despised the lowlife tenor of the *Odyssey*, scoffed that Homer 'was instructed by rustics and little old women in Ithaca and Chios'.[3] Charles Perrault, a snob and acolyte of Louis XIV, felt 'indignation and disgust' when he discovered that Odysseus 'sleeps with pigs in the evening and has a fistfight the next day with an ugly tramp over the scraps from Penelope's kitchen'.[4]

The *Odyssey* portrays sudden reversals of fortune leading to violent movements up or down the social pyramid. The most brutal of these occur in the stories told to Eumaeus by Odysseus in his fictional persona as a displaced Cretan. He says that he since he was the illegitimate son born by a slave to a prosperous Cretan, he was given only a small peasant holding on his father's death. He had fought at Troy, but was thereafter press-ganged into forced labour in Egypt, before insinuating himself into the favour of the pharaoh. He was then misled into taking a voyage with a Phoenician crook who sold him into slavery, but a shipwreck meant that he arrived as a free man in Thesprotia. He was kidnapped again, and faced slavery if he had not escaped and swum ashore to Ithaca (14.191–359). This compelling tale is calculated to make its audience remember that in the ancient Mediterranean, liberty was always a fragile status.

On arrival in Ithaca, Odysseus disguises himself as the poorest type of free individual. For nearly ten books the perspective of the poem fuses that of a king with that of a tramp (see Fig. 10.2). It is in this context that the audience listens to the insults loaded upon the vulnerable outsider by Melantho, herself a slave (19.66–9), when she demands to know if he intends to malinger at the house, prowling around and staring at the women: 'Go away, you loser, and eat your supper outside, or you will soon find yourself beaten away with a blazing torch.' Odysseus' response would alone explain why his poem has attracted so many class-conscious readings:

> Strange woman, what is the reason for such anger with me? Is it because I am dirty, and dressed in rags, and go begging from people? I have to do this out of necessity. That's what indigent men and beggars usually do. There was a time when I too was a wealthy man, who could hold my head high as master of my own flourishing household; in those days I often used to give things to tramps who lived as I do know, regardless of who they were or what it was that they needed (19.71–7).

The *Odyssey* insists that its audience remember that there, but for the grace of the gods, go they.

Yet scholars have disagreed about the class agenda of the *Odyssey*, and the point is an important one, since the poem informed all ancient ideology through its role in education. The class politics of the *Odyssey* have been seen as either fundamentally conservative or fundamentally radical.

The most important statement of the former position, which argues that the poem affirms the necessity of a dominant aristocracy, came in Moses Finley's anthropological study *The World of Odysseus*. He said that the socially subordinate characters in the *Odyssey* are presented as mere 'stock types'.[5] In the Ithacan power struggle, as in the *Iliad*, ultimately 'only the aristocrats had roles'. This view has been developed in a brilliant book-length study of class in the *Odyssey* by Thalmann (1998).

Those scholars, however, who think that the poem offers a critique of class society, stress the radical potential of the device through which Ithacan society is inspected from 'the bottom up' while Odysseus is disguised as a beggar. An early proponent of this view was Felix Jacoby, the scholar-son of a wealthy merchant family, writing in 1933 in Germany before anti-semitism forced him to emigrate to England. He praised the *Odyssey* for offering a portrayal of social relations that took in the 'little people' as well as the grand.[6] More recently, this has informed Rose's sophisticated reading (1975), 'Class ambivalence in the *Odyssey*'.[7] Rose denies that it is possible to identify a consistent ideological position underlying a text in any class-torn society since texts express tensions rather than positions. My own view is similar. There are several passages in the *Odyssey* which could be enjoyed by the slaves who heard performances, and felt to contain perspectives personal to them, or which expressed, at least, some fellow feeling. This is suggested by the ways in which the class element of the *Odyssey* has reappeared in its later adaptations. Its reception, from the perspective of the depiction of social class, is certainly different from that of the *Iliad*: no scene in the *Odyssey* contains the same insistence on the gap between aristocrat and commoner as the confrontation between Thersites, the ordinary Greek solider at Troy, and his overlords.[8]

In the *Iliad* it is Odysseus who strikes Thersites with the sceptre – symbol of inherited god-given kingly status – in order to silence him. This point was not lost on Walcott, who includes a painful new scene between the two in his stage version of the *Odyssey*.[9] Moreover, no parallel in the Roman reception of the *Iliad* exists to the moment when in *Satire* 2.5 Horace constructed a humorous dialogue between Ulysses and Tiresias, which exposes the strategies by which lower-class fortune-hunters wheedled their way into the wills of rich old men. Nor is there any ancient burlesqued *Iliad* equivalent to Petronius' transposition of the *Odyssey* to the seedy brothels portrayed in his *Satyrica*, nor the identification of its hero with the simple villagers and fisher-folk to be found in some early Christian narratives (see Chapter 4). Although Renaissance versions of the *Odyssey* saw its hero as an important prince, and lower-class characters as sometimes evil and usually laughable, by the early eighteenth century a proletarian Odysseus had appeared.

This was in the ballad opera *Penelope* by John Mottley and Thomas Cooke, which premiered in London at the Little Haymarket Theatre on 8 May 1728 and is sometimes falsely attributed to the famous ballad opera composer John Gay. The songs of ballad opera (folk tunes, urban popular ditties and famous refrains by composers like Handel), were known on the streets, and the audiences could sing along if they wanted.[10] *Penelope* sets the story of the *Odyssey* in a London working-class tavern; the sign hanging outside reads, 'This is the Royal Oak, the House of Pen,/With Entertainment good for Horse and Men'.[11] The publican is Penelope, wife of Ulysses; he is a sergeant in the grenadiers and has been absent for 19 years. Meanwhile, she has been besieged by suitors: a butcher, a tailor and a parish clerk.

Cooke, although an innkeeper's son, was a classical scholar (indeed, the first translator of Hesiod into English),[12] and the opera is his barbed response to his long-time enemy Alexander Pope's translation of the *Odyssey*, issued in 1725–26.[13] One of the allegations made in the preface, indeed, is that Pope had relied too much on his so-called assistants in the *Odyssey* translation, William Broome and Elijah Fenton. But Mottley, as a Grub Street pamphleteer and the son of an absentee Jacobite soldier, was equipped to write about abandoned women and the seedier under-side of London life. The vigour of the opera derives from the unorthodox Cooke/Mottley collaboration. Its demotic tone is signified when Penelope tells the audience that she has not combed her 'matted locks' for a month, and only put on one clean smock in the last three. Her maid Doll suggests that she seek comfort in the bottle, but neither gin nor whisky can help. Penelope calls Doll a 'silly sow', and Doll recommends that she marry Cleaver the butcher, singing: 'He's tall and jolly,/Believe thy Dolly,/It wou'd be Folly,/To slight his Pain.' Penelope complains that all the suitors are but 'rakehells'; she will not choose one of them until she has finished weaving her cabbage-net. She despises, she says, the hotpots, stout, ale and punch with which they woo her.

Doll favours the butcher because he bribes her with tasty offal; she is less impressed with the tailor's silver thimble, and nonplussed by the parish clerk's Bible and offer of a reserved pew at church. (The man of god, interestingly, is himself sent up for his supercilious speech and respect for the king.) Doll and Cleaver are secretly in love and plotting; Cleaver will marry Penelope, thus acquiring her property, and keep Doll as his mistress. Cleaver is evil but engaging, and able wittily to send up the

Homeric archetype. He is a butcher, and therefore asks, 'Shall I my Fame with whining Sorrows stain,/Whose Arms have Hecatombs of Oxen slain?' But the opera ends as satisfactorily as the *Odyssey*, and with far less bloodshed.

The English working-class Odysseus has reappeared spasmodically in the theatre, notably in Richard Hope's fine play *Odysseus Thump* (1997), performed at the West Yorkshire Playhouse. Norman Nestor is also trying to get back to the pub – the Ship and Anchor in a Lancashire town. Against a setting of football terraces, closed mills and canal banks, Norman observes the destruction of the Northern industrial working class.[14] But in the nineteenth century, the most *déclassé* version of the *Odyssey* appeared in Andreas Karkavitsas's novel *The Beggar* (1896), the earliest novel to be written in demotic modern Greek. Karkavitsas was convinced that if Greece was to inaugurate a worthy national literature, it needed to be in a language understood 'by people both of the drawing-room and the hills'.[15] He used the *Odyssey* as a springboard for his novel about the return of a beggar to an impoverished northern Greek village, a backward area which had only been re-annexed by Greece from the Turks in 1881.

Karkavitsas, himself middle class, had studied ancient Greek mythology at the Gymnasium in Patras, but after enrolment as a medical officer in the Greek army, travelled in the poorest areas and came to sympathize with the miserable conditions under which most Greeks then lived. He was struck by the professional beggars in the area known as Roumeli, and he recorded how strong he found the parallel between their culture and that of Homeric heroes, especially the clever Odysseus. Each beggar went on long journeys, dressed in noxious rags, to acquire the means on which his family subsisted, but returned secretly at night to his home village to attend public festivals. He would hang his beggar's staff from a nail 'in which are preserved all the ancestral staffs, like the weapons of heroes in their arms-rooms ... the trophy by means of which his beggarly cleverness is advertised'. The beggar then appeared in public, clean, freshly dressed, and triumphant and 'whoever sees them the next day in the market will be thunderstruck like Telemachus before his transformed father'.[16]

The Odyssean hero of the novel is the titular beggar, Tziritokostas, a man capable of killing, with steely muscles beneath his rags, a revenge motive and exceptional cunning. Although his ethics are abominable, through him Karkavitsas celebrates the inherent intelligence and potential of the downtrodden serfs of Thessaly, while sparing no detail of the poverty and superstition that plagued them. Karkavitsas's outrageous new hero, by embodying an ironic twist on one of the canonical works of ancient Greek culture, allows his author to make political points without whitewashing the rivalry that existed between starving rural villagers, and their tawdry malice towards one another. One contemporary review, which for political reasons was unfavourable, saw acutely what Karkavitsas was doing in the novel, with its image of the beggar, 'that strange being formed of cunning and naiveté at the same time, guileless and clever, descended in a direct line from that great Greek ancestor from whom we are all descended after all – Odysseus'.[17]

A similar relocation down the social scale is manifest in a novel by Józef Wittlin, the translator of the *Odyssey* for early twentieth-century Poland. During the First World War, Wittlin (like Karkavitsas) had worked in a military hospital, and developed a Polish idiom for the *Odyssey* that would match the trauma he had encountered and suggest the old diction of folk ballads. The same style permeates his novel *The Salt of the Earth* (1935). This hero of this modern Odyssey is an updated equivalent of the swineherd Eumaeus, an illiterate, near idiotic provincial named Piotr Niewiadomski. But his simple moral instincts offer an alternative to the mad nihilism of the war: he is the 'salt of the earth' in the early Christian sense. Piotr's Odyssean voyage is through the trauma of the early twentieth century; his only defence against monsters and lethal seductions is his human decency.

This is the tradition in which cinema has more recently reacted to the *Odyssey*, for almost all the films that over the last 15 years have transplanted its plot to nineteenth- or twentieth-century contexts have made the Odysseus figure lower class, and his travelogue an exploration of the social underbelly of society. Many have set the story in the USA, where democratically minded citizens have had a special affection for Odysseus, or rather Ulysses, since the Revolutionary War. Indeed, the town of Ulysses in Tompkins County, Ithaca, is one of several in a chunk of New York state gifted to soldiers in reward for securing the new nation. The name was chosen by a land commissioner named Robert Harper, who looked to heroic names associated with Greece and Rome after rejecting the associations of either British or Native American nomenclature.

The southern states of the USA have had a paradoxical relationship with the poem ever since the future US president Ulysses S. Grant (who was actually from the Midwest) led the Union forces to victory over the Confederacy in 1864–65. As US president, Grant fiercely supported the Radical Reconstruction policy that imposed martial law, thus allowing the South to get back on its feet without falling into total anarchy. His name was for a whole generation on the lips of every family in the states readmitted to the Union, amongst which are those – Tennessee, Mississippi, Florida – where authors have set new versions of the *Odyssey*. The near-mythic status of the Civil War has become a substitute for the legendary Trojan War.

The earliest Deep South *Odyssey* was Jon Amiel's *Sommersby* (1993), set in Tennessee, the first state to be re-admitted to the Union in 1866. Richard Gere stars as Horace Townsend, who assumes the identity of the deceased Jack Sommersby. Horace knew the dead man intimately, and since he bears a visual resemblance to him, he returns in his place to his wife and son after the Civil War. The movie divided audiences, partly because Townsend's altruistic decision to die at the end fails to persuade, but much of it is powerful and filmed with careful realism. It conveys the desperate situation at the end of the war; there are marauding Confederate soldiers, failed crops, newly liberated but destitute blacks, derelict buildings and grim scenes in the gaol.

The wanderings end with the opening credits, during which the figure of a man – Townsend/Sommersby – is seen trampling through snow and sun. Jack Sommersby's estate has been looted and the Penelope figure Laurel Sommersby (Jodie Foster) is virtually destitute, living on in a dilapidated grand house. The whole community, white and black alike, is starving. The Eumaeus figure is Joseph, a former slave, now a share-cropper, who loyally supports the man he thinks is his former master; Eurycleia is represented by Jack's nanny, a freed slave. The suitor is a Bible-punching minister, played with menace by Jack Pullman, and the showdown between the rivals for Penelope takes place in her rundown barn. The genesis of *Sommersby* can partly explain the poverty of the context in which it is located, since it was conceived as a remake of Daniel Vigne's famous film *Le Retour de Martin Guerre* (1982), set in a sixteenth-century French peasant community.[18] Indeed, *Sommersby* was also written by Vigne in collaboration with Jean-Claude Carrière, screenplay writer for *Martin Guerre*, who regarded the former as a straightforward adaptation of the latter.[19] Between the two films, Carrière had worked with Peter Brook on *The Mahabharata*, learning much about epic convention and its transference to dramatic form.[20]

The relationship of *Sommersby* to the *Odyssey* is explicit: the impostor hero, a former Classics teacher, is given two scenes in which he reads from Homer to the Telemachus figure, Little Rob. He is also forced to kill the household dog, who of course does not recognize him, in a poignant rewriting of the Argos scene with which this chapter began. In the French prototype, the connection with the *Odyssey* constitutes a set of parallels rather than provable influence, although the screenplay writers will have been aware that the judge involved in the case, Jean de Coras, had explicitly compared the couple involved with Odysseus and Penelope.[21] Arnaud de Tihl (Gérard Depardieu) did exist, and did pretend to be the long-lost husband of Bertrande de Rols. In evoking peasant culture, Vigne and Carrière had a novel and historical documents on which to draw, as well as the expertise of a Princeton scholar.[22] Even the breeds of livestock farmed at the time were researched. But the parallels with the *Odyssey* had been noticed, and were elaborated by the time Odysseus – and Arnaud de Tihl – found themselves transplanted to Tennessee.

A similar context to that of *Sommersby* underlies Anthony Minghella's *Cold Mountain* (2003), adapted from Charles Frazier's novel of the same name. It is, again, the end of the Civil War, and a destitute soldier is returning, although this Odysseus, a carpenter called Inman (Jude Law), is no impostor. The state is not Tennessee but the town of Cold Mountain in North Carolina. Here the Penelope figure, Ada Monroe (Nicole Kidman), moves with her ageing preacher father. The class focus of the film emerges less in the romance between the educated Ada and the artisan Inman than in the redemption Ada finds through physical labour and friendship with the lowest-class person in the area, Ruby Thewes. The connection with the *Odyssey* is more explicit in the novel, in the opening hospital sequence of which Inman meets one man who has tried to learn Greek and another who is blind.[23] Meanwhile, Ada is reading Homer's poem to Ruby while she awaits Inman's return, after 'filling Ruby in on who the Greeks were' (in the film the book is changed into a Jane Austen novel). Frazier imagines how the uneducated Ruby would have reacted. 'She had grown impatient with Penelope, but she would sit of a long evening and laugh and laugh at the tribulations of Odysseus, all the stones the gods threw in his pathway.' But as the daughter of a liar, Ruby was suspicious of Odysseus:

> she found his alibis for stretching out his trip to be suspect in the extreme, an opinion only confirmed by the current passage in which the characters were denned up in a swineherd's hut drinking and telling tales. She concluded that, all in all, not much had altered in the way of things despite the passage of a great volume of time.[24]

Frazier here signals the importance of the least aristocratic scene in the whole *Odyssey*, the storytelling in Eumaeus' lowly hut, but he makes his Eumaeus equivalent, Ruby Thewes, articulate the premise of his approach to the mythic undertext – that human nature does not change much at all.

The best *Odyssey* movie set in the American South is the least well known: it is *Ulee's Gold* (1997), written and directed by Victor Nunez. Here the war that has scarred the hero is Vietnam; Ulee Jackson (Peter Fonda) lost all his friends in combat. The location this time is the Florida panhandle of the tupelo swamplands, where Ulee ekes out a livelihood from his ancestral trade of beekeeping. Nunez's camera focuses on Ulee as he performs backbreaking daily chores – working at the hives, repairing wooden crates and moving barrels of honey. In a sense this Odysseus is more of a Laertes, retired to his small-holding, especially since his wife Penelope died several years ago. Ulee struggles to raise his granddaughters, Casey and Penny, abandoned to his care after his daughter-in-law – Helen – vanished two years previously (she is hooked on heroin and staying with lowlife criminals in Orlando). Their father, Ulee's son Jimmy, is in prison serving a sentence for armed robbery after taking to crime during his father's absences. There is a confrontation between Ulee and the criminals, who take a suitor-like role in invading his house and taking the womenfolk captive. Ulee finally rouses himself from his depression and takes violent action to save his family. The film realistically evokes a deprived family, and the realism is not compromised by the mythic authority lent by the parallel with the *Odyssey*.

Tennessee, North Carolina, Florida – in *O Brother, Where Art Thou?* (2000), the Coen brothers' comic take on the *Odyssey*, the hero is from the Deep South, 1930s Mississippi, during the Great Depression. Indeed, the title of the film is taken from Preston Sturges's *Sullivan's Travels* (1941), a movie within which a director named John Sullivan is attempting to make a truthful film account of contemporary social deprivation. Its title is *O Brother, Where Art Thou?* The Coen brothers' heroes reveal their lowly status by opening the movie on the run from a prison work detail: they are Everett Ulysses McGill (George Clooney), Pete (John Turturro) and Delmar (Tim Blake Nelson). Tiresias is a blind black railroad worker; the Eumaeus figure (Mr Hogwallop) is so poor that he serves his visitors horse meat; the *nekuia* is represented by the black guitarist who has sold his soul to the devil in return for the gift of music; the Cyclops' lair becomes a terrifying meeting of the Ku Klux Klan; Poseidon is downgraded to the status of a power-mad local sheriff.

Another darkly comic work is the bizarre *Cannibal: The Musical!*, which uses the *Odyssey* as a framework for its retelling of the true story of Alferd (sic) Packer, a former Union soldier who was involved in the death of some miners in Colorado and convicted of cannibalism. *Cannibal* is itself a stage version of a movie made in 1993 by Trey Parker (creator of

*South Park*), entitled *Packer: The Musical!* The material from the *Odyssey* includes the Cyclops (represented by a Confederate soldier) and the Sirens (Francophone lesbian Indians), while the overall ambience suggests drop-outs and losers, living off their wits in a provincial outback. Class issues could not be more prominent than in Toni Morrison's quest novel *The Song of Solomon*, first published in 1977. Circe is an ex-slave living on in the decaying mansion of her deceased masters. She helps the wanderer Milkman Dead metamorphose from a thuggish narcissist into a sensitive man. Expert healer, midwife and benefactor of stray animals, she helps Milkman Dead find his father's grave and discover his own ancestry, just as the Homeric Circe tells Odysseus how to conjure up the dead. This benevolent servile-class Circe has devoted her life to avenging slavery.[25]

One recent film that reworks material from the *Odyssey* in an American lower-class context, but without invoking the Civil War, is the German Wim Wenders' *Don't Come Knocking* (2005). It was immediately linked with the *Odyssey*,[26] a poem whose evocation of landscape had been praised by Wenders in a speech delivered in 2003.[27] His obsession with the *Odyssey*'s poet was already apparent in the old storyteller, actually named Homer, in the Berlin of his *Der Himmel über Berlin* (1987, usually known outside Germany as *Wings of Desire*). Wenders's Homer 'is the representative and bearer of collective memory, the spirit of history. He is also the spirit of Berlin, who laments the vanishing of the city in the war.'[28] But *Don't Come Knocking*, written by and starring Sam Shepard, is ironically informed by the story pattern of the *Odyssey*. This Odysseus has fallen on hard times. A former star in Westerns, at the age of 60 he has only drugs, booze and sex to help him face his declining career. After yet another debauched night in his trailer, he gallops away from the film set in his cowboy costume to rediscover his soul.

He gradually loses his movie star identity, acquiring the clothes of a ranch hand and taking the most demotic form of transport – the Greyhound – to his hometown in Elko, Nevada. After an odyssey that takes him from his ancient mother's house to seedy bars and a crummy casino, he ends up in a drunken fistfight with another dropout (like Odysseus fighting Irus), collapses in the gutter and spends a night in a drying-out cell. Learning that he has a child in a depressed Montana ghost town, he tracks down his ex-lover and his son. This is only the first part of the plot, which adds another child and Howard's desperate attempts to put his family life into a semblance of order. But the search for self, roots and family after discovering the hollowness of success in 'heroic' roles is a typical Wenders take on a familiar story, echoing the epic pleasure in

travelling through vast American landscapes central to his earlier collaboration with Shepard in *Paris, Texas* (1984), but in a manner both darker
and more amusing.

*Don't Come Knocking* shares with the British example, *Naked* (1993), its
cinematic luxuriance in the habits and residences of the lowest echelons
of society. *Naked*'s director, Mike Leigh, is himself a Northerner, born in
Salford, Lancashire, of Russian emigrant grand-parentage. First known
as an experimental theatre director, he began to make powerful films
about working-class life. In *Naked*, Johnny (David Thewlis) is a Mancunian drifter who, apparently after committing a violent rape, steals a car
and drives to London. He heads for the home of his old girlfriend Louise.
She now works as an office clerk in London, and for the purposes of the
film the 'home' represented throughout is her rented flat.

The film examines inner city decay and the poverty-stricken underbelly of the Thatcher years, but since its release has been linked by critics
with the *Odyssey*. This is a result not of any statement by the director,
nor any mention of such a parallel in the publicity literature. Indeed, the
*intention* of such a parallel would be difficult to prove, since Mike Leigh's
actors often improvise their own lines, a technique of scene development
in which Thewlis's skill is legendary. Yet the oral, improvisational quality
of the film's dialogue, spoken in strong Mancunian over rippling harp
music, is suggestive of the way that the *Odyssey* and such epics were originally composed and performed. This conclusion becomes almost impossible to avoid during the encounter between Johnny and the waitress. She
takes him to the flat she is 'sitting' while its owners are away. The sitting
room is littered with Greek souvenirs, statuettes of gods and hoplites, and
translations of Greek authors including a copy of E.V. Rieu's bestselling
Penguin Classic translation of the *Odyssey*, which Johnny brandishes at
his reluctant hostess. Of the owner of the flat Johnny enquires, mock-
ingly, 'Is he a Homer-sexual, yeah?', and later comments that he doesn't
want 'to sound Homer-phobic', before emphasizing that he likes the *Iliad*
and the *Odyssey*, what with Achilles, 'the wooden horse, Helen of Troy ...
Cyclops'.

Once this intertextual allusion has been made, Johnny's violent past,
his habitual wandering, his serial encounters with weird individuals, and
the constant deferral of domestic closure with his woman begin to resemble a contemporary version of the *Odyssey*, where the monsters and villains
are poverty, unemployment and existential despair. Johnny is a knowing
protagonist, and his references to philosophical questions or literary allusions create a collusive bond between him and the viewer. Thus after his

attempt at dialogue with the foul-mouthed young Scot, Archie, he tells
Archie's girlfriend Maggie that Archie has a wonderful way 'with Socratic
debate'. All this is delivered in a stream of deadpan irony.

While waiting for Louise to come home from work, he has sex with the
temporary lodger, Sophie, a Goth drug addict sporting a Siren-like bird
tattoo. She spends much of the movie trying to regain his sexual attention again, frustrated by his deep emotional bond with Louise. She thus
synthesizes Siren, lotus-eater, Circe and Calypso. Johnny subsequently
leaves the flat after an unsuccessful encounter with Louise, and wanders
off into the night, a new member of the London homeless. A night security guard, Brian, kindly offers him shelter; like Eumaeus, he has tumbled
far down the social scale. He has his own mini-*Odyssey* to reveal, when it
turns out that his wife, whom he has not seen for 13 years, is thousands of
miles away in Bangkok. They watch a woman dancing through a window
in a house opposite the offices, and Johnny visits her. He cools off when he
sees the tattoo on *her* shoulder – a skull and crossbones. She reminds him
not only of his mother, but of his *dead* mother, and of death.

Johnny's sex scenes are intercut with episodes involving the other male
lead. Jeremy, an upper-class sadist, represents the worst aspects of the
suitors. Indeed, he moves in to Louise's flat and extracts brutal sex from
Sophie by pretending to be the landlord. Meanwhile Johnny, after being
mugged, turns up at the flat. The scene is set for what should be the showdown in which Johnny, loved by both women, discovers his inner hero and
ousts the rival. In Mike Leigh's universe, however, there is no such thing
as a traditional male hero, and Johnny fails miserably. He suffers blows to
the head, resulting in a fit, regresses into a childlike state and is humiliated. It is the marvellous Louise whose raw courage and psychological
cunning drive Jeremy away.

The film is Leigh's most Existentialist work, and Johnny is a working-
class philosopher with traits inherited from Sartre as well as Homer and
John Osborne. The questions Johnny raises include the existence of god,
the imminent demise of the human race and the impossibility of reincarnation. The film is an account of Johnny's quest for meaning. His enemy
is boredom (unemployed and working class, he comments wryly on how
much training is required for manual tasks). His failure to deal with his
emotional past, symbolized by the hooligan who daubs 'cancelled' signs
over adverts reading 'Therapy', means that he is *psychologically* more 'on
the run' than any other cinematic Odysseus. He left Louise because he
thought she was pregnant; in the opening scene, he symbolically throws
away a toddler's pushchair. At the end, Johnny and Louise tenderly sing

together a song about going back up North, concluding with the lines: 'I don't want to roam,/I want to get back home,/To rainy Manchester.' But their reunion proves fleeting because Johnny staggers off again at the film's conclusion to life as a London vagrant.

A more light-hearted story told with gritty urban realism is the Dutch movie made for television *Bijlmer Odyssee* (2004), certainly inspired by Leigh's film and yet more explicit in its debt to the epic. It is set in a low-income high-rise housing estate on the outskirts of Amsterdam. Two young lovers lose each other in labyrinthine blocks of flats and undergo comical adventures before being reunited in a happy ending that contrasts sharply with Leigh's alienation of Johnny from Louise.

Homer has been able to transcend class barriers because people of all social classes, at least at times, have had access to him. In recent decades this has been through the films connected with the *Odyssey*, but the history goes back further than cinema. Victorian popular theatre, which attracted a cross-class audience, enjoyed light entertainments based on the *Odyssey*, such as Burnand's *Patient Penelope* (Strand Theatre, 1863).[29] Homer, as well as Dante and Shakespeare, was read by nineteenth-century African-American literary societies.[30] Jonathan Rose's brilliant history of the reading habits of the British working class (2001) has drawn attention to the excitement that many people have experienced when they began to read Homer in translation – the thrill of imaginative discovery. There could be no better way to conclude this chapter than with the words of an autodidactic stonemason called Hugh Miller (born in 1802), who recalled his childhood pleasure in reading Pope's translations: 'Old Homer wrote admirably for little folk, especially in the *Odyssey* ... I saw, even at this immature period, that no other writer could cast a javelin with half the force of Homer. The missiles went whizzing athwart his pages.'[31]

# PART III
# MIND AND PSYCHE

# 11

# BRAIN POWER

The human being is the most helpless thing produced by the earth ... For as long as the gods give him courage and plant vigour in his limbs, he thinks that he will never come to any harm in the future; when the blessed gods do indeed bring grief upon him, he has to bear it, reluctantly, but with endurance (*Odyssey* 18.130–7).

W hen Odysseus expresses this metaphysical opinion, he is still dressed in rags. He anticipates by centuries the canonical figures of the shabby philosopher (Socrates, Diogenes) and the sage of low-class origins (Aesop). The *Odyssey* and philosophy have been inseparable since antiquity, partly because the Platonic tradition built Homer up as a semi-divine wise man, a tendency encouraged by epic episodes dealing with song. It was god who made Demodocus able to offer delight, 'however his heart might impel him to sing' (8.44–5). This passage was felt to imply the power of the bard's mind to move in space and time, assisted by the Sirens who 'know all that happens on the rich earth' (12.191), partakers in the supernatural power of the bard's mind to transcend normal limitations of time and place.

The Homer scholar Heraclitus insisted that beneath the mythical stories lurked 'Homer's philosophical mind' (*Homeric Problems* 26.3),[1] and Montaigne saw Homer as the highest philosophical authoriy.[2] But it was Odysseus himself that the twelfth-century Byzantine bishop Eustathius called 'The Philosopher'.[3] Odysseus negotiates a compromise between curiosity (travel for the sake of it) and *applied* intelligence geared to the achievement of identified goals. This tension is expressed in the Sirens episode, where Odysseus both acquires knowledge for its own sake (there is no actual need for him to hear their song) and protects his own safety and his men's. The solution is technological – wax ear-stoppers and bonds attached to the mast. Here Odysseus becomes a model even for scientific inventiveness. There are still a few intelligent heroes today. James Bond can extricate himself from danger by using his brain as well as his brawn

– scientific knowledge in addition to his weapons arsenal. But cerebral powers are more likely to be split off and allocated to a member of a team, such as Mr Spock in *Star Trek*, or to a friendly robot.

Marina Warner laments that we have forgotten the role model of the trickster,[4] and it is true that the intellectual Odysseus did not get a good press in the twentieth century. In Homer's epic, however, only once does Odysseus allow uncontrolled curiosity to get the better of him, when he crosses from the Island of Goats to the Cyclopes' land (9.166–76). As the wily hero, beloved of Athena, the goddess of applied technology and strategic planning (see Fig. 11), Odysseus always attracted the attention of those seeking to define cerebral activity. Wordsworth was thinking of Odysseus when he described a statue of Isaac Newton as 'The marble index of a mind for ever/Voyaging through strange seas of Thought, alone'.[5] Even Everett Ulysses McGill, the con-artist hero of the Coen brothers' movie 'based on the *Odyssey* by Homer', *O Brother, Where Art Thou?* (2000), argues he should lead his fellow escaped convicts, since that honour should go to 'the one with the capacity for abstract thought'. The philosophical quality of the *Odyssey* was underscored by the sententious pet serpent in Eden Phillpotts's novella *Circe's Island*; he has no interest in how long travel may take, 'since time and space are only relative values of no signification'.[6] Odyssean intellectualism was also parodied in Jean Giraudoux's novel *Elpénor* (1919), especially in the reworking of the Cyclops sequence; the blinding fails because Polyphemus asks his father to restore his sight, and Ulysses has to work out how to subdue not his body but his mind. Giraudoux's annoying Ulysses then inflicts on Polyphemus a philosophical workout: he has no proof that the Cyclops actually exists, since he can only be certain of his own existence, and all else could simply be appearance.

Odysseus convinces Polyphemus that everything he can perceive by his senses, including the Greeks, is an image created by his imagination. Since neither space nor time exists, he can release these figments. In the final scenes of the encounter, Ulysses boasts that Polyphemus has lost 'every comfort of your shepherd's life, for where Greeks have worked on a soul no fresh grass ever grows again'. The Cyclops' encounter with the Cartesian ego, with philosophical solipsism, and with Western rational argumentation, has wrecked him forever. In Giraudoux's novel the Cyclops proves Ulysses wrong by rediscovering colour, taste and sensual joy in his surroundings.[7] But the tragic undertow remains present in the implied corruption of colonial subjects' relationship with their environment – their alienation – under the influence of Western intellectualism.

The central action of the *Odyssey* also underlies a trajectory in German philosophy focused on the concept of *Heimat*. Its meaning oscillates between 'home' and 'homeland' and yet means neither precisely; originally a legal concept, it became a political one in the eighteenth century. It has come under suspicion because of its elision by Nazi ideologues with the ideas of *Lebensraum* and the German nationalist cult of regionalism, but it also has a philosophical resonance that transcends nationalities and can help explain the intellectual stamina of the *Odyssey*.[8] It was the German Romantic poet and thinker Novalis (Friedrich von Hardenburg) who first defined all philosophy as homesickness, in a reflective fragment dating from notes he made in the winter of 1798–99: 'Philosophie ist eigentlich Heimweh, ein Trieb, überall zu Hause zu sein' (Philosophy is really homesickness, an urge to be at home everywhere).[9]

For Heidegger, in his seminal lecture 'The Origin of the Work of Art' (1936), *Heimat* is a mystical entity bound to locality. Yet *Heimat*, for Heidegger, only exists from the perspective of one who has already lost it, and becomes therefore the domain of poetry: everything that great poets say is viewed from the perspective of homesickness and is summoned into language by pain. Heidegger's poetic *Heimat* is thus the melancholy recollection of a lost aspect of life;[10] a more upbeat version of this view of home-as-art is caught in Borges's poem 'Ars Poetica' (1960):

They tell how Ulysses, glutted with wonders,
Wept with love to descry his Ithaca
Humble and green. Art is that Ithaca
Of green eternity, not of wonders.[11]

When the Jewish philosopher Emmanuel Lévinas meditated on *Heimat*, he drew a distinction between two types of exilic experience. The work of the human subject 'is in essence a movement of the Same toward the Other that never returns to the Same. To the myth of Ulysses returning to Ithaca, I would oppose the history of Abraham leaving his country forever for an unknown land, and forbidding his servant to lead even his son back to this point of departure.'[12] Ulysses repudiates openness to new experiences and cultural difference. After Lévinas's onslaught, it took Gadamer's radical critical theory to recuperate Odysseus for the spirit of open-ended enquiry: instead of art's object, he argued that *Heimat* could be seen as a conceptual *instrument* for understanding aesthetic experience. When we read a text or look at an image, we leave the realm of the familiar and must find anew the security of understanding. Consequently, gaining new insights can be described as the event of homecoming.[13]

The *Odyssey* also caused a significant difference of opinion in German philosophy after the Second World War, when Adorno and Horkheimer in *The Dialectic of Enlightenment* had identified this epic as the founding text of imperialism, capitalism and fascism (see Chapter 7). The *Odyssey* was not rehabilitated for the Left until *Principle of Hope* was published in 1952–59 by Ernst Bloch, the Marxist thinker who developed the notion of humanity's capacity for utopian thinking, and our drive to transcend the limitations imposed by any particular phase of society, through a longing for an imaginary community where such repressions do not apply. Bloch argued that the wanderer Odysseus symbolized man's questing, utopian impulse. This discussion appears under the subheading 'Wishful images of the fulfilled moment', which captures Bloch's conception of myth as a clue to the perfected social order for which man universally longs. Any desired mythical destination, Ithaca or otherwise, is thus, philosophically speaking, 'a hypostatized utopia'.[14]

The intellectual nature of the original homecoming poem reflects its composition in centuries when the ancient Greeks still used myth to answer mental problems, for they had not yet invented the self-conscious art of philosophical enquiry that emerged in the fifth century BCE. Yet cognitive processes are addressed more emphatically in the *Odyssey* than in other archaic poetry. The poem's interest in shape-shifting means that objects of perception are often 'on the verge of being distorted or disappearing',[15] and its domestic contexts, unlike the battlefields of the *Iliad*, are characterized by physical intimacy and peering closely, which leads to examining the nature of things; the nurse notices the scar and recognizes the man (19.468); the dog notices his master and dies (17.326–7).[16] Scrutiny, inductive reasoning, and drawing inferences from the particular to the general are characteristics of the *Odyssey*'s mental landscape.

When the Greeks did invent formal philosophy, categories of question emerged that are still addressed by philosophers today: how should we live? (ethics), what is being? (ontology, which later became a branch of metaphysics), and how do we know things? (epistemology). But the *Odyssey* had already explored all three questions and contains such a pronounced philosophical element that when Forrest Cookson, former president of the American Chamber of Commerce, defined what he saw as the difference between Western deductive and Islamic inductive modes of philosophical reasoning, he based his claim on the *Odyssey* and Joyce's *Ulysses*.[17] In the English-speaking world Odysseus/Ulysses' reputation as philosopher was made in 1604, with the first production of Shakespeare's *Troilus and Cressida*, in Act I.iii of which Ulysses delivers a superb oration justifying what we would call the class system. His reactionary political theory legitimizes 'The primogenity and due of birth,/Prerogative of age, crowns, sceptres, laurels', through spectacular comparisons with the natural world.

Here Ulysses shows himself not only a superb rhetorician, but a clear-thinking political theorist. Political theory was one of the earliest branches of philosophical ethics, and indeed it has recently been argued that the underlying political argument of the *Odyssey* needs more attention.[18] Rutherford (1986) has also shown how the *Odyssey* serially presents its audience with ethical dilemmas. As early as the fifth century BCE, moreover, the founder of the Cynic school of philosophers, Antisthenes, promoted Odysseus as a moral *exemplum* of the sage. The imperial Roman letters attributed to the Cynics use Ulysses in rags as the incarnation of the austerity they advocated.[19] The Stoics, influenced by the Cynics, also saw the much-enduring hero as a model of morality.[20]

Plutarch's *Gryllus* stages a conversation between Odysseus, Circe and Gryllus, transformed into a pig and reluctant to be changed back into a man. The dialogue reminds the reader of a Platonic enquiry. Gryllus ('Grunter') argues that he and his fellow beasts are correct in preferring their present existence.[21] He achieves an impressive defence of zoomorphic being. Beasts are more courageous because they fight without guile (987e). Female beasts are braver than female humans. Animals are more temperate and do not desire material possessions; animals have no need for perfumes; animals do not deceptively commit adultery; animals do not have sex except in order to procreate and do not practise homosexuality or sex outside their species (which Gryllus contrasts with the human deviants who practise zoophilia); animals stick to simple diets, have the right amount of intelligence for their natural conditions of life and therefore must be credited with rationality. The life of the animal as defined by Gryllus indeed, resembles the life of an ascetic philosopher; here Plutarch is turning on its head for comic effect the entire tradition of philosophizing the *Odyssey* ethically.

The portrayal of dynastic rule in Monteverdi's *Il ritorno d'Ulisse* marked a new turn in the musical expression of ethical and political theory. Ulisse is no symbol of ideal monarchy, endowed with divine gifts. Rather, he combines 'the shrewdness of the con man with the lofty goals of the epic hero ... a musical sketch of Machiavelli's ideal prince', his realm 'the historical world of mutability and interdependence'.[22] Other post-Renaissance political theorists have also found the *Odyssey* useful, including John Locke (see p 91) and Spinoza in his *Political Treatise* (1677), which argues that the laws of a nation should not be subject to arbitrary alteration by its monarch. The laws should be considered the king's 'eternal decrees', which render null and void any individual command of his that subverts them. A king's ministers are thus being obedient to a king if they obey his laws, even when he commands them to break them (Chapter 7, section 1): the example he offers is Ulysses' order to his comrades to untie him when he is captivated by the Sirens' song.[23]

The despotic image of the unaccountable French monarchy also lurks behind Voltaire's *Candide* (1759). The novel engages in a constant counterpoint with the *Odyssey*, and in Chapter 25 Candide admires the copy of Homer he discovers in the Venetian aristocrat's library.[24] Yet Candide's wanderings are not those of a resourceful man, for he is an innocent abroad, a 'hero of truly monumental ineptitude'.[25] Voltaire's Candide, desperate to return to his mistress Cunégonde, is convinced of the truth of Leibniz's philosophical doctrine of optimism as propounded by his mentor Pangloss. En route he encounters the Phaeacia-like, utopian province of El Dorado as well as menacing examples of excessive religious zeal – unchristian Benedictines, Franciscans and Jesuits. But Candide's philosophical views are ridiculed as much as religious extremism. As his doubts set in, and he begins to wonder whether what he sees around him can really be Leibniz's 'best of all possible worlds', Voltaire dismantles contemporary philosophical speculations. It was a satirical touch to do this by inspecting them from the perspective of an innocent.

In his *Odyssey*-inspired travelogue, Voltaire also took the opportunity, through the naive Candide's expectation that all men, being equal, should be treated as such, to attack the hierarchies of feudal France and its monarchy. But Homeric epic was far more often seen as monarchist in sympathy, and usually adopted by those wishing to argue *against* republics and radical democracies.[26] It was only in the early twentieth century that the *Odyssey* began to be used to make more progressive political points in fiction, poetry and theatre, a tendency exemplified in Kafka's story *Poseidon*. Here even the sea-god's administration of the waters becomes oppressive, white-collar bureaucratic labour, required by the imperial/capitalist institutional apparatus.[27] Another example is Tony Hoagland's poem 'In the Land of the Lotus Eaters' (1993), where man-pigs, Sirens' songs and blind archery become symbols for a brutal Western society which manufactures arms but deludes itself into forgetting the pain suffered by the rest of the world.[28]

With Odysseus' rejection of Calypso's offer of immortality the poem marks its status as a *metaphysical* text, concerned with the world beyond the limitations of the human lifespan. The idea of the immortal female who can offer the canny male traveller the secret of eternal life has proved durable. The most famous example is Ayesha in Rider Haggard's *She* (1887). Ayesha is partly a conduit for Haggard's fascination with the Aryanist theosophy of his contemporary Madame Blavatsky, an occultist and esoteric philosopher. But the archetypal female in whose mould Ayesha is cast is from the *Odyssey*, an epic to which Haggard wrote a sequel, *The World's Desire* (see pp 192–3). The influence exerted by Haggard's Ayesha extended to Freud, who was struck by her offer of an *eros* that promised to transcend *thanatos*, as well as her identity as she who must be obeyed – and destroyed.[29] Freud uses *She* in *The Interpretation of Dreams* to decode his own dream about the interior of the maternal body.[30] Not to be outdone, Jung's seminars of 1925 illustrated the concept of the *anima* by a reading of the symbolism in *She*, which Jung associated with cases 'of men returning from the colonies after long association with native women'.[31]

Haggard's Ayesha has lived for 2,000 years in her African cave, the 'womb of the Earth'.[32] Another admirer of *She* – as he was of the *Odyssey* – was C.S. Lewis. He was impressed with the power of Ayesha (who he felt embodied an 'authentic' mythic quality) to bestow on her human lover the 'wild, transporting ... forbidden hope' of 'immortality in the flesh'.[33] A fourth important fan was J.R.R. Tolkien, who learned much about the art of storytelling from the device of the polyglot potsherd with which *She* opens.[34] It is in this totemic object, passed down through many generations, that Haggard reveals his intuition that classical texts can help create the allure necessary to bestselling fiction.[35]

*She* was made into a movie starring Ursula Andress and directed by Robert Day in 1965, two years after the link between beauty, myth and immortality had been made in a film more directly dependent upon the *Odyssey*, Godard's *Le Mépris* (*Contempt*, 1963). Here the hope is for the deathlessness bestowed on the makers of an enduring artwork. In the extended scene in the projection room, there is a focus on the existential status – ontology – of stories, texts, images and movies. The view that 'Homer's *Odyssey* is an ontological adventure, an attempt to show the ultimate nature, order and essence of reality', is one with which most commentators would agree,[36] although few except Godard have documented. Yet his Lang and Prokosch ask how the *Odyssey* – which exists in language – can continue to 'be' the *Odyssey* if presented in the moving pictures of cinema?

The hero of the *Odyssey*, by rejecting immortality, comes to understand mortal existence. This was the reason why his journey through physical space came, early in the history of philosophy, to be understood allegorically as the journey across time – the journey of consciousness each of us embarks on at birth. In a modern updating of the allegorical reading of the *Odyssey* as psychic biography, 'Ulysses, Too, Was Sometimes Down at Heart', Marvin Bell even reads it as the experience of a man undergoing periods of psychological illness, negotiating in his ship the twin perils undergone by every individual suffering from manic depression.[37] But whenever any of us thinks in terms of a 'personal odyssey', we are placing ourselves in a tradition that goes back certainly as far as Plato, and probably earlier. In the last book of the *Republic*, Odysseus becomes both model and example in the Myth of Er (10.614b–621d), which is patterned on the *nekuia* in Book 11 of the *Odyssey* and carries metaphysical implications in its vision of the workings of the universe beyond human cognitive powers.

Er dies in battle and his soul departs his body, before returning to life and telling what had happened to him. He describes the judgement of the souls of the departed in an aperture between the Underworld and heaven. The process continues for a thousand years before the souls are reincarnated. Er then tells of the planetary system of the cosmos, the spindle of Necessity, and her daughters, the Fates, spinning out destinies: one of them, Lachesis, told all the souls to choose a lot of a life. Ajax chose to become a lion, and Thersites a monkey, but Odysseus chose the life of a private man to whom nothing much happens – a more powerful statement of his preference for mortality with the middle-aged Penelope to deathlessness with Calypso. Plato had learned from Homer that myth could be a useful vehicle for examining metaphysical subjects inaccessible to the senses and the intellect, such as the nature of the soul and the distant past and future.[38] It has been argued that the *Odyssey* journeys, above all the 'shamanistic' pattern exhibited in the journey to the Underworld, underlie all Plato's cosmological dialogues – the *Phaedrus* as well as the *Timaeus* and *Critias*.[39]

Even before Plato, the early Pythagorean philosophers, whose doctrines included reincarnation, developed an allegorical interpretation of the *Odyssey* which encompassed epistemology and metaphysics as well as the abstemious ethics propounded by the Cynic/Stoic tradition. An echo of their allegorizing method can be heard in Plutarch's *Sympotic Questions*, where the topic is the Sirens.[40] The Pythagoreans argued that their music represented the unearthly bliss that the soul seeks after death, and that even during mortal existence a few souls who have overcome carnal appetites can hear, however faintly. It is hard to overestimate the importance of such allegory to the status of the *Odyssey* amongst philosophers and

its susceptibility to providing polysemic symbols to future generations of
poets.

The tradition came to a climax with Neoplatonism, which fused the
study of Plato with Pythagorean readings of Homer, and had an ines-
timable impact on Christian ideas.[41] Plotinus, the 'father of Neoplatonism' in the third century CE, suggested that Odysseus' desire to go to
his beloved homeland and away from Circe and Calpyso, despite their
charms, is Homer saying 'with a hidden meaning' (*ainittomenos*) that man
needs to return to his spiritual fatherland, tearing himself away from the
beautiful sensory world. Ithaca thus metaphorically represents union with
the divine.[42] Another Neoplatonist, Porphyry, wrote the most dazzling
allegory of the *Odyssey* in his treatise *On the Cave of the Nymphs*, which
begins by quoting the description of the Ithacan cave in which Athena
tells Odysseus to hide his goods (*Odyssey* 13.102–12). This cave is an allegory, according to Porphyry, of the physical universe – it is lovely but it
is also murky. The olive tree represents the divine wisdom that informs
the universe and yet is separate from it. When Athena tells Odysseus
to hide his goods in the cave, Homer is saying that we need to lay aside
our outward possessions in order to think about how to cut away all the
destructive passions of the soul.

There were many more Neoplatonic allegories of the *Odyssey*: Calypso,
whose name comes from a root verb *kaluptein* ('conceal'), stands for our
body, which is the fleshly envelope of the soul. She retains Odysseus as
the flesh fetters man; her island is encircled by water and planted with
trees because the body has liquid flowing round it and is made of a matter
similar to wood.[43] In the fifth century CE the Neoplatonist systematizer
Proclus, whose work influenced Islamic thought as much as Christian
concepts, stressed that Ithaca represents the metaphysical destination at
which any philosophical person is striving to arrive. The soul thus goes on
*an epistemological odyssey* as it passes through the successive stages by which
knowledge is attained – sensations, images, opinions, sciences, discur-
sive reasoning, to pure Intellect. The allegorical approach to the *Odyssey*
as inherited from the Neoplatonists also dominated its Renaissance and
Early Modern reception at least until Giambattista Vico.[44]

When it comes to that third major branch of philosophy, epistemology,
it was originally through the problem posed by disguise and recognition
that the poem expresses its fascination with the problem of acquiring true
knowledge. As if to remind the listener that appearances can be deceptive,
it is in disguise as Mentes that Athena tells Telemachus that he bears a
startling resemblance to Odysseus (1.208–9); Telemachus' glum response is

to question another possible source of knowledge – information imparted verbally: he says that he has no way of knowing for certain who his father is, whatever his mother may say (1.215–16).

As early as the fifth century BCE, the poet Pindar and the historian Herodotus used Homer when drawing distinctions between truthful reportage and exaggeration or fable; Herodotus is adamant that Homer knew the truth about Helen of Troy (that she had spent the war in Egypt), but that he had rejected the truth as inappropriate to his poetic purpose (2.112–20).[45] The *Odyssey* fascinated Aristotle, who wrote a book devoted to Homer, his *Homeric Questions*.[46] In this he examined the internal rules which governed the world of myth and the world of empirically discernible reality: to the question of how a god (Poseidon) and a sea nymph produced a one-eyed giant child (Polyphemus), the answer is given that although this is an impossible occurrence in the world of reality, myth does not follow the same rules: other mythical figures produced children biologically unlike themselves. Scientific intellectual muscles are also being flexed when Aristotle suggests that the seven flocks of 50 cattle belonging to Helios represented the solar days of the lunar year.[47]

The *Odyssey* holds an honoured place in the logician Gottlob Frege's most influential paper on the philosophy of language, *On Sense and Reference* ('Über Sinn und Bedeutung', 1892). When drawing his crucial distinction between sense and reference, Frege looked for an example of a sentence that contains a name that has never had any real-world bearer. Assuming, with a logician's ruthlessness, that there is not (and never was and never will be) any such person as Odysseus, Frege took as a key example a sentence from the *Odyssey*: 'Odysseus was set ashore at Ithaca still sound asleep' (13.116–21). Frege asserted that such a sentence fails to be true or false: it has a sense that we can understand, but no reference in the real world.[48] This led Frege to conclude that the reference of a sentence is its truth-value: he stated that the True and the False are objects, and that all sentences either name one of these two objects, or else they are names that fail to name anything. He concluded that we ought to invent a special term for verbal signs like 'Odysseus' that only have a sense, and not an actual object of reference.[49]

The connection between truth, falsehood and the *Odyssey* took on a more dangerous form when Paul Rassinier appropriated the epic hero as the archetypal liar. Rassinier, a survivor of Buchenwald and Dora concentration camps, always decried the brutality he had seen, and had his health broken by the experience. He nevertheless maintained in a strident stream of books including *The Lies of Odysseus* (1951) and *Ulysses Betrayed by His Own* (1960) that the Holocaust itself was a fabrication (he was not Jewish).[50] He claimed that his titles were inspired by something a Czech fellow-inmate at Buchenwald had said to him:

> You have to reckon with the complex of Ulysses' lie, which is everyone's, and so it is with all of the internees ... each one embroiders his own Odyssey without realizing that the reality is quite enough in itself.[51]

Rassinier himself compared each deportee, after the liberation, with Ulysses; they added a new adventure to their Odysseys, as much to please public taste as to justify their long absence.[52] The vast majority of people, who have no doubts about the historicity of the concentration camps or of the Holocaust, might think that the real liar here was Rassinier himself. Yet the most sinister picture of Odysseus as manipulator of falsehood for self-advantage ever conceived is the Odysseus of Barry Unsworth's novel *Songs of the Kings*, in which Odysseus exploits a war situation in order to spin Iphigenia to her death because he derives pleasure from controlling other people's minds.[53] Perhaps it was falsehoods of this politically motivated type that Heiner Müller had in mind in his wonderful poem 'Tales of Homer', where the old poet warns an enquiring youngster that truth is unchangeable:

> Truth is an arrow, poisoned to all hasty archers!
> Even bending the bow is much. The arrow will still be an
> Arrow if found among rushes. Truth dressed as a lie is still truth.
> And the bow won't die with the archer. Said it and rose.[54]

Thinkers whose ideas were about as far from Frege and Müller as it would be possible to be – Surrealists – have also been attracted to the *Odyssey*. The earlier Surrealists believed that the truest understanding of existence could be attained through artistic expression of the images produced by the unconscious mind. One of the strangest Surrealist texts is *The Odyssey of Ulysses the Palmiped* (palmiped means 'web-footed'), a notorious theatrical piece in four scenes by Roger Gilbert-Lecomte (1957).[55] The drama defies logical analysis. In the first scene, Ulysses 'in his aquarium' announces 'I'll accord no credence to the authenticity of CAUSAL LINKS until I CAN HANG MYSELF BY MEANS OF THE AFORESAID', but there is no object identifiable as 'aforesaid'. The author draws attention to the *absence* of causal links in the dreamlike world of Surrealism. In the third scene a stage direction dictates that Ulysses hang on a gibbet 'instead of a rope: the causal link', while a sardine in a can, whose presence remains unexplained, says 'De Profundis!' In the fourth scene the 'disincarnated Ulysses' is ecstatic in eternal bliss, but can't find the words to say so. Perhaps this means that language is the wrong way to go about trying to communicate the nature of reality. Or there again, perhaps not!

In John Ashbery's short Surrealist play *The Heroes*, first performed in New York in 1953, Ulysses is the hero who finds it hardest to find anything new to say. When he runs into Circe, he says that there is 'nothing. When two ancient personages meet. Known to everybody in the world, disfigured by trash of centuries.'[56] Ashbery is thinking about the impossibility of poetic innovation through the figure of the hero who has been used in more artistic innovations than any other. Ulysses insists, 'I have seen too many places. Too many children know my story.'[57] As Frege would have said, the word 'Odysseus' may not have a *reference*, but it has an indisputable *sense* for most people, a fact also exploited by Wilson Harris in his obscure reading of Odysseus' myth, informed by quantum physics, in *The Four Banks of the River of Space* (1990).[58]

Although Plato himself used Penelope's weaving and unweaving as an image for the unphilosophical man who constantly re-ties his soul to his body (see p 123), a Neoplatonist allegorical interpretation actually represents Penelope as *Philosophia*, a personification of philosophy, with weaving symbolic of the act of pursuing truth, and unweaving representing the philosophers' assault on assumptions by testing propositions and definitions.[59] A woman weaving in some frames from an old reel of film from about 1910 constitutes the opening image of Theo Angelopoulos's film *Ulysses' Gaze* (1995), and the chief philosophical interest in this cerebral late twentieth-century response to the *Odyssey* is the nature of experience and its representations.

'A' (the same initial, of course, as Angelopoulos himself) travels through the Balkans; the relationship of humans to the space they inhabit is articulated in the several scenes where tiny figures wander in immense natural expanses of land by the roadside or the riverbank.[60] We can make some sense of 'A' and his journey through prior knowledge of the *Odyssey*. But his need to discover the reels of film is a metaphor for his need to constitute himself through memory of his past. The viewer is uncertain about the chronological sequence of events, what scenes have represented memories or flashbacks, which have been fantasies, dreams or nightmares.[61] At times parts of the same screen space represent different points in linear time. Angelopoulos invites his viewers to meditate, through his Balkan *Odyssey*, on the twentieth-century relationship between cinema and the way that each of us comes to know both history and our individual selfhood.

Contemporary philosophers of the Self argue that its most important constituents are time, space, a sense of physical embodiment and
the stories that fire the imagination.[62] For black descendants of slaves in
North America, their culture's past is even less recoverable than the life
of the Balkan peasant in 1910. Yet Ellison believed that the *Odyssey* was so
important because the search for identity was not just the Black American, but rather '*the* American theme. The nature of our society is such that
we are prevented from knowing who we are. It is still a young society, and
this is an integral part of its development.'[63] In fact, Ellison saw the figure
of Proteus as a more important key even than Odysseus to the nature
of American society and the problems that it faces. In an interview he
advised American writers 'who struggle with form and with America' to
remember Eidothea advising Menelaus to seize Proteus and hold him fast
whatever shapes he might assume:

> Our task then is always to challenge the apparent forms of reality – that
> is, the fixed manners and values of the few – and to struggle with it until
> it reveals its mad, vari-implicated chaos, its false faces, until it surrenders
> its insight, its truth. We are fortunate as American writers in that with
> our variety of racial and national traditions, idioms and manners, we are
> yet one.[64]

In the figure of Proteus, the philosophical, the aesthetic and the political
have here become eloquently fused. In the next chapter, the subjective and
emotional resonances of the themes of exile and return will be added to
the picture.

# 12

# EXILE FROM ITHACA

When Hermes travelled to Calypso's island cave (5.81–4), 'He did not find great Odysseus. The man sat crying on the headland, as often before, racking his soul with tears, groaning in agony, weeping as he scanned the horizon of the barren sea.' The significance of the *Odyssey*'s exile theme has often been a matter of personal experience. During the earlier part of the twentieth century, it became a key text not only for the Dubliner Joyce but for Pound, Eliot and all the North American writers who during or after the First World War found themselves in self-imposed exile on the European continent – the so-called Expatriates or Lost Generation, immortalized in Malcolm Cowley's autobiographical *Exile's Return: A Literary Odyssey of the 1920s* (1934). But since the Second World War, the poem's focus on the agony endured by its displaced hero, and by the Ithacan community that has lost him, has become more dominant in its reception.

Derek Walcott, who lives in Boston, far from his Caribbean birthplace, has said that 'the taste on the exile's tongue is the taste of his childhood … there is an interior exile, however sublimated, in every writer who is not in his own territory'.[1] The great Ugandan singer Geoffrey Oryema, who lives in Paris but sings in his native Acholi and English, composed his album *The African Odysseus* because as a young man he had to be smuggled out of his own country in a car boot when his father was murdered by the dictator Idi Amin. The last song, 'Exile', expresses his sense that wherever he lives, within his soul his bag is always packed and waiting at the door. One of the most important poetic responses to the *Odyssey* was written in Greek, by a Greek who did not live in Greece. It is Constantine Cavafy's *Ithaca*, published in 1911. This is John Mavrogordato's translation of its third, penultimate stanza:

> You must always have Ithaka in your mind.
> Arrival there is your predestination.
> But do not hurry the journey at all.

Better that it should last many years;
Be quite old when you anchor at the island,
Rich with all you have gained on the way,
Not expecting Ithaka to give you riches.
Ithaka has given you your lovely journey.
Without Ithaka you would not have set out.
Ithaka has no more to give you now.[2]

Cavafy (see Fig. 12) here inaugurated the idea of the Ithaca of the Mind that underlies the modern understanding of the *Odyssey* as spiritual biography. The poem, formally speaking Symbolist, reveals Cavafy discovering his later, more self-aware and cynical voice.[3] The voyage to Ithaca symbolizes his journey through life as a poet, the point of which is adventure and discovery rather than arrival.

Cavafy had been working on it since 1894. The poem travelled with him for 16 years. During most of them he lived in Alexandria with his mother and two of his brothers, Paul (who was, like Constantine, homosexual) and John-Constantine (who was, like Constantine, a man of letters). After their mother died in 1899, Constantine continued to live with Paul, but suffered further bereavements that left him ever more alone: between 1886 and 1905 he also lost two close friends, his uncle, his grandfather and four of his brothers. He must have felt as if he had wandered ever further from Ithaca, his comrades falling around him. He finally let his own personal quest go, and published the poem, shortly after the great turning-point in his life, which occurred when Paul left Alexandria to travel abroad in 1908, never to return. Constantine first began living on his own at the age of 45. He cut back on his social activities and devoted himself to writing poetry. He had finally discovered his own authentic voice – had found his Ithaca, his *raison d'être* – and most of his great poems were written subsequently.

Every aspect of Cavafy's life expresses his hybridity. His family had historical roots in Constantinople (Istanbul), Alexandria, Trebizond, Chios, Trieste, Venice and Vienna as well as London. His family name Kavafis derives not from Greek but from the Turkish word for shoemaker, and yet the spelling that he personally used, and by which he is known – Cavafy – is an Anglicization. He adopted this spelling when his widowed mother took him at the age of nine, along with her other sons, to live in Liverpool (they subsequently moved to London). During the five years he spent in England, he seems to have attended school and spent vacations in Dover.

Yet his poetry always wrestles with his love for the city of Alexandria, which he scarcely left between 1895 and his death. Ithacas are often in the mind, but sometimes they are a matter of topography. Cavafy was also aware that Alexandria, founded by Alexander the Great, had *always* been part of the Hellenic diaspora, indeed originally a colony of Macedon. Cavafy was certain to have known that the ancient biographer of Alexander, Plutarch, attributed the foundation of the city to Alexander's love of the *Odyssey*: when Alexander had conquered Egypt, and had begun to measure out ground in order to build the great city he wanted to bear his name, he changed his plans suddenly. This was after an ancient, grey-haired man (Homer) appeared to him in a dream to recite lines from the *Odyssey* about the location of the island of Pharos (4.354–5). Alexander woke up, travelled to Pharos and decreed that his city would be built on that spot; the reasons for admiring Homer, he said, included his excellence as an architect (*Life of Alexander* 26.3–5).

In 1914 Cavafy wrote a poem (unpublished in his lifetime) entitled 'Return from Greece', in which an Alexandrian philosopher admits his discomfort when residing in Greek culture, and his relief on returning to a place where his 'Asiatic' side feels comfortable. It is this exilic tension between spiritual home, cultural-ethnic ancestry, and chosen residence that Cavafy understood, and which underlies all the *Odyssey*'s afterlife in the hands of migrants and exiles. The poem is often discussed in connection with the idea of *nostalgia* in its literal sense of painful longing for home, but the term is not an ancient one. It was coined in 1688, to translate the German *Heimweh*, or 'home pain'. Some think that it was first used medically, to designate the disease suffered by Swiss soldiers serving in the militias of other nations. They were ill because they were not, so to speak, 'at home'. In the *Odyssey*, the Greek word *nostos* signifies both the action of returning and the story about the person who returns by sea.[4] Odysseus achieves his *nostos* but the poem about him will also be called a *nostos*.

The word *nostos* is related to the name Nestor – a man who returned satisfactorily to his homeland after the Trojan expedition. But it is also related to other important words occurring in the *Odyssey*, especially *neomai* (come, go, arrive) and *noein* (to have an accurate mental perception of a person or situation). All three terms seem to derive from a root in what linguists call Proto-Indo-European (PIE), the common ancestral language that needs to be hypothesized in order to make sense of the similarities between Greek and Sanskrit. The connection between *neomai* and *nostos* is obvious, but the connection between *nostos* and *noein* is more difficult to understand. The answer probably lies in the shared idea of a result, a successful outcome – you cannot arrive back home safely (which is what a *nostos* implies) without having used your mental capacities to assess correctly all the difficulties that an absence at sea entailed in antiquity. Odysseus achieves a successful homecoming because he has a record of exceptionally accurate mental perceptions of situations, and the ability to act on those perceptions. Cunning Odysseus of the many resources is presupposed by the Odysseus who can successfully return.

The traditional Mediterranean story of the return by sea is earlier by far than the Homeric epics. An ancient Egyptian prose tale called *The Shipwrecked Sailor* has been preserved on a papyrus of the Middle Kingdom (i.e. dating from between 2050 and 1750 BCE).[5] An acolyte of the pharaoh tells how a storm killed his companions, and he arrived at an island where he encountered an enormous snake. The snake comforted him, prophesied that he would return to Egypt, and bestowed gifts on him. The prediction proved true and the man returned home. The person to whom he relates this tale is another *nostos*-man, an Egyptian sea captain who has returned from an ill-fated voyage to Nubia and dare not tell the pharaoh. Besides resemblances between this story and several of the tales both true and false about Odysseus in the *Odyssey*, there are parallels with the autobiographical story related by Menelaus to Telemachus – one *nostos*-man to another – in Books 3–4.[6] The parallels include the relationship between narrator and listener, the episode of the lethal storm, the encounter with a zoomorphic oracular figure, the safe return and the acquired wealth. The exciting *nostos* story was no exclusively Greek tradition.

There were also Greek *nostos* poems that preceded the creation of the great Homeric epics.[7] But in the Greek tradition the Troy story provided a mythical peg on which a series of *nostos*-stories could be hung, all of which told of the returns from Troy of Greek heroes (Pausanias 10.28.7). Some scholars think that there was once a single, recognizable epic called *Returns* in the plural, a cycle of loosely connected tales of individual heroes produced by a longstanding tradition of oral performance.[8] Greeks in the ninth and eighth centuries had the *nostoi* in their heads.[9] But the only one that has survived to make its voyage across time and thus become the archetypal story of absence and return is the *Odyssey*, the *Return* (*nostos*) of Odysseus.

The journey homeward is the permutation of the quest myth that has attracted attention from Jungian psychoanalytical theorists. The hero's journey has always had the propensity to be seen as a double quest, both literal and metaphorical: it often requires an expedition home not only to the place whence the hero departed but to a state of being that was in his heart all along.[10] The outward journey of the hero thus requires an inward journey to occur simultaneously. Jungians see the mythical return as 'encoding' the psychic journey that must be taken by every fully formed adult. The ego emerges from a pre-egoic state, but can learn what is necessary for individuation and maturation by exploring that early state of blissful unity and inexperience. Trying to regain spiritual unity with humankind and to pursue happiness – to return to Eden – is thus in one sense a return, but it is return to a home that we have remade because we can never regain preconsciousness. We learn to distinguish good from evil, and cannot return to innocence, but we *can* 'go home' by facing our collective shadows. As Jung put it, 'the unconscious has a Janus-face: on one side its contents point back to a preconscious prehistoric world of instinct, while on the other side it potentially anticipates the future – precisely because of the instinctive readiness for action of the factors that determine man's fate'. [11]

Jungian cultural critics see the pattern of journey outward, knowledge acquisition, and return as articulated more clearly in Odysseus than in other mythical figures. [12] One Jungian psychologist has published a self-help manual detailing a programme of meditation and encounter groups that use passages from the *Odyssey*; these allow her customers 'movement into the greater life … as we grow our partnership with the mythic hero Odysseus and his Great Friend, the goddess Athena'. [13] During Odysseus' travels, he faces challenges 'in the depth realms' that result in crisis and growth. But his companions succumb to the demands of the unconscious, symbolized in the states of forgetfulness induced by the lotus or Circe's drugs, and fail to achieve the return to the home that is both old and new: an example of a victim of the unconscious desires that impede the Jungian concept of Return would be the tragic figure of Thomas Wilson in Somerset Maugham's short story 'The Lotus Eater' (1935), set in 1913. A former bank manager who abandons the rat race to live a life of leisure in Capri, he ends up poverty-stricken, suicidal, wandering the hills, alone and crazed, far away from anything that could fix his consciousness in a world of recognizable reality.

Some Jungian critics fuse their concept of the evolution of consciousness as instantiated in mythical archetypes with other notions, developed in Perennial Philosophy; this label was given by the German thinker Gottfried Leibniz to the system of ideas universal to mankind, especially those of a mystical nature, that underlie all world religions. It was Aldous Huxley – a great admirer of Homer (see p 46) – who made these ideas accessible to the modern world in *The Perennial Philosophy* (1945). Mackey-Kallis, a movie analyst informed by both Jung and Huxley, has argued that

Odysseus' quest is the archetypal manifestation of the perennial journey taken not only by individual human psyches but by the human race as a whole. As a species we have evolved from Edenic primitive preconsciousness, to consciousness (represented by technological advances and the knowledge economy), and one day will achieve 'transconsciousness', the return home to spiritual harmony after accommodating the great changes that experience has effected in us.[14] Odysseus' exile/return is so important, according to her argument, because it resonates on both individual and collective human levels. Odysseus is repeatedly threatened with forces that will overwhelm him, just as individuals and the human race have been, but he never succumbs, even at the darkest moment of contact with the dead, where he could so easily lose all touch with objective reality and the world of human action. Odysseus' self may be threatened but it is never destroyed. He is perceived to be so important to understanding the fundamental storyline of many American movies that Mackey-Kallis devotes a chapter of her book to analysing the *Odyssey* before discussing them.

Although this psychoanalytical model can seem to non-Jungians rather nebulous, it does at least attempt to explain why a certain kind of plot pattern is felt to be so *perennially* satisfying in cinema, a medium intimately bound up with our fantasy and dream lives. Hundreds of Hollywood films have retold the story of the return journey of a newly wise exile, and their global popularity suggests that they satisfy psychological needs that transcend cultural differences. In Mackey-Kallis's view, it is irrelevant whether it is Odysseus who returns, altered and more mature, to Ithaca, or Dorothy to Kansas in *The Wizard of Oz* (1939), or Scarlett to Tara in *Gone with the Wind* (1939), or Simba to the Pride Lands in *The Lion King* (1994).[15] The return in none of these cases is regressive, because the same home that once was left could not be understood and recognized if the outward journey had not taken place.

The Jungian Ithaca is a positive destination to be sought assiduously, but for many twentieth-century interpreters of the *Odyssey*, especially subsequent to the Second World War, Ithaca inevitably disappoints. An fine example is *The Lost Steps* (1953) by the Cuban Alejo Carpentier, who lived most of his life as an exile in Paris. The novel is suffused with self-conscious references to the *Odyssey*, especially articulated in connection with Yannes, a Greek miner who travels constantly with a copy of the epic. The story of a composer who flees New York on a quest to find an Edenic area of earth untouched by civilization, in the upper reaches of the river Orinoko, Carpentier was clear about its meaning: his hero travels 'to the point of the roots of all life, but when he wants to revisit them, he can't. He's lost the portal to authentic existence.'[16]

The problem with Ithaca is perfectly illustrated by the medical condition clinically known as the Ulysses Syndrome, sufferers from which embark, unnecessarily, on a medical journey that returns them to an Ithaca that may be worse than when they left it.[17] The paediatrician Charles Essex has described this painful odyssey, caused by unnecessary medical intervention, in the following terms. A child falls and hurts his leg. There are no obviously broken bones, but a doctor orders an X-ray 'to be on the safe side'. This shows no fracture, but away from the site of the injury there seems to be an abnormal area of bone. Blood tests and scans fail to identify what it might be, so the opinion of an orthopaedic surgeon is sought. He is certain that this is a 'normal variant', but the parents have worried themselves into believing that their son has cancer, so the surgeon feels obliged to perform a biopsy. The pathologist confirms it is normal but, in the meantime, the child falls again, this time on the slippery hospital floor, and fractures his leg at the site weakened by the biopsy. So he does finally end up with his leg in plaster for six weeks.[18]

The assumption that joy in recovering Ithaca will inevitably be compromised emerged in the painful responses to the *Odyssey* of the 1940s, during which years, as we shall see in Chapter 15, an epistemological shift took place in the relationship all of us have with our psychological homeland. Robert Kroestch has written that 'Homecoming implies a going away. A departure and return. And possibly that is the oldest story ... We began to travel during World War II, and we have not stopped since.'[19] This idea is developed in the delicate story *Return to Zion* (2006) by Tamar Yellin, whose Holocaust-haunted characters often feel stranded within multicultural communities in her native Yorkshire. Her Odysseus is a European Jew, whose conventional British semi-detached house is named Ithaca. He and his son Telemachus (the narrator) are obsessed with returning to Jerusalem. Their planning takes so long that Odysseus dies before he can ever return to the place which, the novella implies, was never really his homeland in the first place. He leaves several suitors hovering round his Penelope, who dreams about a different kind of journey in the form of package holidays offering a fantasy of seaside utopia.[20]

These 'displacement' responses to the *Odyssey* actually began just as the war got underway with Aimé Césaire's *Cahier d'un retour au pays natal* (1939, discussed on pp 96–7), and Thomas Wolfe's novel *You Can't Go Home Again* (1940). Wolfe has been called the most autobiographical novelist of the century,[21] and this novel, with its *denial* of the possibility of a satisfactory return to Ithaca, is his most autobiographical novel. From an early age Wolfe compared himself with Odysseus, and identified his own wanderlust, a response to his miserable childhood and domineering father, as a psychological quest for enchanted islands, or the amnesia-inducing lotus.[22] He was also aware that all the men he wrote about went to sea, and put this down to the mysterious power of Poseidon.[23]

The turning-point of *You Can't Go Home Again*, Chapter 6, is entitled 'The Homecoming'. Summoned to an aunt's funeral, George Webber returns from his successful urban career to the provincial village in Virginia where he had been raised. He is shocked by how small and shabby the house in which he grew up now seems. In the *nekuia* scene in the cemetery, like Odysseus trying and failing to embrace Anticleia, he cannot find his mother's corpse beneath her gravestone, since it has *already* been moved to make room for others less than two years after her burial. As his aunt's coffin is lowered into his grave, he becomes aware of his psychological exile:

> the last tie that had bound him to his native earth was severed, and he saw himself as a creature homeless, uprooted, and alone, with no door to enter, no place to call his own, in all the vast desolation of the planet.[24]

Two characters who would agree with Webber are the middle-aged Czechs returning to the land of their birth, after 20 years abroad, in Milan Kundera's *Ignorance*, originally published in French as *L'Ignorance* (2000).

Kundera, a Czech who has lived in France since 1975, has expressed ambivalence about his place of origin, and in *Ignorance* has woven an intense story around the theme of the long-awaited return to homeland. Many types of Ithaca are explored: is it the return to the mother, to the cradle of the mother language, to the love of one's life (even if remembered after his or her death), or to one's own long-forgotten youth, memories of which can only be recovered by revisiting the physical landscapes in which it was experienced? Irena has been in Paris, and Josef in Denmark. They had met many years before, in a Prague nightclub, but only Irena recalls this. On returning, they meet at the airport and the novel's climax coincides with their increasingly desperate lovemaking in a hotel. They come to understand that they can never resume the history interrupted by their departure. The redemptive reconciliation with their earlier selves, the ones that belonged to Prague, does not occur. This is the point at which the parallel with the *Odyssey*, set out with precision in the first two chapters, lends the novel its tragic weight. The woman who has adopted French culture, and the man whose one true love was Danish, are entirely *ignorant* not only of the directions taken by life and language in their homeland, but of each other. Josef, who has been reading a translation of the *Odyssey* (in his adopted language of Danish),[25] fails to recognize even the buildings and landscape of his homeland. At this agonizing moment, the novel puts its over-arching questions explicitly:

> Would an *Odyssey* even be conceivable today? Is the epic of the return still pertinent to our time? When Odysseus woke on Ithaca's shore that morning, could he have listened in ecstasy to the music of the great Return if the old olive tree had been felled and he recognized nothing around him?[26]

The return of Kundera's Czechs to their homeland can only happen because of the fall of the once mighty Soviet Empire in 1989, and it is this fall which concerns the film *Ulysses' Gaze*, directed by Angelopoulos (1995, see also pp 158–9). Angelopoulos's protagonist is 'A', himself a film director of Greek extraction (played with stillness and gravity by Harvey Keitel), who returns to Greece from the USA. 'A' wants to trace the reels he believes still to exist of the first film shot by the Manakis brothers decades earlier, at the dawn of cinema, when they recorded the peasant culture of the Balkans without regard for the national and ethnic boundaries there that have long been bitterly contested. As a Greek himself, who has used ancient Greek sources in his films,[27] Angelopoulos understands that the old stories of war and its aftermath, told not only in the Homeric epics but in Herodotus, Thucydides and the tragedians, were etched two and a half millennia ago into the psyche of Europe. The impossibility of direct communication between Keitel (who speaks no Greek) and Angelopoulos (who speaks no English) heightened the sense of isolation conveyed in the protagonist's scenes.[28]

There are several embedded tales of personal displacement, most memorably the old lady who is offered a lift in 'A's taxi at the Albanian border. Against a background of deep snow, this frail person is desperate to be reunited with the sister from whom she was separated 47 years previously by the civil war. 'A' and his taxi leave her in the desolate town square of Korytsa, abandoned by Angelopoulos's camera as her family has been abandoned by history.[29] Here the melancholic streak in the *Odyssey* that results from its status as the first 'aftermath of war' text in the Western tradition is exploited. The wanderings of his Odysseus take place amidst the ruins of the 'Troy' of the twentieth century, as statues of the twentieth-century Priam, V.I. Lenin, are pulled down everywhere. A new war rages while that fallen empire fragments: the film, set during the siege of Sarajevo, retrospectively confronts every war that scarred the Balkans during the twentieth century. For Angelopoulos's Odysseus there is no

Ithaca, even when he finally enters the ruined movie theatre, since there can be no return to whatever it was that the Manakis brothers signify to him: there can be no recovery of the pre-industrial world of human values, rooted in the land, nor of the innocence of the gaze through which that world was observed by the newly invented cinema camera.

A different unrecoverable Ithaca – the lost African past of the victims of the transatlantic slave trade – forms the psychological landscape of Walcott's monumental *Omeros* (1990). Following in the footsteps of Aimé Césaire, Walcott's text has reclaimed the story of Odysseus for the entire diasporadic black community wrenched from Africa. As early as Book I, Chapter 2.iii, the narrator tells of the Greek-speaking Antigone who strokes Homer's bust, 'the light webbed/on her Asian cheeks, and her eyes defined with a black/almond's outline': she tells him:

> I'm tired of America, it's time for me to go back
> to Greece. I miss my islands.[30]

This exiled Greek heroine is soon joined by the blind man in Ma Kilman's bar, babbling words that sounded Greek to her, 'Or old African babble'. Philoctete watches the wind turn 'yam leaves like maps of Africa'.[31] Greece (or Asia) to America, the Atlantic islands of the West Indies to Africa: in the visionary world of *Omeros* all displaced persons share a poetic bond.

The dead lie on the seabed beneath the route from Africa to the western side of the Atlantic Ocean; Achille, far out at sea, recalls 'the nameless bones of all his brothers/drowned in the crossing', his and their only inheritance 'that elemental noise/of the windward, unbroken breakers, Ithacas/or Africas'. Achille's spiritual voyage back to his ancestral homeland – the *nekuia* of *Omeros* – is full of the 'homesick shame/and pain of Africa'.[32] He learns from the tribal storyteller who would be the African equivalent of Odysseus,

> who the serpent-god conducted miles off his course
> for some blasphemous offence and how he would pay for it
>
> by forgetting his parents, his tribe, and his own spirit
> for an albino god.[33]

The enforced displacement of slavery is thus patterned after Odysseus' exile, his punishment for offending Poseidon. Like Odysseus, each African was compelled to become 'a nation/in himself, without mother, father, brother', and yet

> they felt the sea-wind tying them into one nation
> of eyes and shadows and groans, in the one pain

that is inconsolable, the loss of one's shore
with its crooked footpath.[34]

But in *Omeros* the Europeans are also displaced. Strange alliances develop
in mutual exile: Maud Plunkett sometimes takes Holy Communion with
Ma Kilman, in whose atavistic soul, however, there was 'an old African/
doubt that paused before taking the wafer's white leaf'. Several of the most
touching passages of the poem relate to Maud, dreaming of Ireland and
playing *Airs from Erin* on her piano.[35]

Walcott has sensed that the Irish, whose history of exploitation by
Britain has necessitated serial waves of emigration, have some affinity
with people of African ancestry whose families have lived for generations
outside Africa. The Erin of the ballads Maud plays is her long-lost Ithaca,
but it is a fantasy. Walcott has intuited that Odysseus, partly because of
Joyce's legacy, means much to Irish expatriates. Theresa Kishkan's *A Man
in a Distant Field* (2004) explores the parallels between psychological
alienation undergone by the victims of atrocity and the physical alienation
of the exile. It features an Irishman who has fled the conflict raging in his
homeland in 1922 after being traumatized by the Black and Tans. He finds
the will to return to confront his ghosts on the remote coast of British
Columbia; there he embarks on a personal translation of the *Odyssey* and
is eventually able to return to Ireland to confront his ghosts and discover
love.

Another Irish Canadian Odysseus is Fergus O'Brien, the protagonist
in Peter Behren's even more recent *The Law of Dreams* (2006). Fergus's
exile from Ireland is a direct result of the 1846 potato blight. There is no
sentiment attached to the brutality with which Fergus is severed from his
family, his roots, his mountain home in County Clare and his sweetheart
Phoebe. This Odysseus, like many exiles, knows he can never go home – a
horrifying sequence involving an outlaw gang's attack on Phoebe's home
removes the last reason for him to hanker after an Irish Ithaca. Fergus's
odyssey takes him across Ireland to England and then over the Atlantic
in a harrowing voyage; his own *nekuia* is his suicidal desperation in a
Montreal hotel. He has sexual relationships, but this *Odyssey*-novel faces
the emotional experiences of exile with more honesty than many. Fergus's
emotional isolation cannot be alleviated, and it is not clear that he could
cope with anything more complicated than a solitary passage through life.
He concludes that 'the world is composite, various, and got along very
well without you. It could sew you up with a couple of stones then drop
you into the ocean. It would not remember your name.'

From the exiled migrant it is only a short conceptual step to the misery of the asylum-seeker. Odysseus arrives anxiously on new islands, unsure of what reception he will receive, helpless and vulnerable. Ariane Mouchkine (herself the daughter of a Russian immigrant to France) subtitled as *Odyssées* the Théâtre du Soleil's *Le Dernier Caravansérail* (2005), her theatrical exploration of the ordeals undergone by refugees, in order to suggest the epic scale of the production as well as ironically to frame the struggle of the world's 11 million displaced persons.[36] A year later, Naomi Iizuka's *Anon(ymous)* was performed by The Children's Theatre Company in Minneapolis. Iizuka, as a Japanese-American dramatist, has specialized in the experiences of mixed-race societies, but she studied Classics at college and wanted to fuse her social agenda with a reading of the *Odyssey*. Her hero Anon, a teenaged immigrant to the USA from an unspecified war-torn South-East Asian country, is searching for his mother, a sweatshop worker. The Cyclops is a one-eyed butcher; there are curry houses, pig-faced barflies and a surfboarding Mentor-Athena.

David Farr's stage version of the epic premiered in Bristol in 2005, and reached a wider audience at the Lyric, Hammersmith in 2006. It began with Odysseus being washed up on a beach, carted off to a detention centre and interrogated by immigration officials. The Cyclops' single eye was a sinister spotlight. But Odysseus was not the only exile: the production emphasized that the unfortunate Trojans could never return to their homelands again. The programme invited spectators to make a connection with asylum-seekers by publishing a human rights lawyer's impassioned article on the injustices being committed under the terms of the UK asylum law,[37] along with an invitation to contact relevant charities.

A Ugandan refugee, an Anglicized Alexandrian with a Turkish surname, ancient Egyptian seamen in the pharaoh's service, Jungian theorists, diaspora Jews, leisured Northern European sun-seekers, a depressed Virginian, forcibly exiled Czechs, Balkan migrants, descendants of Africans abducted in chains from their primeval homeland, starving Irish Catholics, asylum-seekers and Asian Americans – this chapter has touched briefly on some groups for whom Odysseus' archetypal displacement from Ithaca has offered a point of identification and a little comfort. As Walcott has so movingly put it, 'The Classics can console' – just not enough.[38] But at the top of this list will always be the people who come from the same peninsulas and islands as Odysseus himself. The history of the Greeks is one of serial waves of emigration to every continent, both voluntary and enforced: the Greeks hail each other across the globe with their proverb 'The Greeks Are Everywhere'.

Odysseus, after all, is one of many Greek male 'wanderer figures whose houses have revolving doors'.[39] Some of the heroic exile songs of Byzantium – called 'Akritic' after the hero Digenis Akritas – are still performed, as are the heartbreaking Greek folk-laments called *tragoudia tis xenitias*, or Songs of Exile.[40] These reached their tragic fulfilment in the *Rembetika*, or bouzouki-accompanied blues, sung after the entire Greek population of Asia Minor was forcibly ejected in 1922 and lived in miserable tent cities around Athens and Salonica. Another traditional demotic Greek ballad type, which stages a dialogue between a returning seaman and his wife, is fused with allusions to the second half of the *Odyssey* in George Seferis's haunting poem 'The Return of the Exile' (1938), as David Ricks has pointed out.[41] Seferis's diplomatic career entailed many years outside Greece, and almost every Greek in his position (of whom there are millions in Australia, Canada, the USA and – still today – the Black Sea) identifies with Odysseus as ancestral hero. This identification has recently underlain Nickos Jean Lambrou's historical novel *Odysseus: His Americanization* (2002), the story of a Greek who emigrates to Chicago in 1974. From his early mistreatment as a DP (displaced person) by the police, to his new understanding of the tragic relationship between the West and Islam after 9/11, this is a vivid account of immigrant life from an Americanized Greek's perspective. In the background are to be heard the songs of exile with which Greeks have always comforted themselves, from the *Odyssey* to George Dalaras's beautiful 'Asia Minor Lament', a classic *rembetiko*.[42]

Innumerable personal histories are told by Greeks and their descendants of astonishing journeys under titles that invoke the ancient epic,[43] and the periodical founded in 1993 to keep together all the world's 'Philhellenes, Greeks and Greek Americans' is called *Odyssey* magazine: as its online editorial declares, 'For those of us who sit at home and wait for our next trip to Greece, the arrival of *Odyssey* magazine eases the suffering.' Yet the Greek experience of exile, as focused on the mythic figure of Odysseus, has, especially since the Second World War, become universalized. Odysseus is now the paradigmatic mythical exile in the collective imagination of the third-millennial global village, his suffering something to which the inhabitants of every continent can relate.

# 13

# BLOOD BATH

> She found Odysseus among the corpses of the slain, splattered with blood and gore like a lion stalking off after gorging on a household ox, with his chest and both jaws smeared with blood, terrifying to see (*Odyssey* 22.401–5).

This is how the audience of the *Odyssey* visualizes its hero, through the eyes of his nurse Eurycleia, after the last suitor has been slaughtered. The deaths of individual suitors have already been described in cinematic detail, from Antinous, out of whose nostrils a 'thick jet of blood gushed ' (22.18–19), to Leodes, whose throat Odysseus slashes with a sword, leaving his head 'to mingle with the dust' (22.328–9). For Odysseus and his men had 'set upon the suitors and hacked at them right and left through the hall; and as their heads were struck there rose a horrible moaning, and the floor streamed with blood'. Eurymachus, the greatest threat to Odysseus, had died in agony when an arrow pierced his liver, leaving him to writhe (22.83–8). Melanthius, the treacherous goatherd, was suspended from the roof to die a slow death under torture (22.172–200).

In *The Odysseus Poems* (1999), Judith Kazantzis replaces the account of the bloodbath with two verse letters from a mother to an unknown Ithacan. In the first, she writes,

> Absolutely horrified to get your letter
> detailing a massacre of young men
> by a mad old loony in Ithaka,
>
> someone claiming to be King Odysseus,
> possessed of a madman's strength.

But in the second, the mother's understanding of events has altered dramatically:

> The true fairy story ending.
> Ithaka back to peace and rightful government.[1]

Kazantzis is pointing out that there are two ways to read the bloodbath. It either appals or pleases; it must be condemned, as Grotius already condemned Odysseus' unprovoked siege of Ismarus (9.39–44) on the ground that it was the earliest recorded violation of international justice,² or honestly enjoyed. In 1990 Fidel Fajardo-Acosta's revisionist study argued that the *Odyssey* implicitly condemns violence, and has what he calls 'a tragic vision'. He insists that the poem is, like the *Iliad*, an elegiac lament 'for the tragic self-destruction of a set of specific individuals and a whole civilization that they represent'.³ The destruction, beginning with the deaths of Odysseus' crew, culminates in the bloody execution of the suitors. Crucial to his argument is the comparison made between the sound of the bowstring when Odysseus tests it prior to the slaughter, and the song of a swallow (21.404–11; see p 17). Fajardo-Acosta stresses that the swallow's cry was sometimes associated with barbarism, sadness, and especially with the opening of the sailing season in the spring, which he thinks must have had tragic connotations.⁴ Yet in other ancient sources the springtime associations are positive: the swallow is the emblem of regeneration and marital harmony.

Even if Odysseus' activities at Troy were sometimes presented negatively, the story told in the *Odyssey* was in antiquity seen as a success story – an upbeat tale of hardship overcome through heroic valour and cunning intelligence.⁵ Book 22 was a favourite with ancient audiences; when Socrates interviews a professional performer of Homer in Plato's dialogue *Ion*, its opening moment when 'Odysseus appears leaping forth on the floor, recognized by the suitors and casting his arrows at his feet' is selected as one of the three most emotive passages in the epics (the other two, one of which is the violent showdown between Achilles and Hector, are both from the *Iliad*). Ion says that when he recites passages to do with horrors, his hair stands on end and his heart throbs, while his audiences respond not only with pity but 'awe and sternness stamped upon their faces' (535b–e). It can be argued that *Odyssey* Book 22 reads less like an indictment of the tragedy of human conflict than the climax of a Peckinpah movie made during what has been called 'the golden age of American film violence' in the 1960s and early 1970s,⁶ or even a film by a sensationalist director such as Quentin Tarantino. Indeed, more than one critic has suggested specifically Odyssean undertones to what have been called Tarantino's 'kick-ass comeback queen', played by the comeback actress Pam Grier in *Jackie Brown* (1997),⁷ as well as the kick-ass comeback hero played by John Travolta in the exceptionally violent *Pulp Fiction* (1994). But there is no Jackie Brown during the male showdown of the *Odyssey*:

Penelope is asleep upstairs.

Odysseus, detached from his original plot, has featured as a violent action hero in computer games, and earlier in movies such as *Ulysses against Hercules* (1961, also released under the title *Ulysses against the Sons of Hercules*) and *Hercules, Samson and Ulysses* (1963). Yet with the exception of the exuberant discharging of arrows in William Gager's late sixteenth-century *Ulysses Redux*, designed for performance by young Oxford men in festive mood,[8] Book 22 of the epic has been one of the least revisited in post-Renaissance culture, at least in *direct* adaptation. Although understood to be the climax of the poem, and therefore popular with illustrators of printed editions (see Fig. 13) and with the artist Henry Fuseli,[9] time and again stage versions of the play kept the slaughter of the suitors offstage, as necessary justice to be meted out discreetly but not closely investigated. Yet an incalculable *indirect* influence has been exerted by five features of the episode: the cunning making possible what is essentially a strategic ambush, the slow build-up of tension, the moral justification of the violence, the absurdity of the odds faced by the avengers, and the bloodiness of the final retribution.[10] This pattern is especially visible in action movies, above all the sub-genre of Westerns associated with Clint Eastwood and self-consciously epitomized by *The Outlaw Josey Wales* (1976) and *Unforgiven*, directed by Eastwood himself (1992). *Unforgiven* builds up to a climax in which a patient and cunning man (a pig-farmer, actually), avenging an assault on his household, woman, children and property, exacts a brutal reprisal on the hate-object Little Bill Daggett (Gene Hackman). Like Odysseus and the suitors, the hero and the villain in these plots are fundamentally similar: they share the same social class, ethnicity, skills, weaponry and value systems.[11] The major difference between hero and villain in both Clint Eastwood's Westerns and the *Odyssey* is to do, rather, with an ability to resist giving way to either inner desires or outer coercions.[12]

This issue is complicated, because it is certainly not the case that modern audiences want their heroes to be more cerebral and less brutally violent. It is perhaps surprising that Odysseus' assault on the suitors has not proved more attractive to these audiences. For although the trick of the hidden armour is important, what is celebrated in the showdown is not Odysseus' cunning intelligence but his prowess as a warrior. Indeed, it is his prowess as a combat hero against odds so ridiculous that they would put the heroes played by Sylvester Stallone or Arnold Schwarzenegger to shame. This is perhaps connected with the fact that Odysseus' cunning has not been prominent in recent North American responses to the poem. Indeed, there is a real sense in which Odysseus' 'Autolycan' aspect has been effaced. One reason for this is that, as Leo Gurko demonstrated in his 1953 study of the North American popular hero, intellectual qualities are suspected by his compatriots, whose politicians often need to present themselves as less astute as well as less educated than they really are. But it is even more important that, as Marina Warner has argued, boys are no longer 'raised to be cozeners or tricksters – it would be unthinkable to train the future men in lures and wiles and masks and tricks'.[13] Boys' action heroes today – Action Man, Robocop – bristle with weapons and prefer brute force to anything more intellectually polished than a sawn-off shotgun.[14]

It has been argued by John Fitch (2004) that the bloodbath of *Odyssey* Book 22 is the source of an important myth underlying the North American psyche. This myth has been necessary in order 'to qualify and redeem the many moral indiscretions that accompanied the creation of the nation ... the collective guilt of a society that displaced the original residents of the land, enslaved an entire race for its own financial gain, and introduced nuclear warfare to the world'. Fitch proposes that the idea of 'what a man's gotta do' often 'postures as a righteous stance by virtue of its dedication to a high ideal, coupled with the embrace of self-sacrifice'. Yet the moral probity of the violence to which the hero resorts is undermined because he becomes just as ruthless as his adversaries. Fitch concludes that such 'faux moral redemption', through bloodletting rather than within the conscience, sanctions sadistic responses to threat and danger. He laments that in American film, the spirit of Odysseus' bloody return to Ithaca prevails over the other archetypal travel myth – the biblical story of Paul's transformation on his journey to Damascus.[15]

Another critic, who sees the *Odyssey* as the linear ancestor of X-rated movies *via* the moral simplicity and exaggerated violence of Grand-Guignol theatre, has suggested that the showdown of the *Odyssey* offers 'melodramatic satisfaction' in contrast with the properly 'tragic' violence in the *Iliad*.[16] Perhaps it is true that the mass murder of the suitors offers the same gratification as melodrama because 'we experience a momentary compensation for every slight or rejection we have ever suffered, all the way back to our childhood'. This critic suggests that a good parallel to the *Odyssey* bloodbath can be seen in Michael Cimino's *The Deer Hunter* (1978), when the Americans slaughter their Viet Cong captors in a prolonged and gory scene. The degree of emotional engagement with which audiences can watch such bloodbaths is clear from the violent street response to Walter Hill's *The Warriors* (1979), marketed with the tagline 'These are the armies of the night. They are 100,000 strong. They outnumber the cops five to one. They could run New York City. Tonight they're all out to get the warriors.' The warriors, a gang of worthy youths, have been bitterly wronged and are in such danger of death that the film presents them as justified in acting with extreme violence against 'the armies of the night'.

The bloody climax of the *Odyssey* has nevertheless proved almost too vicious for straightforward representation. As Green has pointed out, this is difficult to explain given that modern audiences, prepared to watch Peckinpah's *Straw Dogs* (1971), are usually not at all averse to gore and slaughter.[17] Yet there is an undeniable awkwardness about both film versions of the revenge. In Camerini's, the violence is justified by the addition of a scene in which Telemachus is bullied by the suitors. Penelope is relieved when they are despatched, but horrified by the bloodbath (which in this film she witnesses), and by the terrifying expressions on her husband's face as he strangles one suitor with his bare hands before smashing a metal axe-head onto his skull. She rushes off to ask Athena's statue why Ulysses had to come home so angry and ruthless, his pathway so bloodstained? In Konchalovsky's movie, however, the violence seems incomprehensible given Assante's portrayal of Odysseus as a tender family man. Nor has any film version conveyed, for that matter, the paranoid testing to which the married pair in the epic subject each other at the last minute – Odysseus over her fidelity, and Penelope over his identity.[18] The manifold ways in which their *anagnorisis* (recognition scene) has been dealt with, as well as the psychological reactions of everyone to the violent self-revelation of the returning king, show just how much this whole episode echoes anxieties deep in everyone.[19] There has, indeed, been a plethora of ways of changing the core story.

One has been *substitution* – to portray Odysseus as a genuine impostor but a peace-loving husband and father figure. Notable here is Jon Amiel's *Sommersby*, where the audience knows that 'Jack' cannot be Jack Sommersby, and Laurel remembers her real husband as unpleasant. The impostor, however, makes an affectionate spouse, helps the community and opposes the violence of the local white supremacists. The fistfight with his rival for Laurel's affections does not even end in significant injury. There is no final bloodbath. This screenplay was partly inspired by the true story of Arnaud de Tihl, who tried to take the place of Bertrande de Rols's dead husband Martin Guerre in medieval France, but ended up hanged for it – the story told in Daniel Vigne's excellent movie *The Return of Martin Guerre*.

The canonical study of de Tihl, one of the few known individuals in history to have experienced much of what was undergone by the mythical

Odysseus, is by Natalie Zemon Davis (1983). Arnaud really was a man of Odyssean resourcefulness and resilience. He insisted he was Martin Guerre in the face of the testimony of dozens of witnesses over the course of two trials, and would probably have won his case if the real one had not turned up. Arnaud de Tihl had to be hanged. But if he and Bertrande were in collusion, he died without betraying her: like Penelope in the *Odyssey*, we are not sure how much Bertrande knew, and when. This true story, which contains hardly any violence, can be reconstructed in such detail because the judge in the second trial left a written record, so amazed had he been by the performance of de Tihl – his brain power, his memory and his courage (see pp 137–8).

A second strategy that has been adopted by adaptors uneasy with the original epic storyline has been wholesale erasure. Light-hearted adaptations have routinely resolved the 'problem' of Book 22 by having Odysseus forgive the suitors; in Burnand's burlesque *Patient Penelope* (1863) everyone kisses and makes up, even though the sexually excited Eurymachus has actually climbed in to the marital apartment. The most sanitized Odysseus of all time must be Inman in the novel and movie *Cold Mountain* (also discussed on p 138). In these, violence (whether during the North American Civil War or during its anarchic aftermath) is universally depicted as evil; there is little moral complexity in the film's drawing of the good characters (who hate violence) and the bad ones (who use it constantly). There is only one suitor (Teague), and despite the appalling conduct shown by him and his gang, there is no sense of the emotional need for revenge on the part of either Ada or Inman. There is no neglected child and no failure on the part of the estranged lovers to recognize one another. Inman refrains from sex with anybody until his reunion with Ada, despite opportunities in a whore-house and with an attractive young widow, alongside whom (implausibly) he sleeps fully clothed.

The question of the *Odyssey*'s bloodbath has, paradoxically, been most noisily raised in discussions surrounding the exhilarating Canadian Inuit film *Atanarjuat: The Fast Runner* (2001), directed by Zacharias Kunuk. This deservedly won the Cannes Camera D'Or prize for Best First Feature. The director is the first member of his family to live in a settled community, and one of the first generation of Inuit to become literate and indeed make movies. Entirely in the Inuktitut language spoken by the Canadian Inuit, the film is essential viewing for anybody interested in the *Odyssey*, because it is the product of an oral culture that has leapt in just a generation to cinema from storytelling from memory. This explains the dense mythic feel of the film, based on a legend that has been passed down for generations by nomadic hunter-gatherers, eking out their existence on the Arctic tundra near to the top of the world.[20]

The plot is similar to the second half of the *Odyssey*. The hero is not the strongest warrior, but he is patient, crafty and athletic, excellent at fishing, hunting, managing his dog teams and building igloos. He has previously won his beautiful wife Atuat in a bare-knuckle fight against his rival Oki, but has been forced to leave her and their little son; he returns after a long absence to avenge himself on the murderous rival for his wife's hand (along with the rival's promiscuous sister) and claim the position of tribal leader. The *Financial Times* reviewer wrote that the story 'might as well be the *Odyssey*' as we follow Atanarjuat 'launching his own vengeance mission on the home-destroying, wife-stealing Oki'.[21] Yet what makes this film relevant to the cultural history of the *Odyssey* is not any provable influence flowing either way (rather, the parallels suggest the ubiquity in pre-Christian mythologies of the return of the husband theme) but the alterations to the myth in directions which made it acceptable to modern sensibilities.

Elders of the Inuit people were in other respects consulted on every detail of this painstaking reconstruction of life in the Canadian Arctic before the missionaries came. The legend, perhaps four millennia old, has Atanarjuat set up in a situation, complete with concealed weapons, in which his three enemies are at his mercy. After knocking down Oki, Atanarjuat smashes his skull with a bone club, before doing the same to Oki's two sidekicks. But in the film, Atanarjuat smashes the ice *next* to Oki's head, and improbably exclaims, 'The killing stops now!' He proves that he had the upper hand and could have taken revenge, but chooses not to. The villains, although driven from the community, are alive and forgiven. One interviewer, irritated by this censorship of the blood-retribution, asked the director why he could imply that this '1,000-year-old Inuit myth of lust, betrayal and violence climaxes with a surprisingly pacifistic turn' – citing 'Odysseus' bow-and-arrow heroics during his homecoming' as the type of resolution to be expected in a traditional society. But Kunuk responded that 'Every generation has their version. It was a message more fitting for our times. Killing people doesn't solve anything.'[22]

A more common approach to the now unacceptable retributive violence at the end of the *Odyssey* is the blatant revisionism pioneered by the Polish dramatist Stanislaw Wyspianski in *Return of Odysseus*. This Odysseus' violence against both the suitors and their concubines is needless and lawless savagery (see p 41). The new approach coincided with the first psychoanalytical readings of Odysseus' character resulting from the

Europe-wide impact of Freud's work. Wyspianski's Odysseus is suffering from manic depression, and knows that he is murderously disturbed: 'I have found hell in my own country. I have come into a cemetery, and I am the gravedigger. It reeks of carrion flesh.'[23] The play focuses on tensions between son and father – the Oedipal struggles of Telemachus with Odysseus, and Odysseus with Laertes. Telemachus, indeed, begins to imitate his father's violence once Odysseus returns. Wyspianski's hero is recognized not by the scars that he has suffered, but by the casualness of the violence with which he inflicts scars on others. He kills Eumaeus, leaves a trail of other corpses across Ithaca, has a nervous breakdown when Laertes turns up to stop his merciless slaughter of the suitors, and the play ends as he runs into the sea to join 'The boat of the dead! it is sailing into the hereafter, into oblivion'.[24] A similar approach was taken in Gerhart Hauptmann's German play *The Bow of Odysseus* (1914), where the slaughter assumes a Dionysiac level of manic brutality:[25] these angst-ridden central European Odysseuses, psychotically wedded to violence for its own sake, are incapable of assuming the roles of responsible father, husband or leader.

Odysseus is the central figure in a surprising number of Spanish plays that followed on and commented upon the Spanish Civil War,[26] and in these the violence of the homecoming received particular attention. Gonzalo Torrente Ballaster's *El retorno de Ulises* (1945) deals with the slaughter by showing how Ulises can never match up to the legendary picture of his derring-do that has been constructed in Ithaca during his absence. Ulises is a tired, pathetic figure, who returns a reduced man from exile and withdraws from the archery contest, realizing he is incapable of success in it.[27] The play confronts the brutality of the war, but when Penélope chooses to love Ulises anyway, it suggests one way that Spain can come to terms with its recent history and resolve internal hatreds.[28]

Until recently the most unequivocal 'problematization' of the homecoming was Antonio Buero Vallejo's *La tejedoro de sueños* (*The Weaver of Dreams*, 1952), a powerful tragic drama which demolishes Odysseus' claim to moral legitimacy in the slaughter scene. It depicts Penélope as a sad, disillusioned, woman with a pre-feminist conviction that women's rights are trampled on in her society. She even argues that Clytemnestra was justified in killing the vainglorious, adulterous Agamemnon. Like Clytemnestra, this Penélope has fallen in love. The object of her love is one of the suitors, a spiritual, gentle young man named Alfino, with whom she has not actually had sex. But she is disgusted by her violent, cynical and self-seeking husband, whose approach to the enactment of revenge is given detailed attention. Just like the epic Odysseus, this Ulises plans the slaughter carefully by hiding the suitors' arms and locking the doors. But he is far less convinced that he can win by sheer physical superiority, and cheats in the contest of the bow by trying out his strength secretly beforehand. He kills the suitors (whose number is reduced to five) from the safety of a balcony. The way the play must be staged keeps all of them except Alfino invisible, dying unable to defend themselves, and anonymously, in a manner calculated to suggest the victims of a politically motivated firing squad.

Ulises' intemperate use of violence is further underscored when he tries to batter his way into Penélope's room at the end of the play. Buero Vallejo was himself imprisoned and sentenced to death (a sentence eventually commuted) for his support of the Republicans during the Spanish Civil War, and he elides Odysseus with the repressions of the Franco regime. The conclusion of the play, although superficially representing the triumph of the aggressor Ulises, and his equally violent sidekick Telémaco, undermines it by stressing their failure to win emotionally the objects of their desires (the servant woman loved by his son is executed). Penélope, coerced into reunion with a husband whose narcissism and violence she despises, remains defiantly faithful in spirit to her assassinated lover. The patriarchal monarch of Ithaca has become a twentieth-century totalitarian dictator, and the violence he perpetrates is that of a vindictive tyrant who had been, it is implied, legitimately ousted by more peaceable men.[29]

Since the feminist reappraisal of the *Odyssey* began in the 1970s, such a reading has become nearly ubiquitous in serious art, epitomized by the Northern Irish poet Michael Longley's close paraphrase of the closing scenes in his hexameter poem *The Butchers*.[30] It consists of one long, driving sentence that opens with the suitors 'heaped in blood and dust/Like fish', and moves through the hanging of the maid-servants, the mutilation of Melanthius, the cleansing of the house and the journey of the dead souls to 'bog-meadow full of bog-asphodels/Where the residents are ghosts or images of the dead'. The brutality of the revenge is underlined by the title and the insertion of a few contemporary terms to remind us that such scenes are not safely sealed off in a heroic past: Odysseus sees the need 'for whitewash and disinfectant', so that Hermes can round up the dead 'like a clergyman'. This poem elaborates (slightly) the text of the *Odyssey*, in order to underline its savagery, but the most powerful rewriting of all was the presentation of the episode in Walcott's *The Odyssey: A Stage Version* (1992).[31] Odysseus kills Antinous, who has simply asked for his turn with the bow, and Eurymachus, who is begging on his knees for his life. The slaughter of the rest of the suitors follows, in the form of a terrifying dance that at the play's première one reviewer found 'completely gripping',[32] before Odysseus becomes deluded, convinced that he has gone back in time to the beginning of the Trojan War. He tries to kill even the singer, Billy Blue, and is struggling with insanity when Penelope enters with the curt question, 'You had to wade this deep in blood?' She rebukes Odysseus for turning the house into an 'abattoir', demanding to know whether it was for such a scene that she kept her 'thighs crossed for twenty years', and forbids him to hang the maids.[33]

Walcott's implication that Odysseus is suffering from psychosis, taking the form of flashbacks, delusions and a failure to distinguish past situations from present ones, harks back to Wyspianksi. A related tactic has been the form of adaptation preferred by proponents of pacifism: they have generally portrayed Odysseus as the victim of a social order that sends him into unnecessary wars that inflict what used to be called shell shock and is now diagnosed as post-traumatic stress disorder. An influential figure has been Jonathan Shay, a staff psychiatrist at the Department of Veterans' Affairs Outpatient Clinic in Boston, Massachusetts. What interests him is how to treat – and prevent – psychological injury to military personnel. In *Achilles in Vietnam* (1994), Shay threw fresh light on many of the episodes in the *Iliad* by showing how closely the experiences of the warriors at Troy, especially Achilles, were mirrored by those which he had encountered in his disturbed veterans: the men who went completely berserk and lost all discipline in Vietnam were those who had lost faith in the purpose of the war, had become alienated from their superior officers and had lost one of their closest friends in combat – just as Achilles lost Patroclus.

In *Odysseus in America* (2002), Shay focuses on how veterans often failed to cope with returning home, widening his scope to include also the recorded experiences of American soldiers returning from the War of Independence, the Civil War, Korea and the first Gulf War. He draws harrowing testimony from German veterans of the First World War as distilled in Erich Maria Remarque's *The Road Back* (1931, the sequel to the better known *All Quiet on the Western Front* of 1929), and from Willard Waller's *The Veteran Comes Back* (1944). Shay's reading of the *Odyssey* offers a fresh perspective on Odysseus' obsession with telling lies. To a psychiatrist, Odysseus' behaviour in Book 13 is clearly psychotic: 'he is disoriented and does not recognize Ithaca'. When he meets an unknown civilian youth (actually Athena in disguise), his first instinct is to tell 'a dazzling pack of lies'. He moves around 'in disguise and concealment', and even after being reunited with his son, wife and father is often 'icy or cruel. And then he runs off again!'[34]

Shay approaches the poem from a demobilized soldier's viewpoint. The difficulty suffered by soldiers in adjusting to a peacetime lifestyle, where lethal violence is never appropriate, is underscored by Odysseus' first escapade after Troy – the sacking of another town (Ismarus). The lotus-eaters offer an obvious parallel to the 'horrifyingly large number of Vietnam veterans' who abuse drugs and alcohol: well over 50 per cent.[35] In the Cyclops episode Odysseus creates unnecessary danger by lighting a fire in the cave and by boastfully revealing his name: some veterans become addicted to excitement and often succumb to a life of crime because they have no resources for coping with the boredom of everyday life. Shay also notices details overlooked by less purposeful readers, for example, the paranoid and obsessive way in which Odysseus insists on manning his ship, without sleeping for nine days and nights, after receiving the winds from Aeolus at the beginning of Book 10. He does not know how to delegate and share responsibility. When he finally submits to sleep, the sailors are thus justified in disobediently opening the sack, because he has been displaying such peculiar behaviour. His first reaction to the disaster, moreover, is to contemplate suicide (for the one and only time in the poem), which, tragically, is the way out chosen by many veterans.[36] Odysseus' sexual exploitation of Calypso and violence towards Circe have really unpleasant resonances to anyone who was involved in the American war in Vietnam.

Perhaps in order to protect his clients, Shay does not discuss Odysseus' violence in his own palace in terms of the much publicized domestic murders committed by a very few members of the armed forces at the end of tours of duty; in an awful example, four military wives were killed, allegedly by their husbands, at Fort Bragg in North Carolina in July 2002. The men were Special Forces soldiers who had recently returned from Afghanistan.[37] But Odysseus, unlike the Heracles who kills his wife and children on returning home in Euripides' tragedy *Heracles Gone Mad*, is in control of his mind when the suitors are killed. What interests Shay, rather, are the feelings veterans express towards two particular groups. First, young men who avoided being called up become objects of envy and *schadenfreude*, curiously focused often on the pleasure they can take in regular meals. Secondly, huge rage is felt towards 'Jodies', the civilian men who took advantage of their absence to steal their wives and girlfriends. Like these ordinary, cuckolded Americans, it was 'simply not in Odysseus' character to make peace with anyone who had stolen his victuals and tried to steal his wife'.[38]

The difference between Shay's veterans and Odysseus, however, is that since the United States came into existence it has never been occupied by a foreign power. The suitors' leaders have tried to murder Telemachus. They are numerically far superior. To discover the poem's true emotional resonances you would have to ask a soldier who returned to find his entire community under enemy occupation, with his child's life threatened and his womenfolk under sexual pressure. Salman Rushdie understands this in *Shalimar the Clown* (2005), in which the significantly named Kashmiri protagonist Shalimar Noman eventually assassinates the Jewish American who has seduced his wife, and who symbolizes the forces of American imperialism that have led to Noman's own country suffering from the activities of both Islamic insurgents and the occupying Indian army.[39] When he abandons the theatre to train as an assassin in Afghanistan, it is difficult not to sympathize with his plight, either personal or national.

The *Odyssey* makes perfect emotional sense in certain political contexts. Shelley longed for a return of Odysseus, with all the bloodshed it might entail, if it meant that Greece might expel her Ottoman rulers and be free. Shelley prayed in *Hellas* (1822), early in the Greek War of Independence, that the moment had arrived when 'A new Ulysses leaves once more/Calypso for his native shore.'[40] In 1829, when the Greek uprising had already run into problems, the author of an essay on the influence of Homer on the Greek people has the Odyssean model in mind when he wishes 'that such another could arise and exert upon their present degenerate offspring the purifying, healing influence of genius' so that the Greeks might once again 'fight for liberty!'[41] In other situations, too, liberal qualms about the number of casualties on the enemy side must have seemed absurd. Edward Sackville-West's *The Rescue*, the radio version that urged British forces to support the Greeks against Nazi occupation, was first broadcast in 1943. The representation of the violence through the medium of the radio was explicit; extending over several minutes, the script includes the directions 'yell of pain', 'shrieks', 'yell of agony in distance' as well as 'prolonged music' and 'confused shouting'. Penelope listens bloodthirstily while Eumaeus tells her that Ctesippus 'has fallen on one of the axes and bleeds from the neck'.[42] A similar sense of righteous satisfaction is to be found in Vincent Brun's wartime novel *Untimely Ulysses* (1940), in which Anton, the part-Jewish Austrian hero, returns home from exile and witnesses the death of the Nazi governor in a plane crash. He realizes he is watching a scene like 'the suitors of Penelope dying under the arrows of the well-hitting gods. He laughed aloud. The flames were shooting up ... The angels in heaven must have seen.'[43] Much more recently, it is chastening to discover Chinese agitators urging that in the face of Western economic imperialism, with the North American business empire getting its feet under the table in Shanghai, 'Action is needed. China needs its own Odysseus, urgently!'[44]

No ancient or modern court of law, even in Texas (see pp 97–8), would ever have sentenced *all* the suitors (let alone the 12 maids) to death. Yet anyone who has lived under unwanted occupation will be hard pushed not to identify with Odysseus as he tears off his rags to fight. It is more satisfying than the *Iliad*'s portrayal of either Achilles' revenge on Hector (with whom we have been led to sympathize) or the revenge-motivated sack of Troy, as anticipated by, for example, Priam (*Iliad* 22.38–76).[45] The real problem is not the level of violence inflicted, but our fear of the information about human psychology that the narrative contains. The ancient Greeks were far more capable of emotional honesty in articulating the drive for revenge: Thucydides records that in his speech to his Syracusans before battle with the invading Athenian imperial army, the Sicilian general Gylippus urged them that 'in dealing with an enemy it is most just and lawful to claim the right to slake the fury of the soul on the aggressor … [since revenge provides] the greatest of all pleasures' (7.68). It may be difficult for a modern audience, unlike Homer's, to accept that vengeance killing should be described as a 'pleasure', but it will certainly always be a danger when people's lives, and those of vulnerable members of their family, are threatened. Most of us will never find ourselves in Odysseus' position, and should not be too quick to pious judgement. The *Odyssey*, at least, has the honesty to look this most incendiary situation straight in its human face.

# 14

# SEX AND SEXUALITY

> I drew the sharp sword from beside my thigh, and charged at her as if I
> intended to kill her. Screaming loudly, she slipped underneath the sword,
> grabbed me by the knees, and wailed as she addressed her words to me: '...
> come on, put your sword back in its sheath. Then let us go to bed together, and
> through sexual intercourse learn to trust each other' (*Odyssey* 10.321–35).

O dysseus' account of his first encounter with Circe is the nearest
thing to a description of sexual activity – from a male perspective, of course – that occurs anywhere in the *Odyssey*. It involves a
phallic symbol, physical contact, a beautiful woman being humiliated and
a sado-masochistic undercurrent. In the hero's unsheathing of his sword,
the scene enacts the 'overlapping of sexual control and violence' in the
patriarchal world of the *Odyssey*:[1] now he can sleep with Circe safely, freed
of his previous fear of being rendered 'naked, worthless, and unmanned'
(10.301, 10.341). This is all arguably more exciting than the elegant song
performed by the bard in Phaeacia about the Olympian adultery that
Aphrodite committed with Ares (8.266–366). It offers more detail than
the disappointingly brief statement that when Penelope and Odysseus
finally make it back into their marriage bed (the moment for which everyone has been waiting for many thousand hexameters), 'they took delight
in the charms of lovemaking, and then each gratified the other verbally
by narrating what had happened to them' (23.300–1). In antiquity scholars saw that the Circe episode was the sexiest: Servius responded to it by
concluding that she was a 'very famous prostitute' (*clarissima meretrix*).[2]

Odysseus' 'disloyal' slave women are accused of actually enjoying
'Aphrodite' with the suitors (22.444–5). Unmarried young aristocrats in
the *Odyssey* also have sex on their minds: poor Telemachus, destined to
end his own *Bildungsroman* a virgin still, is given on his departure from
Sparta a beautiful wedding dress for his future bride, raising the hope,
never to be fulfilled, that there is a romance in the offing for our younger
hero. As if to underline the erotic connotations of the gift, its giver is

189

none other than the beautiful adulteress Helen herself (15.123–9). The other nubile young person whose hopes of marriage remain unfulfilled is of course white-armed Nausicaa, whose urge to launder her trousseau in preparation for what she feels is her imminent marriage is implanted in her mind by Athena; it is on this mission that she encounters the charismatic stranger, stark naked except for a twig. With Nausicaa, Odysseus enjoys the equivalent of the unfulfilled love stories in *Brief Encounter* or *Lost in Translation*.³ This has not prevented Nausicaa from experiencing a murky afterlife as the object of fantasy about sudden sexual encounters by men with intense young women, for example in Irving Layton's poetic memory of 'going roughly to it' on a raincoat.⁴

Yet the *Odyssey* glosses over all its hero's sexual unions, not only with Penelope and Circe, but in Calypso's 'arching caverns' (5.154–5). The poem's racy reputation seems to be a result not of sex scenes but of an interest in tension between men and women: Beye argues that Odysseus' adventures are shaped by his (hetero)sexuality, which produces much of the distrust that characterizes the psychological if not the explicitly sexual world of the poem.⁵ Yet Homer's restraint did not stop Circe becoming the symbol of the sins of the flesh in much ancient and Renaissance allegory.⁶ Nor did it prevent her from starring as the eroticized protagonist in several Early Modern dramas about both Odysseus (Calderón liked Circe so much that he wrote two) and other mythical heroes. In his influential tragedy *Circe*, Charles Davenant (then aged 19) exploited the recent arrival of actresses in the Restoration theatre by writing a steamy scene in which Circe tries to seduce the young Orestes.⁷

Odysseus' sexual liaisons in the *Odyssey* also informed the development of the Don Juan figure in Western literature, and have inspired much mildly erotic cinema, literature and art. There is a sexual charge to Radley Metzger's film *Dark Odyssey* (1957), although it is not a vehicle for the sustained soft-core erotica for which he was later to become known. The story of a Greek sailor who jumps ship in New York to avenge the rape and murder of his sister, the wanderings involve various seedy contexts in New York City, and his high-voltage relationship with a Greek immigrant woman named Nike. Far more explicit and in a different idiom, *2069: A Sex Odyssey* (1977), directed by George Tressler, sees science fiction meet sex romp as five resourceful residents of the all-female planet Venus embark on a quest to find fertile Earthmen that takes them across the solar system into a series of erotic encounters necessitating full nudity.

Just as the audiences of *Star Trek* were encouraged by nubile actresses to 'thrill to Kirk's sexual exploits with gorgeous females ... from the stunning lady lawyers, biologists and doctors ... to the vicious and breathtaking Elaan of Troylus, who ruled a planet',[8] so the *Odyssey* itself has always offered film directors the opportunity for mildly sexy scenes. Curiously, both major *Odyssey* movies omitted Helen, whose beauty caused the whole Trojan War in the first place, even though she plays a prominent role in Book 4. It seems that twentieth-century directors did not know what to do with adulterous sluts (however gorgeous) reunited domestically, unpunished, with their middle-aged husbands. Camerini's version did allow both Nausicaa and Circe long 1950s-style clinches with Kirk Douglas, and even an attempt at a kiss between Penelope and the main suitor in that version, Antinous. But in Konchalovsky's movie Nausicaa is taken out of the sexual game altogether, and the fluffy Bernadette Peters, a light comedienne, is so seriously miscast as Circe that the whole sequence becomes laughable – as one critic put it, you might as well cast Dolly Parton as Antigone.[9] It is only in Odysseus' extended visit to Calypso, acted by the stunning singer Vanessa Williams, that there is sexual chemistry and sensual physical contact, including Calypso's suggestive palpation of the boar wound above Odysseus' knee. Indeed, the encounter is sufficiently convincing on a sexual level that this viewer was left truly puzzled as to why Odysseus would leave Calypso for an unknown destiny on a raft in perilous seas. NBC seem to have agreed, for the sole joint publicity photo, which was widely reproduced, is the inter-racial embrace of this unforgettable Calypso and the exhausted Odysseus.[10]

Indeed, political correctness – perhaps with an audience including children in mind – seems to have been a major concern in this movie, as the crotchety octogenarian classicist Peter Green pointed out in his legendary review, in which he came close to explicit homophobia in his objections to 'the campiest pretty-boy Hermes I've ever seen'.[11] A determination to avoid any suggestion of under-age sex may be the reason why there is no attempt to convey the erotic frisson between the Nausicaa and the middle-aged Odysseus. Konchalovsky's film ends with an unconvincing bedroom reunion of Odysseus and Penelope, but has at least set up the problem of Penelope's intense sexual frustration in a scene where Greta Scacchi (an actress with a racy reputation) lies half immersed to her upper thighs in rippling waves, her legs apart, moaning in the darkness. Penelope's sexual needs have actually been subject to speculation since antiquity. A tradition had developed already by Hellenistic times that Penelope had not been faithful, indeed had given birth to the god Pan after sleeping with all the suitors.[12] The interest in Penelope's libido continued with the Australian musical drama *Opa: A Sexual Odyssey*, which played in the

Athenaeum Theatre, Melbourne, in 1994. Penelope's desires for uncomplicated sexual pleasure were expressed in her fantasies as revealed by four actors, 'the Sirens of her unconscious, who lure her into a journey through a forbidden erotic landscape'.[13]

That the *Odyssey* had sexual connotations for some ancient audiences is made clear in Petronius' *Satyrica*. By replacing Odysseus' quest for Ithaca with Encolpius' quest for an erection, and Poseidon's wrath with the anger of Priapus, Petronius establishes his novel as a bawdy *Odyssey* from the outset. Before long the anti-hero finds himself in a brothel, hearing how his acquaintance Ascyltos has narrowly escaped becoming a male prostitute (8). Scenes of mass depravity in the brothel ensue, comprising aphrodisiac potions, a sodomite who 'almost dislocated our buttocks with his poking' (21), wrestling masseurs, an assiduous rent-boy who works away at Encolpius' groin to no purpose (23–4), and even the proposed deflowering of a girl who appears to be no more than seven years old. Torrid rivalry over sexual ownership of the boy Giton rages between Encolpius and Ascyltos, and later between Encolpius and Tryphaena (herself a former lover of Encolpius), who seduces the boy at sea (113). But Encolpius has his own share of sexual opportunities, with the gorgeous Circe (131) and Oenothea, who claims to be able to give any man an erection 'stiffer than horn' (134). Some critics have seen the importance of the sexual scenes in the novel – which include such deviations as scopophilia and sadism as well as different permutations in the biological sex of the partners – as evidence for Petronius' own psychology,[14] while others have taken more sociological or literary lines of approach.[15]

In the mid and late nineteenth century the *Odyssey* became strongly associated with sexual passion. One symptom of this was the appeal of the *Odyssey* to the writers of Victorian burlesque, a mildly risqué form of popular entertainment that offered light-hearted, musical adaptations of famous works of literature. These conventionally included titillating breeches roles for pretty actresses, as well as male drag acts and suggestive innuendo. Thus in Francis Cowley Burnand's *Patient Penelope*, the suitor Eurymachus was played by Maria Simpson, while Ulysses dressed up as Penelope, in her bustle and ribbons, for the boudoir denouement. This show therefore involved a woman dressed as a man climbing in a window, and a man dressed as a woman reclining on a bed to await an amorous encounter.[16]

The late Victorian, eroticized reading of the *Odyssey* from the male sexual subject's perspective found explicit expression in *The World's Desire*, a prose 'sequel' to the epic written by the novelist Rider Haggard, with

some assistance from the classicist Andrew Lang. Lang had himself translated the *Odyssey* and written a book-length prose poem entitled *Helen of
Troy*.[17] The sequel claims to be the record set out long ago by Rei, an Egyptian priest who served the Pharoah Meneptah (Rameses II's son) and his
wife Meriamun. A previous chapter has already explored the importance
of the *Odyssey* to the configuration of Ayesha, the immortal African queen,
in Rider Haggard's most famous novel, *She*, which was first serialized in
1886–87. It was while writing *She* that Haggard first conceived the idea of
a sequel to the *Odyssey*, and indeed wrote a first draft called *The Song of the
Bow*.[18]

In the renamed *The World's Desire*, finally published in 1890, Haggard
imagined the final voyage and death of Odysseus as foretold by Tiresias
(see p 210), but made it sexier than the *Odyssey*. If the presiding goddess of
the *Odyssey* is Athena, she is emphatically ousted in this sequel by Aphrodite. A widowed and disconsolate Odysseus visits Aphrodite's Ithacan
temple, and learns that his new quest entails finding and sleeping with
Helen of Troy, the titular World's Desire. After an erotic dream he sails
off to Egypt and arrives at the palace of the pharaoh. He is tricked into
sleeping with the pharaoh's wife
Meriamun, who lusts after him mightily, possesses the magical power
to transform herself into Helen's double. The central sex scene, in the
tradition of high Orientalizing fantasy, concludes with a snake twin-
ing itself around their bodies, in the very moment of their post-coital
embrace, 'knitting them in the bond of sin'.[19] Meriamun ends up accusing
Odysseus of rape, her lovely hair all dishevelled and her robe ripped across
her breast, and evolving into an un-nuanced stereotype of the Eastern
she-tyrant. She beheads her guards, poisons her husband and attempts
to have the real Helen sacrificed. The novel ends with Odysseus dying in
Helen's arms, after Telegonus (his son by another lover, Circe) mistakenly
launches an arrow at him from on board a ship. But this response to the
*Odyssey* has replaced the very soul of the epic – the virgin goddess of intelligence helping a clever man come home – with the sex goddess helping a
sexually excited man find Helen.

This eroticized sequel to the *Odyssey* was related to the vogue in the
visual arts and photography for scenes from mythology, itself a symptom of
the gender politics of later nineteenth-century society.[20] The women in the
*Odyssey* with whom Odysseus is erotically linked were seen to reflect the
dichotomized view of women as idealized brides and loyal wives (Nausicaa
and Penelope, see Fig. 14.1) or as seedy, sexually demanding *femmes fatales*
(Calypso and Circe, and the Sirens). Consequently, although occasional

attempts were made to confer some respectability on Calypso 'of the beautiful hair braids' (see Fig. 14.2), she was usually presented in unambigu-
ously erotic terms. The sexual symbolism is most blindingly obvious in
the standing, phallic male figure and the vaginal cave aperture of Arnold
Böcklin's *Odysseus und Kalypso* (1883). But Nausicaa, as potential wife,
was routinely desexualized: in Edward Poynter's famous *Nausicaa and her
Maidens Playing at Ball* (1879), the Homeric picture has been significantly
modified. The princess with marriage on her mind, who dares to confront
a naked, outcast stranger on a lonely beach, becomes a prototypical nurse
or companion figure, romping and doing the laundry.[21] Penelope is always
shown grieving, weaving or, in the Madonna-like pose of William Blake
Richmond's *The Death of Ulysses* (1888), in which the hero lies supine in the
lap of his virtuous wife, and the pair are construed less as sexual partners
than as mother and son in a classical *pieta*.

Moreover, for every chaste Penelope in Victorian art there are half
a dozen shady temptresses from Odysseus' wanderings, and in 1989
Kestner argued that this was not simply a reflection of the light-hearted
soft pornography available in the demimondaine entertainments called
*Poses Plastiques*, in which young women posed semi-naked in allegedly
sculptural roles inspired by mythology.[22] The ubiquity of sexually predatory Sirens and Circes in the visual art of this period is to be explained,
rather, in terms of their suitability for 'proving' that women's nature made
them prone to deviant behaviour. Sexually available women were felt
to be dangerously animal-like themselves; this idea is expressed in the
truly bestial Circe scene painted by Arthur Hacker in 1893, where all the
figures – the swarming pigs, the grovelling, dazed Odysseus and Circe
herself, with her protuberant buttocks – are seated or prostrate on the
refuse-strewn earth. Two years later it also underlay the presentation as a
latterday Circe of the earthy Arabella of Hardy's *Jude the Obscure* (called
*Jude the Obscene* by one contemporary reviewer); after coercing Jude into
slaughtering their pig, she leaves him feeling 'dissatisfied with himself as
a man'.[23] There was a belief that women who were sexually responsive were
suffering from a disorder that could cause male impotence. The threat felt
to be posed by Circe and the Sirens to the virile power of Odysseus and
his crewmen expressed this conviction.[24]

The numerous pictures of Sirens painted between 1870 and 1910 always
visualized them as naked young white women (Homer's audience will
have imagined them as semi-birdlike in form). The Victorians, however,
wanted their threatening Sirens to be sanitized: William Etty's *The Sirens
and Ulysses* (1837) disgusted contemporary reviewers on account of the real-

istic flesh of all portrayed, the corpses and skeletons. People did not want to look at Greek myths in order to be reminded of the mortality of their flesh, but to see it aestheticized as in William Edward Frost's idealized *The Sirens* (1849).[25] Sirens were sometimes construed allegorically as representing specific dangers – venereal disease, or the seductions presented to men by prostitutes, or the lure of opium;[26] a court physician wrote in 1876 that the temptation presented by opium to a man 'is not the beautiful Goddess of Love but Circe, the wanton one, and the floating forms are Sirens who allure him – the luckless, the headless – within their deadly embrace'.[27] That the seductive women of the *Odyssey* were personifications of men's own instinctive urges was an idea, ultimately deriving from Neoplatonism, promulgated by John Ruskin: Circe, he wrote, encoded men's 'pure Animal like' sexual drive, which needs to be governed with the moral equivalent of moly to prevent men from turning into beasts.[28]

The erotic appeal of classical women in the visual arts is explored by Joyce in *Ulysses*. Above Molly's bed hangs a painting called *Bath of the Nymph* which makes Leopold Bloom think about naked women. Molly, who was born in Gibraltar, Calypso's traditional home, represents both the lovely nymph and Penelope. In the chapter 'Lestrygonians', Bloom appreciates the sexiness of the statues of classical goddesses in the National Museum, a trope of which the reader is reminded when in 'Eumaeus' Bloom perceives Molly as resembling one of the 'antique statues', with their 'splendid proportions of lips, bosom'.[29] In 'Circe' Joyce takes his readers to the Dublin brothel run by Bella Cohen, the scene of several bestial behaviours. When Bloom is denounced for his perversions by society viragos, one of them is described as 'a Venus in furs', in reference to the novel whose author was later to give masochism its name, Leopold Sacher-Masoch's *Venus in Furs* (1870).[30] Joyce's correspondence reveals his own fantasy about being beaten, and Bloom's own masochism was informed by a scene in which the hero of Masoch's novel reads the *Odyssey* in his honeysuckle gazebo. Just before his meeting with his lover Wanda, he fantasizes about what he calls a 'perfect scene of ancient love', Odysseus' encounter with a beautiful enchantress possessing the power to turn men into animals.[31]

Joyce was fascinated by the ways that sexual activity can be represented in language. The 'Nausicaa' episode contains passages 'where it is necessary to speak about tumescent and detumescent prose rhythms, as well as orgasmic ejaculatory plosive phonemes' during Leopold's masturbation sequence.[32] Joyce also explores sex in language when reflecting on words deriving from Latin roots: both Bloom and Stephen 'admitted the alternately stimulating and obtunding influence of heterosexual magnetism'.[33] The transient nature of the sexual act is mocked by the pomposity of 'the incongruity and disproportion between the self prolonging tension of the thing proposed to be done and the self abbreviating relaxation of the thing done'.[34] This builds to a climax with the hilarious circumlocution offered for the phrases 'he fucked her' and 'she was fucked by him': 'masculine subject, monosyllabic onomatopoeic transitive verb with direct feminine object', and 'feminine subject, auxiliary verb and quasimonosyllabic onomatopoeic past participle with complementary masculine agent'.

For all his libidinal drives, Leopold has not had penetrative sexual intercourse with Molly for ten years, five months and 18 days. The physical alienation between them was caused by their child Rudy's death: in the 'Lestrygonians' chapter, Bloom reflects, 'Could never like it again after Rudy'.[35] This alienation results, on 16 June, in Molly's adulterous sexual encounter with Blazes Boylan. Although desperately unhappy with this development, Bloom does nothing to prevent it, and drifts all day around Dublin as Odysseus wandered the Mediterranean. He has for too many years been taking Molly breakfast instead of physically affirming his marital bond. The novel ends with a shift in the emotional status quo, and a hope that Bloom can restart his sexual relationship with Molly and even try for another child, thus recovering, like Odysseus, his status as man of the household in its fullest sense.[36]

A longstanding controversy relates to Molly's ruminations in the final chapter, 'Penelope'. This notoriously takes the form of a stream-of-consciousness monologue, with no punctuation until the full stop at the end, and only eight paragraph breaks. It begins with the word 'yes', and the word is repeatedly interspersed at an accelerating speed until the chapter ends with words that seem to represent Molly's orgasm, 'and yes I said yes I will Yes'. The contested question is not whether Molly is masturbating, fantasizing or recollecting, but the identity of the man in her fantasy. Is it Blazes Boylan, which would mean that in a final subversive twist to the novel's response to the *Odyssey* Joyce makes Penelope mate with Eurymachus? Or is it indeed Poldy that she is now 'determined to seduce', the husband she loves but has been estranged from for ten years, thus bringing the novel to a close with the imminent sexual reunion of man and wife?[37]

In a brilliant study, Kathleen McCormick has shown how answers to this question have changed dramatically over the decades, parallel with shifts in the status of women and views of obscenity. In its early days, shock at the novel's sexual content clouded the whole issue, but by the 1940s critics were coping with Molly's interest in her own body by identifying her as an Earth Mother, Gaia or Tellus, in whom reproduction and regeneration – not sexual pleasure – were the central issues. In the censorious 1950s, however, critics began to attack the woman they saw as the whorish, overtly sexual wife of the hapless victim Poldy. It was not until the advent of academic feminism that more interesting assessments of Molly's significance began to appear: some have read her as a representation of resistance to masculine discourses; others as stereotyped in her limited world view, her passivity and her preoccupation with the body rather than the mind.[38] But none of this alters the fact that the Homeric *Odyssey* lies behind one of the most important steps ever taken in the representation not only of female sexuality but of the subjective experience of fantasy, desire and orgasm. Who can forget the reconfiguration of the Sirens as the barmaids at the Ormond Hotel, one of whom engages the attention of all the men present as she repetitively moved her hand up and down the 'smooth jutting beerpull'?

There have been few permutations of sexual relationships and partner that have not found expression through responses to the *Odyssey*. In one atypical and beautiful poem entitled 'Penelope', Simon Armitage has expressed the aspirations of a 'suitor' towards the unassailable wife, unless the garden labour suggests, rather, Eumaeus:

> Your man is long gone, and I have loitered
> by your garden gate; weeded the border,
>     turned the soil over, waited on your word.[39]

But the most common scenario is that closest to the *Odyssey*, in which a male subject thinks back on a past relationship, identifying the woman involved with either Circe or Calypso. Thus the speaker of Michael Longley's poem 'Eurycleia II' (1991) remembers,

> I began like Odysseus by loving the wrong woman
> Who has disappeared among the skyscrapers of New York
> After wandering for thousands of years from Ithaca.[40]

On the other hand it is impossible to be sure whether it is Calypso, Circe or even Odysseus himself that is the subject of Pablo Neruda's atmospheric and physically charged poem 'Night on the Island' in *The Captain's Verses*.[41] When it comes to marital sex, nobody has better expressed than Borges the importance to Odysseus of his sexual reunion with Penelope in terms of reaffirming his status as Somebody: sex in its most metaphysical dimension. In his brilliant little poem 'Odyssey, Book Twenty-Three':

> Now in the love of their own bridal bed
> The shining queen has fallen asleep, her head

Upon her king's breast. Where is that man now
Who in his exile wandered night and day
Over the world like a wild dog, and would say
His name was No One, No One, anyhow?[42]

The central theme of the film *The Shipping News* (2001, directed by Lasse Hallström), which was adapted from a novel by E. Annie Proulx (1993), is return, over water, to the ancestral home. But before the home-coming can be achieved and the appropriate wife discovered, the hero Quoyle (played by Kevin Spacey) has to come to terms with the end of his seven-year relationship with a sexual temptress. Quoyle falls hopelessly for a young woman named Petal, who turns out to be psychotic. Throughout the film the emotional misery of sexual infatuation with an undeserving object of desire is paralleled by the memory of nearly drowning as a child when his father pushed him under the surface of dark waters, as Odysseus nearly drowns after leaving Calypso's island. When Petal dies in a car crash, Quoyle is persuaded to move to his ancestral home in Newfound-land, where he works as a reporter and learns how to spin an Odyssean yarn to fill the newspaper columns. Eventually he is saved by the love of a Penelope-like single mother and truly comes home in both the literal and psychological senses of the phrase.

Although Circe's subjectivity had been explored before, it was not until Margaret Atwood's 24-poem cycle 'Circe/Mud Poems' (1974) that Circe talked frankly about sex – or rather, about heterosexual politics. When she surrenders to Odysseus in Atwood's tenth poem, she is still emotionally resistant, and their affair begins with a disturbing mock-rape in which Odysseus holds down her arms and hair. But there is tenderness in poem 15, where she meditates on his flawed body and its scars; in the final poem she imagines walking with him through a November landscape, licking melted snow from his mouth.[43] A similar delicate eroticism infuses Judith Kazantzis's poem in the voice of Penelope, as she reflects on 'the whisper-ing entry' that nobody other than she and Odysseus, her 'groaning earth-shaker', knew about as they reunited in their marital bed.[44]

It is not only the heterosexual female perspective that has been explored by women reacting to sex in the *Odyssey*. In Merkel's novel *An Ordinary Marriage* one of Penelope's more erotic relationships in Odysseus' absence is with a North African slave girl, and lesbian interest in the *Odyssey* has recently been spotlighted by Alison Bechdel's brilliant memoir, in the form of an extended comic-strip narrative, *Fun Home: A Family Tragicomic* (2006). Bechdel is famous for her *Dykes to Watch Out For*, syndicated since 1983, and this new autobiographical work has a huge ready-made readership. Bechdel's father Bruce, a closet homosexual, committed suicide in 1980, just a few months after she had herself 'come out'. The memoir traces her difficult relationship with him, from childhood to teenage angst, and movingly explores the complexity of her feelings for him as paternal subject. These involved anger, intellectual recognition and powerful identification. The father and daughter shared a passion for literature. At college she came across the notice of a course on *Ulysses*, and sensed that its appearance in her life is 'like the goddess Athena's visit to Telemachus, when she nudged him to go find his long-lost dad, Odysseus'.[45] On the same day, she realized that she is gay and also discovered Rieu's Penguin translation of the *Odyssey*. She suddenly stopped playing the role of Telemachus – confused child of an errant father – and became Odysseus:

> I embarked that day on an odyssey which, consisting as it did in a gradual, episodic, and inevitable convergence with my abstracted father, was very nearly as epic as the original.[46]

This involved masturbating as she reads Leopold Bloom's reactions to Gertie MacDowell in the 'Nausicaa' chapter of *Ulysses*, and, it is implied, fantasizing about being Odysseus, with Nausicaa ministering to him.[47]

Bechdel's autobiographical descent to the Underworld, she tells us, was the day she publicized her homosexuality; she felt 'adrift on the high seas' but saw that her course lay 'between the Scylla of my peers and the swirling, sucking Charybdis of my family'; her sexual initiation was with a large, one-eyed anarcho-feminist, whose labia were the Cyclops' cave.[48] When she and her father finally brought themselves – on just one occasion – to discuss their 'shared predilection', it was not 'the sobbing, joyous reunion of Odysseus and Telemachus' but more 'fatherless Stephen and sonless Bloom having their equivocal late-night cocoa at 7 Eccles Street'. This 'Ithaca moment', as she puts it, is illustrated by the very sentence from *Ulysses* quoted above, in which Dedalus and Bloom agree about sex – or at least about the 'alternately stimulating and obtunding influence of heterosexual magnetism'. But in Bechdel's case, there is a handwritten question mark of incomprehension marking the word 'obtunding'.[49]

Bechdel achieves a frank evocation of her emerging sexuality and sexual experiences, and a strange, deep tribute to a man who could never give her the support that she needed, and abandoned her by committing suicide. Yet in a curious way his psychological presence is still inspiration and comfort. Bechdel feels both guilt and elation because she finally became the creative artist that he had longed to be. She realizes that the father of whose help she had despaired had given her a psychological gift of lasting value, and this becomes symbolized by the copy of *Ulysses* that he had given her, the text through which she discovered both the *Odyssey* and ways to come to terms with her own life and psychological development.

Odysseus himself is in the ancient sources emphatically heterosexual. This is used to hilarious effect in Mark Merlis's novel *An Arrow's Flight* (1998), which, although strictly speaking is a response to Sophocles' *Philoctetes,* uses material from the *Odyssey* as well. The novel sets the Greek story of Odysseus, Neoptolemus and Philoctetes in contemporary North American gay culture, with the self-important heterosexual Odysseus confused by its conventions and values. In a world of go-go bars and distinctions he does not understand – between 'sissies', 'fairies', 'hustlers' in cute shorts and effeminate 'queens' – Odysseus is profoundly shocked by a porn magazine centre-fold showing Tydeus' backside, and the laugh is definitely on him.

But Odysseus can be a gay male hero, too: in fact a specialist gay international travel service provider, established in 1984, is called Odysseus. The tragic vulnerability of gay men to becoming HIV-positive was explored in *Odysseus Died from AIDS* at the Edinburgh Fringe in August 2006. Written and directed by Steven Svoboda, the play puts the sexual histories and psychological suffering of a group of AIDS sufferers under a tragicomic spotlight. When Elliot succumbs to AIDS, he finds himself in hospital alongside other mortally ill patients. As a studious young man who identifies with the hero of the *Odyssey*, he assigns roles in the epic to the people around him. The black transsexual Rosean is Athena, the Cyclops is the promiscuous heterosexual bruiser Nick, whose CMV makes him blind, and the all-powerful doctor is Zeus. But the most influential gay *Odyssey* is the 1990 film *Pink Ulysses*, written and directed by Eric DeKuyper. Inspired by the gay cult classic *Pink Narcissus* (1971), *Pink Ulysses* offers a series of episodes based on the idea of an actor in tight jeans preparing for a role in a film of the *Odyssey*. This in turn involves handsome iron-muscled young men, minimally dressed in the loincloth idiom of the disguised homoerotic body culture magazines of the 1950s. Some images from the *Odyssey* – for example, being lashed to a mast – receive new sexual connotations. There is explicit male masturbation to orgasm, and a great deal of rolling on sheets, wrestling in jockstraps and close-ups on Telemachus' buttocks. Ulysses, whose oiled pectorals are displayed to advantage in the archery scene, himself dreams of young men, while remaining – as usual – functionally heterosexual.

The *Odyssey* has also provided material for pornography of more seriously hardcore nature, as anyone tempted to google systematically on the names 'Circe' and 'Calypso' will discover. In the epic, of course there is technically speaking no zoophilia (human sex with animals), since Circe only sleeps with Odysseus, and not the men she has changed into pigs. But a sexual or at least sensual relationship between Circe and the pig-men has been repeatedly implied, certainly ever since Gustave-Adolphe Mossa's Symbolist oil-painting *Circe* (1904), in which the witch, whose red jacket is open in a vertical slash that screams 'vulva' at the viewer, is hard pressed on both sides by fleshy pigs with human features who look as though they are trying to suckle her.[50] Amongst written works with literary credentials, there is no more graphic *Odyssey*-related sex than that between Telemachus' girlfriend Haidee and the narrator (a sex-starved journalist named Pumpkin, travelling with Odysseus) in Clive Sinclair's novella *Meet the Wife* (2002). The scene takes place before Pumpkin accompanies Odysseus to Hades to find Penelope (the titular wife), when both Pumpkin and Haidee have been turned into pigs by a Circe-like hostess on the Island of Transformation. This is not, technically speaking, zoophilia, since no physical human is involved. But the combination of a human consciousness and the subjective description of what it feels like to be a priapic boar covering a hormone-crazed sow on heat is arguably more obscene.[51] It is certainly too full of four-letter words to bear repeating here.

Even in the respectable company of classical and Renaissance scholarship, faint hits of unusual sexual fantasies are occasionally discernible. Several critics have noticed how mud and dirt are inextricably bound up with ideas about the body in the Circe myth, and how painters have combined the dazzling flesh of their Circes with scattered animal droppings.[52] One eminent Homerist chose in 1993, rather disturbingly, to compare the excitement of a textual scholar approaching the *Odyssey* with that of a man approaching the lacerations in the naked *corpse* of a young woman 'of surpassing beauty'.[53] People who enjoy doing sexual things with blood have sometimes found inspiration in the rituals Odysseus performs over the trench before he can speak to the dead in the Underworld. But necrophilia and necromancy lead the argument into the final chapter, which is not addressed to the *Odyssey*'s role in the history of representing sex, but to its ongoing dialogue with death.

# 15

# DIALOGUE WITH DEATH

I am painted here, an ever living city of the dead,
the tomb of every age. It was Homer who explored
the house of Hades, and I am copied from him
as my first original.
(Nicias' painting of the Underworld describes itself in a
poem by Antipater of Sidon).[1]

Odysseus is one of the few figures in our cultural repertoire who talks directly with the dead. In Book 11 of the *Odyssey*, he relates to the Phaeacians how he actually visited the Underworld, by means of frightening rituals, and managed to emerge unscathed.

Odysseus' dialogue with the dead (*nekuia*) was the most influential of all those undergone by the several Greek heroes – Heracles, Theseus and Orpheus – who entered the Underworld, in a story type which goes back to the *Epic of Gilgamesh*. Indeed, conceiving death as a *journey* to a darker location is a phenomenon manifested in almost all the world's myth systems.[2] The 'going down' myth (*katabasis*), imitated by Plato in the tenth book of the *Republic*,[3] created the literary scenario of the conversation with the dead, popular in the dialogues of the Second Sophistic,[4] and satirized in the third book of Swift's *Gulliver's Travels*. From the *Odyssey* the Christian notion of Hell in Augustine and Aquinas derived descriptive detail; Dante's *Inferno* could never have come into being without it. More recently the *nekuia* has been read as the scene of ultimate horror during the Holocaust.

Odysseus and his men arrive at the river Oceanus in the eternal darkness of Cimmerian land. They walk up river and conduct the rites, specified by Circe, which impressed the Modernists. T.S. Eliot said that Tiresias was the unifying figure of the nightmarish *The Waste Land* (1922), at 'the evening hour that strives/Homeward, and brings the sailor home from sea'.[5] In 1935 Ezra Pound, whose first Canto begins with Tiresias, said that the *nekuia* was an atavistic remembering of primeval rites capable of putting us in touch with the earliest Mediterranean sensibilities.[6] Odysseus digs a trench, pours libations of milk, honey, wine, water and barley meal, and intones prayers to their sinister recipients. With his own sword he cuts the throats of a ram and a black ewe. As their dark blood flows into the soil,

> the ghosts of the dead and departed swarmed up out of Erebus – brides, youths, old, exhausted men, teenage girls whose high spirits had been wiped out by sudden mourning, large numbers of warriors wounded in combat, their armour still covered in gore. They came in their hordes from every direction and hovered round the trench, screaming weirdly. I was white with fear (11.38–43).

Wilson Harris's poem *Canje (the River of Ocean)* relocates the *nekuia* to a swing bridge in Guiana, where the villagers are forced to undertake life-threatening fishing expeditions in pursuit of food to stay alive. In this ghostly place Ulysses, with the help of liquor, talks to a fishmonger whose son has drowned.[7] One of the most pain-laden recent reactions to the *nekuia* is by the poet Josephine Balmer, whose collection *Chasing Catullus* explores her inconsolable grief at the death of her little niece Rachel. The poems relate moments in the awful process of the child's illness, from diagnosis to the desperate mourning of her relatives. In 'Letchworth crematorium', where her niece's grave is located, Balmer explores the emotions that revisiting the site evoked in her, through a moving rewriting of this section of the Homeric *nekuia*:

> Now they came from the pit on each side,
> souls of the dead, souls of the dying
> with heart-stop cry. And my fear was green.[8]

Odysseus' dialogue with his first dead associate, Elpenor, is ambivalent. Elpenor lies unburied on Circe's island, where he broke his neck, falling drunkenly from her roof. Yet when he appears to Odysseus on the threshold of the Underworld to ask for proper funeral rites, he does so in heroic language recalling the *Iliad* (11.66–78). He wants cremation with all his weapons, and a stone raised to signify his fame, the tomb itself to be surmounted by the oar which he wielded in life. Elpenor's heroism consisted in his labour as a rower. By beginning the catalogue of the dead whom Odysseus meets with this relatively low-status individual, the human tone of the *nekuia* is established at its outset. Little wonder that this scene produced such an exceptional vase-painting in fifth-century Athens (see Fig. 15).[9]

The idea of the ordinary person who dies an unnecessary death in the margins of history fascinated later poets. For Seferis, in 'Sensual Elpenor' (1944), the drunken sailor becomes a fundamental type of the ordinary man, slave to his physical desires.[10] But in the Homeric text Elpenor's voice has an angry edge: he threatens to haunt Odysseus if he fails to bury him. Anger against uncaring leaders is apparent in Christopher Bakken's 'Last words from Elpenor' (2006), where the dead oarsman curses Odysseus as 'a swine/who would forget/son, wife, home, and me – this last betrayal/most appalling'.[11] When Archibald MacLeish commemorated all the unsung dead of the First World War, in which he served as an ambulance driver, it was in the voice of Elpenor. Elpenor says that he believes he is in Hell, because it is full of important and rich dead people, and

> Also the young men
> Their rears strung out on the fences
> Watching for shifts in the breeze:
>   And beyond under the lee the
>   Actual dead: the millions
> Only a god could have killed (28–33).

The reason they are all dead is the influence of

> Kings, dukes, dictators,
> Heroes, headmen of cities,
> Ranting orations from balconies,
> Boasting to lead us back to the
> Other days (36–40).[12]

The *nekuia* of the Odyssey did indeed find profound reverberations in the catastrophic fatalities of the First World War, partly because it had already affected the thinking of two architects of the twentieth-century mind, Karl Marx and Sigmund Freud. For Marx the terrifying mines and factories of the industrial revolution, the subterranean sites of material production itself, where the suffering proletariat laboured in eternity, were assimilated to the classical vision of the Underworld; the investigator of political economy must symbolically descend into this hell-like place if he is to explain the mechanisms of capitalism.[13] There was a counterpart to the Underworld as envisaged by Marx in the industrial hell lying behind Dickens's fiction, but foregrounded in the Wolverhampton of *The Old Curiosity* Shop. This terrible environment – actually described as 'Hell on Earth' – sees the final miseries of Little Nell and her grandfather.[14] For Freud, it was the active but hidden presence of the subconscious parts of our psyches that was spatially mapped on to the classical Underworld; the journey taken by the psychoanalyst and his patient into the recesses of this subconscious was then configured as a katabatic journey.[15]

It was in the wake of Marx and Freud that Eliot in *The Waste Land* and Joyce in the Hades chapter of *Ulysses* 'represented the material and spiritual dislocations produced by Western capitalism as an infernal condition',[16] and one which led directly to the hellish trenches of the First World War. But a recent study proposes an additional reason why the descent to the Underworld became 'the single most important myth for Modernist authors'.[17] This Modernist *nekuia*, usually traced back to Strindberg's autobiographical *Inferno* (1896), was related to pivotal crises in authors' own lives, during which they underwent personal trips to Hell, and returned changed people.

This is to take the notion of the *nekuia* metaphorically as almost any life-changing journey, experience or encounter that fits a sense of going inwards into the self or downwards into a figurative abyss, rather than upwards or outwards in the manner of the shamanic journeys some scholars think are represented by the ancient myths. Rather different from the story of Persephone's abduction by Hades told in the Homeric *Hymn to Demeter*, which is connected with fertility rites and agricultural renewal, the male *nekuia* is related to rebirth of a more spiritual or intellectual kind. If defined as widely as this, the *nekuia* that ultimately derives from the *Odyssey* was indeed the most important narrative in the literature of the first half of the twentieth century. It can be a topographical, geographical or anthropological *nekuia*, with political overtones, like Marlow's journey into the Belgian Congo in Joseph Conrad's *Heart of Darkness* (1902), which is described with 'the imagery and symbolism of the traditional voyage to Hades'[18]; the rivers that flow out from the African interior are 'streams of death in life', the central station is 'a grove of death', enveloped by a 'spectral forest', and this realm of the dead is inhabited by 'phantoms' and 'shades'.[19] Or the *nekuia* can be psychological, like the consul's submission to alcohol in Malcolm Lowry's *Under the Volcano* (1947), even if Geoffrey Firmin's fate is related to the universal fate of the human race during the Second World War.

Yet in Modernist poetry, the *nekuia* often refers to the process of artistic production itself. In the last poem of Seferis's collection *Mythistorema* (1935), the voices of the dead become symbolic of the poet's vocation.[20] The *nekuia* may offer a metaphor for a literary encounter with writers of the past – the community within which the allusive author continuously exists; for Yeats, in *Sailing to Byzantium* (1928), the poetic voice crosses the seas from the land beyond the 'dying generations' to Byzantium, where he encounters the 'singing-masters' of his soul, and learns how to leave behind his fleshly body for the 'artifice of eternity'. The *nekuia* is a metaphor for the transformation of lived experience into poiesis.[21] Wallace Stevens's thoughtful poem *Large Red Man Reading* (1950), opens:

There were ghosts that returned to earth to hear his phrases,
As he sat there reading, aloud, the great blue tabulae.
They were those from the wilderness of stars that had expected more.

The library is the place at which red man, who is reading 'from the poem of life', meets the dead of the Underworld, who would 'have wept to step barefoot into reality'.[22]

This poem dates from 1950, when the Modernist *nekuia* evolved into the all-pervasive *nekuia* of the later twentieth century. The 'katabatic' hero is now ubiquitous, encountering real or metaphorical underworlds in countless contemporary war movies and thrillers.[23] Falconer has argued that 'we are still very much governed by ... a world-view which conceives of selfhood as the narrative construct of the infernal journey and return'.[24] Western culture is saturated with images of the self being forged out of an infernal journey. Although this partly results from the fusing of the Greco-Roman descent narrative with the medieval Christian tradition achieved by the Florentine Dante Alighieri in his *Inferno*,[25] Falconer believes that since 1945, the katabasis has become identified with the very shape of our individual subjectivities.

Dante opened his *Inferno* with the statement, 'Midway on the journey of our life, I found myself in a dark wood', and these days, Falconer argues, the 'dark wood' can be any crisis, whether caused by divorce, redundancy, disease, bereavement or terror. But, paradoxically, much of this sense has been provided by the collectively held notion that the Second World War somehow represented the greatest journey into darkness ever taken by the human race – the death of millions in Russia, the nuclear bombs in Japan and the Holocaust. Falconer is surely correct in arguing that the war created a rupture in the Western philosophical tradition by making it impossible to conduct metaphysical enquiries *without* the spectre of the Holocaust: we all now feel trapped, like survivors of Hades.[26] This is similar to Adorno's view that the post-war condition *is* a sense of homelessness; an inevitable part of morality today is not to feel completely at home even in one's homeland because of the crisis that produced the Second World War and its horrors.[27]

Indeed, some scholars have suggested that we are all diagnostically *post-traumatic*. One reason may be that transference of traumatic responses operates across generations, since parents traumatized by war have been unable to prevent their treatment of their children becoming affected by their own depression, survivor guilt and isolation.[28] Another may be that trauma is not only a clinical syndrome: in contemporary culture it is 'a strategic fiction that a complex, stressful society is using to account for a world that seems threateningly out of control'.[29] The idea of *survival* has been resonant for those suffering other collective and political traumas and those writing about them: as a black man who had fought for his country but still faced racial discrimination, Ellison began *Invisible Man* just after returning from service at sea during the Second World War, and felt there to be a connection.[30] Odysseus' epithet *polutlas* – 'much-enduring' – has always resounded loudly in the ears of those who feel they are survivors.

In 1943 Eric Nossack watched, from the other side of the river Elbe, the firebomb with which Hamburg was decimated by the Allied bombardment. Three months later he completed his literary response to the experience of total annihilation in *Der Untergang*, translated as *The End*, which includes profound Homeric reverberations. He describes how the women used to cheer in glee when Allied aircraft caught fire and crashed, but that he always felt like Odysseus in the *Odyssey*, forbidding the old nurse to rejoice over the death of the suitors (22.411–16): 'Old woman, rejoice in silence; restrain yourself, and do not make any noise about it; it is an unholy thing to vaunt over dead men.'[31] At such moments of apocalyptic hatred, the distinction between friend and foe, for Nossack (who had anyway opposed National Socialism) had become meaningless. A few years later Nossack again expressed these experiences, but in fictionalized form as *Nekuia: Bericht eines Überlebenden* (*Nekuia: The Report of a Survivor*). The narrator, a lone survivor like Odysseus, wanders alone through a devastated world, unsure whether he is alive or dead, searching for home and family.

It was inmates of the concentration camps of the Second World War – the few who stayed alive – who put the seal on our new meaning of the idea of survival.[32] These survivors have been through the fires of hell and come out alive, against all odds. This vision of the descent to the gas chambers on which the world was sent by fascism has often been mediated through the great medieval *nekuia* in Dante's *Inferno*. Written between 1307 and 1321 in the first person, *The Divine Comedy* tells of the poet's journey through the realm of the afterlife: Hell ('Inferno'), Purgatory and Paradise. Dante will not have been able to read the *Odyssey*, and had acquired his knowledge of Ulysses through the Roman tradition and medieval versions of the Troy story (see pp 14–15). His guide through Inferno and Purgatory is not Homer but Virgil. Amongst the many authors who have presented the Holocaust as *nekuia* the most influential is Primo Levi, whose Italian upbringing meant that Dante's verses ran in his veins. Yet his accounts of his experiences in Auschwitz and on the road home after liberation are also informed by the *Odyssey*.

Chapter 11 of the revised 1958 text of *If This Is a Man* is entitled 'The Canto of Ulysses', and frames the horrors of Auschwitz as a katabatic journey through the Inferno on which, however painfully, Levi had gained understanding.[33] *The Truce*, first published in 1963, was subtitled *A Survivor's Journey Home from Auschwitz*, and has directly Homeric resonances in the illicit gorging on plundered horse-meat, recalling the ravenous crew eating the Cattle of the Sun.[34] Levi recognized that his own clever Odyssean qualities had allowed him to survive (he was known in Auschwitz as *débrouillard et démerdard* – smart, and good at getting out of trouble).[35] But with this recognition went guilt, and in *The Truce* he gives prominence to another Odysseus, on to whom he shifts much of the unscrupulous behaviour required of anyone who survived: this is the deceitful Greek Jew from Salonica, a master-trickster with whom Levi begins what he calls his 'wanderings' after their release.[36] The Red Army soldiers with whom these two Odysseuses shared barracks at the transit camp of Katowice had witnessed terrible tragedies and lost many comrades: they 'were cheerful, sad and tired, took pleasure in food and wine, like Ulysses' companions after the ships had been pulled ashore'.[37]

By the time he wrote *The Drowned and the Saved* (1986) Odysseus/Ulysses has become 'Levi's favourite literary figure and alter ego'.[38] Levi compares his role as witness of the camps with Odysseus' tearful response to the Phaeacians: 'we ... speak also because we are invited to do so ... [like] Ulysses, who immediately yields to the urgent need to tell his story'.[39] In *The Truce* (1963) Levi had confided to his reader that one of the most important things he had learnt in Auschwitz was the imperative to avoid 'being a Nobody',[40] and in *The Search for Roots* (1981) the Cyclops represents the most brutal and unintelligent face of fascism. Levi relates the necessity of naming himself to the obese Kapo, the 'tower of flesh' who takes him to see Pannwitz.[41]

Falconer has shown that even second-generation Holocaust narratives continue to use the same trope of the nightmarish *nekuia*.[42] Indeed, she argues that there was a watershed in Western philosophical thinking immediately after the war, consequent upon which metaphysics can never again be conducted in the absence of the spectral image of the Holocaust: we no longer need to go down to meet the dead, for we cannot escape the reality that the modern world has seen the unprecedented: the industrialization of death on a genocidal scale.[43] The Second World War has forever changed the significance of both Homer's Underworld and Dante's.

In fact, the Homeric dimension of Dante's *Inferno* consists of more than a *katabasis* to the land of the dead, because Dante meets Ulysses in *Inferno* Book 26 (see also p 78): Virgil points out to Dante the figures of Ulysses and Diomedes, burning for the treachery of the Trojan horse and for the sacrileges committed at Troy. Virgil asks for an answer to the question of Ulysses' mysterious death, and it is Ulysses who replies. Even love for his son, father and Penelope could not cure his desire 'to be experienced of the world', and so he had sailed away in one small ship, with an ageing crew, through the Pillars of Hercules into uncharted waters. But when they finally saw land, a whirlwind arose which struck their ship until it sank beneath the waves, drowning all.

In the *Odyssey* itself, a different version of Odysseus' death is predicted by the ghost of Tiresias, prophet of Thebes. After drinking the black blood of the sacrificial animals, he tells Odysseus that if he is finally to placate Poseidon, yet another journey awaits him (11.119–36):

> When in your palace you have killed the suitors, whether by cunning or out in the open with bronze weapons, take up your well balanced oar and go on another journey until you come to men who have no notion of the sea, and do not add salt to their food. These men have no knowledge of ships with crimson cheeks, nor of the poising of oars which serve as wings for ships. I will tell you of a very plain sign that you will not be able to miss. At the moment you encounter another traveller who says that what you carry on your fine shoulder is a winnowing fan, that will be when you must fix your balanced oar in the earth, and perform fine rituals in honour of Lord Poseidon ... Then go back home ... death will come to you from the sea, a very gentle death, which will take you in your comfortable old age.

The very mention of Odysseus' own death here has produced reactions, for example Peter Huchel's atmospheric poem *The Grave of Odysseus*,[44] in which the *Odyssey* becomes a paradigm of the human condition:

> No one will find
> The grave of Odysseus,
> no stab of spade
> the encrusted helmet
> in the haze of petrified bones.
> ...
> All is mine, said the dust,
> the sun's grave behind the desert,
> the reefs full of the sea's roar,
> unending noon that still warms

the pirate's boy from Ithaca,
the rudder jagged with salt,
the maritime charts and lists
of ancient Homer.

The death of Odysseus has recently been updated in the most extreme manner, when in his radio play *Speaking Well of the Dead* Israel Horowitz made his Penelope's philandering husband die on 9/11 at the World Trade Center.[45] But the episode of Odysseus' actual death has always been upstaged by the prediction that Odysseus will leave home to go travelling yet again.

The most significant work in this category is Tennyson's *Ulysses* (1842). This beautiful poem, inspired by the death of Tennyson's best friend Arthur Hallam in 1833, imagines a superannuated hero, bored with Ithaca, his 'aged wife' and the life of 'an idle king'. This Ulysses, like Dante's, is attempting to convince his men that a destiny awaits them beyond the ordinary sphere of 'common duties'; they must be 'strong in will/To strive, to seek, to find, and not to yield' to their ageing bodies. A greater glory awaits them still, he tells them:

'Tis not too late to seek a newer world.
Push off, and sitting well in order smite
The sounding furrows; for my purpose holds
To sail beyond the sunset, and the baths
Of all the western stars, until I die.

Tennyson insisted that the poem expressed a bereaved man's continuing sense, despite his sorrow, of 'the need for going forward, and braving the struggle of life'. But Ulysses may here be echoing Satan's determination to find 'courage never to submit or yield' in his first speech in *Paradise Lost*, and there are other readings. Some critics have interpreted it as a dying man's deathbed ramblings, the guilt-stricken monologue of a dangerous leader in denial about the death of his crew, or the affirmation of an agnostic who must live an independent spiritual life in which he makes his own purpose. It is, of course, the multiplicity of possible interpretations that has given this poem its classic status, and its own influence over writers subsequently.[46]

The Russian poet Osip Mandel'shtam, for example, was an ardent populist after the October Revolution of 1917, but is responding to Tennyson as much as to Dante or Homer in his poem expressing the increasingly difficult situation in which the revolutionaries found themselves by 1922:[47]

So, let's give it a shot: a huge, clumsy,
Creaking turn of the rudder.
The earth swims. Man yourselves, men.
Dividing the ocean like a plough,
We will remember even in Lethe's frost,
That earth was worth a dozen heavens to us.

The 'final voyage of Odysseus' tradition has, however, never received a larger-scale response than Nikos Kazantzakis's modern Greek epic *The Odyssey* (1938). In a staggering 33,333 lines, dominated by the expectation of death,[48] Odysseus sets Ithaca in order, abducts Helen, overthrows Minoan civilization, fails to overthrow the Egyptian kingdom, builds a utopian city, loses it in an eruption, and then gives up on society and becomes an ascetic. He travels to the south of Africa and undergoes mystical experiences embodied in figures representing Don Quixote, Hamlet, Faust, Buddha, the Hedonist, the Poet, the Courtesan and Jesus Christ. Finally he sails in a coffin-shaped boat to the Antarctic and dies alone on an iceberg.

Kazantzakis's epic struggles to provide in Odysseus' protracted journey towards death a spiritual biography of the whole human race. But the same Dante–Tennyson tradition of imagining the old age of the hero, long after his Ithacan homecoming, is connected with the *Odyssey*'s relationship with the genre of autobiography. In 'Last of Ulysses' (1847) Walter Savage Landor had already dramatized the death of Ulysses in a moralizing review of his life and loves.[49] An important theme in the *Odyssey* is the struggle to keep alive recollections of the past. Much of the *Odyssey* consists of Odysseus himself fighting off forgetfulness, by forcing his crewmen to escape from the memory-destroying lotus, by avoiding being turned into an amnesiac swine, and above all by putting together his own adventures into a monologue delivered to the Phaeacians. Odysseus' autobiographical narrative is, however, prompted by the sequence in which he listens to his own exploits at Troy being narrated by Demodocus; these make him weep 'like a woman wailing when she flings herself on the body of her husband' (8.72–4). Only now he is ready to reveal his true identity. The philosopher Hannah Arendt pointed out that this passage is fundamental to the history of notions of subjectivity, since it introduces the first extended autobiography in the Western tradition.[50]

Odysseus only becomes aware of who he really is by listening to the storytelling his exploits and ordeals, and becoming aware of its significance. As a hero, Odysseus' impulse to self-revelation is heightened, but Cavarero thinks there is more than this at stake here, a conundrum she calls 'the Paradox of Ulysses'.[51] Odysseus weeps at the shock of discovering that he *is* – that he has a narratable identity, can be constituted in biography and constitute himself through autobiography. But the discovery that meaningful existence can be affirmed through revelation and self-revelation inevitably brings him face to face with the topic of death. As Foucault noticed in another context, Demodocus and his fellow bards must have been singing of Odysseus before the action of the *Odyssey*, and will sing of him indefinitely after his death; Odysseus, although alive, receives this gift *as a wife receives her dead husband*.[52] This is a textual dance of death, but one that can reproduce itself through potentially infinite narration.[53]

Sterling A. Brown opened his collection *Southern Road* (1932) with his first-person African-American dialect poem 'Odyssey of Big Boy', thus suggesting a mythic view of travel, experience and the road to self-discovery. The memories of the hero-narrator Calvin Big Boy Davis resonate 'with Homeric implications'.[54] Although ballad-like in form, the ballad is not a third-person song narrating the heroic deeds of culture heroes like Casey Jones. It paints, instead, an autobiographical picture of a dying man's consciousness as he remembers his past and travels towards the future, orally reshaping his personal history in the process.[55] One recent novel that uses the *Odyssey* to explore the consciousness of an elderly man is Peter Pouncey's *Rules for Old Men Waiting* (2005), told by a dying octogenarian who keeps himself alive by inventing a story set in the First World War. The Homeric atmosphere pervades the memories of combat, of rescue as a young shipwrecked sailor by a Cornish cove lady, of his relationships with his father and his son, and above all his love for his wife.

If Dante and Tennyson made it inevitable that Odysseus' own voice would be borrowed by writers framing the consciousness of dying men, there have also been expressions of the viewpoints of other deceased characters in the *Odyssey*, including Elpenor (see above). Outstanding amongst these is Margaret Atwood's *Penelopiad*, narrated by Penelope in the Underworld, which also includes lyric choruses sung by the executed maids. Joseph Auslander opened his collection *Cyclops' Eye* (1926) with the observation that while his dead friend is dust, and Odysseus is dust, Polyphemus still 'stokes his eye'.[56] The Swedish poet Gunnar Ekelöf's gloomy meditations on mortality, *Variations*, includes an extended parallel between facing Death and facing Polyphemus, every time 'the one-eyed one stirs his pot again .../... he who eats us one after the other,/tearing us apart as Saturn tore his sons,/completely meaningless!'[57] An idiosyncratic example is a play by Kurt Vonnegut first performed in 1970, entitled *Happy Birthday, Wanda June*. The title character is the ghost of a girl who died at the age of ten, run over by an ice-cream truck. The convoluted domestic comedy involves Penelope, whose macho adventurer husband Harold has been away in the Amazon for many years, but returns on his birthday to discover that his wife is surrounded by eager suitors and his son Paul has run away. A cake has been bought to commemorate his birthday, but it was a bakery leftover and is inscribed with the legend 'Happy Birthday, Wanda June'. It had never been picked up because the little girl had been killed.

Although Vonnegut made his position on violence and 'gun-nuts' pellucidly clear in the preface to the published version, critics have expended much ink debating his aims. To them, the play's grim premise seems at odds with its sustained levity of tone. It dates from 1970, at the height of the American carpet-bombing of Vietnam and Cambodia; its cast includes the ghost of a Nazi called Siegfried von Koningswald and an American colonel who dropped the atom bomb on Nagasaki. Vonnegut had become a committed pacifist after serving time as a German PoW in a Dresden factory, where he witnessed the Allied bombing of Dresden on 13 February 1945, two years after Nossack had watched Hamburg's annihilation (see above). An anti-war message becomes inescapable when the spectre of Wanda June reassures the audience that she is happier dead:

> Everybody up here is happy – the animals and the dead soldiers and people who went to the electric chair and everything … So if you think of killing somebody, don't worry about it. Just go ahead and do it. Whoever you do it to should kiss you for doing it. The soldiers up here just love the shrapnel and the tanks and the bayonets and the dum dums that let them play shuffleboard all the time – and drink beer.[58]

The constant connection between the Second World War, Vietnam and the figure of Homer's surviving soldier Odysseus is here underscored yet again. In Vonnegut's dark vision of the afterlife, the soldiers are still playing wargames.

Odysseus' dialogue with the war dead in Hades is one reason why the *Odyssey* has been seen as the *second* great epic, composed after the *Iliad* and presupposing its dire events.[59] Recently, the poem's status as an 'aftermath' text, a post-war story, has had particular resonance for an age that has defined itself as post-everything: postmodern, post-structuralist, post-colonial. But to conclude on a less serious note, the *nekuia*, by putting the hero of the *Odyssey* in direct contact with the dead through blood-drinking, has also always attracted the attention not only of everyone

drawn to the occult, but to vampires and their close allies, blood fetish-
ists. People who like drinking blood, or try to contact the dead, find their
earliest surviving instruction manual in Book 11 of the *Odyssey*, especially
the crucial information that ghosts need to drink blood before they can
talk.

Once the *Odyssey* had arrived in Western Renaissance culture, esoteric
philosophers were able to consult its *nekuia* as well as the scenes of
ghost-raising and corpse consultation in Aeschylus' *Persians* and Lucan's
*Pharsalia*;[60] a chief conduit for the transmission of knowledge about
ghost-raising from Homer to the general public was the fourth book of *De
Occulta Philosophia* by the Renaissance German *magus* Henry Cornelius
Agrippa. The book may be spurious, but this has not impaired its widespread influence, especially since it appeared in English translation in
1655. The section on necromancy describes rites derived directly from the
*nekuia* of the Odyssey:

> Souls of the dead are not to be called up without blood, or by the
> application of some part of their relict Body. In raising up these shadows,
> we are to perfume with new Blood, with the Bones of the dead, and with
> Flesh, Egges, Milk, Honey and Oile, and such-like things, which do
> attribute to the Souls a means apt to receive their Bodies.[61]

Perhaps we should take this leaf out of Agrippa's book, and let the magic
of the *Odyssey* work its power on its own psychosomatic terms. A host
of different reasons have been advanced during the course of this book
for cultural longevity of this particular narrative – its generic versatility,
its sociological complexity and its philosophical and emotional clout. But
perhaps the issue simply *can't* be fully understood by rational analysis,
because the aesthetic levels on which it is apprehended are too intuitive,
too sensual and too neurological.

Arthur Machen – actor, mystic and author of tales of the supernatural,
admired by writers as disparate as Jorge Luis Borges and John Betjeman
– remains a pioneering cult author in the areas of horror and fantasy. In
*Hieroglyphics* (1902) he developed an aesthetic theory of Ecstasy according to which it is impossible to discuss literature without acknowledging
the numinous and indefinable qualities underlying the extraordinary, and
he believed that the *Odyssey* was the yardstick by which all other great
literature is to be judged. The reason is that nobody can *explain* in what
the excellence of the poem consists: it is *felt* but can never be analysed
adequately. All we can do is 'bow down' before its great music,

> recognizing that by the very reason of its transcendent beauty, by the
> very fact that it trespasses far beyond the world of our daily lives … that

because its beauty is supreme, therefore its beauty is beyond criticism ...
we know that the *Odyssey* surpassed the bounds of its own age and its own
land just as much as it surpasses those of our time and our country.[62]

Half a century earlier, Henry Alford, Dean of Canterbury, had ended a
discussion of the *Odyssey* with the statement:

READER – THIS IS THE GREATEST WORK
OF HUMAN GENIUS[63]

Despite having just expended thousands of words analysing what has made
the *Odyssey* able to surpass the bounds of its own age, I have, in conclusion, to concede that both the Anglican Alford and the Mystic Machen
really had quite a point.

# NOTES

## CHAPTER 1. EMBARKATION

1. Gross (2002), vii.
2. Kenner (1971), 50. See also Barbarese (1999), 275.
3. See e.g. Bloom (1991); Fuchs (1994); Boitani and Ambrosini (1998); Luther (2005); Graziosi and Greenwood (2007).
4. For this debate, and a powerful defence of Book 24, see Wender (1978).
5. Longinus, *On the Sublime* 9.14; John Hall (1652), xix.
6. See McLaren (2000), and below, p 27.
7. Borges (1964 [1960]), 23.
8. See Burkert (1987), West (1999), Graziosi (2002), and, on the tradition of Homer's blindness, Kahane (2005), 29–63.
9. Koliades (1829). Boitani (1994 [1992]), 91, has described *Moby-Dick* as 'one of the greatest and most subversive *Odysseys* ever written'.
10. Tolkien (1966).
11. Pillot (1972), 55, 66. For the most recent of the countless attempts to identify the 'true' Ithaca, see Bittlestone (2005).
12. Liveley (2006), 278–9.
13. The scientist Karl-Heinz Frommolt, quoted in BBC News Online, 19 May 2005.
14. This, indeed, is the title of Knox (1993).
15. See Browning (1992), 136.
16. See the titles of Highet (1949), and Bolgar (1954).
17. Kazantzis (1999), 7. See also Hardwick (2000), 19, on the metaphor of retrieving buried treasure.
18. Quoted in Lahr (1993).
19. Taplin (1989).
20. See von Wilamowitz-Moellendorff (1908), 25; Lloyd-Jones (1982), 177–8; below, Chapter 15.
21. Walcott (1949), 15; see also Walcott (1990), 271.
22. There is a lucid overview in Hardwick (2003), 1–11.
23. Kristeva (1980), 66.

24.  Genette (1997 [1982]), especially 1 and 5.
25.  Vidal-Naquet (1988), 361–80.
26.  Raymond Williams (1977), 120–7.
27.  Bakhtin (1986).
28.  See his essay 'Figura' (1944) as translated by Ralph Manheim in Auerbach (1959), 11–76.
29.  Vernant (1988).
30.  'Tradition and the individual talent', in Eliot (1975), 38.
31.  *Ibid.*
32.  English translation in Niane (1994).
33.  See further Adeleye (1992).
34.  'The mystery of life and its arts' (1868), first published as Ruskin (1869).
35.  Hegel (1923 [1837]), 5.29.
36.  See *Supplementum Epigraphicum Graecum* 30 (1980), 933.
37.  See Marrou (1956), 162, and Pack (1967), nos. 2707, 1208.
38.  See Kindstrand (1973).
39.  Eliade (1976), 22.
40.  See West (1997), 402–17.
41.  Lieberman (1950), 105–14; Zeitlin (2001), 204.
42.  See Fries (1911) and MacDonald (2001).
43.  Published by Yilin Publishing House, in Nanjing, in the translation of Xiao Qian and his wife, Wen Jieruo.
44.  Dupont (1991).
45.  Sieber (2003), 23.
46.  *Ibid.*
47.  *The Immortal*, section IV, in Borges (2004).
48.  See Zamora and Faris (1995), 5–6.
49.  See especially Hardwick (1992), 246.
50.  Frye (1957), 33.
51.  See also the Plutarchean *On Homer*, ed. Kindstrand (1990), 216; Lucian *Imagines* 8.
52.  See de Jong (2001).
53.  For other paintings of the Calypso episode see Reid (1993), vol. II, 743–4.
54.  Flecker (1924), 22.
55.  Text and translation in Paton (1916–18), vol. V, 231–2.
56.  Taylor (1956), 41.
57.  See Lygouri-Tolia (1992), 944, especially the silver goblet in Naples found at Herculaneum (image no. 3; Naples Mus. Naz. 25301). The *Odyssey* was elsewhere configured as a daughter of Homer.
58.  See Appendix, plate 10 in Webster (1967).
59.  Joyce (1993 [1922]), 5. Several decades later, the odious narrator of Martin

Amis's *Money*, John Self, takes this further as he describes a polluted urban sky as 'a smear of God's green snot' (Lodge (1992), 59).

60. See Edith Hall (2006), 267–8.
61. Bristow (1991), 94.
62. See Routh (2000), 294.
63. Borges (1975), 'Prologue'.
64. Boitani (1994 [1992]), 79.
65. 'The Homeric Hexameter described and exemplified' (1799).
66. Quoted from an interview with Edwin Honig in Honig (1985), 97–114.
67. Oldham (1681), 62–3.
68. Reynolds and Wilson (1974), 108–37.
69. For an English translation, with commentary, see Frazer (1966), 119–32.
70. See Finsler (1912), 1–19; Browning (1992), 147–8.

## CHAPTER 2. TURNING PHRASES

1. On the equivalence of the bow and the lyre see Schaeffner (1936), 158.
2. See Chantraine (1999), 797.
3. See Cysarz et al. (2004).
4. Which can be found, with translations, in Warmington (1926), vol. 2.
5. Young (2003), 99–100.
6. See Simonsuuri (1979), 17–73; Moore (2000).
7. Hepp (1968) and (1970); see also D'Amico (2002) on sixteenth-century France.
8. Both men's essays are contained in Arnold (1905).
9. See, for example, Burns (2002) and Young (2003).
10. On Chapman see, for example, Lord (1956) and Sowerby (1992); on Pope see, for example, Carolyn D. Williams (1993) and Rosslyn (1985).
11. See Hainsworth (1970); Matthew Clark (2004).
12. Walcott (1993), 1; see especially Hardwick (2004a), 351–5.
13. See Pucci (1997), 26–9.
14. Walcott (1993), 1.
15. Minchin (2001), 1–31.
16. Bell (2004), 41.
17. See Blok (2002).
18. See Albert Lord (1953), and John Miles Foley (1997).
19. Walcott (1990), 148–50, 289; see also Knox (1994), 337.
20. See Johnson, Hale and Belcher (1997), xviii–xix.
21. Gates (1987), 37.
22. Ellison 1981, xxii–xxiii, discussed in John F. Callahan (2004b), 302–3.
23. Quoted in Gilmore-Baldwin (2006).
24. O'Connell (2006).
25. See especially Segal (1994), 113–83.

26. See, for example, Harriott (1969), 34–51; Walsh (1984), 3–36; Ritoók (1989).
27. See Browning (1992).
28. Buch-Jepsen (2002), 80.
29. See Knox (1994), 283–99.
30. Notopoulos (1965), 338.
31. See Knox (1991), xxii; Andrew Rutherford (1978), 47; Blythe (1963), 80; Cohn (1995), 7–8.
32. Reproduced from Garnett (1938), 710.
33. Cohn (1995), 364.
34. *Ibid.*, 420–2.
35. Garnett (1938), 708.
36. Sutherland (2002), 21–2.
37. Morpurgo (1979), 216.
38. For an appreciation of Fitzgerald's translation, see Brewer (1974).
39. From Heaney (1987), 22.
40. See, for example, Timotheus fragments 779, 780 and 793 in David Campbell (1993).
41. See www.oedilf.com.
42. Calin (1983), 15–16, 68, 436–7.
43. See Stafford (1988); Hall and Macintosh (2005), 193–4.
44. Simonsuuri (1979), 109.
45. See Shapir (1994).
46. See Edith Hall (2007c).
47. Kenner (1971), 377.
48. Kenner (1971), especially 380–1. On the German Modernists see Matzig (1949), especially 36; on Poland, see pp 106, 136.
49. Ellmann (1982), 46.
50. Lamb (1808) was reissued at least 20 times between 1810 and 1940.
51. Respectively, Hacks (1997), Yolen and Harris (2002), McLaren (2000), and Shipton (2004). See also Webb and Amery (1981), Redmond and Kingsland (1992) and Claybourne (1997).
52. Tom Smith (2002).
53. See Rovin (1994), 189.
54. See Marie (1995), 26.
55. Moravia (1955), 81.
56. See Silverman and Farocki (1998), 32.
57. Godard (1985), 249.
58. Silverman and Farocki (1998), 44.
59. Elley (1984), 64–5. For a discussion of the episode of the Cyclops in the film, see Roisman (2007).
60. Kristin Thompson (1999), 44–7.

61. See Hill (1992), 174–5.

## CHAPTER 3. SHAPE-SHIFTING

1. See Scott (1925), 83–92 for references to Proteus in English literature.
2. See the chapter 'Seal shifter' in Jamal (1995), 50–64, and the parallel between the Sirens of the *Odyssey* and the Arctic seals drawn by Purdy (1967), 41.
3. For Periclymenus and Mestra see Hesiod fragments 33 and 43 in Merkelbach and West (1967), 23, 31. For Nemesis see *Cypria* fr. 10 in West (2003), 89–91.
4. See Forbes-Irving (1990), 176–7; Warner (1998a), 266–7.
5. Massey (1976), 21.
6. Emerson (1841), no. 1.
7. Warner (2002), 2.
8. Warner (2002), 208–9; see also Bynum (2001), 19–26, 192–3.
9. See Barta (2000), 6.
10. Gunn (1994), 186–7.
11. Massey (1976), 11–12.
12. Skulsky (1981), 1.
13. On Circe as a test-case for theorists of metamorphosis see Barkan (1986), 107–9.
14. Skulsky (1981), 10–23.
15. Warner (1998a), 37; see especially Rudrum (2003), 84.
16. Warner (1998b), 137.
17. Darrieussecq (1997 [1996]); Edith Hall (2007c).
18. See Lada-Richards (2002), 411.
19. See, above all, Murnaghan (1987).
20. Artemidorus, *Oneirocritica* 4.2.244–6.
21. In Euripides' *Hippolytus*, Sophocles' *Oedipus Tyrannus* and Euripides' *Phoenician Women*.
22. The Cyclops episode also featured in Aristophanes' *Plutus* and Eupolis' *Golden Race*. Antiphanes also wrote a *Cyclopes*.
23. For text and translation see Smyth and Lloyd-Jones (1957), 440–1, 445, 473–5. On *Ghost-Raisers* see Raymond Clark (1979), 64–5.
24. Sophocles fr. 454 *TgrF*; see Marshall (2000).
25. Lord (1977), 94–5.
26. Theopompus fragment 34 *KA*.
27. Cratinus fragments 143–57 *KA*.
28. See Reid (1993), vol. II, 748–52.
29. Ørnsbo (1996), 43.
30. On which see Trevelyan (1981), 163–7.
31. Giraldi Cinthio (1554), 225.

32. Huxley (1949), 3–4.
33. *At a Vacation Exercise in the* College; Milton refers to tales of heroes,
    Such as the wise Demodocus once told
    In solemn songs at king Alcinous' feast,
    While sad Ulysses' soul and all the rest
    Are held, with his melodious harmony,
    In willing chains and sweet captivity.
34. Unpublished MS in Florence; see Clubb (1965), 91–2 n.8.
35. Clubb (1965), 97–9.
36. Gager (1592), Act V. See the translation in Henley (1962), 246–60.
37. Rowe (1706), 64.
38. Hall and Macintosh (2005), 461–87. Warr and Crane (1887), vol. i.
39. Reid (1993), vol. II, 1014–18.
40. For an account see Whittington-Egan (2006), 130–1.
41. Phillips (1902), 11, 26, 88.
42. *Ibid.*, 178.
43. See Figs. 5.1, 8, 9.1, 10.1, 10.2, 11 and 14.2.
44. On Hauptmann see especially Matzig (1949), 63–70, Klańska (1998) and
    Riedel (2000), 267; on Walcott see pp 183–4.
45. Sackville-West (1945), especially 92–3.
46. See pp 182–3.
47. See Selaiha (2006).

## CHAPTER 4. TELLING TALES

1. See Grossardt (1998).
2. Broughton (1998), 11.
3. On Odysseus' false narratives see Maronitis (2004), 147–63.
4. Farrar (1859), 232. See especially Kennedy (1958), 180–99.
5. Huxley (1949), 3–4.
6. Conversation recorded by Georges Borach, cited in Ellmann (1982),
    416–17.
7. Calvino (1986), first published in *La Repubblica* (Rome), 21 October
    1981.
8. Lodge (1992), 74–5.
9. See Paul (2007).
10. See in general McDermott (1989).
11. Reardon (1991), 74, n.50.
12. 1.8.2, 1.8.6, 2.1.1, 2.23.3, 3.10.3, 3.20.4, 6.10.4. See MacDonald (1994a), 322
    n.43.
13. Gove (1941).
14. For example, the marvellous creatures and primitive tribes of India in
    Ctesias' *Indika*, and the *Marvels beyond Thule* of Antonius Diogenes,

which included several strong references to Homer, a Siren's tomb, and the narrator's miraculous return home to Tyre, after being transported, like Odysseus in the ship of the Phaeacians, home in his sleep.

15. See Brian Richardson (2000); Zeitlin (2001), 242–4.
16. See, for example, Ladermann (2002), 6–7; Beard (2004): 'Just like any road movie, *The Odyssey* and its reception is rooted in questions of fidelity and adultery, trust and deception. No wonder it makes a good film.'
17. On Apuleius' Greek sources see especially Mason (1978).
18. See MacDonald (1994b) and (2000) on *Acts* 20 and the Gospel of Mark.
19. The full text has not survived, and has to be reconstructed from fragments including a précis in Gergory of Tours' *Liber de miraculis* (one version of the text is published in M.R. James (1924)), and a story called *The Acts of Andrew and Matthias in the City of the Cannibals*, translated by MacDonald (1990).
20. This has been energetically argued by Dennis MacDonald (1994a).
21. Originally published in German as *Der Sechste Gesang* (1956).
22. The unfinished text is available in Lewis (1966), 127–45.
23. Quoted in Lewis (1966), 148.
24. The tradition that Helen never went to Troy, and spent the entire war in Egypt, was inaugurated by the Greek lyric poet Stesichorus in his *Palinode* of the seventh or early sixth century BCE. See Austin (1994), 90–117.
25. Boitani (1994), 85.
26. 1. 'Telemachus', 2. 'Nestor', 3. 'Proteus', 4. 'Calypso', 5. 'Lotus Eaters', 6. 'Hades', 7. 'Aeolus', 8. 'Lestrygonians', 9. 'Scylla and Charybdis', 10. 'Wandering Rocks', 11. 'Sirens', 12. 'Cyclops', 13. 'Nausicaa', 14. 'Oxen of the Sun', 15. 'Circe', 16. 'Eumaeus', 17. 'Ithaca', 18. 'Penelope'.
27. See Schork (1998); Arkins (1999).
28. Kenner (1971), 44.
29. Eagleton (1990), 316–25; see also Zajko (2004), 314–15.
30. Letter of 21 September 1920 in Ellmann (1975), 271.
31. See Woodcock (1970).
32. Landau (1948), 520.
33. Dickstein (2004), 145.
34. Quoted in Dickstein (2004), 129.
35. See Forrest (2004), 270.
36. Ellison (1965 [1952]), 17, 40.
37. *Ibid.*, 37.
38. Rankine (2006). See also the discussion of the use of the *Odyssey* by both Walcott and the African-American painter Romare Bearden in Davis (2007).

39. For example, the epistolary short story 'Letters from the Phaeacian Capital', as well as a Cyclops soliloquizing, in Couldrey (1914), 73–96, 195–99. See also the translation of 'Odysseus and the swine' in Feuchtwanger (1949), 167–90.
40. Grimwood (2001), 251.
41. Valerie Smith (2004).
42. See Thomsen (2002).
43. Blok (2002), with bibliography. See also ClydeSight Productions' 'Humour Fantasy multimedia HTML E-book', *Idiocy and the Oddity*, which sets the Homeric epics in the world of cats living by the river Clyde. It can be accessed at www.clydesight.com.

## CHAPTER 5. SINGING SONGS

1. Wirth (1921), 19–21; Scott (1925), 19.
2. Scott (1925), 71.
3. See also Savatage, *Sirens* (Sum Records, 1983); Astarte, *Sirens* (Cleopatra, 2004); and Ulysses Siren, *Above the Ashes* (Relentless, 2004).
4. Gundry (1998), ch. 10. The first act of his *The Return of Odysseus* was successfully performed in London in 1940, and revived after the war.
5. In an open letter to Monteverdi preserved in one of the manuscript copies of the libretto; text supplied in Osthoff (1956), 73–4.
6. Glover (1985), 290. For a rich reading of the opera's emotional impact see McDonald (2001), chapter 1.
7. See Anon. (1640), the importance of which was realized by Osthoff (1958).
8. For this translation of the libretto see Badoaro (1972), 49. Rosand (1994), 393–45, points out that the composer and Ulisse are explicitly identified in one of the Bologna sonnets, which concludes by saying that Monteverdi today has 'no peer in stretching the bow of the plectrum': Anon. (1640), 6.
9. See Carter (1993), 3.
10. *Ibid.*, 15. The cultural significance of this opera in aesthetic terms must partly explain the large number of subsequent operas on themes from the *Odyssey*, many of which are listed in McDonald (2001), 37–42.
11. Bjurström (1961), 52.
12. *Ibid.*, 95.
13. Reproduced in *ibid.*, 60, 63–4.
14. *Ibid.*, 95.
15. See Rossi and Fauntleroy (1999), 127–8. The Holograph score is held in the Conservatorio di musica S Pietro a Majella in Naples.
16. *The Morning Chronicle* (London), 13 January 1817, 27.
17. On the enormity of the novel's cultural impact, see Simonsuuri (1979), 27–8.

18. Florence (C.L. Rossi, music by Meucci, 1773), Pisa (C.L. Rossi, music by Gazzaniga, 1776), Venice (Pindemonte, music by Bertoni, 1776), Munich (Serimann, music by F.P. Grua, 1780), Naples (music by Cipolla, 1785), Paris (P. Dercy, music by Le Sueur, 1796) and Venice (Sografi, music by Mayr, 1797).

19. Quoted in Fifield (2005), 131.

20. This is Bruch's own description of the final scene, with its final chorus 'There is nowhere lovelier than the homeland'. See Fifield (2005), 132.

21. *Ibid.*, 135.

22. In 1867 he had composed a *Salamis*, subtitled *A War Song of the Greeks*, for male soloists and chorus, with full orchestra, depicting the triumphant return of the Greek fleet from the defeat of the Persian navy at the Battle of Salamis. This has been said to foreshadow the music and style of his *Odysseus* (Fifield (2005), 62).

23. See the introduction to Bridges, Hall and Rhodes (2007).

24. On the jingoistic tenor of Bruch's *Odysseus* and *Leonidas* see Fifield (2005), 327.

25. See Hust (2005), 301–2.

26. See the photograph reproduced in Hust (2005), 340.

27. Interview in *Excelsior*, 12 June 1922, quoted in Nectoux (1984), 113.

28. Nectoux (1991), 313.

29. For a range of responses, see Nectoux (1984), 267–9.

30. Quoted in Nectoux (1984), 273.

31. For an accessible musical analysis sensitive to the development of the story, see Nectoux (1991), 316–26.

32. Nectoux (1984), 346.

33. Nectoux (1991), 314.

34. Letter quoted in Nectoux (1991), 335.

35. See, for example, Zychowicz (1994).

36. This can be heard at www.rhapsody.com/album/odysseus7radiospaceop era.

37. It premiered at London's Linbury Studio on 26 July 2004, as part of a trilogy on themes connected with Odysseus.

38. This was the work of the opera company Tête à Tête in collaboration with Chamber Ensemble Chroma and Shetland Artisan.

39. McKittrick (2003).

## CHAPTER 6. FACING FRONTIERS

1. Boitani (1994), 3.

2. See Edith Hall (forthcoming); Goldhill (2002), 186–91.

3. Strictly speaking it was Vasco de Balbao, not Hernando Cortez, who was the first Renaissance European to encounter the Pacific.

4. Watkins (1989), 27.
5. On which see Cary and Warmington (1963).
6. Vidal-Naquet (1986), 21, 26; Edith Hall (1989), 49–60.
7. Brown (1961), 291, 296; Bodde (1961), 400–3.
8. Dionysius of Halicarnassus, *Ant. Rom.* 4.45; see also Horace, *Odes* 3.29.8. For a recent discussion of the importance of Odysseus to Latin literature and art, see Perutelli (2006).
9. Farrell (2004), 259.
10. *Ibid.*, 261.
11. *Ibid.*, 262–3. The Sperlonga Cyclops is reproduced in Edith Hall (2007d), 60, fig. 3.4.
12. Canto 26.112–20, translated by Singleton (1971), vol. I, p. 279.
13. Seneca, *Medea* 375–9, translated by Fitch (2002), 377. See Bloch (1986), vol. III, 1026.
14. Translated by Mickle (1776), 1.
15. *Ibid.*, 2.
16. 'Primeiro/Ulysses', *Mensagem* II.1 in Pessoa (1992), 16–17.
17. Norris (1992).
18. See Slotkin (1973), 4.
19. Yeh (1992), 123, 131, 139, 133.
20. 'The Searchers', *Look* magazine, 12 June 1956. See McBride (2004), 557.
21. Mitry (1969), 197.
22. McBride (2004), 47, 509–10, 528.
23. Kalinak (2004), 115.
24. Winkler (2004).
25. McBride and Wilmington (1974), 147–63.
26. Bogdanovich (1967), 91–2.
27. Lehman (1990), 395; see also Eckstein (2004), 26.
28. Lehman (1990), 388–93.
29. Eckstein (2004); Henderson (2004).
30. Purdy (1967), 41.
31. Kroetsch (1995), 14.
32. See Pache (1985), 68; Bertacco (2002), 126.
33. Kroetsch (1989), 157–9.
34. Atherton (1998), viii–ix.
35. See, for example, Nicholson (1948); Moskowitz (1963), 11.
36. Fredericks (1976).
37. Moskowitz (1963), 34.
38. Photius, *Library* codex 166, translated in Stephens and Winkler (1995), 101–57.
39. See, for example, Knight (1967) and Moskowitz (1967).
40. Suvin (1972–3), 372–5; Suvin (1973); Suvin (1979), 3–15.

41. Fredericks (1976).
42. See Bompaire (1958), 659 n.2, for cross-references.
43. Suvin (1979), 155.
44. These stories are reproduced in Moskowitz (1975).
45. Asimov (1952), 49, 81.
46. Jewett and Lawrence (1977), 17.
47. Lafferty (1968), 123.
48. For example, Wheat (2000).
49. See, for example, White (2003), 147–8, 151–2.
50. Landon (2003), 3.
51. See Stableford (1999), and, on Classics and SF, Keen (2006).

## CHAPTER 7. COLONIAL CONFLICT

1. *Cyclops and Poseidon*, in *Dialogues of the Sea-Gods* 2, 292.
2. This summary is from Araki (1978), 1–2; for an English version, see Haugaard and Haugaard (1991).
3. Araki (1978).
4. Bader (2005), 6.
5. See Fellmann (1972), 9–11. The vase painting is reproduced in Edith Hall (2007d), 56, fig. 3.2.
6. Erasmus (1957), 120–9. See further Edith Hall (2007d).
7. For a spectacular example, see the cover of *The Amazing Adventures of Ulysses* (Usborne Publishing, 1981), reproduced in Edith Hall (2007d), 58, fig. 3.3. Hutton (1995) retells only the Cyclops incident.
8. Lamb (1924 [1808]), 148.
9. Zoilus of Amphipolis, a philosopher of the fourth century BCE, wrote an *Encomium of Polyphemus*, which sadly has not survived. See Zoilus, no. 71 in Jacoby (1927), 110, fragment 2.
10. See Friedman (1981), 15 and fig. 7; Edith Hall (1989), 49–50 and (2007d), 62, fig. 3.5.
11. See Arens (1979).
12. See Baudet (1965), 28; Jane (1930), vol. 1, 14–15, 26–7, 32–3 and 50–1.
13. See Leroi (2003).
14. Locke (1993), 228.
15. See the report for December 1835 in Darwin (1988), 282–3, and the fears about cannibalism on p 391. For engraved representations of the defiant Maoris encountered by the *Endeavour* see Joppien and Smith (1985), 36–7, 198–9.
16. See London (2002), 111 and n.3.
17. *Reflexionen zur Anthropologie*, no. 903, in Kant (1966), vol. XV.1, 39–5. Kant's image of the intellectual monocularity of the Cyclops has recently been taken up by feminist theorists: Haraway (1990), Paasonen (2003),

Lehtononen (1994), 259–64.

18. Joyce (1993 [1922]), 284–5.
19. Ellison (1965 [1952], 188, 190.
20. *Ibid.*, 381.
21. Walcott (1993), 63–72. See the discussion of Hardwick (1996); Hamner (2001) thinks that Walcott's Cyclops here is a poetic representation of the Greek dictatorship of 1967–74.
22. Wallace (2002), 177–8.
23. Salman Rushdie, 'Gods and Monsters', *The Washington Post*, 28 June 2002, available online at http://www.washingtonpost.com/wp-dyn/articles/A58700-2002Jun27.html. Soyinka (2002) draws a similar comparison with the Cyclops in reference to Israel's conduct towards Palestine.
24. Davies, Nandy and Sardar (1993), 27.
25. Adams (1889–91), vol. 1, 946. Thanks to Margaret Malamud for this reference.
26. See further pp 41, 182.
27. Adorno and Horkheimer (1997), 67.
28. This view was anticipated in Jean Giraudoux's novel *Elpénor* (1919), but his vision of the Cyclops ultimately ridicules Polyphemus (see pp 59, 149–50).
29. The anticolonial reading of the *Tempest* emerged as a response to José Enrique Rodó's essay *Ariel* (1900), although in his version Ariel represented the virtuous youth of Latin America and Caliban the evil materialism of the United States. See also Mannoni (1956).
30. David Dabydeen's *Coolie Odyssey* (1988), 28.
31. Wynter (2002).
32. Soyinka (1998), 374–5.
33. Wynter (2002), 145, 144, 146.
34. See the remarks made in 1982 by Chris Claremont, the script writer on a subsequent *X-Men* series, quoted at http://en.wikipedia.org/wiki/X-Men. The cover of the original issue of *The X-Men* is reproduced in Edith Hall (2007d), 70, fig. 3.7.
35. See Darius (2002) for a discussion of these and other similar interpretations. Subsequently, Fantasy Art has also conflated the victimized Cyclops with the indigenous North Americans.
36. *Sea Grapes* is the titular poem of the collection Walcott (1976). See Walcott's own discussion of this poem in Walcott (1998).
37. Walcott (1990), 323 (see also 13), with Hamner (1997), 41.
38. Berger (2004). In Hawaii, independence and self-determination are pressing issues, and in a production of Euripides' *Cyclops*, a theatrical adaptation of *Odyssey* Book 9, at the University of Hawaii-Manoa in 2004, the question was asked whether Odysseus was a noble hero or an imperialist aggressor.

39. See Rosello and Pritchard (1995), 20; Toumson and Henry-Valmore (2002), 75–84.
40. Davis (1997), 20–61.
41. Wynter (2002), 154 and the translation in Césaire (1983), 68–9.
42. Césaire (1990), 162.
43. Shewring (1980), 101.
44. The word for 'man' here (*anēr*), elsewhere defines men *in opposition* to monsters (see 21.303); the term *pelōrios*, 'huge', is also used in Homer of such glamorously big males as Achilles, Ajax and Hector.
45. See, for example, Clare (1998).
46. Austin (1983).
47. Ruskin (1902–12), vol. XIII, 136. Turner had been inspired by Pope's translation of the *Odyssey*; see Rodner (1997), 62–3.
48. The painting is reproduced in Edith Hall (2007d), 75, fig. 3.8.
49. Russell (1996–97), 34.
50. Zhirmunsky (1966), 284.
51. See, for example, Page (1972), 29–32; Glenn (1971); Calame (1977).
52. Cyclopia, which is incompatible with life, also occurs (but with extreme rarity) in human foetuses.
53. Harris (2003), 110, 133, 152.
54. Sullivan (2002), 'Absolution Chorus'. For a photograph of Robert Sullivan see Edith Hall (2007d), 77, fig. 3.9.
55. Sullivan (1999), *waka* 36, 89, 88.

## CHAPTER 8. RITES OF MAN

1. See Fränkel (1962), 85–93.
2. Mackie (2006).
3. See Hobbs (2000), 18, 193–8, 239, 256; Richardson (1992), 33–4.
4. See Edith Hall (1998), 224–5.
5. Clemens and Mayer (1999), 18–30.
6. *Ibid.*, 30.
7. Nimmo and Combs (1980), 132.
8. *Ibid.*, 130, 133.
9. *Ibid.*, 153.
10. Joseph Campbell (1956), 30.
11. Slotkin (1985).
12. See Jewett and Lawrence (1977), xx–xxi.
13. Nimmo and Combs (1980), 144.
14. Slotkin (1973), index s.v. 'classical', 'myth' and 'epic'.
15. Nimmo and Combs (1980), 235–8.
16. Steckmesser (1965), 241; see also Jewett and Lawrence (1977), 93.
17. Lang and Trimble (1988), 159.

18.  Letter to N.M. Yazykov, translated in Zeldin (1969), 32.
19.  Zeldin (1969), 33.
20.  *Ibid.*, 36–7.
21.  *Ibid.*, 40.
22.  Stolz (1954).
23.  See the interviews in Stolz (1954).
24.  See Hacks (1997); Kipf (2005).
25.  For example, the ballad dialogue between Ulysses and Telemachus in 'Ulysses', in Masters (1921), 225–31. See also Brodsky (1973), 168; Ted Hughes's 'Everyman's *Odyssey*' in Hughes (2003), 59–60.
26.  On the Telemachus books in ancient education, see Morgan (1998), 105–15.
27.  Vidal-Naquet (1981).
28.  See Helene Foley (2005), 109.
29.  'Ulysses and the Siren', first published in Daniel (1605).
30.  See Carolyn Williams (1993).
31.  See, above all, Jenkyns (1980), 192–226; see also Chapter 14.
32.  Coleridge (1846), vol. I, 254–5.
33.  Gladstone (1869), 392.
34.  Howarth (1973), 49–72.
35.  *Ibid.*, 82–3.
36.  *Ibid.*, 93–7.
37.  *Ibid.*, 110–11.
38.  *Ibid.*, 128.
39.  Stuart Hall (1996), 116.
40.  Although see Tate (2004).
41.  Malamud (1963), 34.
42.  *Ibid.*, 66.
43.  *Ibid.*, for example, 112, 115.
44.  *Ibid.*, 238.
45.  Bly (1990), 4.
46.  See especially Bly (1990), 215–17.

## CHAPTER 9. WOMEN'S WORK

1.  Doherty (2006), 303–4.
2.  Schaps (1979), 18–20.
3.  Jenkins (1985), 110–11.
4.  Bergren (1983), 72.
5.  Jenkins (1985), 113, 115.
6.  See Clayton (2003), 1–19.
7.  See, for example, Fig. 14.1.
8.  Bentley, quoted in Grote (1869), vol. I, 151n.

9. William Golding, in conversation, quoted in Boitani (1994), viii.
10. Dalby (2006).
11. A view supported, for example, by Kenner (1971), 48–9.
12. Shaffer (2004).
13. Hoste (1906), vii.
14. Wolf (1795).
15. See Carr (1961).
16. Ruyer (1977).
17. For the phrase 'feminine of Homer' see Barrett in Hudson and Kelley (1984), 361, and Hurst (2006), 7–10.
18. See Susan Stanford Friedman (1986), also printed in Reynolds (1996), 466–73
19. *Aurora Leigh* 7.468–72; see Reynolds (1996), 228 n.3.
20. See Murnaghan and Roberts (2002).
21. On Dacier's translations of Aristophanes, see Edith Hall (2007a), chapter 1.
22. Dacier (1716), vol. I, lxci–lxx. See also Fig. 13.
23. This view was taken by, for example, Harsh (1950), who stressed that in Book 24 a third interpretation of events is offered by a dead suitor – that she was colluding with Odysseus all along (24.167–9).
24. Roworth (1992), 29, 43, 64, 66, 84.
25. Rowe (1706), 9–10, 14.
26. *Ibid.*, 27.
27. See further Hall and Macintosh (2005), chapter 3. Even in the third millennium versions of Penelope along these lines still appear: see, for example, Ramos (2003).
28. See Heitman (2005), 43–9.
29. See especially Papadopoulou-Belmehdi (1994).
30. See John J. Winkler (1990).
31. See Karydas (1998).
32. Yarnall (1994), 194.
33. Heitman (2005), 108–9.
34. In Killigrew (1686).
35. Steiner (1996), 187.
36. Parker (1939), no. 27.
37. Gregory (1997), 176.
38. Porter (1954), 13.
39. Reproduced in DeNicola (1999), 93–5.
40. Barthes (1975), 64.
41. Miller (1986), 274.
42. Reproduced in DeNicola (1999), 120–1.
43. Heilbrun (1990), 120.

44. *Ibid.*, 126.
45. Heaney (1987), 8.
46. Reproduced in DeNicola (1999), 104.
47. Milligan and Hewlett (2002).
48. Cavarero (1995), 11–30
49. See Dworking (1995).
50. Heilbrun (1990), 128.
51. Duffy (1999), 47–8.
52. In addition to those discussed in this chapter, see Levigne (2001).
53. Merkel (2000 [1987]), 11–12, 13, 24.
54. *Ibid.*, 45, 49.
55. *Ibid.*, 157.
56. *Ibid.*, 331.
57. Quoted in Gerd Schneider's 'Afterword' to Merkel (2000 [1987]), 387.
58. Merkel (2000 [1987]), 95.
59. Atwood (2005), 31, 91, 137.
60. *Ibid.*, 115.
61. John Finley (1978), 3–4.
62. In Pastan (1988); see the excellent study by Murnaghan and Roberts (2002).
63. Reproduced in DeNicola (1999), 135–7.
64. See Murnaghan and Roberts (2002), especially 15–24.
65. See, for example, Heitman (2005).
66. Helene Foley (1978).
67. Murnaghan (1987), 103–13.
68. See the oral histories recorded in Marland and Willcox (1980), 122–31.
69. *Circe* (1992), reproduced in DeNicola (1999), 89.
70. See Ndebele (2003), 108–9.

## CHAPTER 10. CLASS CONSCIOUSNESS

1. Koliades (1829), 1.
2. Ronsand (1989).
3. Scaliger (1561), 11; see also Grafton (1992), 162.
4. Perrault (1688–97), vol. III, 55; see Howard Clarke (1981), 122–5.
5. Moses Finley (1979), 53.
6. Jacoby (1961), 117–19.
7. For a revised version see Peter Rose (1992).
8. See Edith Hall (2007b).
9. Walcott (1993), 4–7.
10. Mellers (1965), 269–70. Thanks to Joseph Platnauer for help on this topic.
11. All references to this text use Mottley and Cooke (1728).

12. Cooke (1728).
13. Peter Lewis (1982).
14. See Kingston (1997).
15. Interview published in a newspaper in 1893, quoted in the appendix to Karkavitsas (1982), 165.
16. Karkavitsas (1973), vol. IV, 1675–6.
17. Anonymous review in the newspaper *To Asty*, 22 October 1897, page 1 coll. 2–3.
18. On the relationship between the two films see Natalie Zemon Davis (1997).
19. Carrière (1994), 144.
20. *Ibid.*, 113.
21. For the parallels with the *Odyssey* drawn by the trial judge see de Coras (1561), 4–5, 16, with the comments of Rabel (2003), 395.
22. Natalie Zemon Davis (1983).
23. Frazier (2003), 3, 6.
24. *Ibid.*, 101.
25. Morrison (1998), 239–47.
26. See, for example, the review in *Frankfurter Allgemeine Zeitung*, for 24 August 2005.
27. Wenders (2003).
28. Kolker and Beicken (1993), 151.
29. See Hall and Macintosh (2005), chapter 12.
30. McHenry (2002), 56, 172–3.
31. Miller (1854), 27–8.

## CHAPTER 11. BRAIN POWER

1. The work of this Heraclitus, who worked in Roman imperial times, has been translated into French by Buffière (1962). See pp 107–8.
2. In *Essays* II.36, 'On the worthiest and most excellent of men', reproduced in Montaigne (1967), 206–8.
3. Eustathius's commentary on the *Odyssey* 1658.25–40 on v.277; see also 1660. 32–6 on v.343.
4. See above p 178.
5. Two verses Wordsworth added to his *Prelude* 30 years after its first version; see Boitani (1994), 93.
6. Phillpotts (1926), 38–9.
7. Giraudoux (1958 [1919]), 22, 24, 31–2.
8. For an excellent discussion see Schlink (2002).
9. See Novalis (1997), 135.
10. The lecture is published in Heidegger (1993), 139–212.
11. From *El Hacedor* (1960), translated in Borges (1964), 89.

12. Lévinas (1994), 190–1, translated by Tracy McNulty. See Lesch (1994), 160–2.
13. 'Heimat und Sprache' (1992), in Gadamer (1993), 366–72; see Hammermeister (2000).
14. Bloch (1986), vol. III, 1025–6.
15. Ferrucci (1980), 40.
16. Gray (1985), 29.
17. Cookson (2005).
18. Deneen (2000).
19. See Montiglio (2005), especially chapter 8.
20. See especially Long (1992).
21. See also p 134.
22. See Rebhorn (1988), 183–9; Bokina (1991), 56. Machiavelli's *The Prince* had been published in 1515.
23. Spinoza (2002), 709.
24. See Novalis's *Logological Fragments*, as translated in Novalis (1997), 57.
25. Rubino (1994), 89.
26. See, for example, Anon. (1829), 99.
27. See the remarks of Bruce Clarke (1995), 19. *Poseidon* is included in Kafka (1994).
28. Reproduced in DeNicola (1999), 108–9.
29. See Grinstein (1980), 395–422.
30. Freud (1953 [1900]), 452.
31. See Jung (1991 [1926]), 139, and 118–19, 136–8, 140–44.
32. Haggard (1991 [1887]), 286–7.
33. Lewis (1982), 99–100.
34. Resnick (1967), 40.
35. He received expert antiquarian help from Dr Hubert Holden and Dr John Raven. For a similar plot device in a more recent thriller dependent on the *Odyssey* see Manfredi (2005).
36. Fajardo-Acosta (1990), 17.
37. Bell (2004), 44.
38. Segal (1978); Brisson (2004), 26–7.
39. Planinc (2003).
40. 9.124.6 = 745d–f. See Pépin (1982).
41. See Lamberton (1986); Lamberton and Keaney (1992), xx.
42. 'On Beauty' (*Enneads* I.6.1), chapter 8.
43. See Brisson (2004), chapter 7.
44. See Howard Clarke (1981), 60–105.
45. See Nicholas Richardson (1992), 31–2.
46. See V. Rose (1886), fragments 142–79; Lamberton and Keaney (1992), xi–xvi.

47. Fragments 172, 173 in Rose (1886).
48. Frege (1892), 33.
49. *Ibid.*, 34. For an English translation, see Geach and Black (1952), 62–3.
50. The important parts of Rassinier's books are collected, in English translation, in Rassinier (1978).
51. *Ibid.*, 35.
52. *Ibid.*, 112.
53. Unsworth (2002); see also Edith Hall (2005), 24–5.
54. See the English translation in Müller (1989).
55. English translation in Benedikt and Wellwarth (1964), 217–20.
56. Ashbery (1960), 58.
57. *Ibid.*, 60.
58. On Wilson Harris see also pp 99–100, 158, 204.
59. See Helleman (1995).
60. See further Anne Rutherford (2002).
61. Makriyannakis (2005).
62. See, for example, Baumeister (1998) and Edith Hall (2007c).
63. Ellison (2004), 41.
64. *Ibid.*, 38–9.

## CHAPTER 12. EXILE FROM ITHACA

1. Quoted in Hamner (1997), 80. See also Knox (1994), 339.
2. Cavafy (1971), 47–8.
3. Liddell (2002), 152–3.
4. Malkin (1998), 2–3.
5. See Lichtheim (1973), 211–15.
6. 3.276–602, 4.351–585: see Morris (1997), 613–14.
7. Durante (1971), 48.
8. West (2003), 17–18; Nagy (1990), 70–9.
9. Malkin (1998), 53.
10. Mackey-Kallis (2001), 1.
11. Jung (1990), 279.
12. See, for example, Izod (2001), 187; the best reading of the *Odyssey* by an expert Jungian is Rüf (1994).
13. Houston (1992), 23.
14. See Mackey-Kallis (2001), 3–4.
15. *Ibid.*, 5.
16. Remark in an interview quoted in Carpentier (2001), ix.
17. Rang (1972).
18. Essex (2005).
19. Kroetsch (1995), 145.

20. *Return to Zion* is included in Yellin (2006).
21. Snyder (1971), xi.
22. Letter written in 1924, published in Wolfe (1956), 64.
23. *Ibid.*, 23.
24. Wolfe (1968), 75, 83, 82.
25. Kundera (2002), 177.
26. *Ibid.*
27. Michelakis (2004), 209.
28. See Barnes (1996).
29. Anne Rutherford (2002).
30. Walcott (1990), 14.
31. *Ibid.*, 18, 20.
32. *Ibid.*, 128, 130, 134.
33. *Ibid.*, 139.
34. *Ibid.*, 150–1.
35. *Ibid.*, 58, 56.
36. See Choate (2006).
37. Francis (2006).
38. See p 6.
39. Sultan (1999), 1.
40. *Ibid.*, 9–12.
41. Seferis (1967), 214–19; Ricks (1989), 147–57.
42. Lambrou (2002), 69.
43. See, for example, Koromila (1994).

## CHAPTER 13. BLOOD BATH

1. Kazantzis (1999), 61–2.
2. See George deForest Lord (1991), 95.
3. Fajardo-Acosta (1990), 117.
4. *Ibid.*, 243–4; see also Borthwick (1988), 19–20.
5. Post (1951); Cook (1995), 149; Wilson (2002), 141.
6. Slocum (2001), 7.
7. Kinder (2001), 83.
8. Gager (1592), Act V; see the translation in Henley (1962), 248–60.
9. See the excellent discussion in Rubens and Taplin (1989), 15, 147–9.
10. Rovin (1994), 189.
11. Cook (1995), 149.
12. See Lateiner (1995), 183–7; Mitchell (2001), 180.
13. Warner (1994), 26.
14. See also the introduction to Jones and Watkins (2000), 10–12.
15. Fitch (2004).
16. Gould (1991), 9, 4.

17. Green (2004), 293.
18. For a sensitive reading, see Meg Harris Williams (2005), chapter 6.
19. On the profound influence of the recognition scenes in the later books of the *Odyssey* see Cave (1988), 10–46 and index under 'Homer, *Odyssey*'.
20. Said (2002).
21. Andrews (2002).
22. Shubow (2003).
23. Wyspianski (1966), 63.
24. *Ibid.*, 71.
25. See Riedel (2000), 267.
26. Paulino (1994).
27. Rogers (1984), 118.
28. Torrente Ballaster (1981), 188–9.
29. On Odysseus in Spanish drama relating to the Civil War see Cazorla (1986), Rogers (1984) and Lamartina-Lens (1986).
30. Included in Longley (1991), 51.
31. Walcott (1993), 153ff.
32. Taplin (1992).
33. Hardwick (2004b), 231–2.
34. Shay (2002), 3–4.
35. *Ibid.*, 36.
36. *Ibid.*, 43.
37. See further Riley (2004), 133–4.
38. Shay (2002), 125.
39. Rushdie (2005), 297, 308.
40. Shelley (1886 [1822]), 52.
41. Anon. (1829), 99.
42. Sackville-West (1945), 89–90
43. Brun (1940), 253, from the chapter entitled 'The Execution'.
44. See the comment on *China Daily Online Community*, posted 26 September 2004 (last accessed 5 May 2005): 'Shanghai was and is now colonized by the west. It has happened already, the barbarians are here, inside the Gates. They will take it, exploit it and corrupt it as much as they possibly can without any moral, humanitarian or ethical consideration … Action is needed. China needs its own Odysseus, urgently.'
45. See Dilworth (1994).

## CHAPTER 14. SEX AND SEXUALITY

1. Wohl (1993), 25.
2. Servius the grammarian's commentary on the *Aeneid* ed. Thilo and Hagen (1881), vol. II, 127.
3. The movie *Brief Encounter* (1945), directed by David Lean, was adapted

from a play of the same name by Nöel Coward. *Lost in Translation* (2003) was written and directed by Sofia Coppola.

4.  'Nausicäa' in Cole (1963), 335.
5.  Beye (1966), chapter 5.
6.  Yarnall (1994), 89–144; Kuhn (2003).
7.  Davenant (1677), Hall and Macintosh (2005), 36–40.
8.  See Lichtenberg, Marshak and Winston (1975), 41; Jewett and Lawrence (1977), 13.
9.  Green (2004), 294.
10.  Paglia (1997), 177–8.
11.  Green (2004), 289.
12.  The Greek for 'all' is *pan* – for sources see Mactoux (1975), 97–102.
13.  Bunting and Bolton (1994).
14.  See J.P. Sullivan (1968), 232–53.
15.  See Gill (1973).
16.  Burnand (1863), 21–2.
17.  See further Ellis (1978), 133.
18.  *Ibid.*, 128–35.
19.  Haggard and Lang (1890), 216.
20.  On Greek mythical settings in early pornographic photography, see Tang (1999), 104–7.
21.  Kestner (1989), 218.
22.  *Ibid.*, 5–6; Hall and Macintosh (2005), 389–90.
23.  Hardy (1974 [1896]), 86.
24.  Kestner (1989), 232, 12, 10; see also Yarnall (1994), 161–8.
25.  Kestner (1989), 70–2.
26.  *Ibid.*, 63–4, 8–9.
27.  Quoted in Haller and Haller (1974), 202.
28.  Ruskin (1902–12), vol. XVII, 213.
29.  Joyce (1993), 592.
30.  *Ibid.*, 441–2.
31.  Sacher-Masoch (2000 [1870]), 18. See also Dijkstra (1986), 393; Yarnall (1994), 174–5; Arkins (1999), 114.
32.  Gray (1985), 233–4.
33.  Joyce (1993), 618.
34.  *Ibid.*, 685–6.
35.  *Ibid.*, 160.
36.  Theoharis (1988), 126–30.
37.  See Gray (1985), 228, 241.
38.  McCormick (1994); see also Clayton (2004), 87–8.
39.  Armitage (1993), 50. Armitage has also written an aclaimed but more light-hearted radio adaptation of the *Odyssey*, performed on BBC Radio

4 in August 2006.

40. Longley (1991), 31.
41. Neruda (1994 [1952]), 42–5.
42. Text and translation by Robert Fitzgerald in Borges (1972), 165.
43. See Yarnall (1994), 187–91.
44. Kazantzis (1999), 69.
45. Bechdel (2006), 202.
46. *Ibid.*, 203.
47. *Ibid.*, 207.
48. *Ibid.*, 209–10, 213, 214–15.
49. *Ibid.*, 221–2.
50. Reproduced in Lafon and Clais (1993), 36.
51. Sinclair (2002), 90–4.
52. Yarnall (1994), 166–8.
53. Dawe (1993), 8.

## CHAPTER 15. DIALOGUE WITH DEATH

1. *Palatine Anthology* 9.792.
2. Eliade (1976), 42–3.
3. See p 154.
4. Bompaire (1958), 365–78.
5. *The Waste Land* 3.220–1, with the note on 3.218: Eliot (1974), 71, 82.
6. See Pound (1971), 274, quoted in Kenner (1971), 147. See also Pratt (2002).
7. Harris (1954), 32–9.
8. Balmer (2004), 50.
9. On this famous vase, now in Boston, see Caskey (1934).
10. For text and translation see Seferis (1967), 316–25.
11. Included in Bakken (2006).
12. 'It is I, Odysseus – Elpenor' (1933), from MacLeish (1963), 275–80.
13. See Pike (1997), 216; Rosalind Williams (1990), 47–9; Falconer (2005), 173–5.
14. Rosalind Williams (1990), 68–9.
15. See Hillman (1979); Falconer (2005), 91, 144–5.
16. Falconer (2005), 27.
17. Evans Lansing Smith (2001), 7.
18. Feder (1955), 280.
19. See Evans Lansing Smith (2001), 28–30.
20. See Ricks (1989), 135–46. For a bilingual edition of *Mythistorema* see Seferis (1967), 1–59.
21. Yeats (1974), 104–5.
22. Stevens (1954), 423–4.

23. See Holtsmark (2001).
24. Falconer (2005), 2; see also 4.
25. *Ibid.*, 2.
26. *Ibid.*, 28.
27. Adorno (1978), 39.
28. Vickroy (2002), 17, 19.
29. Kirby Farrell (1998), 2, 19, 25.
30. Ellison (2004), 39–40.
31. Nossack (2004), 11.
32. See further Edith Hall (2007c).
33. First published in English translation in 1959.
34. Levi (1995 [1963]), 388–9.
35. See the Introduction by Karl Miller to Levi (1995 [1963]), xxi.
36. Levi (1995 [1963]), 269.
37. *Ibid.*, 271.
38. Judt (1999), 32.
39. Levi (1988 [1986]), 121.
40. Levi (1995 [1963]), 275.
41. *Ibid.*, 22; see also Falconer (2005), 84.
42. Falconer (2005), 89–112.
43. *Ibid.*, 28.
44. Translation from poem in German, before 1975, by Peter Huchel, text and this translation in Hamburger (1976), 500–1.
45. The play was broadcast on BBC Radio 4 on the evening of 12 September 2003.
46. See the excellent edition of the poem in Tennyson (1989), 138–45.
47. 'Dusk of Liberty', in *Tristia*: bilingual edition in Mandel'shtam (1987 [1922]).
48. Scouffas (1991), 142. The poem was translated into English by Kimon Friar (1958).
49. Included in Landor (1847).
50. Arendt (1971), 132.
51. Cavarero (2000), 17–32.
52. Foucault (1984), 102.
53. Cavarero (2000), 120.
54. Sanders (1997).
55. Sterling A. Brown (1980), 20–1.
56. Auslander (1926), Preface.
57. Translated in Bly (1975), 99–100.
58. Vonnegut (1970), 53–4.
59. Scott (1925), 59–60.
60. Edith Hall (1996), 151–3.

61.  Agrippa (1655), 70.
62.  Machen (1960 [1902]), 40–1.
63.  Alford (1841), 69; see also Jenkyns (1980), 68.

# BIBLIOGRAPHY

Adams, Henry (1889–91), *History of the United States, 1800–1817*. 9 vols. New York: Scribner

Adeleye, Gabriel (1992), 'The *Odyssey* and the *Sundiata*: similarities and differences in the epics of two cultures', published online at http://department.monm.edu/history/faculty_forum/ADELEYE.htm

Adorno, Theodor W. (1978 [1951]), *Minima Moralia*, translated by E. Jephcott. London: Verso

—— and Max Hoerkheimer (1997), *Dialectic of Enlightenment*. English translation by John Cumming. London: Verso

Agrippa, Henry Cornelius (1655), *Of Occult Philosophy, or Of Magical Ceremonies: The Fourth Book*. Translated into English by Robert Turner. London: John Harrison

Alford, Henry (1841), *Chapters on the Poets of Ancient Greece*. London: Whittaker & Co.

Allen, T.W. (1946, ed.), *Homeri Opera*, vol. 5. Oxford: Clarendon

Andrews, Nigel (2002), 'A blizzard of wonderful things', *Financial Times Arts and Leisure*, 30 January. http://specials.ft.com/timeoff/film/FT3MOOHJ3XC.html

Anon. (1640), *Le glorie della musica celebrate dalla sorella poesia, rappresentandosi in Bologna la Delia e l'Ulisse nel teatro de gl'Illustriss. Guastavillani*. Bologna: Ferroni

Anon. (1829), *Essay on the Influence of the Homeric Poems on the Greek Nation*. Cambridge: R. Bridges

Araki, James T. (1978), 'Yuriwaka and Ulysses: the Homeric epics at the court of Ōuchi Yoshitaka', *Monumenta Nipponica: Studies in Japanese Culture* 33, 1–36

Arendt, Hannah (1971), *The Life of Mind*. New York: Harcourt and Brace

Arens, W. (1979), *The Man-Eating Myth: Anthropology & Anthropophagy*. New York: Oxford University Press

Arkins, Brian (1999), *Greek and Roman Themes in Joyce*. Lewiston, NY: E. Mellen Press

Armitage, Simon (1993), *Book of Matches*. London: Faber & Faber

Armstrong, Richard (2000), review of Inge Merkel, *Odysseus and Penelope*, *Classical and Modern Literature* 21, 73–80

Arnold, Matthew (1905), *On Translating Homer, with F.W. Newman's 'Homeric translation' and Arnold's 'Last words'*. London: New Universal Library

Aryanpur, Manoocher (1967–68), '*Paradise Lost* and the *Odyssey*', *Texas Studies in Literature & Language* 9, 151–86

Ashbery, John (1960), *The Heroes*, in Herbert Machiz (ed.), *Artists' Theatre: Four Plays*, 43–78. New York & London: Grove Press

Asimov, Isaac (under pseudonym of Paul French) (1952), *David Starr, Space Ranger*. New York: Doubleday

Atherton, Catherine (1998, ed.), *Monsters and Monstrosity in Greek and Roman Culture*. Bari: Levante

Atwood, Margaret (2005), *The Penelopiad*. Edinburgh: Canongate

Auerbach, Erich (1953 [1945]), *Mimesis: The Representation of Reality in Western Literature*, translated by Willard R. Trask. Princeton: Princeton University Press

—— (1959), *Scenes from the Drama of European Literature: Six Essays* (= *Theory and History of* Literature, vol. 9). Manchester: Manchester University Press

Auslander, Joseph (1926), *Cyclops' Eye*. New York & London: Harper & Bros.

Austin, Norman (1983), 'Odysseus and the Cyclops. Who is who?', in C.A. Rubino and C.W. Shelmerdine (eds.), *Approaches to Homer*, Austin: University of Texas Press, 3–37

—— (1994), *Helen of Troy and her Shameless Phantom*. Ithaca, NY: Cornell University Press

Bader, David (2005), *One Hundred Great Books in Haiku*. New York: Viking

Badoaro, Giacomo (1972), *Il ritorno d'Ulisse in Patria: An Opera with Libretto by Giacomo Badoaro*, translated by G. Dunn. London: Faber Music

Bailey, James Osler (1972 [1947]), *Pilgrims through Space and Time: Trends and Patterns in Scientific and Utopian Fiction*. Reprint. Westport, CT: Greenwood

Bakhtin, Mikhail (1986), 'Response to a Question from the Novy Mir Editorial Staff', English translation by Vern W. McGee, in Caryl Emerson and Michael Holquist (eds.), *Speech Genres and Other Late Essays*. Austin, Texas, 1–7

Bakken, Christopher (2006), *Goat Funeral*. Lebanon, NH: Sheep Meadow Press

Ballantyne, R.M. (1913), *The Coral Island*, with preface by J.M. Barrie. London: J. Nisbet

Balling, Hans and Anders Klinkby Madsen (2002, eds.), *From Homer to Hypertext: Studies in Narrative, Literature and Media*. Odense: University Press of Southern Denmark

Balmer, Josephine (2004), *Chasing Catullus: Poems, Translations & Transgressions*. Newcastle: Bloodaxe

Barbarese, J.T. (1999), 'The Contemporaneity of Homer's "Odyssey"', *Sewanee Review* 107, 275–83

Barkan, Leonard (1986), *The Gods Made Flesh: Metamorphosis and the Pursuit of Paganism*. New Haven & London: Yale University Press

Barnes, Hugh (1996), 'Head on the block in Bosnia', *The Sunday Telegraph*, *Arts* section, 11 February, 12

Barta, Peter I. (2000, ed.), *Metamorphoses in Russian Modernism*. Budapest & New York: Central European University Press

Barthes, Roland (1975), *The Pleasure of the Text*. New York: Farrar, Strauss & Giroux. Translation by Richard Miller of *Le plaisir du texte* (1973). Paris: Éditions du Seuil

Baudet, Henri (1965), *Paradise on Earth: Some Thoughts on European Images of Non-European Man*, translated by Elizabeth Wentholt. New Haven & London: Yale University Press

Baumeister, R.F. (1998), 'The Self', in D.T. Gilbert, S.T. Fiske and G. Lindzey (eds.), *Handbook of Social Psychology* (4th ed.). New York & Oxford: Oxford University Press, 680–740

Beard, Mary (2004), 'The never ending story', *Guardian*, Friday, 30 April

Bechdel, Alison (2006), *Fun Home: A Family Tragicomic*. London: Jonathan Cape

Bell, Marvin (2004), *Rampant (Poems)*. Port Townsend, WA: Copper Canyon Press

Benedikt, Michael and George E. Wellwarth (1964, ed. and transl.), *Modern French Theatre: An Anthology of Plays*. New York: E.P. Dutton

Bérard, Victor (1902), *Les Phéniciens et l'Odyssée*. 2 vols. Paris: Armand Colin
—— (1924, transl.), *L'Odyssée*, vol. 1. Paris: Association Guillaume Bude

Berger, John (2004), 'UH theater eyes unique take on Greek characters', *Honolulu Star*, 17 September

Bergren, Anne (1983), 'Language and the female in early Greek thought', *Arethusa* 16, 69–95

Bertacco, Simona (2002), *Out of Place: The Writings of Robert Kroetsch*. Bern: Peter Lang

Beye, C.R. (1966), *The Iliad, the Odyssey and the Epic Tradition*. Garden City, NY: Doubleday

Bittlestone, Robert (2005), *Odysseus Unbound: The Search for Homer's Ithaca*. New York & Cambridge: Cambridge University Press

Bjurström, Per (1961), *Giacomo Torelli and Baroque Stage Design*. Stockholm: Almquist & Wiksell

Bloch, Ernst (1986 [1952–59]), *The Principle of Hope*, translated by Neville Plaice, Stephen Plaice and Paul Knight. 3 vols. Oxford: Basil Blackwell

Blok, Rasmus (2002), 'A sense of closure: the state of narration in digital literature', in Balling and Madsen (eds.), 167–80

Bloom, Harold (1991, ed.), *Odysseus/Ulysses*. New York & Philadelphia: Chelsea House Publishers

Bly, Robert (1975, transl.), *Friends: You Drank Some Darkness: Three Swedish Poets (Harry Martinson, Gunnar Ekelöf and Tomas Tranströmer)*. Boston: Beacon Press

—— (1990), *Iron John: A Book About Men*. Rockport, MA: Element

Blythe, R. (1963), 'Sublimated Aladdin', in *The Age of Illusion: England in the Twenties and Thirties*. London: Hamish Hamilton

Bodde, D. (1961), 'Myths of ancient China', in Kramer (ed.), 367–408

Bogdanovich, Peter (1967), *John Ford*. London: Studio Vista

Boitani, Piero (1994 [1992]), *The Shadow of Ulysses: Figures of a Myth*, translated by Anita Weston. Oxford: Clarendon Press

—— and Richard Ambrosini (1998, eds.), *Ulisse: Archeologia dell'uomo moderno*. Rome: Bulzoni

Bokina, John (1991), 'Deity, beast and tyrant: images of the prince in the operas of Monteverdi', *International Political Science Review* 12, 48–66

Bolgar, R.R. (1954), *The Classical Heritage and its Beneficiaries*. Cambridge: Cambridge University Press

Bompaire, J. (1958), *Lucien Écrivain*. Paris: E. de Boccard

Borges, Jose Luis (1962 [1941]), *The Garden of Forking Paths*, in *Ficciones*, translated by Anthony Kerrigan. London: Weidenfeld & Nicolson

—— (1964 [1960]), *Dreamtigers*. English translation of *El Hacedor*, by Mildred Boyer and Harold Morland. Austin: University of Texas Press

—— (1972), *Selected Poems 1923–1967*, edited by Norman Thomas di Giovanni. London: Allen Lane

—— (1975), *La rosa profunda*. Buenos Aires: Emecé

—— (2004), *The Aleph and Other Stories*, translated by Andrew Hurley. Harmondsworth: Penguin Classics

Borthwick, E.K. (1988), 'Odysseus and the return of the swallow', *Greece & Rome* 35, 14–22

Brewer, Reuben (1974), 'A poet's *Odyssey*', in *Mirror on Mirror: Translation, Imitation, Parody*, 96–102. Cambridge, MA: Harvard University Press

Bridges, Emma, Edith Hall and P.J. Rhodes (2007, eds.), *Cultural Responses to the Persian Wars*. Oxford: Oxford University Press

Brisson, L. (2004), *How Philosophers Saved Myths*, translated by C. Tihanyi. Chicago: University of Chicago Press

Bristow, J. (1991), *Empire Boys: Adventures in a Man's World*. London: Harper Collins

Brodsky, (1973), *Selected Poems*, translated by George L. Kline. Foreword W.H. Auden. New York: Harper & Row

Brooke-Rose, Christine (1991), *Textermination*. Manchester: Carcanet

Broughton, T. Alan (1998), 'In the hut of Eumaeus', *Beloit Poetry Journal* 48.3, 10–11

Brown, Sterling A. (1980), *Collected Poems of Sterling A Brown*. London: Harper & Row

Brown, W.N. (1961), 'Mythology of India', in Kramer (ed.) 277–330

Browning, Robert (1992), 'The Byzantines and Homer', in Lamberton and Keaney (eds.), 134–48

Brun, Vincent (1940), *Untimely Ulysses*. London: Jonathan Cape

Buch-Jepsen, Niels (2002), 'What happened to the author? Modernist impersonality and authorial selfhood', in Balling and Madsen (eds.), 77–94

Buereo Vallejo, Antonio (1983), *La tejedora de sueños: drama en tres actor*, 6th edition, edited by Luis Iglesias Feijoo. Madrid: Cátedra

Buffière, F. (1956), *Les mythes d'Homère et la pensée grecque*. Paris: Les Belles lettres

—— (1962, ed.), *Héraclite: Allégories d'Homère*. Paris: Les Belles lettres

Buitron, Diana (1992, ed.), *The Odyssey and Ancient Art: An Epic in Word and Image*. Annandale-on-Hudson, NY: Edith C. Blum Art Institute

Bunting, Andrea and Sue Bolton (1994), 'Tired of waiting for Odysseus', *Green Left* 130, 9 February. Available online at www.greenleft.org.au/1994/130/10407

Burkert, W. (1987), 'The making of Homer in the 6th century BC: rhapsodes versus Stesichorus', in *Papers on the Amasis Painter and his World*. Malibu: Getty Museum, 43–62

Burnand, F.C. (1863), *Patient Penelope; or, The Return of Ulysses. A Burlesque in One Act*. London: Thomas Hailes Lacy

Burns, Christopher Andrew (2002), *Chapman's Homer: A Bibliographical Essay*. Croydon: C.A.B. Publishing

Butcher, S.H. and A. Lang (1879), *The Odyssey of Homer Done into English Prose*. London: Macmillan

Butler, Samuel (1900), *The Odyssey: Rendered into English Prose for the Use of Those who Cannot Read the Original*. London: A.C. Fifield

—— (1967 [1897]), *The Authoress of the Odyssey*, edited by D. Grene. Chicago & London: University of Chicago Press

Bynum, Caroline Walker (2001), *Metamorphosis and Identity*. New York: Zone Books

Calame, Claude (1977), 'Les légendes du Cyclops dans le folklore Européan et extra-Européan: Un jeu de transformation narrative'. *Études de Lettres* (Bull. de Fac. des Lettres Lausanne), ser. 3. 2, 45–79

Calin, William (1983), A *Muse for Heroes: Nine Centuries of the Epic in France*. Toronto: University of Toronto Press

Callahan, John F. (2004a, ed.), *Ralph Ellison's Invisible Man: A Casebook*. Oxford: Oxford University Press

—— (2004b), 'Ellison's *Invisible Man*', in Callahan (2004a, ed.), 287–322

Callahan, John M. (1991), 'The ultimate in theatre violence', in James Redmond (ed.), *Violence in Drama*. Cambridge: Cambridge University Press, 165–75

Calvino, Italo (1986 [1981]), 'The Odysseys within the *Odyssey*', in *The Uses of Literature*, English translation by Patrick Creagh. San Diego, New York & London: Harvest, 135–45

Campbell, David (1993, ed.), *Greek Lyric* vol. 5. Cambridge, MA & London: Harvard University Press

Campbell, Joseph (1956 [1948]), *The Hero with a Thousand Faces*. New York: Meridian

Carpentier, Alejo (2001 [1953]), *The Lost Steps*, translated by Harriet de Onís. Minneapolis: University of Minnesota Press

Carr, Winifred (1961), 'Opera at the foot of the Acropolis', *Daily Telegraph*, 7 September

Carrière, Jean-Claude (1994), *The Secret Language of Film*. Translated from the French by Jeremy Leggatt. New York: Pantheon Books

Carter, Tim (1993),' 'In love's harmonius consort?' Penelope and the interpretation of *Il ritorno d'Ulisse in patria*', *Cambridge Opera Journal* 5, 1–16

Cary, M. and E.H. Warmington (1963), *The Ancient Explorers*. 2nd edition. Harmondsworth: Penguin

Caskey, L.D. (1934), 'Odysseus and Elpenor on a pelike in Boston', *American Journal of Archaeology* 38, 399–400

Cavafy, C.P. (1971), *Poems*, translated by John Mavrogordato, with an Introduction by Rex Warner. London: Chatto & Windus

Cavarero, Adriana (1995 [1990]), *In Spite of Plato: A Feminist Rewriting of Ancient Philosophy*, translated by S. Anderlini-D'Onifrio and Áine O'Healy. London: Polity

—— (2000 [1997]), *Relating Narratives: Storytelling and Selfhood*, translated by Paul Kottman. London: Routledge

Cave, Terence (1988), *Recognitions: A Study in Poetics*. Oxford: Clarendon

Cazorla, Hazel (1986), 'El retorno de Ulises: dos enfoques contemporaneous del mito en el teatro de Buero Vallejo y Antonio Gala', *Hispanófila* 87, 43–51

Césaire, Aimé (1969), *Une tempête: théâtre d'après La tempête de Shakespeare: adaptation pour un théâtre nègre*. Paris: Seuil

—— (1983), *The Collected Poetry of Aimé Césaire*, translated and edited by

Clayton Eshleman and Annette Smith. Berkeley, Los Angeles, London

—— (1990), *Lyric and Dramatic Poetry 1946–82*, translated by Clayton Eshleman and Annette Smith. Charlottesville: University Press of Virginia

Chafe, Rick (2000), *The Odyssey: A Play Adapted from Homer.* Toronto: Playwrights Canada Press

Chalkondylas, Demetrios (1488, ed.), *Homerou Poiesis apasa.* 2 vols. Florence: Demetrius Mediolanensis

Chantraine, Pierre (1999), *Dictionnaire étymologique de la langue grecque.* 2nd edition. Paris: Klincksieck

Choate, E. Teresa (2006), 'Le dernier caravansérail (Odyssées) (review)' *Theatre Journal* 58, 95–99

Clare, Ray (1998), 'Representing monstrosity: Polyphemus in the *Odyssey*', in Atherton (ed.), 1–17

Clark, Matthew (2004), 'Formulas, metre and type-scenes', in Fowler (ed.), 117–38

Clark, Raymond J. (1979), *Catabasis, Vergil and the Wisdom-Tradition.* Amsterdam: B.R. Grüner

Clarke, Bruce (1995), *Allegories of Writing: The Subject of Metamorphosis.* Albany, NY: SUNY Press

Clarke, Howard (1981), *Homer's Readers: A Historical Introduction to the* Iliad *and the* Odyssey. Newark, NJ: University of Delaware Press

Clauss, James (1999), 'Descent Into Hell – John Ford's "The Searchers"', *Journal of Popular Film and Television*, Fall. Available online at www.findarticles.com/p/articles/mi_m0412/is_3_27/ai_58470118

Claybourne, Anna (1997), *The Adventures of Ulysses.* London: Usborne

Clayton, Barbara (2004), *A Penelopean Poetics: reweaving the feminine in Homer's Odyssey.* Lanham, MD: Lexington Books

Clemens, John K. and Douglas F. Mayer (1999), *The Classic Touch: Lessons in Leadership from Homer to Hemingway.* Revised edition. Chicago, IL: Contemporary Books

Clubb, Louise George (1965), *Giambattista della Porta: Dramatist.* Princeton, NJ: Princeton University Press

Coates, John D. (2003), ' The "Spiritual quest" in Rider Haggard's *She* and *Ayesha*', *Cahiers victoriens & édouardiens* 57, 33–54

Cohen, Beth (1995, ed.), *The Distaff Side: Representing the Female in Homer's Odyssey.* New York & Oxford: Oxford University Press

Cohn, Maren Ormseth (1995), *T.E. Lawrence and Odysseus: A Study of Translation, Identity, and Heroic Action.* Chicago, IL

Cole, William (1963, ed.), *Erotic Poetry.* London: Weidenfeld & Nicolson

Coleridge, Henry Nelson (1846), *Greek Classic Poets.* London: Murray

Cook, Erwin (1995), *The Odyssey in Athens: Myths of Cultural Origins*. Ithaca and London: Cornell University Press

Cooke, Thomas (1728, transl.), *The Works of Hesiod*. London: T. Green

Cookson, Forrest (2005), 'Democracy and Islam', *Bangladesh Independent*, 2 September

Couldrey, Oswald (1914), *The Mistaken Fury and Other Lapses*. Oxford: B.H. Blackwell

Cowper, W. (1791), *The Iliad and Odyssey*. Translated into English blank verse. 2 vols. London: J. Johnson

Curtin, Kevin Thomas (1985), '*The Natural*: our *Iliad* and *Odyssey*', *Antioch Review* 43, 225–41

Cysarz, Dirk et al. (2004), 'Oscillations of heart rate and respiration synchronize during poetry recitation', *American Journal of Physiology: Heart and Circulatory Physiology* 287, 579–87

Dacier, Anne (1716 [1708]), *L'Odyssée d'Homère traduite en François, avec des Remarques par Madame Dacier*. 3 vols. Paris: L'Imprimerie Royale

Dalby, Andrew (2006), *Rediscovering Homer: Inside the Origins of the Epic*. New York & London: W.W. Norton

D'Amico, Silvia (2002), *Heureux qui comme Ulysse: Ulisse nella poesia francese e neolatina del XVI secolo*. Milan: Pubblicazioni della facoltà di lettere e filosofia dell' Università di Milano

Daniel, Samuel (1605), *Certaine Small Poems Lately Printed: with the Tragedie of Philotas*. London: S. Waterson

Darius, Julian (2002), 'X-Men is not an allegory of racial tolerance', *Sequential Culture* 3, 25 September

Darrieussecq, Marie (1997), *Pig Tales*. London: Faber & Faber. English translation by Linda Coverdale of *Truismes* (Editions P.O.L. 1996)

Darwin, Charles (1988), *Diary of the Voyage of H.M.S. Beagle*, edited by Richard Darwin Keynes. Cambridge: Cambridge University Press

Davenant, Charles (1677), *Circe, A Tragedy*. London: Richard Tonson

Davies, Merryl Wyn, Ashis Nandy and Ziauddin Sardar (1993), *Barbaric Others: A Manifesto on Western Racism*. London & Boulder, CO: Pluto Press

Davis, Gregson (1997), *Aimé Césaire*. Cambridge: Cambridge University Press

—— (2007), 'Reframing the Homeric: Images of the *Odyssey* in the art of Derek Walcott and Romare Bearden', in Lorna Hardwick and Chris Stray (eds.), *The Blackwell Companion to Classical Reception*. Oxford: Blackwell, 401–14

Davis, Natalie Zemon (1983), *The Return of Martin Guerre*. Cambridge, MA & London: Harvard University Press

—— (1997), *Remaking Impostors: from Martin Guerre to Sommersby*. Natalie

Hayes Robinson lecture, 1. Egham: Royal Holloway, University of London

Dawe, R.D. (1993), *The Odyssey: Translation and Analysis*. Lewes: Book Guild

de Coras, Jean (1561), *Arrest Memorable, du parlement de Tolose*. Lyon: Antoine Vincent

de Jong, Irene (2001), *A Narratological Commentary on the Odyssey*. Cambridge & New York: Cambridge University Press

della Porta, Giambattista (1978 [1591]), *La Penelope*, edited by Raffaele Sirri. Naples: Editrice Ferraro

Deneen, Patrick J. (2000), *The Odyssey of Political Theory: The Politics of Departure and Return*. Lanham: Rowman & Littlefield

DeNicola, Deborah (1999, ed.), *Orpheus and Company: Contemporary Poems on Greek Mythology*, Hanover, NH: University Press of New England

Dickstein, Morris (2004), 'Ralph Ellison, race, and American culture', in Callahan (ed.), 125–48

Dijkstra, Bram (1986), *Idols of Perversity*. New York: Oxford University Press

Dilworth, Thomas (1994), 'The fall of Troy and the slaughter of the suitors: ultimate symbolic correspondence in the Odyssey', *Mosaic* 27.2 (June), 1–33

Divus, Andreas (1538), *Odyssea*. Leiden: Vince[n]tius de Portonariis

Doherty. Lillian E. (1990), 'Joyce's Penelope and Homer's: feminist reconsiderations', *Classical and Modern Literature* 10, 343–9

—— (1995), *Siren Songs: Gender, Audience, and Narrators in the* Odyssey. Ann Arbor: University of Michigan Press

—— (2006), 'Putting the women back into the Hesiodic *Catalogue of Women*', in Zajko and Leonard (eds.), 297–325

Dougherty, Carol (2001), *The Raft of Odysseus: The Ethnographic Imagination of Homer's Odyssey*. New York: Oxford University Press

Duffy, Carol Ann (1999), *The World's Wife: Poems*. London: Picador

Dupont, Florence (1991), *Homère et Dallas*. Paris: Hachette

Durante, M. (1971), *Sulla preistoria della tradizione poetica greca*, vol. 1. Rome: dell'Ateneo

Dworkin, Craig Douglas (1995), 'Penelope reworking the twill: patchwork, writing, and Lyn Hejinian's *My Life*', *Contemporary Literature* 36, 58–81

Eagleton, Terry (1990), *The Ideology of the Aesthetic*. Oxford: Blackwell

Eckstein, Arthur M. (2004), 'Introduction: main critical issues in *The Searchers*', in Eckstein and Lehman (eds.), 1–45

—— and Peter Lehman (2004, eds.), *The Searchers: Essays and Reflections on John Ford's Classic Western*. Detroit: Wayne State University Press

Edwards, Viv and Thomas J. Sienkewicz (1990), *Oral Cultures Past and Present:*

*Rappin' and Homer*. Oxford: Basil Blackwell

Eliade, Mircea (1976), *Occultism, Witchcraft, and Cultural Fashions*. Chicago: University of Chicago Press

Eliot, T.S. (1974), *Collected Poems 1909–1962*. London & Boston: Faber & Faber

—— (1975), *Selected Prose*, edited with an introduction by Frank Kermode. New York: Farrar, Strauss & Giroux

Elley, Derek (1984), *The Epic Film: Myth & History*. London: Routledge

Ellis, Peter Berresford (1978), *H. Rider Haggard: A Voice from the Infinite*. London & Henley: Routledge Kegan Paul

Ellison, Ralph Waldo (1965 [1952]), *Invisible Man*. London: Penguin

—— (1981), *Invisible Man*. Reprint with new introduction by the author. New York: Random House

—— (2004), 'Ralph Ellison on *Invisible Man*', in Callahan (ed.), 23–63

Ellmann, Richard (1975, ed.), *Selected Letters of James Joyce*. New York: Viking

—— (1982), *James Joyce*. 2nd edition. Oxford: Oxford University Press

Emerson, Ralph Waldo (1841), *Essays* (first series). Boston: J. Munroe & Co.

Emlyn-Jones, C., Lorna Hardwick and J. Purkis (1992, eds.), *Homer, Readings and Images*. London: Duckworth & the Open University

Erasmus (1957), *Ten Colloquies of Erasmus*, translated with an Introduction and Notes by Craig R. Thompson. New York: Liberal Arts Press

Erskine, John (1929), *Penelope's Man: The Homing Instinct*. London: Eveleigh Nash & Grayson

Essex, Charles (2005), 'Ulysses syndrome', *British Medical Journal* 330 (28 May), 1268

Fagles, Robert (1996, transl.), *The Odyssey*. New York: Viking Penguin

Fajardo-Acosta, Fidel (1990), *The Hero's Failure in the Tragedy of Odysseus: A Revisionist Analysis*. Lewiston, Queenston & Lampeter: Edwin Mellen Press

Falconer, Rachel (2005), *Hell in Contemporary Literature: Western Descent Narratives since 1945*. Edinburgh: Edinburgh University Press

Farrar, Frederic W. (1859), *Julian Home: A Tale of College Life*. Edinburgh: Adam and Charles Black

Farrell, Joseph (2004), 'Roman Homer', in Fowler (ed.), 254–71

Farrell, Kirby (1998), *Post-traumatic Culture: Injury and Interpretation in the Nineties*. Baltimore & London: Johns Hopkins University Press

Feder, Lillian (1955), 'Marlow's descent into Hell', *Nineteenth Century Fiction* 9, 280–92

Fellmann, Berthold (1972), *Die antiken Darstellungen des Polyphemabenteuers*. Munich: Wilhelm Fink

Felson-Rubin, Nancy (1994), *Regarding Penelope: From Character to Poetics*.

Princeton, NJ: Princeton University Press

Ferrucci, Franco (1980), *The Poetics of Disguise: The Autobiography of the Work in Homer, Dante and Shakespeare*, translated by Ann Dunnigan. Ithaca, NY & London: Cornell University Press

Feuchtwanger, Lion (1949), *Odysseus and the Swine and Other Stories*. English translation. London: Hutchinson International Authors

Fifield, Christopher (2005), *Max Bruch: His Life and Works*. 2nd edition. Woodbridge, Suffolk & Rochester, NY: Boydell Press

Finley, John H. (1978), *Homer's Odyssey*. Cambridge, MA & London: Harvard University Press,

Finley, Moses (1979), *The World of Odysseus*. 2nd edition. London: Penguin

Finsler, Georg (1912), *Homer in der Neuzeit von Dante bis Goethe: Italien, Frankreich, England, Deutschland*. Leipzig & Berlin: Teubner

Fitch, John (2002, transl.), *Seneca, Tragedies* vol. 1. Cambridge, MA & London: Harvard University Press

—— (2004), 'Archetypes on the American screen: heroes and anti-heroes', *Journal of Religion and Popular Culture* 7, Summer. Available online at http://www.usask.ca/relst/jrpc/art7-archetypes-print.html

Fitzgerald, Robert (1961), *The Odyssey*. Garden City, NY: Anchor Press/ Doubleday

Flecker, James Elroy (1924), *The Bridge of Fire: Poems*. London: Elkin Mathews

Foley, Helene (1978), 'Reverse similes and sex role in the *Odyssey*', *Arethusa* 11, 7–26

—— (2005), 'Women in ancient epic', in John M. Foley (ed.), *A Companion to Ancient Epic*. Oxford: Blackwell, 105–18

Foley, John Miles (1997), 'Oral tradition and its implications', in Ian Morris and Barry Powell (eds.), *A New Companion to Homer*. Leiden: Brill, 146–73

Forbes-Irving, P.M.C. (1990), *Metamorphosis in Greek Myth*. Oxford: Oxford University Press

Forrest, Leon (2004), 'Luminosity from the lower frequencies', in Callahan (ed.), 267–86

Foucault, M. (1984), *The Foucault Reader*, ed. Paul Rabinow. New York: Pantheon

Fowler, Robert (2004, ed.), *The Cambridge Companion to Homer*. Cambridge: Cambridge University Press

Francis, Rebecca (2006), 'UK: safe haven?', programme essay for David Farr's *The Odyssey: A Trip based on Homer's Epic* at the Lyric Hammersmith. London

Fränkel, Hermann (1962), *Early Greek Poetry & Philosophy*, translated by Moses Hadas and James Willis. New York: HBJ

Frazer, R.M. (1966, transl.), *The Trojan War: The Chronicles of Dictys of Crete and Dares the Phrygian*. Bloomington, IN & London: Indiana University Press

Frazier, Charles (2003), *Cold Mountain*. London: Hodder and Stoughton

Fredericks, S.C. (1976), 'Lucian's *True History* as SF', *Science Fiction Studies* no. 8 = vol. 3.1 (March)

Frege, Gottlob (1892), 'Über Sinn und Bedeutung', *Zeitschrift für Philosophie und philosophische Kritik* 100, 25–50

Freud, Sigmund (1953 [1900]), *The Interpretation of Dreams*, translated and edited by James Strachey in *The Standard Edition of the Complete Psychological Works of Sigmund Freud*, vols. IV–V. London: Hogarth Press

Friedman, John Block (1981), *The Monstrous Races in Medieval Art and Thought*. Cambridge, MA: Harvard University Press

Friedman, Susan Stanford (1986), 'Gender and genre anxiety: Elizabeth Barrett Browning and H.D. as epic poets', *Tulsa Studies in Women's Literature* 5, 217–23

Fries, Carl (1911), 'Das Buch Tobit und die Telemachie', *Zeitschrift für Wissenschaftliche Theologie* 53, 54–87

Frye, Northrop (1957), *Anatomy of Criticism*. Princeton, NJ: Princeton University Press

Fuchs, Gotthard (1994, ed.), *Lange Irrfahrt-grosse Heimkehr: Odysseus als Archetyp – zur Aktualität des Mythos*. Frankfurt: Josef Knecht

Gadamer, Hans-Georg (1993), *Gesammelte Werke*, vol. VIII [= *Ästhetik und Poetik* I]. Tübingen: J.C.B. Mohr (Paul Siebeck)

Gager, William (1592), *Ulysses Redux. Tragoedia Nova*. Oxford: J. Barnes

Garnett, D. (1938, ed.), *The Letters of T.E. Lawrence*. New York: Doubleday

Gates, Henry Louis, Jr (1987), *Figures in Black: Words, Signs, and the 'Racial' Self*. New York & Oxford: Oxford University Press

Geach, Peter and Max Black (1952, eds.), *Translations from the Philosophical Writings of Gottlob Frege*. Oxford: Basil Blackwell

Genette, Gérard (1997 [1982]), *Palimpsests: Literature in the Second Degree*, translated by Channa Newman and Claude Doubinsky. Lincoln and London: University of Nebraska Press

Gill, C. (1973), 'The sexual episodes in Petronius' Satyricon', *Classical Philology* 68, 172–85

Gilmore-Baldwin, Molly (2006), 'Jazz man is down-to-earth', *The Olympian*, 10 January

Giraldi Cinthio, G. (1554), *Discorsi ... intorno al comporre de I romanzi, delle comedie, e delle tragedie, e di altre maniere di poesie*. Venice: Gabriel Giolito de Ferrari et fratelli

Giraudoux, Jean (1958 [1919]), *Elpenor*, translated by Richard Howard. New

York: Noonday Press

Gladstone, William (1869), *Juventus Mundi. The Gods and Men of the Heroic Age*. London: Macmillan & Co.

Glenn, J. (1971), 'The Polyphemus folktale and Homer's Kyklopeia', *TAPA* 102, 133–85

Glover, Jane (1985), 'The Venetian operas', in Denis Arnold and Nigel Fortune (eds.), *The New Monteverdi Companion*. London & Boston: Faber & Faber, 288–304

Glück, Louise (1996), *Meadowlands*. Hopewell, NJ: Eco

Godard, Jean-Luc (1985), *Jean-Luc Godard par Jean-Luc Godard*, edited by Alain Bergala. Paris: Cahiers due Cinéma-Éditions de l'Étoile

Gogol, Nikolai (1969), *Selected Passages from Correspondence with Friends*, translated by Jesse Zeldin. Nashville: Vanderbilt University Press

Goldhill, Simon (2002), *Who Needs Greek? Contests in the Cultural History of Hellenism*. Cambridge: Cambridge University Press

Goltz, A. (2005), '*Odyssee*-Rezeption im Film – moralische Normen und Konflikte in Epos und Adaptation', in Luther (ed.), 109–24

Gould, Thomas (1991), 'The use of violence in drama', in James Redmond (ed.), *Violence in Drama*. Cambridge: Cambridge University Press, 1–13

Gove, Philip B. (1941), *The Imaginary Voyage in Prose Fiction*. London: Holland Press

Grafton, Anthony (1992), 'Renaissance readers of Homer's ancient readers', in Lamberton and Keaney (eds.), 149–72

Gray, Wallace (1985), *Homer to Joyce: Interpretations of the Classic Works of Western Literature*. New York: Macmillan

Graziosi, Barbara (2002), *The Invention of Homer: The Early Reception of Epic*. Cambridge: Cambridge University Press

—— and Emily Greenwood (2007, eds.), *Homer in the Twentieth-Century: Between World Literature and the Western Canon*. Oxford: Oxford University Press

Gregory, Eileen (1997), *H.D. and Hellenism: Classic Lines*. Cambridge: Cambridge University Press

Green, Peter (2004), 'Homer for the kiddies', in *From Icaria to the Stars*, 288–96. Austin, TX: University of Texas Press

Grimwood, Jon Courtenay (2001), *Pashazade*. London: Earthlight

Grinstein, Alexander (1980), *Sigmund Freud's Dreams*. New York: International Universities Press

Gross, John (2002, ed.), *After Shakespeare: An Anthology*. Oxford & New York: Oxford University Press

Grossardt, Peter (1998), *Die Trugreden in der Odyssee und ihre Rezeption in der antiken Literatur* (= *Sapheneia* 2). Bern: P. Lang

Grote, George (1869), *A History of Greece*. 12 vols. New edition. London: John

Murray

Gundry, Inglis (1998), *Last Boy of the Family: A Musical Memoir*. London Thames Publishing

Gunn, Thom (1994), *Collected Poems*. New York: Farrar, Strauss & Giroux

Gurko, Leo (1953), *Heroes, Highbrows and the Popular Mind*. Indianapolis & New York: Bobbs-Merrill

Hacks, Peter (1997), *Prinz Telemach und sein Lehrer Mentor*. Berlin: Eulenspiegel

Haggard, H. Rider (1991 [1887]), *She*, ed. Daniel Karlin. Oxford: Oxford University Press World's Classics

——— and Andrew Lang (1890), *The World's Desire*. London: Longman's, Green & Co.

Hainsworth, Brian (1970), 'The criticism of an oral Homer', *Journal of Hellenic Studies* 90, 90–8. Shortened version in Emlyn-Jones, Hardwick and Purkis (1992, eds.), 65–75

Hall, Edith (1989), *Inventing the Barbarian: Greek Self-Definition through Tragedy*. Oxford: Oxford University Press

——— (1996), *Aeschylus' Persians, edited with a Translation and Commentary*. Warminster: Aris & Phillips

——— (1998), 'Literature and performance', in Paul Cartledge (ed.), *The Cambirdge Illustrated History of Ancient Greece*. Cambridge: Cambridge University Press

——— (2005), 'Iphigenia and her mother at Aulis: a study in the revival of a Euripidean classic', in J. Dillon and S. Wilmer (eds.), *Rebel Women: Staging Ancient Greek Drama Today*. London: Methuen, 3–41

——— (2006), *The Theatrical Cast of Athens. Interactions between Ancient Greek Drama and Society*. Oxford: Oxford University Press

——— (2007a), 'Introduction' to Edith Hall and Amanda Wrigley (eds.), *Aristophanes in Performance*. Oxford: Legenda, 1–29

——— (2007b), 'Putting the class into classical reception', in Lorna Hardwick and Christopher Stray (eds.), *The Blackwell Companion to Classical Reception*. Oxford: Blackwell, 386–97

——— (2007c), 'Subjects, selves and survivors', *Helios* 34, 125–59

——— (2007d), 'The survival of culture', in E. Shuckburgh (ed.), *Survival*. Cambridge: Cambridge University Press, 53–79

——— (forthcoming), 'Navigating the realms of gold: translation as access route to the Classics', in Zajko and Lianeri (eds.)

——— and Fiona Macintosh (2005), *Greek Tragedy and the British Theatre 1660–1914*. Oxford: Oxford University Press

——— F. Macintosh and A. Wrigley (2004, eds.), *Dionysus since 69: Greek Tragedy at the Dawn of the Third Millennium*. Oxford: Oxford University Press

Hall, John (1652), *Peri hypsous, or Dionysius Longinus of the height of eloquence*.

*Rendered out of the originall*. London: Francis Eaglesfield

Hall, Stuart (1996), Editorial in *Soundings* 3, 116–18

Haller, John S. and Robin M. Haller (1974), *The Physician and Society in Victorian America*. New York: Norton

Hamburger, Michael (1976, ed.), *German Poetry 1910–1975*. New York: Urizen Books

Hammermeister, Kai (2000), 'Heimat in Heidegger and Gadamer', *Philosophy and Literature* 24.2, 312–26

Hammond, Paul (1983), *John Oldham and the Renewal of Classical Culture*. Cambridge: Cambridge University Press

Hamner, Robert D. (1997), *Epic of the Dispossessed: Derek Walcott's Omeros*. Columbia: University of Missouri Press

—— (2001), 'Creolizing Homer for the stage: Walcott's *The Odyssey*', *Twentieth-Century Literature*, Fall

Haraway, Donna (1990), *Simians, Cyborgs and Women: The Reinvention of Nature*. London: Free Association

Hardy, Thomas (1974 [1896]), *Jude the Obscure*, with an Introduction by Terry Eagleton and Notes by P.N. Furbank. London: Macmillan

Hardwick, Lorna (1992), 'Convergence and divergence in reading Homer', in Emlyn-Jones, Hardwick and Purkis (eds.), 226–48

—— (1996), 'A Daidalos in the late-modern age? Transplanting Homer into Derek Walcott's *The Odyssey: A stage version*', online article available at http://www2.open.ac.uk/ClassicalStudies/GreekPlays/conf96/cctoc.htm

—— (2000), *Translating Words, Translating Cultures*. London: Duckworth

—— (2003), *Reception Studies* [= *Greece & Rome New Surveys in the Classics* 33]. Oxford: Oxford University Press

—— (2004a), ' "Shards and suckers": contemporary receptions of Homer', in Fowler (ed.), 344–62

—— (2004b), 'Greek drama and anti-colonialism: decolonizing Classics', in Hall, Macintosh and Wrigley (eds.), 219–42

Harriott, Rosemary (1969), *Poetry and Criticism Before Plato*. London: Methuen

Harris, Wilson (1954), *Eternity to Season: Poems of Separation and Reunion*. Georgetown, Guiana

—— (1990), *The Four Banks of the River of Space*. London: Faber & Faber

—— (2003), *The Mask of the Beggar*. London: Faber & Faber

Harsh, Philip (1950), 'Penelope and Odysseus in *Odyssey* XIX', *American Journal of Philology* 71, 1–21

Hartog, François (2001), *Memories of Odysseus: Frontier Tales from Ancient Greece*. Edinburgh: Edinburgh University Press

Haugaard, Erik, and Masako Haugaard (1991), *The Story of Yuriwaka: A*

*Japanese Odyssey*. Nowot, CO: Roberts Rinehart

Hauptmann, Gerhart (1914), *Der Bogen des Odysseus*. Berlin: Fischer

Heaney, Seamus (1987), *The Haw Lantern*. London: Faber & Faber

Hegel, G.W.F. (1923 [1837]), *Vorlesungen über die Philosophie der Weltgeschichte* ed. Georg Lasson. Leipzig: F. Meiner

Heidegger, Martin (1993), *Basic Writings*, ed. David Farrell Krell. 2nd edition. London & New York: Routledge

Heilbrun, Carolyn (1990 [1985]), 'What was Penelope unweaving?', in *Hamlet's Mother and Other* Women. New York: Columbia University Press, 103–11

Heitman, Richard (2005), *Taking Her Seriously: Penelope and the Plot of Homer's Odyssey*. Ann Arbor: University of Michigan Press

Helleman, W.E. (1995), 'Penelope as Lady Philosophy', *The Phoenix* 49, 283–301

Helmbold, W.C. and E.N. O'Neil (1959), *Plutarch's Quotations*. Baltimore, MD & Oxford

Henderson, Brian (2004), '*The Searchers*: An American Dilemma', in Eckstein and Lehman (eds.), 47–74

Henley, Elton F. (1962, ed.), *William Gager: Ulysses Redux (1592). A facsimile edition and an English translation*. PhD Diss. Florida State University

Hepp, Noémi (1968), *Homère en France au XVIIe siècle*. Paris: Klincksieck

—— (1970), *Deux amis d'Homère au XVIIe siècle. Textes inédits de Paul Pellison et de Claude Fleury*. Paris: Klincksieck

Heubeck, Alfred, Stephanie West and J.B. Hainsworth (1988–1992), *A Commentary on Homer's Odyssey*. 3 vols. Oxford: Clarendon

Highet, Gilbert (1949), *The Classical Tradition: Greek and Roman Influences on Western Literature*. London: Oxford University Press

Hill, Geoffrey (1992), *Illuminating Shadows: The Mythic Power of Film*. Boston & London: Shambhala

Hillman, James (1979), *The Dream and the Underworld*. New York: Harper & Row

Hobbes, Thomas (1686, transl.), *Homer's Odyssey, Translated out of the Greek*. 3rd edition. London: W. Crook

Hobbs, Angela (2000), *Plato and the Hero: Courage, Manliness, and the Impersonal Good*. Cambridge: Cambridge University Press

Holtsmark, Erling B. (2001), 'The *katabasis* theme in modern cinema', in Martin M. Winkler (ed.), *Classical Myth & Culture in the Cinema*. Oxford: Oxford University Press, 23–50

Honig, Edwin (1985, ed.), *The Poet's Other Voice: Conversations on Literary Translation*. Amherst: University of Massachusetts Press

Hoste, Mary R. (1906), *Nausicaa: An Idyll of the Odyssey, Adapted and Arranged as a Play*. London: David Nutt

Houston, Jean (1992), *The Hero and the Goddess: The* Odyssey *as Mystery and Initiation*. London & New York: Aquarian Press

Howarth, Patrick (1973), *Play Up and Play the Game: The Heroes of Popular Fiction*. London: Eyre Methuen

Hudson, Ronald and Philip Kelley (1984, eds.), *The Brownings' Correspondence*. Winfield, KS: Wedgestone Press

Hughes, Ted (2003), *Collected Poems*, ed. Paul Keegan. London: Faber & Faber

Hurst, Isobel (2006), *Victorian Women and the Classics: The Feminine of Homer*. Oxford: Oxford University Press

Hust, Christoph (2005), *August Bungert: Ein Komponist im deutschen Kaiserreich*. Tutzing: Hans Schneider

Hutton, Warwick (1995), *Odysseus and the Cyclops*. New York: Simon & Schuster

Huxley, Aldous (1949), 'Tragedy and the whole truth', in *Music at Night and Other Essays*. London: Chatto & Windus, 3–18

Izod, John (2001), *Myth, Mind and Screen: Understanding the Heroes of our Times*. Cambridge: Cambridge University Press

Jacoby, F. (1927, ed.), *Die Fragmente der griechischen Historiker*, vol. II. Berlin: Weidmannsche Buchhandlung

—— (1961 [1933]), 'Die geistige Physiognomie der *Odyssee*', in H.J. Mette (ed.), *Kleine philologische Schriften*. Berlin: Akademie-Verlag, 107–38

Jamal, Michele (1995), *Deerdancer: The Shapeshifter Archetype in Story and in Trance*. Harmondsworth: Penguin/Arkana

James, Edward (2000), 'Before the novum: the prehistory of science fiction criticism', in Patrick Parrinder (2000, ed.), *Learning from Other Worlds*. Liverpool: Liverpool University Press, 19–35

James, M.R. (1924, transl.), *The Apocryphal New Testament*. Oxford: Clarendon Press

Jane, Cecil (1930, ed. and transl.), *Select Documents Illustrating the Four Voyages of Columbus*. London: Hakluyt Society

Jenkins, I.D. (1985), 'The ambiguity of Greek textiles', *Arethusa* 18, 109–32

Jenkyns, Richard (1980), *The Victorians and Ancient Greece*. Oxford: Basil Blackwell

Jewett, Robert and John Shelton Lawrence (1977), *The American Monomyth*. Garden City, NY: Anchor Press/Doubleday

Johnson, Eyvind (1952), *Return to Ithaca: The Odyssey Retold as a Modern Novel*, translated from Swedish by M.A. Michael. London: Thames & Hudson

Johnson, John William, Thomas A. Hale and Stephen Belcher (1997, eds.), *Oral Epics from Africa: Vibrant Voices from a Vast Continent*. Bloomington & Indianapolis: Indiana University Press

Jones, Dudley and Tony Watkins (2000, eds.), *A Necessary Fantasy? The Heroic Figure in Children's Popular Culture*. New York & London: Garland

Joppien, Rüdiger and Bernard Smith (1985), *The Art of Captain Cook's Voyages*, vol. 1. New Haven & London: Yale University Press

Joyce, James (1993 [1922]), *Ulysses*, edited by Jeri Johnson (Oxford World's Classics). Oxford: Oxford University Press

Judt, Tony (1999), 'The courage of the elementary', *TLS*, 20 May, 31–8

Jung, Carl (1990), *The Archetypes and the Collective Unconscious*, translated by R.F. Hull. Princeton, NJ: Princeton University Press

—— (1991 [1926]), *Analytical Psychology: Notes of the Seminar Given in 1925*, edited by William McGuire. London: Routledge

KA = Kassel, R. and C. Austin (1983–, eds.), *Poetae Comici Graeci*. Berlin: de Gruyter

Kafka, Franz (1994), *Poseidon: und andere kurze Prosa*, edited by Jürgen Born. Frankfurt am Main: Fischer Taschenbuch Verlag

Kahane, Ahuvia (2005), *Diachronic Dialogues: Authority and Continuity in Homer and the Homeric Tradition*. Lanham, Boulder, New York: Lexington Books

Kalinak, Kathryn (2004), ' "Typically American": music for *The Searchers*', in Eckstein and Lehman (eds.), 109–43

Kant, I. (1966), *Gesammelte Schriften*, edition of the Deutsche Akademie der Wissenschaften zu Berlin, vol. XV.1, Berlin

Karkavitsas, Andreas (1973), *Apanta* (Complete Works). Athens: Kapopoulos

—— (1982 [1897]), *The Beggar*, English translation of *O Zitianos* by William F. Wyatt, Jr, with an appendix by P.D. Mastrodemetres. New Rochelle, NY: Caratzas Brothers

Karydas, C.H.P (1998), *Eurykleia and her Successors: Female Figures of Authority in Greek Poetics*, Lanham

Katz, Marilyn Arthur (1991), *Penelope's Renown: Meaning and Indeterminacy in the Odyssey*. Princeton, NJ: Princeton University Press

Kazantzakis, Nikos (1958 [1938]), *The Odyssey: A Modern Sequel*, English translation by Kimon Friar/ New York, NY: Simon & Schuster

Kazantzis, Judith (1999), *The Odysseus Poems: Fictions on the Odyssey of Homer*. Tregarne, Cornwall: Cargo Press

Keen, Tony (2006), 'The "T" stands for Tiberius: models and methodologies of classical reception in science fiction', paper delivered at the 2006 meeting of the Classical Association in Newcastle upon Tyne, available online at http://tonykeen.blogspot.com/2006/04/t-stands-for-tiberius-models-and.html

Kennedy, Margaret (1958), *The Outlaws on Parnassus*. London: Cresset Press

Kenner, Hugh (1971), *The Pound Era*. Berkeley, CA: University of California

Press

Kestner, Joseph (1989), *Mythology and Misogyny: The Social Discourse of Nineteenth-Century British Clasical-Subject Painting*. Madison, WI: University of Wisconsin Press

Kidd, Michael (1999), *Stages of Desire: The Mythological Tradition in Classical and Contemporary Spanish Theater*. Philadelphia: Pennsylvania State University Press

Killigrew, Anne (1686), *Poems*. London: Printed for Samuel Lowndes

Kinder, Marsha (2001), 'Violence American style: the narrative orchestration of violent attractions', in Slocum (ed.), 67–100

Kindstrand, Jan Fredrik (1973), *Homer in der zweiten Sophistik*. Uppsala: Uppsala University Press

—— (1990, ed.), *[Plutarchus] de Homeri*. Leipzig: Teubner

Kingston, Jeremy (1997), 'Homer is the hero, home to Oldham', *The Times*, 29 September

Kipf, Stefan (2005), 'Ein mythische Gestalt mit pädagogischer Kraft oder nur Odysseus' Sohn? Telemach in der neuzeitlichen Kinder- und Jugendliteratur', in Luther (ed.), 95–108

Kishkan, Theresa (2004). *Man in a Distant Field*. Toronto: Simon and Pierre Fiction

Klańska, Maria (1998), 'Der Bogen des Odysseus von Gerhart Hauptmann als Beispiel seiner Auffassung der Antike', in R. Bernhardt (ed.), *Gerhart Hauptmann. "Nu jaja! Nu nee nee!" Beiträge eines Colloquiums*. Lübeck-Travemünde [= *Travemünder Protokolle* 4], 13–42

Knight, Damon Francis (1967), *In Search of Wonder: Essays on Modern Science Fiction*. 2nd edition. Chicago: Advent Publishers

Knox, Bernard M.W. (1991), 'Introduction' to T.E. Lawrence (transl.), *The Odyssey of Homer*. New York: Oxford University Press

—— (1993), *The Oldest Dead White European Males and Other Reflections on the Classics*. New York & London: W.W. Norton

—— (1994), *Backing into the Future: The Classical Tradition and its Renewal*. New York & London: Norton

Koliades, Constantine (1829), *Ulysses Homer; or, a Discovery of the True Author of the Iliad and Odyssey*. London: John Murray

Kolker, Robert Phillip, and Peter Beicken (1993), *The Films of Wim Wenders: Cinema as Vision and Desire*. Cambridge: Cambridge University Press

Koromila, Marianna (1994), *In the Trail of Odysseus*, translated by Nigel Clive. Norwich: Michael Russell

Kramer, S.N. (1961, ed.) *Mythologies of the Ancient World*. Garden City, NY: Doubleday

Kristeva, Julia (1980), *Desire in Language: A Semiotic Approach to Literature and Art*, edited by L.S. Roudiez. Oxford: Blackwell

Kroetsch, Robert (1989), *The Lovely Treachery of Words: Essays Selected and New*. Toronto: Oxford University Press

—— (1995), *A Likely Story: The Writing Life*. Alberta, Canada: Red Deer College Press

Kuhn, Barbara (2003), *Mythos und Metapher: Metamorphosen des Kirke-Mythos in der Literatur der italienischen Renaissance*. Munich: W. Fink

Kundera, Milan (2002), *Ignorance: A Novel*, translated from French by Linda Asher. London: Faber & Faber

Lada-Richards, Ismene (2002), 'The subjectivity of Greek performance', in Pat Easterling and Edith Hall (eds.), *Greek & Roman Actors: Aspects of an Ancient Profession*. Cambridge: Cambridge University Press, 395–418

Laderman, David (2002), *Driving Visions: Exploring the Road Movie*. Austin: Texas University Press

Lafferty, R.A. (1968), *Space Chantey*. London: Dennis Dobson

Lafon, Sylvie and Anne-Marie Clais (1993), *Gustave Adolf Mossa: La Scène Symboliste*. Nice: Z'éditions

Lahr, J. (1993), 'Inventing the Enemy', *New Yorker*, 18 October, 103–6

Lamartina-Lens, Iride (1986), 'Myth of Penelope and Ulysses in *La tejedora de sueños*, *¿Por qué corres, Ulises?*, and *Ulises no vuelve*', *Estreno* 12, 31–4

Lamb, Charles (1808), *The Adventures of Ulysses*. London: The Juvenile Library, republished in Percy Fitzgerald (1924, ed.), *The Life, Letters and Writings of Charles Lamb*, vol. v, 141–250. London: Navarre Society

Lamberton, Robert (1986), *Homer the Theologian: Neoplatonist Allegorical Reading and the Growth of the Epic Tradition*. Berkeley & London: University of California Press

—— and John J. Keaney (1992, eds.), *The Hermeneutics of Greek Epic's Earliest Exegetes*. Princeton, NJ: Princeton University Press

Lambrou, Nickos Jean (2002), *Odysseus: His Americanization*. San Jose and New York: Writers' Press

Landau, Rom (1948), *Odysseus: A Novel*. London: Macdonald

Landon, Brooks (2003), 'Bodies in Cyberspace', in Pharr (ed.), 3–13

Landor, Walter Savage (1847), *The Hellenics*, enlarged and completed edition. London: E. Moxon

Lang, Jeffrey S. and Patrick Kimble (1988), 'Whatever happened to the man of tomorrow? An examination of the American monomyth and the Comic Book Superhero', *Journal of Popular Culture* 22, 157–73

Lateiner, Donald (1995), *Sardonic Smile: Nonverbal Behaviour in Homeric Epic*. Ann Arbor: University of Michigan Press

Lawrence, T.E. (1926), *Seven Pillars of Wisdom. A Triumph*. London: Jonathan Cape

—— (1932, transl.), *The Odyssey of Homer*. London: Oxford University Press

Lehman, Peter (1990), 'Texas 1868/America 1956: *The Searchers*', in Peter Lehman (ed.) *Close Viewings: An Anthology of New Film Criticism*. Tallahassee: Florida State University Press, 387–415

Lehtonen, Mikko (1994), *Kyklooppi ja kojootti*. Tampere: Vastapaino

Leroi, Armand Marie (2003), *Mutants: On the Form, Varieties and Errors of Human Body*. London: HarperCollins

Lesch, Walter (1994), 'Philosophie als Odyssee: Profile und Funktionen einer Denkfigur bei Lévinas, Hokheimer, Adorno und Bloch', in Fuchs (ed.), 157–88

Levi, Primo (1984 [1975]), *The Periodic Table*, translated by Raymond Rosenthal. New York: Schocken Books

—— (1988 [1986]), *The Drowned and the Saved*. English translation by Raymond Rosenthal. London: Joseph

—— (1995 [1958], [1963]), *If This is a Man* & *The Truce*, translated by Stuart Woolf, with an Introduction by Karl Miller. London: Abacus

—— (2001 [1981]), *The Search for Roots*, translated by Peter Forbes. London: Penguin

Levigne, Michelle (2001), *The Dark One* (eBook). ISBN: 1-55316083-5

Lévinas, Emmanuel (1994), *En Découvrant l'existence avec Husserl et Heidegger*. Paris: Vrin

Lewis, C.S. (1966), *Of Other Worlds: Essays and Stories*, edited by Walter Hooper. London: Geoffrey Bles

—— (1982), 'The mythopoeic gift of Rider Haggard', in *On Stories and Other Essays on Literature*, edited by Walter Hooper, 97–100. New York: Harcourt

Lewis, Peter (1982), 'Burlesque of contemporary drama in *Penelope*', *Notes & Queries* 227, 5301

Lichtenberg, J., Sandra Marshak and Joan Winston (1975), *Star Trek Lives!* New York: Bantam

Lichtheim, M. (1973), *Ancient Egyptian Literature*, vol. 1. Berkeley: University of California Press

Liddell, Robert (2002), *Cavafy: A Critical Biography*. 2nd edition, with an Introduction by Peter Mackridge. London: Duckworth

Lieberman, S. (1950), *Hellenism in Jewish Palestine*. New York

Liveley, Genevieve (2006), 'Science fiction and cyber myths: or, do cyborgs dream of Dolly the sheep', in Zajko and Leonard (eds.), 275–94

Lloyd-Jones, Hugh (1982), *Blood for the Ghosts: Classical Influences in the Nineteenth and Twentieth Centuries*. London: Duckworth

Locke, John (1993 [1690]) *Two Treatises of Government*, edited by Mark Goldie. London: Everyman

Lodge, David (1992), *The Art of Fiction*. London: Penguin

London, Norrell A. (2002), 'Curriculum and pedagogy in the development of colonial imagination: a case study', in *Pedagogy, Culture, and Society* 10, 95–121

Long, A.A. (1992), 'Stoic readings of Homer', in R. Lamberton and J.J. Keaney (eds.), *Homer's Ancient Readers*, Princeton: Princeton University Press, 41–66

Longley, Michael (1991), *Gorse Fires*. London: Secker & Warburg

Lord, Albert (1953), 'General Introduction', *Serbo-Croatian Heroic Songs*, 1, 3–20

Lord, George deForest (1956), *Homeric Renaissance: The Odyssey of George Chapman*. London: Chatto & Windus

—— (1977), *Heroic Mockery: Variations on Epic Themes from Homer to Joyce*. Newark, NJ & London: University of Delaware Press

—— (1991), 'The *Odyssey* and the western world', in Bloom (ed.), 89–102

Luther, Andreas (2005, ed.), *Odysseerezeptionen*. Frankfurt am Main: Verlag Antike

Lygouri-Tolia, Effie (1992), 'Odysseia', *Lexicon Iconograpgicum Mythologiae Classicae* vol. VI.2, 943.4. Zurich: Artemis

McBride, Joseph (2004), *Searching for John Ford*. London: Faber & Faber

—— and Michael Wilmington (1974), *John Ford*. London: Secker & Warburg

McCormick, K. (1994), 'Reproducing Molly Bloom: a revisionist history of the reception of "Penelope"', in R. Pearce (ed.), *Molly Blooms*. Madison, WI: Wisconsin University Press, 17–39

McDermott, Hubert (1989), *Novel and Romance: The Odyssey to Tom Jones*. Basingstoke & London: Macmillan

MacDonald, Dennis R. (1990, ed. and transl.), *The Acts of Andrew and the Acts of Andrew and Matthias in the City of the Cannibals*. Atlanta, GA: Scholars Press

—— (1994a), *Christianizing Homer: The* Odyssey, *Plato and The Acts of Andrew*. Oxford: Oxford University Press

—— (1994b), 'Luke's Eutychus and Homer's Elpenor: *Acts* 20:7–12 and *Odyssey* 10–12', *Journal of Higher Criticism* 1, 5–24

—— (2000), *The Homeric Epics and the Gospel of Mark*. New Haven, CT: Yale University Press

—— (2001), 'Tobit and the Odyssey', in Dennis R. MacDonald (ed.), *Mimesis and Intertextuality in Antiquity and Christianity*. Harrisburg, PA: Trinity Press International, 11–40

McDonald, Marianne (2001), *Sing Sorrow: Classics, History and Heroines in Opera*. Westport, CT: Greenwood Press

Machen, Arthur (1960 [1902]), *Hieroglyphics*. New edition. London: Unicorn Press

McHenry, Elizabeth (2002), *Forgotten Readers: Recovering the History of*

*African American Literary Societies*. Durham, NC & London: Duke University Press

Mackey-Kallis, Susan (2001), *The Hero and the Perennial Journey Home in American Film*. Philadelphia: University of Pennsylvania Press

Mackie, C.J. (2006), 'Men of darkness', in W. Haslem, C.J. Mackie and A. Ndalianis, *Super/Heroes*. Washington, DC: New Academia

McKittrick, Ryan (2003), 'Homer on the highway', *ARTicles Online* 1.3b, February. Available at http://www.amrep.org/articles/1_3/homer.html

McLaren, Clemence (2000), *Waiting for Odysseus: A Novel*. New York: Atheneum Books for Young Readers

MacLeish, Archibald (1963), *The Collected Poems*. Boston: Houghton Mifflin

MacLennan, Hugh (1941), *Barometer Rising*. Toronto: Collins

—— (1958), *The Watch that Ends the Night*. Toronto: Macmillan

Mactoux, Marie Madeleine (1975), *Pénélope: légende et mythe*. Paris: Belles Lettres

Makriyannakis, Vangelis (2005), 'Angelopoulos' *Ulysses Gaze*: where the old meets the new', *Forum* 1. Online Edinburgh University journal, available at http://forum.llc.ed.ac.uk/

Malamud, Bernard (1963 [1952]), *The Natural*. London: Eyre & Spottiswoode

Malkin, Irad (1998), *The Returns of Odysseus: Colonization and Ethnicity*. Berkeley: University of California Press

Mandel'shtam, Osip (1987 [1922]), *Tristia*, translated by Bruce McClelland. Barrytown, NY & Station Hill, New York, NY: Talman

Manfredi, Valerio Massimo (2005), *The Oracle*. English translation by Christine Feddersen-Manfredi. London: Pan Macmillan

Mannoni, Octave (1956), *Prospero and Caliban: The Psychology of Colonization*, translated by Pamela Powesland. London: Methuen

Marie, Michel (1995), *Le Mépris: Jean-Luc Godard*. Paris: Nathan

Marland, Michael and Robin Willcox (1980, eds.), *While They Fought: An Anthology of Prose and Verse Exploring The Lives of Those Who Did Not Fight, But Who Had to Endure the Second World War*. London: Longman

Maronitis, D.N. (2004), *Homeric Megathemes: War–Homilia–Homecoming*. English translation by David Conolly. Lanham, MD: Lexington Books

Marrou, H.-I. (1956), *A History of Education in Antiquity*, translated by George Lamb. New York: Sheed & Ward

Marshall, C.W. (2000), 'The point of Sophocles, fr. 453', *Eranos* 98, 1–8

Mason, H.J. (1978), 'Fabula Graecanica: Apuleius and his Greek sources', in B.L. Hijmans and R. Th. van der Paardt (eds.), *Aspects of Apuleius' Golden Ass*. Groningen: Boama, 1–15

Massey, Irving (1976), *The Gaping Pig: Literature and Metamorphosis*. Berkeley, Los Angeles & London

Masters, Edgar Lee (1921), *The Open Sea*. New York: Macmillan Co.

Matzig, Richard B. (1949), *Odysseus: Studie zu antiken Stoffen in der modernen Literatur, besonders im Drama*. Thal-St. Gallen: Pflugverlag

Maugham, W. Somerset (1978 [1935), 'The Lotus Eater', in *Collected Short Stories*, vol. IV. Harmondsworth: Penguin

Mellers, Wilfrid (1965), *Harmonious Meeting: A Study of Music, Poetry and Theatre in England, 1600–1900*. London: Dobson

Merkel, Inge (2000 [1987]), *Odysseus and Penelope: An Ordinary Marriage*. Riverside, CA: Ariadne Press (translation by Renate Latimer of *Eine ganz gewöhnliche Ehe*. Salzburg: Residenz Verlag)

Merkelbach, R. and M.L. West (1967, eds.), *Fragmenta Hesiodea*. Oxford: Clarendon Press

Merles, Mark (1998), *An Arrow's Flight*. New York: St Martin's Press

Michelakis, Pantelis (2004), 'Greek tragedy in cinema', in Hall, Macintosh and Wrigley (eds.), 199–242

Mickle, William Julius (1776, transl.), *The Lusiad; or, The Discovery of India*. 5th edition. Oxford: Cadell

Mikics, David (1995), 'Derek Walcott and Alejo Carpentier: nature, history and the Caribbean writer', in Zamora and Faris (eds.), 371–404

Miller, Hugh (1854), *My Schools and Schoolmasters*. Edinburgh: Johnstone and Hunter

Miller, N.K. (1986), 'Arachnologies: the woman, the text, and the critic', in N.K. Miller (ed.), *The Poetics of Gender*. New York: Columbia University Press, 270–95

Milligan, Peter and James Hewlett (2002), *Tank Girl: The Odyssey*. London: Titan Books

Minchin, Elizabeth (2001), *Homer and the Resources of Memory*. Oxford: Oxford University Press

Mitchell, Lee Clark (2001), 'Violence in the film western', in Slocum (ed.), 176–91

Mitry, Jean (1969), 'Interview with John Ford', in Andrew Sarris (ed.), *Interviews with Film Directors*. New York: Avon

Montaigne, Michel de (1967), *Oeuvres Complètes*, edited by Robert Barral and Pierre Michel. Paris: Éditions du Seuil

Montiglio, Silvia (2005), *Wandering in Ancient Greek Culture*. Chicago: University of Chicago Press

Moore, Fabienne (2000), 'Homer revisited: Anne Le Fevre Dacier's preface to her prose translation of the Iliad in early eighteenth-century France', *Studies in the Literary Imagination*, Fall 2000. Available online at www.findarticles.com/p/articles/mi_qa3822/is_200010/ai_n8910338

Moravia, Alberto (1955), *A Ghost at Noon*, translation of *Il Disprezzo* by Angus Davidson. New York: Farrar, Strauss & Young

Morgan, T. (1998), *Literate Education in the Hellenistic and Roman Worlds*. Cambridge: Cambridge University Press

Morpurgo, E. (1979), *Allen Lane, King Penguin: A Biography*. London: Hutchinson

Morris, Sarah (1997), 'Homer and the Near East', in I. Morris and B. Powell (eds.), *A New Companion to Homer*. Leiden: Brill, 599–623

Morrison, Toni (1998 [1977]), *The Song of Solomon*. London: Vintage

Moskowitz, Sam (1963), *Explorers of the Infinite: Shapers of Science Fiction*. Westport, CT: Hyperion

—— (1967), *A Sense of Wonder: Three Science Fiction Stories*, edited with an introduction, London: Sidgwick & Jackson

—— (1975, ed.), *A Martian Odyssey and Other Science Fiction Tales*. Westport, CT: Hyperion

Mottley, John and Thomas Cooke (1728), *Penelope: A Dramatic Opera*. London: Thomas Green

Müller, Heiner (1989), *The Battle: Plays, Prose, Poems*, edited and translated by C. Weber. New York: Performing Arts Journal Publications

Murnaghan, Sheila (1987), *Disguise and Recognition in the Odyssey*. Princeton, NJ: Princeton University Press

—— and Deborah H. Roberts (2002), 'Penelope's song: the lyric Odysseys of Linda Pastan and Louise Glück', *Classical and Modern Literature* 22, 1–33

Murray, A.T. (1919), *The Odyssey*. 2 vols. Loeb translation. London: Heinemann

Nagy, G. (1990), *Pindar's Homer: The Lyric Possession of an Epic Past*. Baltimore, MD: Johns Hopkins University Press

Ndebele, Njabulo S. (2003), *The Cry of Winnie Mandela*. Claremont

Nectoux, Jean-Michel (1984, ed.), *Gabriel Fauré: His Life through his Letters*, English translation by J.A. Underwood. New York: Marion Boyars

—— (1991), *Gabriel Fauré: A Musical Life*, English translation by Roger Nichols. Cambridge: Cambridge University Press

Neruda, Pablo (1994 [1952]), *The Captain's Verses*, translated by Brian Cole. London: Anvil Press Poetry

Niane, Djibril Tamsir (1994, ed.), *Sundiata: An Epic of Old Mali*, translated by G.D. Pickett. Harlow: Longman African writers

Nicholson, Marjorie Hope (1948), *Voyages to the Moon*. New York: Macmillan

Nimmo, Dan and James E. Combs (1980), *Subliminal Politics: Myths and Mythmakers in America*. Englewood Cliffs, NJ: Prentice-Hall

Norris, Paul Byron (1992), *Ulysses in the Raj*. Bacsa: London

Nossack, Hans Erich (1947), *Nekyia: Bericht eines Überlebenden*. Hamburg: Wolfgang Krüger

—— (2004 [1948]), *The End: Hamburg 1943*, translated by Joel Agee. Chicago & London: University of Chicago Press

Notopoulos, James A. (1965), 'The tragic and the epic in T.E. Lawrence', *Yale Review*, Spring, 331–45

Novalis [= Friedrich von Hardenburg] (1997), *Novalis: Philosophical Writings*, translated and edited by Margaret Mahony Stoljar. New York: SUNY Press

O'Connell, Erin (2006), 'Homer and rap: epic iconographies', in Angela Ndalianis, Chris Mackie, and Wendy Haslem (eds.), *Super/Heroes*, Washington, DC: New Academia

Ogilby, John (1665, transl.), *Homer, his Odysses*. London: Thomas Roycroft

Oldham, John (1681), *Some New Pieces never before publisht*. London

Ørnsbo, Jess (1996), *Odysseus from Vraa: A Traditional Comedy*, translated by Hugh Matthews, in Hans Christian Andersen (ed.), *New Danish Plays*. Norwich: Norvik Press, 29–123

Osthoff, Wolfgang (1956), 'Zu den Quellen von Monteverdis "Ritorno di Ulisse in Patria"', *Studien zur Musikwissenschaft* 23, 67–78

—— (1958), 'Zur Bologneser Aufführung von Monteverdi's "Ritorno di Ulisse" im Jahre 1640', *Mitteilungen der Kommission für Musikforschung* 11, 155–60

Paasonen, Susan (2003), 'Cyborg and Cyclops: the vision of a man-machine', in Tanja Sihvonen and Pasi Väliaho (eds.), *Experiencing the Media: Assemblages and Cross-Overs*. Turku, 236–54

Pache, Walter (1985), 'The fiction makes us real: aspects of postmodernism in Canada', in A.L. MacLeod (ed.), *Canadian Literature in English*, 149–79. Mysore: University of Mysore Press

Pack, Roger Ambrose (1967), *The Greek and Latin Literary Texts from Greco-Roman Egypt*. 2nd edition. Ann Arbor

Page, Denys (1972), *Folktales in Homer's Odyssey*. Cambridge, MA: Harvard University Press

Paglia, Camille (1997), 'Homer on film: a voyage through *The Odyssey, Ulysses, Helen of Troy*, and *Contempt*', *Arion* 5.2, 166–97

Panger, Daniel (1982), *Black Ulysses*. Athens, OH: Ohio University Press

Papadopoulou-Belmehdi, Ioanna (1994), *Le Chant de Pénélope*. Paris: Belin

Parker, Dorothy (1939), *Sunset Gun. Poems*. New York: Sun Dial Press

Pastan, Linda (1988), *The Imperfect Paradise*. New York: Norton

Paton, W.R. (1916–18), *The Greek Anthology*. 5 vols. London: William Heinemann

Paul, Joanna (2007), 'Homer and cinema: translation and adaptation in *Le Mépris*', in Zajko and Lianeri (2007, eds.)

Paulino, José C. (1994), 'Ulises en el teatro español contemporáneo: una revision panorámica', *Annales de la Literatura Española Contemporánea* 19, 327–42

Pépin, Jean (1982), 'The Platonic and Christian Ulysses', in Dominic J. O'Meara (ed.), *Neoplatonism and Christian Thought*. Norfolk, VA, 3–18

Perrault, Charles (1688–97), *Parallèle des anciens et des modernes*. 4 vols. Paris: Jean Baptiste Coignard

Perutelli, Alessandro (2006), *Ulisse nella cultura Romana*. Florence: Le Monnier Universita

Pessoa, Fernando (1992), *Message*, bilingual edition, translated by Jonathan Griffin, with an Introduction by Helder Macedo. London: Menard Press

Pharr, Mary (2003, ed.), *Fantastic Odysseys. Selected Essays from the Twenty-Second International Conference on the Fantastic in the Arts*. Westport, CT: Praeger

Philips, Stephen (1902), *Ulysses: A Drama in a Prologue and Three Acts*. New York & London: Macmillan

Phillpotts, Eden (1926), *Circe's Island, and The Girl & The Faun*. London: Grant Richards

Pike, David L. (1997), *Passage through Hell: Modernist Descents, Medieval Underworlds*. Ithaca, NY & London: Cornell University Press

Pillot, Gilbert (1972), *The Secret Code of the Odyssey: Did the Greeks Sail the Atlantic?* translated from the French by Francis E. Albert. London, New York & Toronto: Abelard-Schumann

Planinc, Z. (2003), *Plato through Homer: Poetry and Philosophy in the Cosmological Dialogues*. Columbia & London: University of Missouri Press

Pope, Alexander (1725–26), *The Odyssey*. Translated into English verse by A. Pope, W. Broome, and E. Fenton, with observations by W. Broome. 5 vols. London: Bernard Lintot

Porter, Katherine Anne (1954), *A Defense of Circe*. New York: Harcourt, Brace & Co.

Post, L.A. (1951), *From Homer to Menander*. Berkeley: University of California Press

Pouncey, Peter R. (2005), *Rules for Old Men Waiting*. London: Chatto & Windus

Pound, Ezra (1971 [1950]), *Selected Letters of Ezra Pound, 1907–1941*, edited by D.D. Paige. New York: New Directions

Pratt, William (2002), 'Pound's Hells, real and imaginary' in William Pratt (ed.), *Ezra Pound: Nature and Myth*. New York: AMS Press

Pucci, Pietro (1997), *The Song of the Sirens: Essays on Homer*. Lanham, MD: Rowman & Littlefield Publishers

Purdy, Al (1967), *North of Summer: Poems from Baffin Island*. Toronto & Montreal: McClelland and Stewart

Rabel, Robert J. (2003), 'Impersonation and identity. *Sommersby, The Return of Martin Guerre* and the *Odyssey*', *IJCT* 9, 391–406

Ramos, Janell Marie (2003), *Waiting for Odysseus*. Victoria, BC: Trafford

Rang, M. (1972), 'The Ulysses syndrome', *Journal of the Canadian Medical Assocation* 106, 122–3

Rankine, Patrice D. (2006), *Ulysses in Black: Ralph Ellison, Classicism, and African American Literature*. Madison, WI: Wisconsin University Press

Rassinier, Paul (1978), *The Holocaust Story and the Lies of Odysseus*, translated from the French by Adam Robbins. Costa Mesa, CA: Institute for Historical Review

Reardon, B.P. (1991), *The Form of the Greek Romance*. Princeton, NJ: Princeton University Press

Rebhorn, W.A. (1988), *Foxes and Lions. Machiavelli's Confidence Men*. Ithaca, NY: Cornell University Press

Redmond, Diane and Robin Kingsland (1992), *The Comic Strip Odyssey*, retold by Diane Redmond and illustrated by Robin Kingsland. Harmondsworth: Viking

Reid, Jane Davidson (1993), *The Oxford Guide to Classical Mythology in the Arts*. 2 vols. New York & Oxford: Oxford University Press

Resnick, Henry (1967), 'An interview with Tolkien', *Niekas* 18, 37–43

Reynolds, L.D. and Nigel Wilson (1974), *Scribes and Scholars: A Guide to the Transmission of Greek & Latin Literature*. 2nd edition. Oxford: Oxford University Press

Reynolds, Margaret (1996, ed.), *Aurora Leigh: Elizabeth Barrett Browning*. New York & London: W.W. Norton

Richardson, Brian (2000), 'Make it Old: Lucian's *A True Story*, Joyce's *Ulysses*, and Homeric Patterns in Ancient Fiction', *Comparative Literature Studies* 37, 371–83

Richardson, Nicholas (1992), 'Aristotle's reading of Homer', in Lamberton and Keaney (eds.), 30–40

Ricks, David (1989), *The Shade of Homer: A Study in Modern Greek Poetry*. Cambridge: Cambridge University Press

Riedel, Volker (2000), *Antikerezeption in der deutschen Literatur*. Stuttgart & Weimar: J.B. Metzler

Rieu, E.V. (1945 – actually 1946), *The Odyssey. Homer*. Harmondsworth: Penguin Books

—— (1974), *The Odyssey*. Translated by E.V. Rieu. Lithographs by Elisabeth Frink. London: Folio Society

—— (1995), *The Odyssey (Penguin Audiobooks)*, narrated by Alex Jennings and

Derek Jacobi. Harmondsworth: Penguin

—— (2003), *The Odyssey. Homer.* New edition, revised by D.C.H. Rieu, with introduction by Peter Jones. London: Penguin

Riley, Kathleen (2004), 'Heracles as Dr Strangelove and GI Joe: male heroism deconstructed', in Hall, Macintosh and Wrigley (eds.), 113–41

Ritoók, Z. (1989), 'The views of early Greek epic on poetry and art', *Mnemosyne* 42, 331–48

Rodner, William S. (1997), *J.M.W. Turner: Romantic Painter of the Industrial Revolution.* Berkeley & London: University of California Press

Rodó, José Enrique (1929 [1900]), *Ariel*, edited by William F. Rice. Chicago: Chicago University Press

Rogers, Elizabeth (1984), 'Myth, man and exile in *El Retorno de Ulises and ¿Por qué corres, Ulises?*', *Annales de la Literatura Española Contemporánea* 9, 117–30

Roisman, Hanna M. (2007), 'The *Odyssey* from Homer to NBC: The Cyclops and the gods', in Lorna Hardwick and Chris Stray (eds.), *The Blackwell Companion to Classical Reception.* Oxford: Blackwell, 315–26

Romm, James S. (1992), *The Edges of the Earth in Ancient Thought: Geography, Exploration, and Fiction.* Princeton: Princeton University Press

Rosand, Ellen (1989), 'Iro and the interpretation of *Il ritorno d'Ulisse in patria*', *Journal of Musicology* 7, 141–64

—— (1994), 'The bow of Ulysses', *Journal of Musicology* 12, 376–95

Rose, Peter (1975), 'Class ambivalence in the *Odyssey*', *Historia* 24, 129–49

—— (1992), *Sons of the Gods, Children of Earth: Ideology and Literary Form in Ancient Greece.* Ithaca, NY: Cornell University Press

Rose, V. (1886, ed.), *Aristotelis qui ferebantur librorum fragmenta.* Leipzig: Teubner

Rosello, Mireille and Annie Pritchard (1995 ed. and transl.), *Aimé Césaire: Notebook of a Return to My Native Land.* Newcastle upon Tyne: Bloodaxe

Rossi, Nick and Talmage Fauntleroy (1999), *Domenic Cimarosa: His Life and Operas.* Westport, CT & London: Greenwood Press

Rosslyn, Felicity (1985), *Pope's Iliad: A Selection with Commentary.* Bristol: Bristol Classical Press

Routh, Chris (2000), 'Peter Pan: flawed or fledgling "hero"?', in Jones & Watkins (eds.), 291–307

Rovin, Jeff (1994), *Adventure Heroes: Legendary Characters from Odysseus to James Bond.* New York

Rowe, Nicholas (1706), *Ulysses. A Tragedy.* London: Jacob Tonson

Roworth, Wendy Wassyng (1992, ed.), *Angelica Kauffman: A Continental Artist in Georgian England.* Brighton & London: Reaktion Books

Rubens, Beaty and Oliver Taplin (1989), *An Odyssey round Odysseus: The Man and his Story Traced through Time and Place*. London: BBC Books

Rubino, Carl A. (1994), 'The Obsolescence of the Hero: Voltaire's Attack on Homeric Heroism', *Pacific Coast Philology* 29, 85–94

Rudrum, Alan (2003), 'Ethical vegetarianism in 17th century Britain: its roots in 16th century European theological debate', *The Seventeenth Century* 18, 76–92

Rüf, Elisabeth (1994), 'Der lange Weg nach Hause: die *Odyssee* in tiefenpsychologischer Entfaltung', in Fuchs (ed.), 189–238

Rushdie, Salman (2002), 'Gods and monsters', *The Washington Post*, 28 June, available online at http://www.washingtonpost.com/wp-dyn/articles/A58700-2002Jun27.html

—— (2005), *Shalimar the Clown: A Novel*. London: Jonathan Cape

Ruskin, John (1869), *The Mystery of Life and its Arts: Being the Third Lecture of Sesame and Lilies*. New York: J. Wiley

—— (1902–12), *The Works of John Ruskin*, edited by E.T. Cook and A. Wedderburn. 39 vols. London: Allen

Russell, James R. (1996–97), 'Polyphemos Armenios', *Revue des Études Arméniennes* 26, 25–38

Rutherford, Andrew (1978), *The Literature of War: Five Studies in Heroic Virtue*. London: Macmillan

Rutherford, Anne (2002), 'Precarious boundaries: affect, mise en scène and the senses in Angelopoulos' Balkans epic', in Richard Candida Smith (ed.), *Art and the Performance of Memory: Sounds and Gestures of Recollection*. London & New York: Routledge

Rutherford, Richard (1986),'The philosophy of the Odyssey', *JHS* 106, 145–62

Ruyer, Raymond (1977), *Homère au feminine*. Paris: Copernic

Sacher-Masoch, Leopold (2000 [1870]), *Venus in Furs*, translated by Joachim Neugroschel. New York & London: Penguin

Sackville-West, Edward (1945), *The Rescue: A Melodrama for Broadcasting based on Homer's Odyssey*. London: Secker & Warburg

Said, S.F. (2002), 'Northern exposure', *Sight and Sound* 71 (February). Available online at http://www.bfi.org.uk/sightandsound/feature/71/

Sanders, Mark A. (1997), 'Sterling A. Brown and the Afro-modern moment', *African American Review* 31, 393–7

Scaliger, J.C. (1561), *Poetices libri septem*. Lyons: Antonius Vincentius

Schaeffner, André (1936), *Origine des instruments de musique: Introduction ethnologique à l'histoire de la musique instrumentale*. Paris: Peyot

Schaps, David M. (1979), *Economic Rights of Women in Ancient Greece*. Edinburgh: Edinburgh University Press

Schell, Edwin A. (1913), 'Tennyson's *Ulysses*', *Methodist Review* 95.2 (March), 192–5

Schlink, Bernhard (2002), *Heimat als Utopie*. Frankfurt am Main:

Suhrkamp

Schnabel, Ernst (1958 [1956]), *The Voyage Home*, English translation by Denver Lindley. London: Victor Gollancz

Schork, Richard J. (1998), *Greek and Hellenic Culture in Joyce*. Gainesville, FL: University of Florida Press

Scott, John A. (1925), *Homer and his Influence*. London: George G. Harrap & Co.

Scouffas, George (1991), 'Kazantzakis: Odysseus and the "cage of freedom"', in Bloom (ed.), 133–43

Seferis, George (1967), *Collected Poems 1924–1955*, with a translation by Edmund Keeley and Sherrard. London: Jonathan Cape

Segal, C.P. (1978), ' "The Myth was Saved": reflections on Homer and the mythology of Plato's *Republic*', *Hermes* 106, 315–36

—— (1992), 'Bard and audience in Homer', in Lamberton and Keaney (eds.), 3–29

——(1994), *Singers, Heroes, and Gods in the Odyssey*. Ithaca & London: Cornell University Press

Selaiha, Nehad (2006), 'Still harping on war', *Al-Ahram Weekly Online*, issue no. 815, 6 October

Shaffer, Elinor (2004), 'Butler, Samuel (1835–1902)', *Oxford Dictionary of National Biography*, Oxford University Press [http://www.oxforddnb.com/view/article/32217, accessed 31 March 2006]

Shapir, M.I. (1994) (in Russian), 'The hexameter and pentameter in the poetry of Katenin', *Philologica* 1, 43–114. English translation available online at http://www.rvb.ru/philologica/01eng/01eng_shapir.htm

Shay, Jonathan (2002), *Odysseus in America: Combat Trauma and the Trials of Homecoming*. New York: Scribner

Shelley, Percy Bysshe (1886 [1822]), *Hellas: A Lyrical Drama*. London: Reeves and Turner

Shewring, Walter (1980, transl.), *The Odyssey*, introduced by G.S. Kirk. The World's Classics. Oxford: Oxford University Press

Shipton, Paul (2004), *The Pig Scrolls*. London: Puffin

Shubow, Justin (2003), 'Cold Comfort: the misrepresentation at the center of *The Fast Runner*', *The American Prospect Online*, 28 February. http://www.prospect.org/webfeatures/2003/02/shubow-j-02-28.html

Sieber, Sharon L. (2003), 'Time and the fantastic: simultaneity in Borges, Cortázar, Lezama Lima, and Paz', in Pharr (ed.), 23–8

Silverman, Kaja and Harun Farocki (1998), *Speaking about Godard*. New York & London: New York University Press

Simonsuuri, Kirsti (1979), *Homer's Original Genius: Eighteenth-Century Notions of the Early Greek Epic (1688–1798)*. Cambridge: Cambridge University Press

Sinclair, Clive (2002), *Meet the Wife*. London: Picador

Singleton, Charles S. (1971, trans. and ed.), *The Divine Comedy: Inferno*. London: Routledge & Kegan Paul

Skulsky, Harold (1981), *Metamorphosis: The Mind in Exile*. Cambridge, MA & London: Harvard University Press

Slocum, J. David (2001, ed.), *Violence and American Cinema*. New York & London: Routledge

Slotkin, Richard (1973), *Regeneration through Violence: The Mythology of the American Frontier, 1600–1860*. Middletown, CT: Wesleyan University Press

—— (1985), *The Fatal Environment: The Frontier Myth in the Age of Industrialization 1800–1890*. New York: Atheneum

Smith, Evans Lansing (2001), *The Descent to the Underworld in Literature, Painting, and Film, 1895–1950: The Modernist Nekyia*. Lewiston, Queenston & Lampeter: Edwin Mellen

Smith, Tom (2002), *The Odyssey*. New York: Playscripts Inc.

Smith, Valerie (2004), 'The meaning of narration in Ralph Ellison's *Invisible Man*', in Callahan (ed.), 189–220

Smyth, Herbert Weir and Hugh Lloyd-Jones (1957), *Aeschylus* vol. 2, revised edition with an appendix by Hugh Lloyd-Jones. Cambridge, MA: Harvard University Press

Snyder, William (1971), *Thomas Wolfe: Ulysses and Narcissus*. Athens, OH: Ohio University Press

Sowerby, Robin, (1992), 'Chapman's discovery of Homer', *Translation and Literature* 1 (1992), 26–51

Soyinka, Wole (1998), 'Ulysses Britannicus in Africa', in Boitani & Ambrosini (eds.), 367–79

—— (2002), 'Beware the Cyclops', *Guardian*, *Saturday Review*, Saturday 6 April, 1–2

Spence, Joseph (1726), *An Essay on Pope's Odyssey: In Which Some Particular Beauties and Blemishes of that Work are Considered*. London: J. and J. Knapton, etc.

Spinoza, Benedict de (2002), *Complete Works*, translated by Samuel Shirley and edited by M. Morgan. Indianapolis & Cambridge: Hackett

Stableford, Brian M. (1971), *In the Kingdom of the Beasts* [part II of the *Dies Irae* trilogy]. London: Quartet books

—— (1999), 'Proto science fiction', in John Clute and Peter Nichols, *The Encyclopedia of Science Fiction*. Corrected edition. London: Orbit, 965–7

Stafford, Fiona (1988), *The Sublime Savage: A Study of James Macpherson and the Poems of Ossian*. Edinburgh: Edinburgh University Press

Stanford, W.B. (1968 [1954]), *The Ulysses Theme: A Study in the Adaptability of a Traditional Hero*. 2nd edition. Oxford: Blackwell

—— and J.V. Luce (1974), *The Quest for Ulysses*. London: Phaidon

Steadman, John M. (1959), *Milton's Epic Characters*. Chapel Hill, NC: University of North Carolina Press

Steckmesser, Kent Ladd (1965), *The Western Hero in History and Legend*. Norman: University of Oklahoma Press

Steiner, George (1996), *Homer in English*, edited with an introduction and notes by George Steiner, with the assistance of Aminadav Dykman. Harmondsworth: Penguin

Stephens, Susan A. and John J. Winkler (1995), *Ancient Greek Novels: The Fragments*. Princeton, NJ: Princeton University Press

Stevens, Wallace (1954), *The Collected Poems*. New York: Alfred A. Knopf

Stolz, Lois Meek et al. (1954), *Father Relations of War-Born Children: The Effect of Postwar Adjustment of Fathers on the Behavior and Personality of First Children Born While the Fathers Were at War*. Stanford: Stanford University Press

Sullivan, J.P. (1968), *The Satyricon of Petronius: A Literary Study*. London: Faber & Faber

Sullivan, Robert (1999), *Star Waka*. Auckland, NZ: Auckland University Press

—— (2002), *Captain Cook in the Underworld*. Auckland, NZ: Auckland University Press

Sultan, Nancy (1999), *Exile and the Poetics of Loss in Greek Tradition*. Lanham, Boulder & New York: Rowman & Littlefield

Sutherland, John (2002), *Reading the Decades: Fifty Years of the Nation's Bestselling Books*. London: BBC Worldwide

Suvin, Darko (1972–73), 'On the poetics of the science fiction genre,' *College English* 34

—— (1973), 'Science fiction and the genealogical jungle', *Genre* 6, 251–73

—— (1979), *Metamorphoses of Science Fiction: on the Poetics and History of a Literary Genre*. New Haven & London: Yale University Press

Tang, Isabel (1999), *Pornography: The Secret History of Civilisation*. London: Macmillan

Taplin, Oliver (1989), *Greek Fire*. London: Cape

—— (1992), 'Derek Walcott: *The Odyssey*', unpublished review; typescript available for consultation at the APGRD, Oxford University

Tate, Claudia (2004), 'Notes on the invisible women in Ralph Ellison's *Invisible Man*', in Callahan (ed.), 253–66

Taylor, E.G.R. (1956), *The Haven-Finding Art: A History of Navigation from Odysseus to Captain Cook*. London: Hollis & Carter

Tennyson, Alfred (1989), *A Selected Edition*, edited by Christopher Ricks. London: Longman

*TgrF* = Snell, Bruno and Richard Kannicht (1971–2004, eds.), *Tragicorum Graecorum Fragmenta*. Göttingen: Vandenhoeck & Ruprecht

Thalmann, William G. (1998), *The Swineherd and the Bow: Representations of Class in the Odyssey*. Ithaca, NY & London: Cornell University Press

Theoharis, Theoharis Constantine (1988), *Joyce's Ulysses: An Anatomy of the Soul*. Chapel Hill: University of North Carolina Press

Thilo, George and Hermann Hagen (1881, eds.), *Servii grammatici qui feruntur in Vergilii carmina commentarii*. Leipzig: Teubner

Thompson, Craig R. (1957), *Ten Colloquies of Erasmus, Translated with Introduction and Notes*. Indianapolis: Bobbs-Merrill

Thompson, Kristin (1999), *Storytelling in the New Hollywood: Understanding Narrative Technique*. Cambridge, MA & London: Harvard University Press

Thomsen, Mads Rosendahl (2002), 'Attention: tender tension. On composite poetics of narratives', in Balling and Madsen (eds.), 127–35

Tolkien, J.R.R. (1966), 'On fairy-stories', in *The Tolkien Reader*. New York: Ballantine, 3–84

Torrente-Ballaster, G. (1981), *El retorno de Ulises*, in *Teatro II*. Barcelona: Destino, 115–89

Touchefou-Meynier, Odette (1992), 'Odysseus', *Lexicon Iconographicum Mythologiae Classicae*, vol. VI.1, 943–70. Düsseldorf: Artemis

Toumson, Roger and Simonne Henry-Valmour (2002), *Aimé Césaire: Le Nègre inconsolé. Biographie*. Châteauneuf-le-Rouge: Vents d'ailleurs

Trevelyan, H. (1981), *Goethe and the Greeks*. 2nd edition. Cambridge: Cambridge University Press

Trevelyan, R.C. (1901), *Polyphemus & Other Poems*, with designs by R.E. Fry. London: R. Brimley Johnson

Unsworth, Barry (2002), *The Songs of the Kings*. London: Hamish Hamilton

Vernant, Jean-Pierre (1988). 'The tragic subject: historicity and transhistoricity', in Vernant and Vidal-Naquet (1988), 237–47

—— and Vidal-Naquet, Pierre (1988). *Myth and Tragedy in Ancient Greece*, English translation by Janet Lloyd. New York: Zone Books

Vicaire, Paul (1960), *Platon: critique littéraire*. Paris: C. Klincksieck

Vickroy, Laurie (2002), *Trauma and Survival in Contemporary Fiction*. Charlottesville & London: University of Virginia Press

Vidal-Naquet, Pierre (1981), 'Land and sacrifice in the Odyssey: a study of religious and mythical meanings, in R. Gordon (ed.), *Myth, Religion & Society*. Cambridge: Cambridge University Press, 80–94

—— (1986), *The Black Hunter: Forms of Thought and Forms of Society in the Greek World*. English translation. Baltimore & London: Johns Hopkins University Press

—— (1988). 'Oedipus in Vicenza and in Paris: two turning points in the history of Oedipus', in Vernant and Vidal-Naquet (1988), 361–80

Vogler, Christopher (1999), *The Writers' Journey: Mythic Structure for Writers*. 2nd edition. London: Pan Books

von Wilamowitz-Moellendorff, Ulrich (1908), *Greek Historical Writing, and Apollo. Two Lectures Delivered before the University of Oxford*, translated by Gilbert Murray. Oxford: Oxford University Press

Vonnegut, Kurt (1970), *Happy Birthday, Wanda June*. New York: Delacorte Press

Walcott, Derek (1949), *Epitaph for the Young*. Bridgetown: Barbados Advocate

—— (1976), *Sea Grapes*. London: Cape

—— (1990), *Omeros*. London: Faber & Faber

—— (1993), *The Odyssey: A Stage Version*. London: Faber & Faber

—— (1998), 'A sail on the horizon', in Boitani and Ambrosini (eds.), 47–56

Wallace, Maurice O. (2002), '"What ails you Polyphemus?" Toward a new ontology of vision in Frantz Fanon's *Black Skin White Masks*', in *Constructing the Black Masculine: Identity and Ideality in African American Men's Literature and Culture, 1775–1995*. Durham, NC & London, 170–8

Walsh, George B. (1984), *The Varieties of Enchantment: Early Greek Views of the Nature and Function of Poetry*. Chapel Hill & London: University of North Carolina Press

Warmington, E.H. (1926), *Remains of Old Latin*. London: Loeb

Warner, Marina (1994), *Managing Monsters: Six Myths of our Time: The 1994 Reith Lectures*. London: Vintage

—— (1998a), *No Go the Bogeyman: Scaring, Lulling and Making Mock*. London: Chatto & Windus

—— (1998b), 'The enchantments of Circe: Odysseus's refusal, Gryllus' choice', in Boitani and Ambrosini (eds.), 135–52

—— (2002), *Fantastic Metamorphoses, Other Worlds: Ways of Telling the Self*. Oxford: Oxford University Press

Warr, G.C. (1887), *Echoes of Hellas: The Tale of Troy & The Story of Orestes from Homer & Aeschylus*, with introductory essay & sonnets by George C. Warr; presented in 82 designs by Walter Crane. London: M. Ward

Watkins, D.P. (1989), *Keats' Poetry and the Politics of the Imagination*. Rutherford: Associated University Presses

Webb, Vivian and Heather Amery (1981), *The Amazing Adventures of Ulysses*, illustrated by Stephen Cartwright. London: Usborne

Webster, T.B.L. (1967), *Hellenistic Art*. London: Methuen

Wender, Dorothea (1978), *The Last Scenes of the Odyssey*. Leiden: Brill

Wenders, Wim (2003), 'In defense of places', *Directors' Guild of America Magazine* 28.4, November

West, Martin (1997), *The East Face of Helicon: West Asiatic Elements in Greek Poetry and Myth*. Oxford: Clarendon Press

—— (1999), 'The invention of Homer', *Classical Quarterly* 49, 364–82

—— (2003, ed.), *Greek Epic Fragments. From the Seventh to the Fifth Centuries BC*. Cambridge, MA: Loeb

Wheat, Leonard F. (2000), *Kubrick's 200: A Triple Allegory*. Lanham, MD: Scarecrow Press

White, Fred D. (2003), '*2001: A Space Odyssey* and the betrayal of language', in Pharr (ed.), 147–53

Whittington-Egan, Richard (2006), *Stephen Phillips: A Biography*. High Wycombe: Rivendale Press

Williams, Carolyn D. (1993), *Pope, Homer, and Manliness: Some Aspects of Eighteenth-century Classical Learning*. London: Routledge

Williams, Marcia (1996), *The Iliad and the Odyssey, Retold and Illustrated*. London: Walker

Williams, Meg Harris (2005), *The Vale of Soulmaking: The Post-Kleinian Model of the Mind and its Poetic Origins*. London: Karnac Books

Williams, Raymond (1977), *Marxism and Literature*. Oxford: Oxford University Press

Williams, Rosalind (1990), *Notes on the Underground: An Essay on Technology, Society and the Imagination*. Cambridge, MA & London: MIT Press

Wilson, Donna F. (2002), *Ransom, Revenge and Heroic Identity in the Iliad*. Cambridge: Cambridge University Press

Winkler, John J. (1990), 'Penelope's cunning and Homer's', in *The Constraints of Desire: The Anthropology of Sex and Gender in Ancient Greece*. New York: Routledge, 129–61

Winkler, Martin M. (1991), 'Tragic features in John Ford's *The Searchers*', in M.M. Winkler (ed.), *Classical Myth & Culture in the Cinema*. Lewisburg, PA: Bucknell University Press, 185–208

—— (2004), 'Homer's *Iliad* and John Ford's *The Searchers*', in Eckstein and Lehman (eds.), 145–70

Wirth, Hermann (1921), *Homer und Babylon*. Freiburg: Herder & Co.

Wohl, Victoria (1993), 'Standing by the stathmos: sexual ideology in the *Odyssey*', *Arethusa* 26, 19–50

Wolf, F.A. (1795), *Prolegomena ad Homerum, sive De operum Homericorum prisca et genuina forma variisque mutationibus et probabili ratione emendandi*. Halle: Libraria Orphanotrophei

Wolfe, Thomas (1956), *The Letters of Thomas Wolfe*, edited by E. Nowell. New York: Scribner

—— (1968 [1947]), *You Can't Go Home Again*. London: William Heinemann

Woodcock, George (1970), 'A nation's Odyssey: the novels of Hugh MacLennan', in *Odysseus Ever Returning: Essays on Canadian Writers and Writing*. Toronto & Montreal: McClelland & Stewart, 12–23

Wynter, Sylvia (2002), ' "A different kind of creature": Caribbean literature, the Cyclops factor and the second poetics of the *propter nos*', in Timothy J. Reiss (ed.), *Sisyphus and Eldorado: Magical and Other Realisms in Caribbean Literature*. 2nd edition. Toronto, NJ & Asmara, Eritrea, 143–67

Wyspianski, Stanislaw (1966 [1907]), *The Return of Odysseus: A Drama in Three Acts*, translated with an introduction by Howard Clarke. Indiana University publications. Russian and East European series, 35. Bloomington: Indiana University Press

Yarnall, Judith (1994), *Transformations of Circe: The History of an Enchantress*. Urbana & Chicago: University of Illinois Press

Yeats, W.B. (1974), *Selected Poetry*. Edited with an introduction and notes by A. Norman Jeffares. London: Pan Books

Yeh, Max (1992), *The Beginning of the East*. Boulder: Fiction Collective Two

Yellin, Tamar (2006), 'Return to Zion', in *Kafka in Brontëland, and Other Stories*. New Milford, CT: Toby Press

Yolen, Jane and Robert J. Harris (2002), *Odysseus in the Serpent Maze*. London: Collins Voyager

Young, Philip H. (2003), *The Printed Homer: A 3,000-Year Publishing and Translation History of the* Iliad *and the* Odyssey. Jefferson, NC & London: McFarland & Co.

Zajko, Vanda (2004), 'Homer and *Ulysses*', in Fowler (ed.), 311–23

—— and Miriam Leonard (2006, eds.), *Laughing with Medusa: Classical Myth and Feminist Thought*. Oxford: Oxford University Press

—— and Alexandra Lianeri (2007, eds.), *Translation and the Classic*. Oxford: Oxford University Press

Zamora, Lois Parkinson and Wendy B. Faris (1995, eds.), *Magical Realism: Theory, History, Community*. Durham, NC: Duke University Press

Zeitlin, Froma (2001), 'Visions and revisions of Homer', in Simon Goldhill (ed.), *Being Greek Under Rome: Cultural Identity, the Second Sophistic and the Development of Empire*. Cambridge: Cambridge University Press, 195–266

Zeldin, Jesse (1969, transl.), *Selected Passages from Correspondence with Friends by Nikolai Gogol*. Nashville, TN: Vanderbilt University Press

Zhirmunsky, Victor (1966), 'The epic of "Alpamysh" and the return of Odysseus', *Proceedings of the British Academy* 52, 267–86

Zychowicz, James L. (1994), 'The Odyssey of Kurt Weill's "Ulysses Africanus" ', *American Music Research Center Journal* 4, 77–97

# INDEX